RECKLESS RITES

JEWS, CHRISTIANS, AND MUSLIMS

FROM THE ANCIENT TO THE MODERN WORLD

Edited by
MICHAEL COOK, WILLIAM CHESTER JORDAN, AND PETER SCHÄFER

RECKLESS RITES

PURIM AND THE LEGACY OF JEWISH VIOLENCE

Elliott Horowitz

PRINCETON UNIVERSITY PRESS
PRINCETON AND OXFORD

Third printing, and first paperback printing, 2008
Paperback ISBN: 978-0-691-13824-4

The Library of Congress has cataloged the cloth edition of this book as follows

Horowitz, Elliott S.
Reckless rites : Purim and the legacy of Jewish violence / Elliott Horowitz.
p. cm.—(Jews, Christians, and Muslims from the ancient to the modern world)
Includes bibliographical references and index.
ISBN-13: 978-0-691-12491-9 (alk. paper)
ISBN-10: 0-691-12491-4 (alk. paper)
1. Violence—Religious aspects—Judaism—History. 2. Purim. 3. Bible. O.T.
Esther—Criticism, interpretation, etc. 4. Judaism—Relations—Christianity.
5. Christianity and other religions—Judaism. I. Title. II. Series.

BM538.P3H67 2006
296.3'697–dc22   2005048752

British Library Cataloging-in-Publication Data is available

This book has been composed in Galliard Typeface
Printed on acid-free paper. ∞
press.princeton.edu
Printed in the United States of America

3   5   7   9   10   8   6   4

To my parents
for their boundless encouragement
and to my children
for their boundless tolerance

If it be permitted by human sagacity to discover the causes which have influenced the singular fate of the Jewish people, it must be sought by a more intimate knowledge of their feelings and history, than has fallen to the share of ridiculing Polytheists, of hostile Christians, and of doting Rabbins.

—ISAAC D'ISRAELI, *The Genius of Judaism* (1833)

I and the public know
What all schoolchildren learn,
Those to whom evil is done
Do evil in return.

—W. H. AUDEN, "September 1, 1939"

The most odious form of moral bias is found in the history that loudly condemns the crimes and persecutions of one side, and conceals or defends those of the other.

—G. M. TREVELYAN, "Bias in History" (1947)

Contents

Illustrations

Acknowledgments

THIS book has been researched and written over more than a dozen years on three continents, with the aid of research fellowships from several institutions: a year at the Center for Advanced Judaic Studies at the University of Pennsylvania (1994–1995), and subsequent semesters at the Hebrew University's Institute for Advanced Studies (1996), the Oxford Centre for Hebrew and Jewish Studies in Yarnton (1998), and Harvard University's Center for Jewish Studies (2002). I thank the directors and staff of each, especially David Ruderman of the University of Pennsylvania—a true friend and esteemed colleague with whom I have enjoyed a special relationship on both sides of the Atlantic for over two decades.

This is also a time to pay homage to the great libraries I have used in Israel, England, and the United States, especially the Jewish National and University Library in Jerusalem, the Bodleian Library in Oxford, Harvard's Widener Library, the New York Public Library, and the Library of the Jewish Theological Seminary of America. Furthermore, I would like to acknowledge the helpful staff of the Judaica Reading Room at the Jewish National and University Library in Jerusalem, who over many years have extended to me countless courtesies.

In that reading room I often saw Jacob Katz, with whom I was privileged to enjoy a relationship for two decades. Although I was not formally his student, Professor Katz showed a keen and supportive interest in my work since the beginning of my academic career, and was able, shortly before his death in 1998, to read and comment on a Hebrew version of what became chapter 6 of the present volume. He is the intended reader whose absence I most lament.

Friendship, both professional and personal, has played no small role in the writing (and especially completing) of this book. Daniel Boyarin, my former neighbor and colleague in the Negev, first encouraged me to work on the subject of Purim. Among current neighbors in Jerusalem Richard Cohen, Elchanan Reiner, Moshe Rosman, and Stuart Schoffman have generously lent me their ears over beers and other beverages, and have been highly supportive at crucial junctures. Yisrael Yuval, who unfortunately lives in a different neighborhood, has sympathetically shared the trials and tribulations, as well as the bittersweet pleasures, of writing responsibly about painful subjects. Jordan Penkower, another Jerusalemite, has provided numerous references over the years, and helped at the end with photography. Peter Miller, my neighbor in New York, provided crucial support in the final stages.

Myra Noveck's deft editing of my final draft has contributed considerably to the book's readability. She also saved me from embarrassing errors connected with recent Israeli history. Natalie Dohrmann and Jerome Balsam graciously saved me from some equally embarrassing typographical errors. At Princeton University Press Brigitta van Rheinberg has shown the perfect combination of patience, impatience, and enthusiasm over more years than I care to mention. All three readers for the Press provided highly constructive criticism, and I thank them for their efforts. It was also a pleasure to work with Clara Platter and my copyeditor, Jon Munk.

Several chapters of this book's latter half are based on previously published material. An earlier version of chapter 5 appeared as "From the Generation of Moses to the Generation of the Messiah: Constructions of Amalek in Jewish History" (in Hebrew), *Zion* 64 (1999): 425–54. Earlier versions of chapter 6 appeared first as "The Jews and the Cross in the Middle Ages: History and Historiography" (in Hebrew), 118–40, in Y. Assis, O. Limor et al., eds., *The Jews of Europe and the First Crusade* (Jerusalem: Zalman Shazar Center and Dinur Center, 2000), and then "The Jews and the Cross in the Middle Ages: Towards a Reappraisal," 114–31, in Tony Kushner and Nadia Valman, eds., *Philosemitism, Antisemitism, and "the Jews"* (Ashgate, 2004). Chapter 7 also draws upon two previously published articles: "A 'Dangerous Encounter': Thomas Coryate and the Swaggering Jews of Venice," *Journal of Jewish Studies* 52:2 (2001): 341–53, and "'They Fought Because They Were Fighters and They Fought Because They Were Jews: Violence and the Construction of Modern Jewish Identity," in Peter Medding, ed., *Jews and Violence: Studies in Contemporary Jewry* 18 (2002): 23–42. Chapter 8 is partially based on "'The Vengeance of the Jews Was Stronger Than Their Avarice': Modern Historians and the Persian Conquest of Jerusalem in 614," *Jewish Social Studies* 4, no. 2 (1998): 1–39. Chapter 9 draws on two articles: "The Rite to Be Reckless: On the Perpetration and Interpretation of Purim Violence," *Poetics Today* 15 (1994): 9–54, and "And It Was Reversed: Jews Confront Their Enemies in Their Purim Festivities" (in Hebrew), *Zion* 59 (1994): 129–68.

RECKLESS RITES

1. The photograph, taken in the Jerusalem neighborhood of Meah She'arim on Purim of 1993, shows an ultra-Orthodox young man following the Torah reading for Purim morning, which features the Amalekite attack on the Israelites at Rephidim. As Lieut. (Res.) Moshe Horowitz informs me, the toy gun being used as a pointer is an AK-47, commonly used by terrorists. From Alex Levac, *Photographs* (in Hebrew) (Tel-Aviv, 1994), 45. Courtesy of Alex Levac.

Introduction

BETWEEN REPHIDIM AND JERUSALEM

IN the spring of 2004, as this book was slouching toward completion, Jeffrey Goldberg reported in the *New Yorker* about a series of disturbing interviews he had recently conducted with Jewish settlers in the West Bank and Gaza. "The Palestinians are Amalek," he was told by Benzi Lieberman, chairman of the Council of Settlements. "We will destroy them," Lieberman continued. "We won't kill them all. But we will destroy their ability to think as a nation. We will destroy Palestinian nationalism." And Moshe Feiglin, a leading Likud activist, told Goldberg: "The Arabs engage in typical Amalek behavior. I can't prove this genetically, but this is the behavior of Amalek."

Goldberg explained to his readers that the Amalekites were a "mysterious Canaanite tribe that the Bible calls Israel's enemy." In the book of Exodus, he added, "the Amalekites attacked the Children of Israel on their journey to the land of Israel. For this sin, God damned the Amalekites, commanding the Jews to wage a holy war against them." Although the *New Yorker*'s legendary fact-checking staff allowed no flagrant errors to enter this thumbnail portrait, I would like to make clear to my own readers that in the Bible the Amalekites are neither Canaanites nor particularly mysterious. They are desert-dwelling descendants of Esau, the elder son of Isaac, through his own eldest son Eliphaz (Gen. 36:12). And although it would not be incorrect to say that they "attacked the Children of Israel on their journey to the land of Israel," the book of Deuteronomy chose rather to stress that the attack, at Rephidim, occurred as the "faint and weary" Israelites "came forth out of Egypt" (25:17–18).

The Amalekites, their distant cousins, were the first enemy they encountered in their forty-year trek through the desert. Although by the battle's end the militarily inexperienced Israelites, led by Joshua (with Moses looking on from a hilltop), somehow "mowed down Amalek and his people with the edge of the sword" (in the mellifluous rendition of the Revised Standard Version [RSV]), enough Amalekites survived for God to vow that He would continue to wage war with Amalek "from generation to generation" (Exod. 17:8–17). In the book of Exodus the perpetual struggle with Amalek is described as God's war, but in Deuteronomy the Israelites themselves are commanded to "blot out the remembrance of Amalek from under heaven."

In his *New Yorker* article Goldberg gallantly came to the defense of the Jewish tradition, asserting—again not quite accurately—that the commandment to exterminate the Amalekites "is perhaps the most widely ignored command in the Bible." He did not mean that it was ignored in the Bible itself but that "the rabbis who shaped Judaism," who, according to Goldberg, "could barely bring themselves to endorse the death penalty for murder, much less endorse genocide," solved the moral problem by ruling "that the Amalekites no longer existed."[1] This, however, is patently false. Not only did the "rabbis who shaped Judaism," that is, the Talmudic sages, never make such an assertion, but even Maimonides, in his great twelfth-century code, clearly suggested—as many commentators noted—that unlike the "seven nations" of ancient Canaan, who were also doomed to extermination by biblical command, the Amalekites were still alive and kicking.[2]

How seriously the command to "utterly destroy" Amalek was taken in biblical religion may perhaps best be seen from the account, in the first book of Samuel, of Saul's ill-fated war against the Amalekites. Saul, Israel's first king, was commanded in God's name by the prophet Samuel, again following the RSV,[3] to "go and smite Amalek, and utterly destroy all that they have; do not spare them, but kill both man and woman, infant and suckling, ox and sheep, camel and ass" (1 Sam. 15:2–3). Although Saul and his army did indeed defeat the Amalekites, whom they "utterly destroyed . . . with the edge of the sword" (1 Sam. 15:8–an intertextual allusion to Exod. 17:13) they spared both King Agag, who was taken captive, and "the best of the sheep and of the oxen and of the fatlings," purportedly in order to sacrifice them to God (1 Sam. 15:9). Samuel powerfully expressed God's ire at this partial fulfilment of His command and then dramatically executed the Amalekite king in the presence of his belatedly repentant Israelite counterpart (1 Sam. 15:22–33).

What does this have to do with relations between Israelis and Palestinians in the twenty-first century? Very little or a great deal, depending on how one defines the term "Amalekite." If it is defined genealogically, the

---

[1] Jeffrey Goldberg, "Among the Settlers: Will They Destroy Israel?" *New Yorker* (May 31, 2004).

[2] Maimonides, *Mishneh Torah*, Laws of Kings, 5:4–5.

[3] Hereafter I will sometimes follow the Revised Standard Version (1946–1952), sometimes the new translation of the Jewish Publication Society published under the title *Tanakh* (1985), and sometimes an eclectic combination of the two.

Palestinians, as Arabs and descendants, in biblical terms, of Ishmael (Isaac's half-brother), have no relation to Amalek, the grandson of Isaac's elder son, Esau. In fact, for centuries, as we shall see, Amalek was associated by Jews with the Roman Empire and its medieval Christian inheritors. If, however, Amalek is seen as a moral or metaphysical category—a notion that first merged in Jewish thought, as we shall see, in the Middle Ages—Palestinians may be classified as Amalekites. This is evidently what the Australian-born Feiglin meant when he told Jeffrey Goldberg that although he could not link the Arabs with Amalek "genetically," their "behavior" was "typical" of Amalek. Indeed, the association of Arabs with Amalekites has become widespread enough for at least one Israeli-Arab journalist to have developed the habit of referring to himself, with some measure of irony, as an Amalekite.[4] Not surprisingly, after the death of Yasser Arafat, in November of 2004, "Pikuach Nefesh," an association of some two hundred rabbis who oppose territorial concessions on the part of Israel, announced that "the day of Arafat's death should be a day of rejoicing," since the Palestinian leader was "the Amalek and the Hitler of our generation."[5]

Several months earlier Goldberg had published a short piece in the Op-Ed section of the *New York Times* ("Protect Sharon from the Right," August 5, 2004) that began with the description of a circumcision ceremony he had recently attended. The ceremony had taken place in a trailer that served as the synagogue of an outpost outside one of the Jewish settlements on the West Bank. Like other Jewish outposts in the area, many of which are technically illegal, this one too was home to a handful of families who belonged to what Goldberg aptly described as "the avant-garde of radical Jewish nationalism, the flannel-wearing, rifle-carrying children of their parents' mainstream settlements, which they denigrate for their bourgeois affectations . . . and their misplaced fealty to the dictates of the government in Jerusalem."

Not surprisingly, the young father—a goat farmer—found occasion, when he rose to speak, to raise the (to him) timely subject of Amalek. "I am looking at our life today, and what Amalek wants to do is swallow up the people of Israel," he said. Then, using an image that had been first developed in the *Zohar*, he added: "This is the snake. This is the snake"—although "serpent" would arguably have been a better translation, since the Zoharic allusion is to the sly and slithering creature in the book of Genesis. Goldberg then turned to a young acquaintance seated next to him, Ayelet, a pregnant (married) teenager who wore a long skirt and carried a semiautomatic M-16, and asked her whether she thought Amalek

---

[4] Sayed Kashua in *Kol ha-'Ir*, June 8, 2001; November 19, 2004.

[5] *Haaretz*, November 12, 2004.

was alive today. "Of course," she replied, and pointed toward one of the Arab villages in the distance. "The Amalekite spirit is everywhere," she added, "it's not just the Arabs." When asked by Goldberg who else might be part of Amalek, she replied, "Sharon isn't Amalek, but he works for Amalek."

The teenaged Ayelet was hardly the first Jewish ideologist to suggest that misguided fellow Jews might be in league with Amalek. Ironically, in fact, this position had been advanced by such fervent opponents of Zionism as the renowned Lithuanian Talmudist Elhanan Wasserman, who early in the twentieth century asserted that Amalekites could be found among those Jews who had "cast off the burden of the Torah," both in the Diaspora and the Holy Land. By the time Rabbi Wasserman was killed by the Nazis in 1941, the latter had become the universally recognized Amalekites of their day, temporarily blotting out the memory of all others. Yet late in the twentieth century the notion of Jewish Amalekites again gained currency, finding expression, for example, in an article by the Bar-Ilan professor and West Bank resident Hillel Weiss that appeared in *Ha-Zofeh*, the newspaper published by Israel's National Religious Party, on Purim of 1994. On that very day Dr. Baruch Goldstein—another West bank resident—opened fire, with his army-issued semiautomatic rifle, on dozens of Muslims who were praying inside the mosque at the Tomb of the Patriarchs in Hebron, killing twenty nine.[6]

At the time, I was living in Jerusalem, barely an hour's drive north from Hebron, and was working on a Hebrew version of an article about the history of Purim violence that became the genesis of this volume.[7] The realization, as the news came in sometimes contradictory spurts over the radio, and as I saw the raucous celebrations in the center of Jerusalem continuing unabated, that there was a clear connection between past Purims and the present one was both exhilarating and disturbing. It became clear to me that another chapter had written itself into the history of Purim—a carnivalesque holiday of reversal that celebrates the triumph of the Jews, during the days of Mordecai and Esther, over the genocidal plot of their archenemy Haman, who was hanged on the gallows that he had planned for Mordecai.

Haman is referred to repeatedly in the book of Esther as an Agagite— that is, descendant of the Amalekite king Agag. The Torah reading for the morning of Purim is taken from the account in Exodus (17:8–16) of the battle at Rephidim, after which God vowed that He would have war with Amalek "from generation to generation." And the Sabbath before Purim, called the "Sabbath of Memory," is even more infused with mordant

---

[6] See Horowitz, "From the Generation of Moses," 428, 454, and the sources cited there.
[7] Horowitz, "And It Was Reversed," 129–68.

memories of Israel's encounters with its archenemy. The special Torah reading, drawn from the book of Deuteronomy (25:17–19), from which that Sabbath draws its name, opens with the command to "remember what Amalek did" and concludes with the ringing (yet to some chilling) exhortation to "blot out the remembrance of Amalek from under heaven." And the reading from the Prophets for the Sabbath before Purim is taken from the aforementioned account (in 1 Sam. 15) of Saul's ill-fated war against the Amalekites, from which their king alone was spared until the prophet Samuel dramatically "hewed Agag in pieces before the Lord in Gilgal."

Although my article on Purim, whose treatment began in the fifth century, stretched ambitiously into the nineteenth, I decided after the Hebron massacre of 1994 to be even more ambitious and extend my story to the present. The editors of the journal *Zion*, published by the Historical Society of Israel, wisely advised me to delete the hastily written appendix, which was not sufficiently integrated with the rest of the article. A decade later, however, I feel that there is no longer any excuse for me, as a historian or as a Jew, "to keep silence at such a time as this" (Esther 4:14). I have therefore chosen, somewhat recklessly, to begin not at the beginning, but at the end, inspired, in part by the words of Esther herself (Esther 4:14), "if I perish, I perish."

In May of 1982, shortly before I immigrated to the state of Israel, the "Karp Commission" issued its findings regarding Jewish violence on the West Bank—under Israeli control since 1967—including events that had transpired in Hebron over the (extended) holiday of Purim, 1981. Although at that point the Jewish presence in Hebron itself had not yet been renewed—most Jews had abandoned the "City of the Patriarchs" after the massacre of 1929, and the last had departed in 1947—on Friday (March 20), the first day of Purim, settlers from neighboring Kiryat Arbah came to celebrate the holiday in Beit Hadassah, which had once housed a Jewish infirmary and a synagogue. By Friday evening they had managed, allegedly through their spirited dancing, to bring the roof down over the Arab-owned upholstery shop downstairs. Since Purim in Hebron is traditionally celebrated over two days (the fourteenth and fifteenth of Adar) the settlers settled down in Beit Hadassah for another day of boisterous festivity, which in 1981 coincided with the Jewish Sabbath.

The Arab upholsterer, who had closed his shop before noon on Friday as was his custom, returned the next day to find a large hole in his ceiling, and proceeded to the local (Israeli) police station, but did not file a formal complaint—hoping, he later explained to investigators, that after repairing the hole quiet could be restored. He began work on repairing the ceiling, as he had been advised by the (Arab) municipality, but his new neighbors upstairs insisted that he stop, "on account of the sanctity of the Sabbath." When the upholsterer returned on Saturday evening, he was forcibly prevented by the settlers from continuing with the repairs. Around midnight an officer from the (Israeli) military governor's office arrived and saw that the entire ceiling had collapsed, and that young settlers were removing the contents of the shop. When he asked them what was going on, they replied that the shop's ceiling had collapsed and that they were removing the cotton fabric so that it would not get soiled. When the same officer returned some two and a half hours later, after having been informed that the shop's door was open, one of the settlers reportedly told him (in Hebrew) that he was witnessing the renewal of Hebron's Jewish community.

On Sunday the upholsterer returned to find his shop devastated. While he was sitting at its entrance mourning his fate, three armed settlers emerged from Beit Hadassah and asked him to leave. When he replied that it was his shop, they pushed him away violently. He then returned to the police station and filed a formal complaint. The police investigation was completed nearly a year later, in February of 1982. The state attorney's office decided the following March to close the case, both on the grounds of insufficient evidence and because the Arab upholsterer had by then received financial compensation. The Karp Report, however, found it both "highly disturbing" and worthy of note that, according to the police superintendent's affidavit, Hebron's military governor had instructed the commander of the local police station not to investigate the incident.[8]

On Purim of 1986, five years after the festive reconquest of Beit Hadassah, Jewish settlers paraded through Hebron carrying puppets of various images from the book of Esther, including, of course, that of Haman. When they arrived at Beit Romano, one of the other local buildings that had been owned by Jews prior to 1948, one of the settlers, as reported by *Haaretz* correspondent Ori Nir, placed a *kaffiyeh* on the effigy of Haman, which was being hung. The local Arabs, understandably, took offense, and only the timely intervention by a representative of the military government—who demanded that the settlers remove the *kaffiyeh*—prevented a violent confrontation. It is not unlikely that Dr. Baruch Goldstein, who immigrated from the United States to Kiryat Arbah in 1983—and who by 1984 already had a police record in Hebron—participated in the Purim parade of 1986.[9]

Three years later, according to the same correspondent's report, the (by then) traditional Purim parade through Arab Hebron was even more

---

[8] The Karp Report was issued by Israel's Ministry of Justice on May 23, 1982. On the events of March 1981 in Hebron, see 8–11.

[9] See Elimelekh Horowitz, "Hag Purim; Simha ve-Sasson oh Sinah ve-Sasson," 324–25, in *Ha-Mishak*, ed. Emilia Peroni (Tel Aviv, 2002).

provocative. Jewish settlers carried a skeleton with a *kaffiyeh* on its head and a noose around its neck, and also burned Palestinian flags. Some Jewish children carried toy rifles, which they pointed menacingly at their Palestinian counterparts. From the city's central square the festive settlers, many in masquerade, continued to the Tomb of the Patriarchs into which they sought to introduce a Torah ark—contrary to regulations—during the time normally set aside for Muslim prayer. "The shoving match . . . continued for some time," reported Nir, "and provided such surreal scenes as [Israeli soldiers] struggling with [Jewish] settlers dressed as Arabs, in an effort to protect the 'real' Arabs who were in the vicinity."[10]

The following year, in 1990, the Purim parade departed from Beit Hadassah toward the Tomb of the Patriarchs, and in that year, too, Palestinian flags were burned in the streets of Arab Hebron. Some of the Jewish participants were again provocatively dressed as Palestinians, but Noam Arnon, then spokesman for the settler organization Gush Emunim, chose to wear a "Peace Now" t-shirt with a *kaffiyeh* on his head—suggesting an inner affinity between those two sartorial objects. Four years later the holiday of Purim coincided with the first Friday of Ramadan—as delicate a situation as one could imagine in the embattled city of the Patriarchs. On that fateful Friday morning Dr. Goldstein brought his semiautomatic rifle with him to Purim prayers at the Tomb of the Patriarchs and fired into the neighboring room where Muslims were at prayer. Since then, for me and for many others, Purim has never been the same.

In Hebron, however, little changed, even after the murder, in November 1995, of Prime Minister Yitzhak Rabin by Yigal Amir, a law student at Bar-Ilan University (where I was then teaching) and an admirer of Goldstein.[11] On Purim of 1997, according to *Haaretz* correspondent Amira Segev, Hebron's traditional Purim parade, which by then departed from the Jewish "neighborhood" of Tel Rumeida, was headed by a Lubavitch "mitzvah tank," and Noam Arnon, who by then had become spokesman for the Jewish community of Hebron, (cross-) dressed as the outspoken left-wing parliamentarian Shulamit Aloni, who had been a minister in Rabin's government. One young woman was dressed as Margalit Har-Shefi, a Bar-Ilan law student and West Bank resident who had been arrested in connection with her classmate's assassination of Yitzhak Rabin.

In 1998 the Purim parade again stretched from Tel Rumeida to the Tomb of the Patriarchs, the site of the 1994 Purim massacre. Noam Federman, a Kahanist resident of Tel Rumeida, was dressed, according to *Haaretz* correspondent Tami Sokol, as Leah Rabin in witch's garb, with

---

10 Ibid., 325.

11 On Amir's admiration for Goldstein see Michael Karpin and Ina Friedman, *Murder in the Name of God: The Plot to Kill Yitzhak Rabin* (New York, 1998), 10, 15–16.

a sticker that ominously read "Shalom, Leah"—a ghoulish allusion to Bill Clinton's famous words of farewell to Yitzhak Rabin at the latter's funeral. And one of the settler children was dressed as the local Jewish saint, Dr. Baruch Goldstein, wearing a stethoscope and carrying a rifle. He was apparently one of many local Jewish children that year who chose that macabre masquerade—presumably with the approval of their parents.[12]

Purim in Hebron after 1994 was like Purim in Hebron since 1981, only more so—with a new Jewish hero for Jewish children to dress up as. And in Jerusalem the fashion of categorizing fellow Jews as Amalekites reached new highs—or lows. In late February of 1996, after a bus blew up on Jaffa road, a reporter for *Ma'ariv* heard a passerby exclaim: "This is all due to the leftists of Meretz. We will take care of them. For us they are Amalek."[13] Four years later Israel's controversial Education Minister Yossi Sarid, one of the founders—with the aforementioned Shulamit Aloni—of Meretz, had the distinction of being designated an Amalekite by no less an authority than Rabbi Ovadiah Yosef, the founder and spiritual leader of Israel's Shas party, and the most widely respected rabbinical figure among Oriental and Sephardic Jews throughout the world. In a public address delivered in March of 2000, shortly before the holiday of Purim, Rabbi Yosef compared the veteran left-wing politician to Haman, adding that "he is wicked and satanic and must be erased like Amalek." The office of Israel's attorney general pursued a criminal investigation (on grounds of possible incitement to violence) but the great rabbi was never charged.[14]

In contemporary Israel, it is not only Haman who is conjured, but also his stubborn nemesis Mordecai, whose refusal to bow before the evil minister has reverberated for centuries, as we shall see, both among Jews and Bible-reading Christians. In the spring of 2003 the Israeli painter Moshe Gershuni, who was to receive the coveted Israel Prize on Independence Day of that year, announced that he would not attend the ceremony in order to avoid shaking hands with Education Minister Limor Livnat, with whose government's policies he sharply disagreed. Livnat, in response, decided to revoke the prize. Writing in *Haaretz* the conductor Itai Talgam compared the story to the book of Esther, and asked rhetorically: "Why couldn't Ahashverosh's chief minister abide this one exception and write off Mordechai as just an eccentric old geezer?" Talgam saw Gershuni as a contemporary Mordecai who represents "the Jewish spirit, that does not give in; and the temptation to try to break this spirit cannot be assuaged by all the pleasures and power of authority."[15]

---

[12] Horowitz, "Hag Purim," 327.
[13] Horowitz, "From the Generation of Moses," 454.
[14] See Kamil, "Ovadia Yosef."
[15] *Haaretz*, April 20, 2003.

In modern America, too, the ancient book of Esther could be brought to bear upon contemporary politics. In southern California during the Watergate investigations of the 1970s, members of a left-leaning *Havura* (prayer community) accompanied the reading of the Megillah with a dramatic enactment of the Esther story. One of the participants, the local campus Hillel rabbi, chose for himself the role of Haman. Rather than merely masquerading as the biblical villain, he chose to impersonate Richard Nixon's senior aide H. R. (Bob) Haldeman—whose surname also began with an H. In addition to wearing a three-piece suit and a hat, he walked onstage carrying a briefcase on which was written H. R. "Bob" Haman, and from which audiotape trailed. Riv-Ellen Prell, the participant-observer who has described the performance, notes that the character had no spoken lines. "His entire performance was visual and succeeded because of his ability to effectively associate Haldeman with Haman and Haman with Haldeman." Both had access to the highest corridors of power and both had been stripped of it when their evil intentions were uncovered.[16] On the East Coast not long afterward members of the Jewish Defense League in Brooklyn decided, on Purim of 1977, to burn in effigy another person who had ascended to the highest corridors of power under Richard Nixon—their coreligionist Henry Kissinger![17] This, however, was not as paradoxical as might appear, for as we have already seen, it had long been claimed that Jews too could be Amalekites.

This book, however, is not only about Jewish myths and their legacies, but also about myths told and retold concerning the Jews, whether about their "passionate hostility to violence," as Jean Paul Sartre put it, or their predilection for particularly peevish forms of predation, such as the ritual murder of children. As recently, in fact, as March 2002 the Saudi scholar Umayna Ahmad al-Jalahma revived the canard that Jews require the blood of non-Jews for their Purim pastries. But whereas in the nineteenth century, especially after the "Damascus Affair" of 1840, the claim had been made that Purim was one of the occasions for which Jews required the blood of Christians, Dr. al-Jalahma seems to have been the first to discover that Muslim blood can also be used for filling the three-cornered *Hamantaschen*.[18] Both Purim and the book of Esther, as we shall

[16] Riv-Ellen Prell, "Laughter That Hurts: Ritual Humor and Ritual Change in an American Jewish Community," 214–15, in *Between Two Worlds; Ethnographic Essays on American Jewry*, ed. Jack Kugelmass (Ithaca, 1988).

[17] Shifra Epstein, "From Tel-Aviv to Borough Park: Purim in the Twentieth Century," 51, in *Purim: The Face and the Mask* (no editor stated) (New York, 1979).

[18] His article "The Jewish Holiday of Purim," published originally in *Al-Riyadh*, March 10, 2002, is quoted in Gabriel Schoenfeld, *The Return of Anti-Semitism* (San Francisco, 2004), 17–18.

frequently see, are subjects that have impelled both apologists and anti-Semites to show their true colors, as they have impelled me to show mine in this introduction.

In the fall of 2004 the local news in Israel again inserted itself into my narrative. On Sunday, October 10, when the Armenians in Jerusalem's Old City were observing the "Exaltation of the Holy Cross" (or "Holy Cross Day"), a cross was carried by the local archbishop in the traditional procession near the Church of the Holy Sepulchre. Natan Zvi Rosenthal, a twenty-one-year-old student at the (ultranationalist) Har Hamor yeshiva, happened to be passing by, and spat upon both the processional cross and the archbishop, who responded by slapping Rosenthal. Both were consequently questioned by the police—who decided, however, to charge only the student with assault. An editorial two days later in *Haaretz* under the title "Jerusalem's Disgrace" saw the incident as revealing "a little bit of the increasingly wild Jewish-nationalist-religious atmosphere" in the city.[19]

Some have suggested that it is the spatial proximity of the Armenian Quarter to that of the Jews in Jerusalem's Old City that has been responsible for Jewish attacks upon religious processions and clergymen. Yet Rosenthal, who has since apologized for his action,[20] encountered the Holy Cross procession neither in the Jewish Quarter nor the Armenian one, but near the Church of the Holy Sepulchre, in the Christian Quarter. I would suggest, therefore, that acts of enmity toward Armenian processions and clergymen should be seen against the background of a long Jewish tradition reaching back to the tenth century, whereby Armenians were referred to, not always in a hostile manner, as "Amalekites."[21]

This tradition, which shall be examined in greater detail in chapter 5, was still very much alive in the nineteenth century. In 1839 the British missionary Joseph Wolff, who was active in both Palestine and Yemen, found it "remarkable that the Armenians, who are detested by the Jews as the supposed descendants of the *Amalekites*, are the only Christian church who have interested themselves for the protection and conversion of the Jews." Similarly, in their 1842 account of their extensive missionary efforts among Jews in both Europe and the Middle East, the Scottish missionaries Bonar and McCheyne suggested that "the peculiar hatred which

---

[19] See Amiram Barkat in *Haaretz*, October 11, 2004, October 12, 2004.
[20] Barkat, *Haaretz*, October 18, 2004. See also E. J. Greenberg, "Church Flap in Jerusalem: Bad Blood—and Saliva," *Forward*, October 22, 2004. A more recent spitting incident against an Armenian priest occurred early in January 2005. See Barkat in *Haaretz*, January 7, 2005.
[21] See Horowitz, "From the Generation of Moses," 431, 450–51.

the Jews bear to the Armenians may arise from a charge often brought against them, namely that Haman was an Armenian, and that the Armenians are the *Amalekites* of the Bible."[22]

On Saturday, March 11 1995, when a procession of Armenian priests was making its way, with a large cross, from Jerusalem's Armenian Quarter to the Church of the Holy Sepulchre, Moshe Ehrenfeld, a Jewish resident of the city, spat conspicuously as the procession passed. Although newspaper reports concerning the 1995 incident—for which Ehrenfeld, who was found guilty of "interfering with a religious ritual," was fined and given a (suspended) two-month prison sentence—failed to mention that it occurred on *Shabbat Zakhor*, the Sabbath before Purim, there can be little doubt that Ehrenfeld himself was aware of that momentous date.[23]

Moreover, the hostility to the cross that he evinced was by no means limited, even then, to a small group of fanatics. In the spring of 1992 a minor crisis had erupted in Israel when representatives of the education ministry discovered, to their horror, that a film marking five hundred years since the expulsion of Spanish Jewry that had been commissioned from Israel Television contained scenes in which some of the major figures (e.g., Ferdinand, Isabella, and Torquemada) wore crosses. What was particularly upsetting was that the film was to be shown in connection with that year's International Bible Quiz for Youth in Jerusalem, whose dominant theme was the Spanish Expulsion. The education ministry demanded that the film be reedited and the crosses removed.[24] We shall return in chapter 6 to the Jewish relationship with, and history of violence against, the cross, which for centuries was commonly referred to as an "abomination."

In its editorial on the recent spate of anti-Christian incidents in Jerusalem *Haaretz* referred to "the increasingly wild Jewish-nationalist-religious atmosphere" in the city, which, I might add, is equally true of Hebron. In both holy cities holy tombs have become sites of religious violence, and in both cities acts of violence against non-Jews have clustered around the days between *Shabbat Zakhor* and Purim. It was over the holiday of Purim that religious settlers from Kiryat Arbah festively reconquered Beit Hadassah from an Arab upholsterer in 1981, it was on that holiday that Dr. Goldstein of Kiryat Arbah gunned down twenty-nine prostrate Muslims at the Tomb of the Patriarchs in 1994, and it was on the Sabbath before that holiday that one year later Moshe Ehrenfeld spat conspicuously in the presence of an Armenian procession in Jerusalem. It

---

[22] See Joseph Wolff, *Journal of the Rev. Joseph Wolff* (London, 1839), 255; Bonar and McCheyne, *Narrative of a Mission*, 706.

[23] See Shahar Ilan in *Haaretz* February 21, 1997; Moshe Reinfeld, *Haaretz*, February 27, 1997.

[24] Avital Nitzan in *Haaretz*, March 31, 1992.

may be added that Daniel Rossing, a former advisor on Christian affairs to Israel's Religious Affairs Ministry, recently told a reporter that anti-Christian incidents tend to occur at "certain times of the year, such as during the Purim holiday." Rossing, in fact, knows Christians in Israel "who lock themselves indoors during the entire Purim holiday."[25] Some may derive a measure of solace from recalling that for centuries Jews in Christian countries would do the same between Good Friday and Easter.[26] Others may be upset that I am packing so much dirty laundry between the covers of an academic book instead of leaving it to fade on the pages of soon-to-be-forgotten newspapers or consigning it to the dreary darkness of the microfilm room. But in doing so I am following in the path of many worthy predecessors, including the biblical author of the book of Esther.

LUTHER AND HIS LEGACY

At the end of the book of Esther's seventh chapter Haman is hanged "on the gallows which he had prepared for Mordecai," and the anger of King Ahasuerus abated. Had the author abated his (or her) account there, Martin Luther would never have commented, in his infamous essay "On the Jews and Their Lies" (1543), on how much the Jews "love the book of Esther, which so well fits their bloodthirsty, vengeful, murderous greed and hope," nor would his eighteenth-century countryman Johann David Michaelis have accused Esther herself of "insatiable vindictiveness."[27] But that is not what the author of Esther did. He/she went on to report not only that the "Jews had light and gladness and joy and honor" (Esther 8:16), but that they "smote all their enemies with the sword, slaughtering and destroying them, and did as they pleased to those who hated them" (Esther 9:5), with the consequence that more than seventy-five thousand of these "enemies" were slain. And not only was Haman, but also his ten sons were hanged (Esther 9:7–10), presumably because they, like their "Agagite" father, were descendants of Amalek.

Not only in his 1543 essay did Luther criticize the book of Esther, but also in his "table talk" he condemned it, together with 2 Maccabees, for being "too Jewish" (my translation) and containing "too much heathen corruption," prompting him to express the wish that both books "did not

[25] Barkat in *Haaretz*, October 12, 2004.

[26] See, among others, Parkes, *Conflict of the Church and the Synagogue*, 327, 330, 332; Guido Kisch, *The Jews in Medieval Germany* (Chicago, 1949), 183–84, 300–301; Solomon Grayzel, *The Church and the Jews in the XIIIth Century* II, ed. K. R. Stow (New York, 1989), 162, 242, 255, 257–59, 261, 267, 270; Nirenberg, *Communities of Violence*, 209–12.

[27] See H. Bornkamm, *Luther and the Old Testament*, trans. E. W. Gritsch and R. C. Gritsch (Philadelphia, 1969), 188–89; Bickerman, *Four Strange Books*, 215–16.

exist"—a wish that continued to command respect, as we shall see, well into the twentieth century.[28] And the eminent bible scholar and polyhistor Michaelis, who taught at Göttingen for nearly half a century until his death in 1791, not only accused Esther of "insatiable vindictiveness," but also complained that Haman had been put to death without trial. His attitude toward the Jewish queen was evidently colored by his rather negative stance vis-à-vis her co-religionists in eighteenth-century Germany, the granting of citizenship to whom he publicly opposed. Michaelis, whose position toward the Jews has convincingly been described as "racial antisemitism with a theological pedigree,"[29] was an ardent believer—like his older contemporary Montesquieu—in the impact of climate upon peoples and their cultures. As products of a "southern climate," he argued, the Jews could never be fully assimilated into a German state. Moreover, he felt that their religious obligations prevented them from fully merging with any another nation. "As long as the Jews keep the laws of Moses, as long as for instance they do not take their meals with us," he wrote, "or with simple folk, over a glass of beer, are not able to make friends, they will never . . . fuse with us."[30]

It is not clear which law of Moses, according to Michaelis, stood in the way of Jews sharing a glass of beer with "simple folk"—except, of course, during the holiday of Passover. And it is rather ironic that whereas Esther had been guilty, in his view, of "insatiable vindictiveness," he saw her modern co-religionists as "a people that [on account of the Sabbath] cannot bear arms, and defend the state under which they live," and therefore "can never be on a footing with other citizens, nor enjoy equal rights."[31]

[28] "Ich bin dem Buch und Esther so feind, dass ich wollte sie wären gar nicht vorhanden; denn sie judenzen zu sehr und haben viel heidnische Unart" (*Tischreden*). Among the many scholars who have quoted Luther's remarks with varying degrees of approval or disapproval, see Samuel Davidson, *An Introduction to the Old Testament: Critical, Historical, and Theological*, 3 vols. (London, 1862–63), 2: 172–73; R. H. Pfeiffer, *An Introduction to the Old Testament*, (New York, 1941), 747; B. W. Anderson, S. V. "Esther" in *The Interpreter's Bible* (New York, 1954), 3:830; Bickerman, *Four Strange Books*, 212; Clines, *Ezra, Nehemiah, Esther*, 255. On Luther's influence among modern scholars, see also Hans Bardtke, *Luther und das Buch Esther* (Tübingen, 1964); Wolfram Herrmann, *Ester im Streit der Meinungen* (Frankfurt, 1986).

[29] J. H. Hess, "Johann David Michaelis and the Colonial Imaginary: Orientalism and the Emergence of Racial Antisemitism in Eighteenth-Century Germany," *JSS*, n.s. 6 (2000): 93.

[30] On the dispute between Michaelis and Christian Wilhelm von Dohm regarding the suitability of Jews for citizenship, see, among others, Jacob Katz, *Out of the Ghetto: The Social Background of Jewish Emancipation, 1770–1870* (Cambridge, Mass., 1973), 89–94; Hess, "Johann David Michaelis," 57–58. Both Katz and Hess quote the same passage, but I have followed the former's translation.

[31] He asserted furthermore: "They must be subjected to more taxes, in order to make up with their purses, for what they are not in a situation to do with their swords and their hands."

In a later chapter we shall return to the question of European attitudes concerning the suitability of Jews for warfare, and the implications of that question for the historiography of Jewish violence.

Early in the nineteenth century W.M.L. De Wette of the University of Berlin, who is considered to have "inaugurated a new era in critical Old Testament scholarship," wrote of Esther that it "refers nothing to the operation and direction of God, and contains no religious element." This assertion went hand in hand with De Wette's view that the book displayed a "blood-thirsty spirit of revenge and persecution."[32] Although he was forced in 1822, on account of his critical views, to abdicate his professorship at Berlin, De Wette's scholarship, like that of many nineteenth-century biblical scholars, was informed by a strain of enlightened Protestant piety that posited a stark dichotomy between religiosity and revenge. A book that was full of one, he evidently believed, would necessarily be quite empty of the other. De Wette's student Friedrich Bleek also saw the absence of God's name as "characteristic of the untheocratic spirit" of Esther, in which a "very narrow minded and Jewish spirit of revenge and persecution" prevailed, to the extent that "no other book of the Old Testament" was "so far removed . . . from the spirit of the Gospel."[33]

In referring to the book's "very narrow minded and Jewish spirit of revenge," Bleek seems to have meant, by way of hendiadys, its "very narrowmindedly Jewish spirit of revenge." For many nineteenth-century German Bible scholars (and some even in the twentieth) the words "Jewish," "narrow-minded," and "revenge" formed an unholy trinity that characterized the reified religion of narrow legalism and rough justice that Jesus came to rectify.[34] And the text that was seen as most typifying this

---

See J. D. Michaelis, *Commentaries on the Laws of Moses*, trans. Alexander Smith, 4 vols. (Aberdeen, 1814), 3:180–81.

[32] W. M. L. De Wette, *A Critical and Historical Introduction to the Canonical Scriptures of the Old Testament*. trans. Theodore Parker, 2 vols (Boston, 1843), 2:339–40, 46.

[33] Friedrich Bleek, *An Introduction to the Old Testament*, ed. J. Bleek and A. Kamphausen, translated from the second German edition of 1865 by G. H. Venables, 2 vols. (London, 1875), 1:450. On De Wette (1780–1849) and his disciple Bleek (1793–1859), see Cheyne, *Founders*, 31–53, 142–48, and John Rogerson, *Old Testament Criticism in the Nineteenth Century* (London, 1984), 28–49. For a broader view of De Wette as a German Romantic intellectual, see T. A. Howard, *Religion and the Rise of Historicism* (Cambridge, 2000), 23–109.

[34] For two of the classic critiques of this position see Solomon Schechter, "The Law and Recent Criticism," *JQR*, o.s. 3 (1890–1891): 754–66; Israel Abrahams, "Professor Schürer on Life under Jewish Law," *JQR*, o.s. 11 (1898–1899): 626–42. See the discussion of both in Horowitz, "Israel Abrahams," 143–47.

preredemptive state of Judaism was the book of Esther, which Bleek—and many others after him—explicitly contrasted with "the spirit of the Gospel."[35] Later in the nineteenth century Heinrich Ewald famously remarked that in moving to Esther from the other books of the Hebrew Bible "we fall as it were, from heaven to earth"—and this acerbic comment continued to echo for decades.[36]

Even during the Hitler years German biblical scholarship saw little reason to reconsider the harsh condemnation of Esther and its "spirit" that had become standard during the nineteenth and early twentieth centuries. In 1934 Otto Eissfeldt of the University of Halle (who was an ordained Protestant minister) asserted that Esther's inclusion into the biblical canon could only be explained by "the close connection between Jewish religion and the Jewish national spirit."[37] Four years later his younger colleague Johannes Hempel, at the University of Berlin, published *Das Ethos des Alten Testaments*, in which he described the book of Esther as showing, through its "hate-inspired wish-fulfilment" (*hassdurchglühte Wunschtraum*) how far the fantasy of pursuing vengeance could go among the Jews. In 1964 Hempel, who had been associated during the Nazi years with the infamous *Institut zur Erforschung des jüdischen Einflusses auf das deutsche kirchliche Leben* (Institute for the Study and Eradication of Jewish Influence on German Religious Life) established by the German Christian movement, published a second edition of his *Das Ethos des Alten Testaments*. Yet even in that revised edition he saw no need to change his earlier description of the book of Esther as showing, through its "hate-inspired wish-fulfilment" how far the fantasy of pursuing vengeance could go among the Jews.[38]

In 1953, the year of my own birth, Curt Kuhl, writing in German, asserted that the book's enthusiastic embrace by the Jews, among whom it "became a great favorite," testified to their "narrow-minded and fanatical

---

[35] Contrast, however, Paul (formerly Selig) Cassel, a nineteenth-century Jewish convert to Christianity, who bravely wrote that "Esther and Mordecai must not be judged by the standard of the gospel, nor must we expect to find in them the tolerating spirit of Jesus Christ." Cassel, *Esther*, xvi–xvii.

[36] See, for example, Driver, *Introduction*, 457; Washington Gladden, *Seven Puzzling Bible Books* (London, 1897), 94; Davies, *Ezra, Nehemiah, and Esther*, 293. On Ewald (1803–1875) see Cheyne, *Founders*, 66–118; Rogerson, *Old Testament Criticism*, 91–103.

[37] O.W.H.L. Eissfeldt, *Einleitung in das Alte Testament* (Tübingen, 1934), 566–67. On Eissfelt (1887–1973), see G. Wallis in *DBI*, 1: 327.

[38] J. Hempel, *Das Ethos des Alten Testaments*, 2nd ed. (Berlin, 1964 [1938]), 30, 105. On the Institut and its activities between 1939 and 1945, see Max Weinreich, *Hitler's Professors: The Part of Scholarship in Germany's Crimes Against the Jewish People* (New York, 1946), 62–67, and Susannah Heschel, "When Jesus Was an Aryan: The Protestant Church and Antisemitic Propaganda," in *Betrayal: German Churches and the Holocaust* (1999), 68–70, 83. On Hempel (1891–1964), see also C. T. Begg in *DBI*, 1:493.

nationalism."[39] I had been conceived in the city of Tel-Aviv, which may well have been seen by Professor Kuhl as a different sort of testimony to the narrow-minded and fanatical nationalism of the Jews. But if not for a different nation's narrow-minded and fanatical nationalism I probably would have been conceived and born in Germany, and perhaps even studied there. And then, had I become a Bible scholar, perhaps I too would ask rhetorically, as Werner Schmidt of the University of Bonn has recently done, "Does not the book [of Esther] emphasize too much the superiority of Judaism?" Since, however, I had the good fortune to be born and bred in New York, I regard Professor Schmidt's narrow-minded question as akin to a Teutonic tourist asking of that city's sometimes self-applauding residents, Do they not emphasize too much the superiority of the Yankees?

POSTBIBLICAL PURIM VIOLENCE

This book deals not only with the theme of Amalek and responses—Christian as well as Jewish—to the book of Esther over the centuries, but also with Jewish violence connected with the holiday of Purim, from the early fifth century to the late twentieth. This is a subject fraught with historiographical complexities. For Jewish scholars living in Christian countries writing about Jewish violence against Christians or abuse of Christian symbols on Purim—especially by linking the similar fates of Haman and Jesus—was, as we shall see, no simple matter.[40]

Christian scholars, of course, discussed these matters more openly, and sometimes also quite enthusiastically. In his widely read *Lectures on the History of the Jewish Church*, based on lectures delivered originally in his capacity as professor of ecclesiastical history at Oxford, Arthur Penrhyn Stanley, who was appointed Dean of Westminster Abbey in 1864, referred to the "natural objection of the civilised—we may add, of the Christian—conscience, to the Book of Esther and the Feast of Purim."[41] Stanley, who acknowledged that "every Jew throughout the world felt with Mordecai, and has felt in many a time of persecution since, as he raised . . . his loud and bitter cry [Esther 4:1]," but this did prevent him from asserting that "the continuance of that bitter animosity in the Jewish nation renders the

---

[39] Kuhl also explicitly endorsed Luther's rejection of Esther, stating categorically that the book had "nothing to say to the Protestant believer." Curt Kuhl, *The Old Testament: Its Origins and Composition*, trans. C. T. M. Herriott (Edinburgh and London, 1961 [German original, 1953]), 271.

[40] On the connection between Haman and Jesus, see Thornton, "Crucifixion of Haman."

[41] Stanley, *Lectures*, 3:176–78. The first edition appeared between 1863–1876. On Stanley (1815–1881) see R. E. Clements in *DBI*, 2:502–3.

Feast of Purim the least pleasing of their festivals." He noted also that Purim "was long retained in all its intensity as the natural vent" of the hatred that Jews felt towards "their heathen or Christian oppressors in each succeeding age"[42]—anticipating, thereby, the central argument of this book, which, I suspect, the learned dean would have found more "pleasing" than the Jewish holiday upon which it focuses (although I am not sure how much that pleases me).

Both Dean Stanley and other nineteenth-century scholars who commented on Purim as the "natural vent" of Jewish hatred toward "Christian oppressors" had in mind particularly the 408 edict issued early in the reign of Theodosius II instructing the governors of all provinces in the Roman Empire to "prohibit the Jews from setting fire to Aman in memory of his past punishment, in a certain ceremony of their festival, and from burning with sacrilegious intent a form made to resemble the saint cross in contempt of the Christian faith."[43] Even before it was discussed in Stanley's *Lectures on the History of the Jewish Church*, the fifth-century edict had featured prominently in Henry Hart Milman's treatment, in his pioneering *History of the Jews*, of Jewish-Christian relations in the Roman Empire after its Christianization under Constantine.

Both Stanley and Milman, moreover, shared similar biographies. Milman (1791–1868) had prepared for Oxford at Eton whereas the younger Stanley (1815–1881) "came up" from Rugby. Both were ecclesiastical historians as well as Anglican divines who became deans of leading cathedrals. Milman was appointed Dean of St. Paul's in 1849 and fifteen years later, as noted above, Stanley became Dean of Westminster. It was during the decade of his tenure as professor of poetry at Oxford (1821–1831) that Milman composed his *History of the Jews*, in which he wrote memorably of the "furious collision" that occurred between Christians and Jews early in the fifth century after "great, and probably not groundless, offence" was taken by the former "at the public and tumultuous manner in which the Jews celebrated the holiday of Purim."[44]

A third polyhistoric Victorian to address the subject was the religiously eccentric though enormously learned naturalist Philip Henry Gosse (1810–1888), whose *History of the Jews* drew heavily on Milman's popular work—though Gosse's pungent (and ardently alliterative) prose had its own distinct character. Describing the relations between Jews and Christians

---

[42] Stanley, *Lectures*, 3:177.

[43] I follow the translation of Linder, *Roman Imperial Legislation*, 237.

[44] Milman, *History*, 3:192–93. On Milman and his work, see most recently R. E. Clements, "The Intellectual Background of H. H. Milman's *History of the Jews* (1829) and Its Impact on English Biblical scholarship," 246–71, in *Biblical Studies and the Shifting of Paradigms, 1850–1914*, ed. H. G. Reventlow and W. Farmer (Sheffield, 1995).

during the reign of Theodosius II, Gosse noted that the resentment of the former "against the contempt and hatred of their opponents found vent in a singular manner, when no other opportunity presented itself of avenging themselves." This was done, explained Gosse (a member of a strictly Calvinist sect known as "the Brethren"), through the feast of Purim, which "has not infrequently been celebrated with bacchanalian orgies more befitting the worship of an idol-demon than a thanksgiving to Jehovah." During the fifth century, he asserted, the holiday "was made the vehicle of much that was outrageous and offensive to Christians." The Jews represented Jesus "under the similitude of Haman . . . and the gibbet on which they were accustomed to hang the effigy of their enemy, they now made in the form of the cross."[45]

Gosse's own Calvinist hostility to the veneration of the cross ("the object of idolatrous adoration") seems to have equipped him with a rare degree of empathy for the "outrageous and offensive" conduct of the Jews. He also understood intuitively that the Jews of late antiquity had not only conflated Haman with Christ, but also the ancient Amalekites with contemporary Christians. "The smart of personal insult would add pungency to the indignities with which the infuriated and intoxicated Jews would avenge the old and the new quarrel, venting their impotent malice at once upon Haman and Christ, upon the Amalekites and the Nazarenes; and blasphemies would be uttered, which might make the ears of those who heard tingle."[46]

As we have seen, infuriated (and sometimes intoxicated) Jews in the Holy Land are still avenging "the old and the new quarrel" against those they consider to be "Amalekites," but their malice is hardly as impotent as it was in the distant days of Theodosius II, and the concept of Amalek has been amplified to include not only "Nazarenes" but also Ishmaelites and even some Israelites. And while some of the statements recorded by contemporary journalists would indeed make the ears tingle, I must confess that many of the hostile comments about the book of Esther that I encountered in the learned tomes that I consulted in some of the world's greatest libraries made my blood curdle, and sometimes caused my hand to shake as I transcribed them. Readers, I suppose, will often hear the jingle-jangle of these discordant voices reverberating between the lines of this book, not to mention vague traces of Bob Dylan and Billie Holiday. I hope, however, that this will not prevent them from also hearing what the Victorian poet and translator Edward Fitzgerald felicitously called "the brave music of a distant drum."[47]

[45] Gosse, *History*, 227–28; Edmund Gosse, *The Life of Philip Henry Gosse* (London, 1890), 219–20; idem, *Father and Son: A Study of Two Temperaments* (1972 [1907]), 9.
[46] Gosse, *History*, 228.
[47] Edward Fitzgerald, trans. *The Rubáiyát of Omar Khayyám* (London 1859).

A Brief Guide (and an Apologia)

What I have herein performed, I had rather the Reader should tell
me at the end, then I tell him at the beginning of the Book.

—Thomas Fuller, *Pisgah-Sight of Palestine* (1650)

This book is divided into two sections; the first is devoted primarily to the
book of Esther and the difficult questions it posed—and continues to
pose—for both Jews and Christians since late antiquity. Was it a book that
promoted cruel vengeance or one that sought primarily to show the hidden
hand of God in history (chap. 1)? Was Esther a greater heroine than
Vashti or vice versa (chap. 2)? Did Mordecai "the Jew" do the right thing
in refusing to bow before Haman (chap. 3), and was the latter's enmity
against the Jews personal or tribal (chap. 4)? Chapter 5 moves from the
book of Esther to the biblical theme of Amalek and examines the ways in
which this archenemy of the Jews (and their God) was defined and imagined
over the centuries. Since according to Jewish law the Amalekites,
including women and children, had to be utterly destroyed, thinking
about Amalek involved, as we have seen, thinking about the possibilities
of, and justifications for, Jewish violence.

Chapter 6, which opens the second part, examines one specific form of
Jewish violence over many centuries—the desecration of the cross and
other Christian images. The following chapter examines discussions over
the centuries, in both Jewish and Christian literature, as to whether Jews
were by nature—or divine punishment—less capable of violence than
other peoples. The impact of such discussions upon the historiography of
Jewish violence informs chapter 8, devoted to violence against Christians,
sometimes within the context of Purim festivity, in the fifth–seventh centuries. Chapter 9 carries the subject of Purim violence into medieval and
early modern Europe, especially against the background of the often violent rites of Carnival. The final chapter is devoted to the history of local
Purims, to the question of their origins, and to the problems of continuity and discontinuity in "invented traditions."

Along the way we shall encounter such diverse figures as Saint Augustine,
Bernard Berenson, Miguel de Cervantes, Benjamin Disraeli, James Frazer,
Blu Greenberg, Adolf Hitler, Christopher Isherwood, Lyndon Johnson,
Meir Kahane, Benny Leonard, Cotton Mather, Friedrich Nietzsche,
George Orwell, Philip Roth, Harriet Beecher Stowe, Alfred Lord
Tennyson, Pope Urban II, John Wesley, and Leopold Zunz, and this
sometimes dizzying diversity will undoubtedly annoy some readers as

much as it delights others. Hopefully the latter will outnumber the former, to whom I offer my apologies in advance. And I should perhaps add, following the great (though controversial) French scholar Ernest Renan, that any reader who thinks that the word "perhaps" has not been used frequently enough "can fill it in at his own discretion."[48]

[48] Renan, *History* 1:xvii–xviii.

PART ONE

BIBLICAL LEGACIES

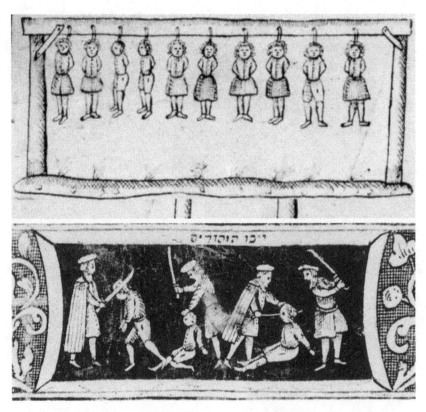

2. Two scenes from an eighteenth-century Italian illustrated scroll of Esther. From Israel Museum 182/175. Courtesy of the Israel Museum, Jerusalem.

I

The Book of Esther

FOR AND AGAINST

Eminent (and Less Eminent) Victorians
Encounter the Book of Esther

NO BOOK in the Old Testament, it has been aptly observed, "has occasioned more antipathy for some readers, and more enjoyment for others, than the book of Esther."[1] Among the Jews it was a great favorite, especially when they found themselves threatened by a new "Haman" of their own generation. Its status was both reflected and buttressed by the authoritative statement of Maimonides in the twelfth century that, alone among the Bible's non-Pentateuchal books, Esther would never become obsolete, even in the Messianic era?[2] Among Christians it has been treated, especially before Luther, either "as an allegory or as a prophetic . . . statement regarding Christ and the Virgin," in which Mordecai featured as the former and Esther as the latter, or, particularly among Protestants, "with bewilderment and with scorn for its sanctioning of . . . barbarous deeds against non-Jews."[3]

The latter position, however, was not limited to believers. "We close the blood-stained Book of Esther with feelings of loathing and disgust," wrote Austin Holyoake in his brief but pungent pamphlet tellingly titled *The Book of Esther: A Specimen of What Passes as "the Inspired Word of God."* Holyoake (1826–1874), together with his older brother George Jacob, was a leading figure in the British secularist movement, and author also of *Thoughts on Atheism* (1870) and *Ludicrous Aspects of Christianity* (1873). His laundry list of incidents recorded in the book of Esther included "drunkenness, domestic tyranny, lust, ambition, vacillation,

---

[1] Fuerst, *Ruth, Esther*, 32.
[2] Maimonides, *Mishneh Torah*, Hilkhot Megillah, 2:18.
[3] Fuerst, *Ruth, Esther*, 32.

revenge, and wholesale and brutal murder of innocent men, women and children," and he described Queen Esther as a "tigress" of "diabolical ferocity"[4]—a subject to which we shall return in the next chapter. In nineteenth-century England, then, one did not have to be a believing Christian to loathe the book of Esther.

Against the background of robust condemnations of Esther by both representatives of the church (such as Dean Stanley) and its opponents (such as Holyoake), what were Victorian Jews to do? In 1877 Ellis Davidson published—under the explicit "sanction" of Britain's Chief Rabbi Nathan Marcus Adler—*The Bible Reader . . . Adapted for the Use of Jewish Schools and Families, With the Addition of Questions on the Text, and Moral Reflections on Each Chapter.* As the subtitle of his reader made clear, Davidson recognized that there were biblical passages that provoked "moral reflection," but he did not necessarily feel obligated to include all of these in a work intended primarily for the use of "Jewish schools and families." Thus Davidson's bowdlerized version of Esther omitted not only the information that its eponymous heroine "was fair and beautiful" (Esther 2:7), but also much of the brutality in the book's penultimate chapters, in which the Jews took ample advantage of the permission granted them by Ahasuerus "to destroy, to slay, and to annihilate any armed force . . . that might attack them, with their children and women" (8:11).[5] Although he quoted the royal decree, Davidson deleted the gory details of the ensuing casualties.

The "moral reflections" that followed Davidson's excerpts from the book of Esther focused primarily on questions of propriety. In reading the book, he acknowledged, "we are likely to feel surprised that Esther, a Jewess, should enter the palace, and become the wife of an idolater, however exalted his position." He reminded his readers, however, that "she lived in a country where the word of the king was law, and where none dared dispute the royal will." The massive revenge taken by the Jews was not seen as a moral problem, since Esther, according to Davidson, "did not ask for revenge," only that her people "should be allowed fairly to defend themselves." Nor were the hangings of Haman, the king's chief minister, and his ten sons (Esther 9:25) seen as acts of Jewish vengeance. The hanging of the former—on the gallows that he had prepared for Mordecai (7:10)— was not, according to Davidson, "at Esther's request," and his ten sons "were slain in the battle" and only afterwards hanged "to show the people how utterly the whole house of Haman was degraded, and in order that future assaults might be prevented."[6]

[4] Holyoake, *Esther*, 2–3, 11.
[5] E. A. Davidson, *The Bible Reader . . .* (London, 1877), 359–63.
[6] Ibid., 366–67.

Rather different in his approach was Davidson's younger co-religionist and contemporary, Claude Goldsmid Montefiore. "Among the thousands and thousands of Jews who have celebrated and still celebrate the festival [of Purim]," wrote Montefiore in 1896, "it is likely that very few have paid any heed to the moral and religious worth of the book on which the festival now depends."[7] Montefiore (1858–1938), a leading figure in the world of Anglo-Jewry, was the great-nephew of the renowned Sir Moses (1784–1885) and grandson of Sir Isaac Lyon Goldsmid (1778–1859), who had been made a baronet by Queen Victoria in 1841—the first professing Jew in England to be awarded a hereditary title. In 1878, following in the footsteps of his brother Leonard and together with such talented young men as George Nathaniel Curzon (the future viceroy of India)—Claude Montefiore entered Balliol, "the most stimulating Oxford college of the time, and a kindergarten for aspiring politicians and diplomats." Its master since 1870 had been the legendary—though controversial—Benjamin Jowett, who had been instrumental in bringing modern biblical criticism to Oxford, but was also remembered by one of Balliol's first Jewish students as having "had a preference for those Jews who were staunch to their faith, and rather regarded with contempt the renegade type." While Curzon obtained a "first" in the Mods examination but only a "second" in the more demanding Greats (*Literae Humaniores*), Montefiore received a coveted "first" in the latter.[8] After Oxford he studied in Berlin with the great rabbinic scholar Solomon Schechter, whom, being independently wealthy, he was able to bring back to London as his private tutor. Montefiore also used his fortune to found, with his friend Israel Abrahams, the *Jewish Quarterly Review* in 1888, and four years later he delivered—at Jowett's invitation—the prestigious Hibbert Lectures at Oxford.[9] In his *Bible for Home Reading*, a two-volume anthology "with comments and reflections for the use of Jewish parents and their children" first published in 1896, Montefiore prefaced the text of Esther (which he

[7] Montefiore, *BHR*, II, 2:386.

[8] On Balliol during Jowett's years and his impact on the college, see Peter Hinch, *Benjamin Jowett and the Christian Religion* (Oxford, 1987), esp. 96–120. On Curzon's experiences at Balliol, see most recently David Gilmour, *Curzon* (London, 1994), 23f. For a discussion of Jowett's intellectual impact from the perspective of one of Balliol's first Jewish students, see O. J. Simon, "The Master of Balliol (Professor Jowett): In Memoriam," in his *Faith and Experience: A Selection of Essays and Addresses* (London, 1895), 238–48 [originally published in the *Jewish Chronicle*, October 6, 1893]; Simon, "Jowett's Religious Teaching," *JQR*, o.s. 8 (1896): 245–59.

[9] On Montefiore, see Lucy Cohen, *Some Recollections of Claude Goldsmid Montefiore: 1858–1938* (London, 1940); Chaim Bermant, *The Cousinhood* (New York, 1972), 313–27; Edward Kessler, *An English Jew: The Life and Writings of Claude Montefiore* (London, 1989);

included in its entirety) with some "comments and reflections" on the book's historicity and moral implications, as well as those of the holiday of Purim with which it was intimately linked. He asserted that although "in the case of the Bible, as well as in the case of every other book, our duty is to do homage to the God of truth and of goodness," most commentators on Esther had, in his view, erred in one direction or the other:

> On the one hand, its religious and moral deficiencies have been ignored or explained away; on the other they have been exaggerated and falsely labelled. Just because of these very deficiencies it has been called by enemies of the Jews and of the Jewish religion the most specifically Jewish book of the Hebrew Bible, and it is still so called to this day. But this is both inaccurate and unjust.[10]

As part of his firm commitment to what he (perhaps naïvely) called "the God of truth and of goodness," Montefiore was willing to acknowledge that Judaism possessed both "excellencies" and "defects," but insisted that it would be "monstrous" to single out the latter "and to say that in these, and only in these, lie the characteristics of our faith." Doing so, he claimed, would be akin to describing a person exclusively on the basis of his faults— a practice that, as a Victorian gentleman, Montefiore considered "shamefully unfair." Moreover, he argued, what if on one specific day a person's "peculiar faults resulted in some specially objectionable deed." Would it not be "grossly unjust," he asserted, "to say that that particular day was the most characteristic day of his life! Yet this is precisely what some non-Jewish critics do as regards Judaism and the Book of Esther."[11]

Christian critique of the book of Esther went back, as we have seen, to Martin Luther in the sixteenth century. By the late nineteenth century it had received prominent expression not only in German scholarship but also in the works of such esteemed British scholars as Arthur Penrhyn Stanley (1815–1881) and Samuel Rolles Driver (1846–1914), both of whom served as canons of Christ Church at Oxford simultaneously with their academic appointments at the university. The former, in his widely read if quaintly titled *Lectures on the History of the Jewish Church*, had referred to the "natural objection of the civilised—we may add, of the Christian—conscience, to the Book of Esther and the Feast of Purim."[12]

A. H. Friedlander in *DBI* 2:160–61. Montefiore's Hibbert Lectures, on "The Origin and Growth of Religion as Illustrated by the Religion of the Ancient Hebrews," were extensively covered in *The Jewish Chronicle* (see especially "The Hibbert Lectures: A Retrospect," in the issue of June 10, 1892, 11–13) and were soon published in book form.

[10] Montefiore, *BHR*, 2:386. On Montefiore's treatment of the book of Esther see Jonathan Magonet, "The Liberal and the Lady: Esther Revisited," *Judaism* 29 (1980): 167–76.

[11] Montefiore, *BHR*, 2:386–87.

[12] Stanley, *Lectures*, 3:176–78.

Driver, who had begun his Hebrew studies as a schoolboy at Winchester, had since 1883 been Regius Professor of Hebrew at Oxford, a position to which he was appointed by Prime Minister William Gladstone.[13] In his *Introduction to the Literature of the Old Testament*, first published in 1891 (a ninth edition was published in 1913), Driver informed his readers that "much fault has been found with the temper displayed in the Book of Esther," which was "said, for instance, to breathe a spirit of vengeance and hatred, without any redeeming feature; and to be further removed from the spirit of the gospel than any other Book of the OT [Old Testament]." Driver also commented on the absence of God's name in the book, which he saw as reflective of its "purely secular" point of view; "the preservation of the [Jewish] race as such, and its worldly greatness, not the perpetuation or diffusion of its religion," he asserted, "are the objects in which the author's interest is manifestly centred."[14]

Driver's decidedly negative comments on the book of Esther, which reflect, as we have seen, the liberal-Anglican consensus in late nineteenth-century England, may be contrasted with those of his Oxford colleague the Assyriologist Archibald Henry Sayce—over whom, ironically, he had been chosen for the Regius professorship by the religiously conservative Gladstone, who considered the latter "too unsound in the faith."[15] In 1885 Sayce had contributed a volume on Ezra, Nehemiah, and Esther to a series published by the Religious Tract Society in which, without polemicizing against those who had dismissed the book of Esther, he defended its religious utility as providing "a useful illustration of a fact which is oft forgotten"—that "God's inspiration is not confined to a particular kind of literary work or a particular description of narrative." Thus, "secular as it seems to be in tone," asserted Sayce, the book of Esther "has been made an instrument through which God has revealed His will to us, and prepared the way for the work of Christ."[16]

---

[13] On Driver, see most recently the essay by J. A. Emerton, 122–38, in *A Century of British Orientalists, 1902–2001*, ed. C. E. Bosworth (Oxford, 2001). On biblical scholarship in nineteenth-century England, see Gerald Parsons, "Biblical Criticism in Victorian Britain: From Controversy to Acceptance," in *Religion in Victorian Britain*, ed. Parsons, 4 vols (Manchester, 1988), 2:238–57; R. E. Clements, "The Study of the Old Testament," 3:109–41, in *Nineteenth-Century Religious Thought in the West*, ed. Ninian Smart et al., 3 vols (Cambridge, 1985).

[14] Driver, *Introduction*, 456–57.

[15] See A. S. Peake, *Recollections and Appreciations*, ed. W. F. Howard (London, 1938), 74. On Sayce (1845–1933), see also Cheyne, *Founders*, 232–33, where he is described as having served, in his more popular writings, as "a pillar of traditional views of the Bible" and even "an orthodox apologist."

[16] A. H. Sayce, *An Introduction to the Books of Ezra, Nehemiah, and Esther* (4th ed., London, 1893), 120.

These pious words seem to have convinced neither Driver nor Walter Adeney, professor of New Testament exegesis and church history at London's New College (not to be confused with Oxford's, where Driver had been a fellow), who soon afterward contributed a similar volume on Ezra, Nehemiah, and Esther to the *The Expositor's Bible*. In his opening comments on Esther he stressed the "striking contrast between the high estimation" with which the book was "cherished among the Jews" and the "slighting treatment that is often meted out to it in the Christian church." Adeney, who had earlier served as a Congregational minister in London (Acton) from 1872–1889, made no secret of the fact that he considered the "slighting treatment" of Esther to be the correct one. "It is indisputable," he wrote, "that the book is not characterised by the pure and lofty spirit that gives its stamp to most of the other contents of the Bible."[17]

The book of Esther, Adeney further asserted, "is dedicated to nothing higher than the exaltation of the Jews," and "this practical deification of Israel permits a tone of heartless cruelty." While acknowledging that Haman was richly deserving of punishment, he felt that the Jews had gone too far in making him "the recipient of unrestrained scorn" and impaling his sons "on their father's huge stake." Of the Jews' "legalised slaughter of their 'enemies'" (his quotation marks), Adeney tellingly commented: "We cannot imagine a scene more foreign to the patience and gentleness inculcated by our Lord," by whom he meant, of course, Jesus Christ. Although the Jews had been faced with an "order of extermination," this, Adeney asserted, "does not excuse the savagery" of their actions, "but it amply accounts for their conduct. They were wild with terror, and they defended their homes with the fury of madmen." The wanton violence of the wild—and somehow no longer mild—Jews was nonetheless more understandable to Adeney than "the responsible part taken by Mordecai and Esther in begging permission for this awful massacre." As a consequence of their intervention, he asserted, "the last pages of . . . Esther reek with blood."[18]

In his own comments on the book's final chapters, in *The Bible for Home Reading*, Claude Montefiore was hardly less critical of his coreligionists and their alleged behavior than had been Dean Stanley, Canon Driver, and Rev. Adeney:

> We can hardly dignify or extenuate the operations of the Jews by saying that they were done in self-defense. For we are told that all the officials helped the Jews, and that none durst withstand them. Moreover, the slain apparently included both women and children. There is no fighting, but just as

---

[17] Adeney, *Ezra, Nehemia, and Esther*, 351, 355.
[18] Ibid., 357–59.

there was to have been a massacre of unresisting Jews, so now there is a massacre of unresisting Gentiles.[19]

Montefiore may well have been the first Jew to describe the events chronicled at the end of Esther as "a massacre of unresisting Gentiles," but as a critically trained scholar whose Oxford education had been leavened by exposure to German *Wissenschaft*, he was able to seek some measure of solace in the book's widely questioned historicity. "But in truth, as the slaughter is purely a paper one," he wrote, "so we need not imagine the [biblical] writer to have been so bloodthirsty as he seems at first sight. . . . A stroke of a pen did not hurt a single human being, and yet it was so tempting to increase the numbers!"[20] Of course, from our own historical perspective it is hard to concur that strokes of a pen cannot hurt human beings—as Montefiore, who died in 1938 and lived to see the publication of both *The Protocols of the Elders of Zion* and *Mein Kampf*, probably came to realize.

Despite his attempts to lessen the impact of Esther's last chapters by questioning their historicity, Montefiore, who explicitly agreed with Adneney that they "reek with blood," acknowledged in his final verdict "that if the Bible had not included the Book of Esther, it would have gained rather than lost in religious value and moral worth." To the obvious question of why he had nonetheless included it, in its entirety, in his *Bible for Home Reading* he replied somewhat lamely that "the book is too well known and the festival of Purim is still too well celebrated, for such an omission." Montefiore, always the gentleman, added as a codicil to his comments on Esther that if he had perhaps been too severe in his criticisms, the reader, having been given the entire book, "has the same material as I for forming a better judgement."[21]

FAREWELL TO PURIM?

If the holiday of Purim was "still . . . well celebrated" in 1896, when *The Bible for Home Reading* was first published, this was despite its author's own controversial efforts, eight years earlier, to bring its observance to an end. Early in March of 1888 Montefiore, who was then thirty years old, had contributed an article entitled "Purim Difficulties" to the London *Jewish Chronicle*, which opened with the statement that "for those who regard Judaism as a religion pure and simple, and the Jews as merely the members

[19] Montefiore, *BHR*, 2:403.
[20] Ibid., 388, 403. For some recent discussions of Esther's historicity—or lack thereof—see Moore, *Esther*, xxxiv–xlvi; Fox, *Character and Ideology*, 131–138.
[21] Montefiore, *BHR*, 2:405.

of a religious brotherhood, any festival which . . . lacks an inward and essential religious justification presents serious difficulties and objections. Such a festival is Purim." It was, he argued, "surely of doubtful propriety to give public thanks to God for a triumph which probably never existed . . . , or which, if it be a fact, is yet not lifted up out of the religion of crude vengeance by any grand and signal religious issue." And so Montefiore, who had written to his former tutor Solomon Schechter the previous summer that he was "meditating all while upon the effect of Biblical Criticism upon our conception of Judaism,"[22] made it publicly known before Purim of 1888 that, for his part, he would "not be sorry" if a festival celebrating probably fictitious events "and which . . . while merely representative of the national element in Judaism represents even that in its most unpleasing aspect, were gradually to lose its place in our religious calendar."[23]

One may detect in Montefiore's remarks an echo of the description of Purim by Stanley (a fellow graduate of Balliol) as the "least pleasing" of the Jewish festivals. Although he had been careful, in his 1888 essay, to stop short of explicitly calling for the abolition of Purim, some of his co-religionists reacted rather angrily to his article. Samuel Montagu—the future first Baron Swaythling and then Liberal MP for Whitechapel—who was widely known for his religious orthodoxy, wrote to the *Jewish Chronicle* that he had read it "with painful feelings, almost approaching disgust," and Oswald Simon, who had been Montefiore's contemporary at Balliol, asserted that Jews had always observed their national triumphs "religiously and not otherwise." Simon, who was to become co-founder with Montefiore and Israel Abrahams of the reformist Jewish Religious Union, claimed—as we shall see, not entirely accurately—that "Jews have never gone about the streets on the fourteenth of Adar with an effigy of Haman," but have rather, following the call of the psalmist, "gone into the House of God with prayer and entered his courts with thanksgiving."[24]

The more Orthodox—and short lived—*Jewish Standard* published, under the title "Purim Difficulties," the text of a sermon in response to Montefiore's eponymous article that had been delivered at London's St. John's Wood Synagogue. Its author, the Rev. [Berman] Berliner, acknowledged that "unfortunately, the Feast of Purim is neglected by some of our

---

[22] *Lieber Freund: The Letters of Claude Goldsmid Montefiore to Solomon Schechter*, ed. J. B. Stein, (Lanham, 1988), 6.

[23] C. G. Montefiore, "Purim Difficulties," *Jewish Chronicle*, March 2, 1888, 8.

[24] *Jewish Chronicle*, March 9, 1888, 6. On Montagu, who in 1887 had established the Federation of Synagogues, see L. P. Gartner, *The Jewish Immigrant in England, 1870–1914* (Detroit, 1960), 114–15, 203–6, and E. C. Black, "Edwin Montagu," *TJHSE* 30 (1987–1988), 200–204. On Simon, see David Cesarani, *The Jewish Chronicle and Anglo-Jewry, 1841–1991* (Cambridge, 1994), 71, 90, 94, and note 8, above.

coreligionists, from whom a better example might be expected," but he nonetheless felt that "almost every sentence" in the article—the name of whose author he evidently dared not speak—"requires revision and emendation." Regarding the alleged "feeling of vengeance which is fostered by this festival [of Purim]," Berliner replied, "I challenge anyone to point out in our service any words of rejoicing for the large number of people who were killed." And although he admitted that there had been a "slaughter," Berliner confidently asserted that it had been perpetrated "in self defence," adding, with more than a touch of pathos, "It is quite a mistake to think that there were not then, as there have been in every age, thousands of men who would gladly wreak their vengeance upon the defenceless Jew."[25] In these last remarks Berliner would appear to have been alluding to the wave of pogroms that had assaulted Eastern European Jewry just a few years earlier, following the assassination of Czar Alexander II in 1881— shortly, in fact, before the holiday of Purim.[26]

Although Montefiore did not explicitly respond to his critics, when he returned in 1896, in his *Bible for Home Reading*, to the question of Purim's observance, his attitude had softened somewhat. This, however, seems to have had more to do with the comments of Walter Adeney (which he approvingly quoted) than with the criticisms of his co-religionists. "The worthiness of the festival," Adeney had written,

> will vary according to the ideas and feelings that are encouraged in connection with it. When it has been used as an opportunity for cultivating pride of race, hatred, contempt, and gleeful vengeance over humiliated foes its effect must have been injurious and degrading. When, however, it has been celebrated in the midst of grievous oppressions, though it has embittered the spirit of animosity towards the oppressor, it has been of real service in cheering a cruelly afflicted people. Even when it has been carried through with no seriousness of intention, merely as a holiday devoted to music, dancing, and games, and all sorts of merrymaking, its social effect in bringing a gleam of light into lives that were as a rule dismally sordid may have been decidedly healthy.[27]

Ironically, then, it was a Congregationalist minister rather than the rabbi of the St. Johns Wood Synagogue who helped bring Montefiore to the realization that over the centuries Purim may indeed have been "of

---

[25] *The Jewish Standard*, March 16, 1888. The sermon had been delivered on March 10. On Berliner, who had previously been minister of a synagogue in Bristol, see V. D. Lipman, "The Age of Emancipation, 1815–1880," in Lipman, ed., *Three Centuries of Anglo-Jewish History* (Cambridge, 1961), 85, 101.

[26] Among recent studies, see Aronson, *Troubled Waters*; Klier and Lombroza, *Pogroms*.

[27] Adeney, *Ezra, Nehemia, and Esther*, 401–2; Montefiore, *BHR*, 2:405–6.

real service in cheering a cruelly afflicted people," and in "bringing a gleam of light into lives that were as a rule dismally sordid." Yet there was one aspect of the festival's fury openly acknowledged by Adeney that Montefiore chose to omit—hostility toward Christians. The former had written that although Purim "has embittered the spirit of animosity towards the oppressor—*the Christian Haman in most cases*—it has been of real service in cheering a cruelly afflicted people" (emphasis added). In the long passage from Adeney's comments on Esther that he included in his *Bible for Home Reading*, Montefiore furtively deleted (without ellipsis!) the reference to Jewish animosity toward "the Christian Haman." Thus, despite his stated determination to present his imagined reader with the entire book of Esther, warts and all, so that he would have "the same material as I for forming a better judgement," Montefiore felt it both necessary and justifiable to withhold Adeney's passing reference to anti-Christian elements in the observance of Purim, even when these appeared "in the midst of grievous oppressions."

In his *Liberal Judaism* (1903), published shortly after he helped to establish England's reformist Jewish Religious Union, Montefiore discussed the major and minor Jewish holidays. Among the latter he included "Purim and the Fast of Ab, which, though not mentioned in the Pentateuch, once played an important part in Jewish life, but . . . are now dropping into desuetude." The only non-Pentateuchal festival which, in his view, was "likely to maintain itself," was that of Hannukah. By linking Purim with the equally waning Ninth of Ab Montefiore alluded only to its declining observance rather than its moral repugnance. Similarly, in his *Outlines of Liberal Judaism* published nine years later, Montefiore asserted that "of the non-Pentateuchal festivals . . . the only which [English] Liberal Judaism should retain," was, to his thinking, that of Hannukah, which celebrated "the heroism of the Maccabean martyrs and warriors, and the preservation of the Jewish religion at a season of utmost peril."[28] Although he had switched from a descriptive tone to a more prescriptive one, Montefiore was still more careful than he had earlier been to avoid explicit criticism of Purim's moral character.

"Ungodly Confidence"

Montefiore's shift may perhaps be explained by the strident criticisms of Esther and Purim that were being expressed in liberal Protestant circles. In 1891, as we have already seen, S. R. Driver, the Regius Professor of Hebrew

---

[28] Montefiore, *Liberal Judaism* (London, 1903), 134–35; idem, *Outlines of Liberal Judaism: For the Use of Parents and Teachers* (London, 1912), 258–59.

at Oxford, expressed the view that "it seems . . . impossible to acquit Mordecai of permitting, and the Jews of engaging in, an unprovoked massacre."[29] Early in the twentieth century Thomas Witton Davies, a professor of Semitic Languages at University College in North Wales who had previously been principal of a Baptist college in Nottingham, approvingly cited Luther's reservations concerning the book of Esther and also Heinrich Ewald's comment that one was "falling from heaven to earth" when moving to Esther from the other books of the Hebrew Bible.[30]

In truth, however, the influence of the latter two had, in German scholarship, continued unabated throughout the latter half of the nineteenth century. Ewald's contemporary Ernest Bertheau, who was a professor at Göttingen, asserted that Esther and Mordecai "are full of a spirit of revenge and hostility not [merely] to Gentile ways, but to the Gentiles themselves . . . and of ungodly confidence in a victory over the world."[31] Bertheau's words were published in 1862, two decades after A. H. Hoffmann had composed *Deutschland, Deutschland, über alles*, and the very year in which Otto von Bismarck was appointed prime minister of Prussia. Upon entering office Bismarck famously declared that "the great questions of the day" were decided "not by parliamentary speeches and majority votes," but rather "by iron and blood." If any entity could in those years be seen as harboring an "ungodly confidence in a victory over the world," it was Bismarck's Prussia, which under the aegis of the newly established German Reich annexed Alsace-Lorraine in 1871, together with its more than a million and a half residents—prompting some to remark that "Europe has lost a mistress and gained a master."[32] By 1884, when Heinrich von Treitschke declared that "colonization was a matter of life and death," the German Reich had established its first colonies in Africa, soon to be followed by protectorates in the Pacific—including the northeastern part of New Guinea.[33]

And yet German Bible scholars continued to rant against the arrogant nationalism of the book of Esther. Emil Friedrich Kautzsch, who became professor of theology at Halle in 1888, asserted that the book of Esther "expresses such national arrogance and such hatred of other nations" that

---

[29] Driver, *Introduction*, 456.

[30] Davies, *Ezra, Nehemiah, and Esther*, 293.

[31] E. Bertheau, *Die Bücher Esra, Nechemia, und Ester* (1862), quoted in Keil, *Ezra, Nehemiah, and Esther*, 315.

[32] See L. L. Snyder, *Roots of German Nationalism* (Bloomington, Ind., 1978), 55–74; Peter Pulzer, *Germany, 1870–1945: Politics, State Formation, and War* (Oxford, 1997), 11–15, 40–45.

[33] Snyder, *Roots of German Nationalism*, 75–91; G. A. Craig, *Germany: 1866–1945* (Oxford, 1978), 116–24.

it was easy to understand "the strong objections to its canonicity which have been raised."[34] Similarly, Carl Heinrich Cornill, who succeeded Kautzsch to the professorship at Halle upon the latter's death, wrote in 1891 that "the Christian expositor of the Old Testament would prefer to pass over the Book of Esther altogether," asserting furthermore that "the framers of the canon [here] committed a serious blunder. All the worst and most unpleasing features of Judaism are here displayed without disguise."[35]

Although some might argue that in Cornill's comments on Esther "all the worst and most unpleasing features" of German Protestant biblical scholarship are "displayed without disguise," by the end of the nineteenth century, as we have seen, such evaluations of the book had become standard in the Anglo-American world as well. It must also be acknowledged that there were also some German Jews who, like Claude Montefiore later in the nineteenth century, expressed deep misgivings about the book of Esther and the holiday with which it was linked. Abraham Geiger (1810–1874), the great scholar and reformer, not only expressed doubts about Esther's historicity, but also described it as "lacking in taste and morality" (*geschmack-und gesinnunglos*).[36] This went hand in hand with his sense, as early as 1861, that "Amalek and his alleged descendant Haman can no longer instil in our hearts the same aversion" that they could in earlier times.[37]

ESTHER AND ETHICS

Early in the twentieth century the British Baptist Thomas Davies, who had earned his doctorate in Leipzig, pointed, as had many German scholars, to the presence throughout the book "of a low ethical standard . . . . Nothing seems wrong if only it furthers the advancement of the Jews." One reflection of the book's "low ethical standard," according to Davies,

[34] E. F. Kautzsch, *An Outline of the History of the Old Testament*, trans. John Taylor (London 1898 [German original, 1897]), 131. On Kautzsch, see C. T. Begg in *DBI*, 2:17.

[35] C. H. Cornill, *Introduction to the Canonical Books of the Old Testament*, trans. G. A. Box (New York, 1907 [German original, 1891]), 257. On Cornill, see R. Smend, in *DBI*, 1:227. Note also the remark by Hermann Gunkel (1862–1932) that the book "cannot be read by a Christian or a non-Jew without great distaste." Gunkel, *What Remains of the Old Testament, and Other Essays*, trans. A. K. Dallas (New York, 1928), 16.

[36] A. Geiger, *Nachgelassene Schriften* ed. L. Geiger, 5 vols (Berlin 1875–1878), 170; Bickerman, *Four Strange Books*, 217. The volume reference given by the latter (ibid., 239n56) is incorrect, and I thank Jay Harris for providing me with the correct one. I have also translated Geiger a bit more literally than had Bickerman.

[37] Geiger, "Nothwendigkeit und Maas einer Reform des jüdischen Gottesdientes," (1861) reprinted in Geiger, *Nachgelassene Schriften* 1:203–29. See especially 209, 223.

was Esther's concealment of her Jewish identity at Mordecai's behest [Esther 2:10, 20], after being brought to the king's palace to compete in the royal beauty contest after proud Vashti's deposal. "To have been known as Jewish must at the time . . . have meant some disadvantages," he charitably conceded," and to "have concealed these things from the king, the eunuchs, and her rivals required extraordinary adroitness." Nonetheless, doing so exhibited, in his view, "but little steadfastness of principle on the part of Esther or her cousin [Mordecai]."[38]

Needless to say, at the time that Davies was writing his commentary on Esther, elements of British society—and of Europe as a whole—were experiencing considerable uneasiness at the prospect of contemporary Jews who were utilizing sometimes "extraordinary adroitness" in order to hide their origins and "pass" as members of polite society. In 1910, the year after which his commentary appeared, the narrator of G. K. Chesterton's novel *The Ball and the Cross* reflected on two types of Jews—those who changed their names and those who did not. "For though there are no hard tests for separating the tares and wheat of any people; one rude but efficient guide is that the nice Jew is called Moses Solomon and the nasty Jew is called Thornton Percy." A year later, in an address to London's West End Jewish Literary Society Chesterton (1874–1936) distinguished between the "broad-minded Jew" and his more likeable "narrow-minded" co-religionist: the former was "a difficulty and an offence in Europe," but "the narrow-minded Jew was an excellent fellow, whom one admired and regarded with an amount of veneration as one did any other great relic of antiquity, such as the pyramids."[39] And within a decade T. S. Eliot would invoke the specter of "Rachel *née* Rabinovich," the Jewish femme fatale who "tears at the grapes with murderous paws."[40] In the early twentieth century Jews were widely perceived as more pernicious when their identity was less obvious—a judgement with which Haman himself would certainly have concurred.

READING ESTHER AFTER THE RISE OF NAZISM

Although Hitler, who was widely associated with Haman, proved more successful in his genocidal plans than the latter, the Holocaust had little effect on the treatment of Esther by Christian scholars in the years immediately after World War II. In the late 1940s the Danish scholar Aage

---

[38] Davies, *Ezra, Nehemiah, and Esther*, 318.
[39] Bryan Cheyette, *Constructions of "the Jew" in English Literature and Society: Racial Representations, 1875–1945* (Cambridge, 1993), 181.
[40] Ibid., 250–51.

Bentzen described the book as "a very unpleasant example of how persecutions and suppressions have poisoned the soul of a nation," and approvingly quoted Luther's negative judgment. Bentzen, who had been Professor of Theology at the University of Copenhagen since 1930, also considered it "morally unsound" that Esther "conceals her nationality [Esther 2:10, 20] and so secures her high position [as queen] or at least avoids an unpleasant handicap"[41]—that handicap, of course, being anti-Semitism.[42] A similar criticism of Esther's dishonesty had been leveled in 1898 by the Dutch scholar Gerrit Wildeboer who had described her as having been "worldliwise but not honorable." The latter, however, has been taken to task by the American scholar Carey Moore, who wrote that "Wildeboer's observation . . . is rather unfair, and fails to take into consideration the complexity of life in the Golah."[43]

The "Golah," a Hebrew word that occurs in the book of Esther (2:6), is the Exile—or, to use a Greek word, Diaspora—where life has indeed been complex and where Jewishness, as some readers might remember, has often constituted what Bentzen so gingerly called "an unpleasant handicap." It was one thing for Wildeboer in the late nineteenth century to criticize Esther for concealing her identity, but for a Danish scholar to do so shortly after his country emerged from four years of Nazi occupation required considerably more obtuseness. Such obtuseness, however, was hardly in short supply among European Bible scholars both during and after World War II.

In 1937, four years after Hitler's rise to power, the German scholar Wilhelm Vischer saw the book of Esther as presenting "the Jewish question in the sharpest form." Although in his own view the "answer" was provided by the cross, which linked Haman and Jesus and which, he asserted, could establish "peace, instead of deadly hatred, between Jew and non-Jew,"[44] other Christian scholars continued to carelessly condemn the book of Esther for its nationalism and vindictiveness. In that same year Henry Wheeler Robinson, a Baptist divine and reader in biblical criticism at Oxford, described the book of Esther as "an exaltation of nationalism at its worst,"[45] and the Methodist scholar W. L. Northridge saw it as

---

[41] Bentzen, *Introduction to the Old Testament*, 2:194. There was no change in the second edition published in 1952. On Bentzen (1894–1953), see A. S. Kapelrud in *DBI*, 1:122.

[42] On Mordecai's motives in commanding Esther to keep her identity secret, see Fox, *Character and Ideology*, 32–33.

[43] G. Wildeboer, *Das Buch Esther* (Tübingen, 1898), 181; Moore, *Esther*, 28. On Wildeboer, who was a professor of Old Testament at Groningen between 1884–1907, see S. J. DeVries in *DBI*, 2:645.

[44] W. Vischer, *Esther* (Munich, 1937), 14, quoted in J. D. Levenson, "The Scroll of Esther in Ecumenical Perspective," *JES* 13 (1976): 441.

[45] H. W. Robinson, *The Old Testament: Its Making and Meaning* (London, 1937), 74.

revealing "Jewish vindictiveness at its worst" and as "setting the contrast between unworthy elements in Judaism and the Christian spirit of love to all." Claude Montefiore, who, as we have seen, had many reservations about the moral message of the book of Esther, nonetheless replied sharply (but politely) to his Methodist colleague in the monumental *Rabbinic Anthology*, which he published (with Herbert Loewe) shortly before his death in 1938: "There is a good deal of glass in both our houses," wrote Montefiore. "We had better not throw stones at one another."[46]

His co-editor Loewe, who had succeeded Israel Abrahams as reader in rabbinics at Cambridge, was a bit more forthright, although his bluntness was tastefully relegated to a footnote. "What seems so terrible in Dr. Northridge's arguments," Loewe remarked, "is the fact that they were written in 1937, when current events should have taught him to take a different view." In the best tradition of the Oxbridge debating hall, he then posed a rhetorical question: "Let us assume that the Book of Esther 'typifies Jewish vindictiveness at its worst' . . . shall we then go on to say that Hitler's barbarity typifies 'Christian vindictiveness at its worst'?" As far as the contemporary relevance of the book was concerned, Loewe ventured to say that "if we take the description of the events narrated [in Esther] at face value, we have a situation not very different from that which confronts Jews in Germany today."[47]

Even during the darkest years of the Holocaust, as we have already seen, German scholars such as Johannes Hempel continued unequivocally to condemn the vengeful spirit of the book of Esther. In 1940 Paul Heinisch, a Silesian-born Catholic scholar who was teaching in the Netherlands, published a German book on Old Testament theology which appeared in English a decade later, blessed with the Benedictine order's stamp of approval. In his book, which was reprinted (with the same order's imprimatur) in 1955, Heinisch grumbled that in Esther "Christian sensibilities are gravely wounded at the joy which the Jews showed when they were enabled to revenge themselves upon their enemies," adding that "here the Old Testament is definitely inferior to the New Testament."[48] In 1957 Artur Weiser, who had taught at the University of Tübingen since 1930, was still able to state that Luther's condemnation of the book "is a testament to the impartial clarity of the Christian verdict."[49]

---

[46] For the quotation from Northridge and Montefiore's response, see *A Rabbinic Anthology*, ed. C. G. Montefiore and H. Loewe (London, 1938), 614–15.

[47] Ibid., 679–80.

[48] Paul Heinisch, *Theologie des Alten Testaments* (Bonn, 1940), 182; idem, *Theology of the Old Testament*, trans. W. G. H. Heidt (Collegeville, Minn., 1950, 1955), 215. On Heinisch (1878–1956), see C. T. Begg in *DBI*, 1:491.

[49] Artur Weiser, *Introduction to the Old Testament*, trans. by D. M. Barton (on the basis of the 4th German ed., 1957) (London, 1961), 313. On Weiser (1893–1978), see H.-D. Neef in *DBI*, 2:626–27.

Not long afterward, Ernest Sellin's classic *Introduction to the Old Testament* was reissued—"completely revised and rewritten"—by Georg Fohrer. In the original edition Sellin, who taught at the University of Berlin from 1921, had referred to the "exclusive fanatical spirit" which animates the book of Esther, but which—he charitably conceded—could be excused "to a certain extent . . . by the equally fanatical persecution of the Jews." In Sellin's view, the book showed "the direction which was taken by the natural development of the Jewish mind; and how wide was the departure" by the time of its composition "from the path pointed out by . . . the prophets."[50] This, of course, according to the by then standard theological narrative of Protestant biblical scholarship,[51] made necessary the coming of Christ. Sadly, however, Sellin, who became an opponent of Hitler, was eventually forced by the direction taken by (what some might call) the "natural development of the German mind" to forfeit his emeritus status at the University of Berlin, where Johannes Hempel, not surprisingly, had no trouble maintaining his post.

When Sellin's Old Testament introduction was reissued (in German) by Fohrer in 1965, it still described the book of Esther as "the product of a nationalistic spirit, seeking revenge upon those that persecute the Jews." And that nationalistic spirit was portrayed, moreover, as having "lost all understanding of the demands and obligations of Yahwism, especially in its prophetical form."[52] The Christian subtext of Fohrer's remarks may be better understood by citing a passage from his essay on "The Jewish Question and Zionism," in which he argued that the latter was not a solution to the former:

> With the advent of the New Covenant, the Old Covenant is outdated. Christian revelation, on the other hand, is eternally young. But, with its coming, the existence of those who prepared it [the Jews] has lost any real meaning. It is in a sense paradoxical that the Old Testament people of God, despite this obsolescence, should continue to exist simultaneously with the people of the New Testament.[53]

[50] E. Sellin, *Introduction to the Old Testament*, trans. W. Montgomery (London, 1923 [German original, 1912]), 231–32.

[51] For a dissenting Catholic perspective, see, for example, Johannes Schildeberger O.S.B., *Das Buch Esther* (Bonn, 1941), 47.

[52] Sellin, *Introduction to the Old Testament*, "completely revised and rewritten by Georg Fohrer," trans. D. E. Green (Nashville, 1968), 255. Fohrer's German original had appeared in 1965, and the English translation was reprinted in 1976. On Sellin (1867–1946), see W. Thiel in *DBI*, 2:453–54; on Fohrer, see A. Siedlecki. *Ibid.*, 1:401–402.

[53] G. Fohrer, "Die Judenfrage und der Zionismus," in Fohrer, *Studien zur alt-testamentlichen Theologie und Geschichte, 1949–66* (Berlin, 1969), 44, quoted by Charlotte Klein, *Anti-Judaism*

"If," to quote again the words of Esther herself (Esther 7:4), "we had been sold merely as slaves . . . I would have held my peace," but Professor Fohrer has determined that "with the advent of the New Covenant," the existence of those who brought the (now obsolete) religion of prophetic Yahwism to the world "has lost any real meaning." One can certainly understand why a former denizen of the Third Reich might be made especially uncomfortable by a "nationalistic spirit seeking revenge upon those that persecute the Jews," but it also took considerable chutzpah for a scholar of Fohrer's background to continue to demean the book of Esther for "having lost all understanding of the demands and obligations of Yahwism." To those who insist on evaluating the book of Esther through the refracting glass of the Gospels, perhaps the best advice has recently been given by the British scholar D. J. Clines, who has sagely written that "the undoubted 'Jewishness' of the book is something it shares with the whole of the Old Testament; if that is an 'offence' in Christian eyes, it is a stumbling block that must be surmounted before any part of the Old Testament is appropriated for Christian use."[54]

Clines may have been alluding to criticisms of Esther found not only in the writings of nineteenth- and early twentieth-century scholars, but also in those of his own older contemporaries. In *The Growth of the Old Testament*, first published in 1950, Harold Rowley of the University of Manchester—who had served as a Baptist missionary in China during the 1920s—asserted that the book "breathes a spirit of intense nationalism," an allegation that remained unchanged in both the second (1958) and third (1967) editions of his influential work.[55] Rowley, who was professor of Semitic languages at Manchester between 1945–1959, was co-editor (for the Old Testament) of the second edition of *Peake's Commentary on the Bible*, for which he selected his former colleague Laurence Browne, who had since become Vicar of Highbrook (in Sussex), to write the commentary on Esther. Browne had spent several years in the *raj* (teaching in Lahore during 1930–1934), and had later been professor of comparative religion at Manchester (1941–1946) and professor of theology at Leeds (1946–1952) before accepting the vicarage at Shadwell, near Leeds, where he served until moving to Highbrook.[56] There is no record,

---

in Christian Theology, trans. E. Quinn (London, 1978), 8. For other choice passages from Fohrer's writings, see Klein, *Anti-Judaism*, 16–18, 42–45.

[54] Clines, *Ezra, Nehemiah, Esther*, 256.

[55] H. H. Rowley, *The Growth of the Old Testament* (London, 1950), 154. The first and second editions were each reprinted at least twice, and the third in 1969. On Rowley (1890–1969), see R. E. Clements in *DBI*, 2:423–24.

[56] All information on Browne, who was born in 1887, is taken from the British edition of *Who's Who 1981*, 340–41.

however, of his ever having any published anything on Esther until his 1962 contribution to the new *Peake's Commentary on the Bible*, which is perhaps best described as "over the top."

"The Book of Esther," wrote Browne by way of introduction, "occupies the same place in sacred scripture as the villainous rogue in a story or play which has been written with a moral purpose." Both Gentiles and Jews, he claimed, "are represented in the story as actuated by the basest motives of pride, greed, and cruelty," and the book's only useful place in the Bible "is as a picture of unredeemed humanity." Moreover, the "ultra-nationalist" book, Browne asserted, contained "no noble character," not even Mordecai, who "only thought of personal advancement." The latter's reason for refusing to bow before Haman, "though not explicitly stated," was "evident" according to Rev. Browne "from the whole tone of the book: Haman, the enemy of the Jews, was typical of all Gentiles, only fit for destruction."[57] Less than two decades after the Holocaust a Cambridge-educated Anglican vicar and former university professor was thus able to perversely present Mordecai as a Jewish proto-Hitler, for whom "all Gentiles" were fit only "for destruction."

Ironically, in his 1919 commentary on Esther for the original *Peake's Commentary on the Bible*, Archibald Duff trenchantly observed that "the literature on the book, while for the most part valuable, is marred by anti-Semitic prejudice which passes too unfavourable a judgement on the Jews." Duff, a Scottish scholar who a decade earlier had published a *History of Old Testament Criticism*, expressed admiration for the stress by Esther's author—whom he believed to be a contemporary of the Maccabees—upon the Jews' strict abstention from taking any booty, which added, he felt, "a touch of fine national self-respect." It was also an indication, according to Duff, of "what sort of society Jesus arose among, and sought to bless."[58] Duff clearly shared with many of the scholars whose views of the book he courageously condemned as "marred by anti-Semitic prejudice" a propensity to impose upon it a Christian perspective—one which, as we have seen, was accepted, even in "critical" biblical scholarship, for many decades.

ESTHER IN AMERICA

In his survey of *The Jewish Scriptures* (1896) Amos Kidder Fiske, a Harvard-educated journalist who wrote for the *New York Times*, informed his readers that the book of Esther was "saturated with pride of race in its most offensive guise," and asserted confidently that there was "surely

[57] Browne, "Esther," 381–85.
[58] Duff, "Esther," 336, 339–40.

nothing" in it "of the spirit of Christianity, or even of the better spirit of Judaism."[59] Less than a decade later John Edgar McFadyen, then professor of the Old Testament at Knox College in Toronto, published an *Introduction to the Old Testament* (1905) in which he described the book of Esther as characterized by "aggressive fanaticism and fierce hatred of all that lay outside of Judaism." Although McFadyen, who had been educated at Oxford and Glasgow, recognized the book's "attractive literary qualities," these, he asserted, "cannot blind us to its religious emptiness and moral depravity." The book's considerable popularity, he felt, was due primarily "to the power with which it expresses some of the most characteristic, if almost odious, traits of Judaism." A decade later, in his *Old Testament and the Christian Church*, McFadyen referred to the "violent and revengeful temper" of Esther, which could "only be condemned and deplored by the Christian conscience."[60]

Similarly, in *The Interest of the Bible* (1922), published after his return to Scotland, where he became a professor at the United Free Church College in Glasgow, McFadyen saw the book of Esther's "sanguinary temper," like Samson's dying prayer for vengeance upon the Philistines, as "separated by a whole moral world from the dying prayer of Jesus for forgiveness upon his enemies."[61] In *The Approach to the Old Testament* (1926) McFadyen returned once more to the book of Esther, citing approvingly the opinion of the American Bible scholar Lewis Paton that Esther's request from Ahasuerus for a "second butchery" shows "a malignant spirit of revenge more akin to the teaching of the Talmud than to the teaching of the Old Testament."[62] Paton, who taught at the Hartford Theological Seminary, had cited the view of Maimonides that in the Messianic era all non-Pentateuchal books of the Bible would become obsolete except for Esther, but asserted unequivocally that "with this verdict of late Judaism modern Christians cannot agree. The book is so conspicuously lacking in religion that it should never have been included in the Canon of the O.T." Paton claimed, moreover, that there was "not one noble character in this book," adding for good measure that "the verdict of Luther is not too severe."[63]

---

[59] A. K. Fiske, *The Jewish Scriptures: The Books of the Old Testament in the Light of their Origin and History* (London, 1896), 343–45. On Fiske (1842–1921), see J. D. Wade in *DAB*, 6:416–17.

[60] McFadyen, *Introduction*, 310–11, 315; McFadyen, *Old Testament and the Christian Church* (New York, 1915), 309.

[61] McFadyen, *The Interest of the Bible* (London, 1922), 22. He also referred in that work to the "peculiarly unlovely and indeed repulsive form" that the assertion of "national individuality" took in that book (113).

[62] McFadyen, *The Approach to the Old Testament* (London, 1926), 141; Paton, *Esther*, 287.

[63] Paton, *Esther*, 96–97.

In 1912 Hinckley Mitchell, an ordained Methodist minister and professor at Tufts College, published *The Ethics of the Old Testament*, in which
he castigated Esther for "paying the [sexual] price of her cousin's
advancement"—a subject to which we shall return in the next chapter.
Worse, however, in Mitchell's view was her request from Ahasuerus, in the
book's penultimate chapter (Esther 9:13), for a second day of Jewish
revenge and the hanging of Haman's sons. "There are many 'hard say-
ings' in the Old Testament," wrote Mitchell, "but for malice and cruelty
there is none that is more abhorrent to the humane reader than this heartless petition."[64]

Two years later, in *The Religion of the Hebrews*, Rev. John Peters of
St. Michael's (Episcopal) Church in New York, who like Mitchell had
pursued graduate study at the University of Leipzig, described Esther as
representing "the extreme narrow school of Judaism," and as exhibiting
a particularly "bitter hatred of foreigners."[65] Peters's book, it may be noted,
was reprinted, without change, by Harvard University Press in 1932. Six
years earlier Columbia University Press had published Julius Bewer's *The
Literature of the Old Testament in Its Historical Development* as part of its
renowned (and widely used) "Records of Civilization" series. Bewer, a
German-born professor at New York's Union Theological Seminary,
described the Jews of the Persian period, whose world, he believed, was
reflected in the book of Esther, as characterized by "clannishness and religious arrogance, which had found expression in the insistence on the
exclusive character of the Jewish race and its destiny as ruler of the world."
And the book itself, he asserted, was dominated by a "spirit of hate and
revenge," which explained its popularity during the Maccabean period
when "the jingo spirit became prevalent."[66]

"Jingoism," a term which originated with the blustering patriotism of
those who had sought to push Britain into war with Russia in the late
1870s, was again on the rise in Europe of the 1920s, finding expression,
for example, in the assassination of Germany's (Jewish) foreign minister
Walter Rathenau in 1922—the same year in which Bewer, who had earned
his Ph.D. at Columbia, was awarded another doctorate (in Theology) by
the University of Göttingen. Four years later, upon the publication of *The
Literature of the Old Testament in Its Historical Development*, he was made

---

[64] Mitchell, *Ethics*, 373–74. On Mitchell (1846–1920), an 1873 graduate of Wesleyan who
earned his doctorate at Leipzig in 1879, see R. H. Pfeiffer in *DAB*, 13:47–48.

[65] J. P. Peters, *The Religion of the Hebrews* (Boston, 1914), 23–24. On Peters (1852–1921),
who had been ordained in 1877 and studied in Berlin and Leipzig during the years
1879–1883, see M. P. Graham in *DBI*, 2:274–75.

[66] J. A. Bewer, *The Literature of the Old Testament in its Historical Development* (New York,
1926), 302–7. On Bewer (1877–1953), see J. M. Bullard in *DBI*, 1:125–26.

an honorary member of the same German university, few of whose faculty, one assumes, took offense at his reference in that work to the "clannishness and religious arrogance" of the ancient Jews. Bewer's book was reprinted without change (by Columbia University Press) in 1933.

One would perhaps have thought that the events in Europe between 1933 and 1945 would have chastened some of the criticisms of the book widely considered (by non-Jews) to be the "most Jewish" in the Old Testament. This, however, was hardly the case in Mary Ellen Chase's *The Bible and the Common Reader* (1944), which she graciously dedicated to her "students at Smith College who have enjoyed with me the reading and study of the King James Bible." Chase, a writer of both fiction and nonfiction previously best known for her novels about sea-faring families in her native Maine, expressed distaste for "the atmosphere of hatred and lust for blood which runs throughout" the book of Esther, in which "a narrow and fanatical patriotism everywhere takes the place of religious feeling."[67] Although Chase was hardly a respected Bible scholar, her popular book (a second edition of which appeared in 1960) undoubtedly did much to perpetuate the pernicious view of Esther that had become standard in America since the late nineteenth century.

In 1946, two years after the initial appearance of Chase's aforementioned work, Mortimer Cohen, who was rabbi of Philadelphia's Beth Shalom Synagogue, published *Pathways through the Bible*. His volume was an official project of the Jewish Publication Society of America, intended "primarily for the young," though it was believed that "adults will find in it interest, instruction, and enjoyment." Cohen had been ordained at New York's Jewish Theological Seminary in 1919, and the volume of biblical selections he edited was approved by a broad committee consisting of representatives not only of that institution and its allied (Conservative) Rabbinical Assembly, but also of the (Reform) Hebrew Union College and its allied Central Conference of American Rabbis, B'nai B'rith, and the National Council of Jewish Education. In his forward Cohen expressed the hope that the "general reader, as well as the teacher, will find here those classic passages of the Holy Scriptures which combine both literary beauty and the enduring ethical and religious values of Judaism."[68]

One may presume that it was in the interest of the latter that Rabbi Cohen had the king's decree, in the eighth chapter of Esther, grant the Jews the right only "to gather together and protect their lives," whereas the biblical original informs us, as noted above, that they were also granted the right to "destroy, to slay, and to annihilate any armed force . . . that might attack them, with their children and women" [Esther 8:11]. Cohen,

---

[67] Chase, *Bible*, 200–201. In the revised edition of 1960 none of these words was changed.
[68] M. J. Cohen, ed., *Pathways through the Bible* (Philadelphia, 1946), x.

who in his introduction to Esther had referred to the similarities between ancient and modern anti-Semitism, informed his readers that "on the fourteenth day of the month of Adar the Jews rested and made it a day of feasting and rejoicing," but even some of the younger ones must have asked themselves what the Jews were joyously resting from. The answer, of course, could be found in the (uncensored) book of Esther itself (9:5–16), where it was reported that the Jews of Shushan had over two days, killed eight hundred men, and "the other Jews who were in the king's provinces . . . slew seventy-five thousand of those who hated them."[69]

Not all American-Jewish authors of the postwar period were as eager as Cohen to suppress the number of casualties reported in the book of Esther. In *A Treasury of Jewish Holidays* (1952), Hyman Goldin found room in his summary of the book's plot to inform readers both of the eight hundred casualties in Shushan and that elsewhere "the Jews with the help of the king's officers killed seventy-five thousand of their enemies."[70] Whereas Cohen was the rabbi of a well-heeled Conservative congregation in Philadelphia, Goldin, who had emigrated to the United States from his native Lithuania, was an Orthodox rabbi who lived in Brooklyn and led a considerably less charmed life. He had served both as principal of two Jewish schools in Borough Park and chaplain of the Great Meadow Prison in Comstock, New York (1932–1947)—an experience that allowed him, among his many other literary projects, to co-edit *The Dictionary of American Underworld Lingo* (1950).[71] Goldin seems to have understood that attempts to keep sensitive information under wraps often led to the lid being, sometimes unpleasantly, blown off.

From these two American rabbis, one Conservative and one Orthodox, we may move, in conclusion, to their younger Reform colleague, Samuel Sandmel, who was a highly respected biblical scholar. In a general survey of the Hebrew Bible which he published in 1963, Sandmel, who was then provost of the Hebrew Union College—Jewish Institute of Religion, appended a personal postscript to his discussion of Esther:

> If a personal word is not out of order, the Scroll of Esther seemed to me at one time to have no place in Scripture, both because of its barbarity and what seemed to me then its unreality. But Hitler was a Haman *redivivus*, and the generation of those who were adults in 1932 discovered that the legends about the age of Xerxes came to be a traumatic modern experience.[72]

---

[69] Ibid., 499–500, 509–11.

[70] H. E. Goldin, *A Treasury of Jewish Holidays* (New York, 1952), 125–26.

[71] See the entry on Goldin in the 1973–1982 supplement to the *Encyclopedia Judaica*, 266.

[72] Samuel Sandmel, *The Hebrew Scriptures: An Introduction to their Literature and Religious Ideas* (New York, 1963), 504.

Sandmel had graduated from the University of Missouri in 1932 and was ordained at the Hebrew Union College four years later.[73] His formative years as a rabbinical student took place under the shadow of Hitler's rise to power, and this experience still shaped his view of the book of Esther some three decades later. Yet by the time he published *The Enjoyment of Scripture* in 1972, Sandmel had evidently reverted to his prewar position. "On the affirmative side," Sandmel wrote there, "the book [of Esther] offers encouragement to a beleaguered community; on the negative side it has a vindictive, even ferociously vengeful spirit in which retaliation becomes possible and lamentably indiscriminate." He then added: "I have no fondness for the close of the book, which describes the slaughter of foes."[74] Was it Israel's occupation of Palestinian territories, the emergence of the Jewish Defense League, Nixon's bombing of Cambodia—or some combination of these—that caused Sandmel to change his tune? Whatever the case, it is clear that any attempt, whether Jewish or Christian, to rescue the book of Esther from opprobrium by making it newly relevant runs the risk of reassigning it—when the winds of memory change direction—to the bookshelf of barbarism.

[73] On Sandmel (1911–1979), see M. J. Cook in *DBI*, 2:438.
[74] Samuel Sandmel, *The Enjoyment of Scripture* (New York, 1972), 35–36. Sandmel made no mention there of his earlier position in favor of the book, but he did assert: "I have elsewhere written that I should not be grieved if the book of Esther were somehow dropped out of Scripture" (44). It is not clear to which publication he was alluding.

2

A Pair of Queens

On the seventh day, when the heart of the king was merry with
wine, he commanded . . . the seven eunuchs . . . to bring Queen
Vashti before the king with her royal crown, in order to show
the peoples and the princes her beauty; for she was fair to
behold. But Queen Vashti refused to come at the king's command
conveyed by the eunuchs. At this the king was enraged,
and his anger burned within him.

(ESTHER 1:10–12)

OH, VASHTI, NOBLE VASHTI!

DID Vashti do the right thing? In his *Exposition of the Old and New Testament*, first published in the early eighteenth century, the English nonconformist divine Matthew Henry wrote that "perhaps it was not her wisdom" to deny the king's request, since "the thing was not in itself sinful; and therefore to obey had been more her honour."[1] Later in that century the Calvinist preacher Thomas Scott (1747–1821) also showed some understanding for Vashti's reluctance to obey the king's immodest request, but asserted nonetheless that it had been "highly imprudent . . . to persist in a refusal, which could terminate only in an open contest and the most fatal effects."[2] In nineteenth-century England, however, more positive views of Vashti began to appear, from rather diverse directions. In his *History of the Jews*, first published in 1829, Henry

---

[1] Henry (1662–1714) suggested that perhaps Vashti had "refused in a haughty manner," in which case "it was certainly evil." See Matthew Henry, *An Exposition* . . . , 7th ed., 2 vols. (Edinburgh, 1767), 2:525.

[2] Thomas Scott, *The Holy Bible . . . with Explanatory Notes, Practical Observations, and Copious Marginal References*, 6 vols. (London, 1825), 2:4P. Scott's Bible commentary had first been published in 1788–1792.

Hart Milman wrote admiringly of Vashti as having been motivated, in her refusal, by "a better sense of her own dignity."[3] And Alfred Lord Tennyson, who succeeded William Wordsworth as Poet Laureate in 1850, a year after Milman, whose highly popular *History of the Jews* he may well have read, became Dean of St. Paul's, wrote:

> Oh, Vashti, noble Vashti! Summon'd out
> She kept her state, and left the drunken king
> To brawl at Shushan underneath the palms.[4]

Tennyson's contemporary Austin Holyoake, who, as we have seen, was a leading figure in the British secularist movement, singled out Vashti as the only "estimable or worthy character" in the entire book, who was nonetheless punished for "possessing a virtue [modesty] which is universally admired among enlightened and refined people."[5]

Although their American contemporary Harriet Beecher Stowe expressed admiration for Esther as a woman whose "beauty and fascination were the moving power" in her people's salvation, she also valued Vashti's brave refusal. "The story of Esther," she wrote in 1873,

> belongs to that dark period in Jewish history when the national institutions were to all human view destroyed. The Jews were scattered up and down through the provinces captives and slaves, with no rights but what their conquerors might choose to give them. Without a temple, without an altar, without a priesthood, they could only cling to their religion as a memory of the past, and with some dim hopes for the future.[6]

Mrs. Stowe, who was the daughter, sister, and wife of Protestant clergymen, certainly knew her Bible.[7] She had been married since 1836 to the biblical scholar Calvin Ellis Stowe, author of, among other works, *The Right Interpretation of Sacred Scriptures* (1853), which appeared shortly after *Uncle Tom's Cabin* had catapulted Mrs. Stowe to international fame through its sensitive portrayal of the cruel world of slavery. Her depiction of the Jews in the days of Esther and Mordecai, as "captives and slaves, with no rights but what their conquerors might choose to give them" linked two of her primary areas of interest, but her discussion of the book of Esther (and its eponymous heroine) was also linked to her interest in women and their potential role in the modern world. "Every year the festival of Purim, in

---

[3] Milman, *History,* 2:17.

[4] *The Works of Alfred Lord Tennyson: Poet Laureate* (London, 1909), 184.

[5] Holyoake, *Esther,* 2–3.

[6] Stowe, *Woman,* 195.

[7] Her father was the noted Presbyterian minister Lyman Beecher (1775–1863) and one of her brothers, Henry Ward Beecher (1813–1887), a highly charismatic preacher and opponent of slavery, headed the Plymouth Congregational Church in Brooklyn.

every land and country whither the Jews are scattered," she wrote, "reminds the world that the romance has been a reality and the woman whose beauty and fascination were the moving power in it was no creation of fancy."[8]

Yet Stowe also admired Vashti's principled refusal. "If we consider the abject condition of all *men* in that day before the king," she wrote, "we shall stand amazed that there was a woman found at the head of the Persian empire that dared to disobey the command even of a drunken monarch." The drunken king's request, Stowe asserted, was according to then prevailing Oriental custom, an indecency as great as if a modern husband should propose to his wife to exhibit her naked person." Vashti, therefore, "was reduced to a place where a woman deliberately chooses death before dishonor."[9] Similarly Lyman Abbott, who in 1888 succeeded Stowe's brother Henry Ward Beecher as leader of the Plymouth Congregational Church in Brooklyn, expressed admiration for the "womanly courage" of both Vashti and Esther. Stowe's younger contemporary Helen Hunt Jackson (1830–1885) wrote poems in praise of both Esther and Vashti. Although the Amherst-born poet, who was a friend of Emily Dickinson's, praised Esther's "dauntless heart, which knew no fear—not even of king who slew at pleasure," she had less regard for her personal morality: "Thou heldest thy race too dear, thyself too cheap." Vashti, in this regard, was deemed more honourable:

> How thou wert pure and loyal-souled as fair?
> How it was love which made thee bold to dare
> Refuse the shame which madmen would compel.[10]

Lyman Abbott was not the first American clergyman to praise Vashti's conduct. In 1875 the Methodist minister Milton Terry also praised the deposed queen for refusing "to be treated as an ordinary concubine, and to suffer her person to be immodestly exposed to the promiscuous crowd of half-drunken revellers."[11] During the final decade of the nineteenth century the Ohio Congregationalist clergyman Washington Gladden published two popular books, *Who Wrote the Bible?* and *Seven Puzzling Bible Books.* Gladden, a leading figure in the "Social Gospel" movement, saw the book of Esther as representing "the perfect antithesis of the precepts

---

[8] Stowe, *Woman*, 195.

[9] Ibid., 197. On the close connection of both Calvin and Harriet Stowe to the Hebrew Scriptures and ancient Israel see Edmund Wilson, "The Jews," in Wilson, *A Piece of My Mind* (Garden City, 1958), 90–92.

[10] Abbott, *Life and Literature*, 184, 191; Friedlander, *Standard Book of Jewish Verse*, 333, 336–37.

[11] M. S. Terry, *Kings to Esther*, in D. D. Whelan, ed., *Commentary on the Old Testament*, vol. 4 (New York, 1875), 505. On Terry (1840–1914), see J. R. Tyson in *ANB* 21:464–65.

and spirit of the gospel of Christ," and suggested that it was chiefly useful "as a dark background on which we may see more clearly the brightness of the Christian morality." He stressed that "the name of God is not once mentioned in the book"—adding that "it seems like blasphemy to intimate that the Spirit of God could have had anything to do with its composition."[12] Gladden also had a distinct preference for Vashti over her successor. Between the two queens, he asserted, "Vashti is the character which most demands our sympathy," although the biblical author "seeks to transfer our affection to Esther."[13]

This rehabilitation of Vashti in Anglo-American culture, at the expense not only of Esther but of virtually all the book's other characters, continued well into the twentieth century. "Not one of them, except Vashti, who possessed the courage of good convictions, is worth preservation," sniffed Mary Ellen Chase of Smith College in 1945. Chase saw the book's other characters as "self-seeking, designing, revengeful, and even cruel," each of whom (including Esther) "revolts us by his intolerance, his hatred, and his ruthlessness."[14] Nearly two decades later the Anglican vicar Laurence Browne, whom we also met in the previous chapter, claimed that in the whole book there was no noble character, with the possible exception of Vashti. Her refusal to appear before Ahasuerus was, in Browne's view, "fully justified," and has "for the reader," he claimed, "the unhappy effect of removing so early from the stage the only character who commands his respect."[15]

WOMEN, WINE, AND BLOOD

Although she was admired by the Methodist Terry, the Congregationalist Gladden, and the Anglican Browne, it has been among female feminists that Vashti has found her most ardent fans. Lucy Chandler, one of the contributors to Elizabeth Cady Stanton's controversial *Woman's Bible* (1895–1898), praised Vashti for having "a higher idea of womanly dignity than placing herself on exhibition as one of the king's possessions," describing her as "the first woman recorded whose self-respect and courage enable her to act contrary to the will of her husband . . . the first 'woman who dared.'" Like Harriet Beecher Stowe before her, Chandler—who, in addition to her feminism, was also a proponent of the twin

---

[12] See W. Gladden, *Who Wrote the Bible?: A Book for the People* (Boston, 1891), 165–66; Gladden, *Seven Puzzling Bible Books* (London, 1897), 73–96. On Gladden (1836–1918), see J. H. Dorn in *ANB* 9:97–99; Dorn, "Social Gospel" in the *Oxford Companion to United States History*, ed. P. S. Boyer (Oxford, 2001), 725–26.

[13] Gladden, *Seven Puzzling Bible Books*, 81, 94–95.

[14] Chase, *Bible*, 199.

[15] Browne, "Esther," 381–82.

spiritual movements known as "New Thought" and "Spiritual Purity"—saw both Esther and Vashti as heroines worthy of emulation: "Women as queenly, as noble and as self-sacrificing as was Esther, as self-respecting and as brave as was Vashti," she wrote, "are hampered in their creative office by the unjust statutes of men; but God is marching on; and it is the seed of woman which is to bruise the head of the serpent."[16]

In one of her own essays on the book of Esther, Elizabeth Cady Stanton expressed her regret that "the [biblical] historian allowed Vashti to drop out of sight so suddenly." She speculated that perhaps as a result of Vashti's refusal to appear at the king's banquet "she was doomed to some menial service, or to entire sequestration in her own apartments."[17] The rabbinic sages, however, had been in unanimous agreement, as Louis Ginzberg noted, that Vashti had been executed,[18] and some Jewish illustrators, beginning in the middle ages, even depicted her as being executed naked.[19] This was rooted in the ingenious interpretation of the rabbinic sages that Ahasuerus had commanded Vashti—whom they identified as the granddaughter of Nebuchadnezzar—to appear on the seventh day of his banquet, "with her royal crown"—but wearing nothing else. And this was seen, no less ingeniously, as divine punishment for her having forced Israelite maidens to work on the Sabbath while stripped naked.[20]

Like some of her British contemporaries, Stanton had serious reservations about the holiday of Purim, but these were connected less with the spirit of savagery it allegedly celebrated than with the prominent role of alcohol in its observance. Citing, not quite accurately, the talmudic opinion (*Megillah* 7b) that "in the feast of Purim one may drink until he knows not the difference between 'cursed be Haman' and 'blessed be Mordecai'"—in fact, it was opined that one *must* drink until reaching that lofty level of inebriation—Stanton expressed the suspicion that "the thanksgiving feast of Purim has degenerated in many localities into the same kind of gathering as the Irish wake."[21] Stanton's contemporary, the London

---

16 *The Woman's Bible*, ed. Elizabeth Cady Stanton, 2 vols (1895–1898), 2:86–87, 92. On Cady Stanton's Bible and her various collaborators, see Kathi Kern, *Mrs. Stanton's Bible* (Ithaca, 2001).

17 Cady Stanton, *Woman's Bible*, 2:90.

18 Ginzberg, *Legends*, 4:378–89, 428, 442, 445, 6:456–57.

19 See the *La Biblia de Alba* (facsimile, Madrid, 1992), 390b. Note also Abraham Karp's comment on the scene as depicted in the "Washington *Megillah*," which seems to have been illustrated in eighteenth-century Italy: "Vashti . . . as commentators suggest, was to have appeared without clothes. She refused, but our artist complies." See Karp, ed., *From the Ends of the Earth: Judaic Treasures of the Library of Congress* (New York, 1991), 92.

20 See Ginzberg *Legends*, 4:374–76; 6:455–56; K. P. Darr, *Far More Precious than Jewels: Perspectives on Biblical Women* (Louisville, 1991), 169.

21 Cady Stanton, *Woman's Bible*, 2:90.

3. Execution of Vashti, eighteenth century, Italy. From Israel Museum 182/175. A similar image appeared in one of the Esther scrolls illustrated in early seventeenth-century Ferrara by Abraham Pescarol (Jewish National and University Library, Jerusalem). Courtesy of the Israel Museum, Jerusalem.

Congregational minister Walter Adeney, also used his commentary on Esther—particularly the opening scene of the king's seven-day banquet—as a vehicle for expressing his strong views about the vice of drunkenness:

> The worst effect of this vice . . . is its degrading influence on the conduct and character of men. It robs its victims of self-respect and manliness, and sends them to wallow in the mire with swinish obscenity. What they would not dream of stooping to in their sober moments, they revel in with shameless ostentation when their brains are clouded with intoxicating drink.[22]

Consequently, the drunken king is driven to transgress "the most sacred rules of Oriental etiquette" and the "seclusion of the harem is to be violated for the amusement of the king's dissolute boon companions." Significantly, Adeney too suggested that Vashti might be seen as a protofeminist. "Was it true modesty," he asked, "that prompted her daring refusal, or the lawful pride of womanhood?" If it was indeed the latter, then all women, Adeney felt, "should honour Vashti as the vindicator of their dues." Yet, since Vashti too "gave a banquet for the women in the palace" (Esther 1:9), he also allowed for the possibility that her reckless refusal had no less been fueled by alcohol than had her husband's despicable demand:

> Vashti had been feasting with the women of the harem when she received the brutal request. Had she too lost her balance of judgement under the bewitching influence of the wine-cup? Was she rendered reckless by the

[22] Adeney, *Ezra, Nehemiah, and Esther*, 364.

excitement of her festivities? . . . Since one of the commonest results of intoxication is a quarrelsomeness of temper, it must be admitted that Vashti's flat refusal to obey must have some connection with her previous activities. In that case, of course, something must be detracted from her glory as the martyr of womanliness.

Adeney, who had spent many years at the pulpit, took advantage of the opportunity provided by Vashti's plight to remind his readers that it was "unhappily . . . too frequently the case that, even in a Christian land, womanhood is degraded by becoming the victim of intemperance," adding that "no sight on earth is more sickening."

It was not only Vashti of whom Adeney was of two minds, but also her successor. On the one hand he saw her as "a strong, unselfish woman" to be admired for "conquering almost unsuperable tensions to a life of ease, and choosing a course of terrible danger to herself for the sake of her oppressed people." Yet it also pained him to see "how the woman who had saved her people at the risk of her own life pushed her advantage to the extremity of a bloodthirsty vengeance." In the end, he wrote, "we must confess" that, despite her strength, courage, and unselfishness, "Esther is not a Madonna," and that "the heroine of the Jews does not reach the Christian ideal of womanhood."[23]

ESTHER AMONG CRYPTO-JEWS

Although Adeney considered Esther to be no Madonna she had indeed been held up by medieval Christian moralists as a feminine model of disdain for "worldly dress and finery" (Esther 2:15), whereas Vashti, in her rejection of the king's invitation, was seen as prefiguring the *Synagoga* (Jews), who "invited to the faith [of Jesus], contemned the preaching of the faith."[24] In the fifteenth and sixteenth centuries Esther became a heroine to crypto-Jews (also known as *conversos* or Marranos) of Iberian descent, first in Western Europe and then in the New World, who closely identified with her as a Jew who—like them—was obliged to keep her true identity secret. It has also been reasonably suggested that the cult of Queen Esther among crypto-Jews "may have been, at least in part, a reaction . . . to their Catholic environment, with its exaltation of the

[23] Ibid., 365–66, 383, 391.

[24] D. O. Hughes, "Regulating Women's Fashion," in *A History of Women in the West; Volume 2: Silences of the Middle Ages*, ed. Christiane Klapisch-Zuber (Cambridge, Mass., 1992), 152; Sara Lipton, *Images of Intolerance: The Representation of Jews and Judaism in the Bible moralisée* (Berkeley, 1999), 68.

Virgin Mary."[25] Moreover, although Esther had concealed her Jewishness during her first months in the king's palace, according to both the Greek Additions to Esther (C:26–28), which in the Latin Vulgate (used by Catholics) had been incorporated into the biblical book itself, and the talmudic rabbis (*Megillah* 13a), she did her best to observe what she could.[26]

This too was characteristic of many crypto-Jews in both Iberia and Latin America, who also created new rituals to compensate for those they could observe only partially, or not at all. Eventually, it seems, a special Marrano ritual was compiled, in which "Esther's Prayer"—from the apocryphal Additions to Esther conveniently found in the Vulgate—with what the Anglo-Jewish scholar Lucien Wolf described as "its pathetic avowal of crypto-Judaism and its fierce denunciation of the persecutor and the heathen," figured prominently. In 1525 a new-Christian residing in Spain's Canary Islands was asked by the local Inquisition "how many times he had said the prayer of Queen Esther"—a question that had been put to him since he was "known to have said that Queen Esther was born for the salvation of many."[27] In late sixteenth-century Mexico a seventeen-year-old female new-Christian had allegedly been able to recite "Esther's Prayer" (and other hymns) backward.[28] At around the same time a Brazilian new-Christian was charged by the local Inquisition with having said that "just as the old-Christians are devoted to Saint Catherine of Sienna and other Saints, the new-Christians are devoted to Queen Esther."[29]

Perhaps the clearest sign of that devotion was the observance of the Fast of Esther, which in traditional Judaism was (and is) merely a minor fast on the day before Purim (13 Adar). In what Cecil Roth pioneeringly called "the religion of the Marranos," however, in which fast days

---

[25] M. A. Cohen, *The Martyr: Luis de Carvajal, A Secret Jew in Sixteenth-Century Mexico* (Philadelphia, 1973), 97; On Marrano identification with the character of Esther, see also Yerushalmi, *From Spanish Court*, 38, 112; A. S. Selke, *The Conversos of Majorca: Life and Death in a Crypto-Jewish Community in Seventeenth-Century Spain*, trans. H. J. Maxwell (Jerusalem, 1986), 17–18.

[26] On the (Greek) Additions to Esther, see Moore, *Esther*, lxiiii–lxiv, 103–11; Moore, "Esther, Additions to," in D. N. Freedman, ed., *The Anchor Bible Dictionary*, 6 vols. (New York, 1992), 2:626–33. On the degree of Esther's religious observance, see also Ginzberg, *Legends* 1:386–88.

[27] Wolf, *Canary Islands*, xxiii, 63–64.

[28] H. C. Lea, *The Inquisition in the Spanish Dependencies* (New York, 1908), 203; Roth, *Marranos*, 186, 276. Contrast, however, Liebman, *New World Jewry*, 122.

[29] On the veneration of Esther, see Gitlitz, *Secrecy and Deceit*, 117, 470; Andrea Zanardo, "Il Criptogiudaismo portoghese. Una ipòtesi antropologica," in *L'identità dissimulata: Giudaizzanti iberici nell' Europa cristiana dell'età moderna*, ed. P. C. Ioly Zorattini (Florence, 2000), 356, 365.

played—for both practical and penitential reasons—a particularly prominent role, the fast was observed far more widely than Purim itself "with
an austerity," wrote Roth, "unknown to traditional Judaism."[30] The dominant feature of that "austerity" was the transformation of the Fast of
Esther from a single-day observance to a three-day affair, following the
example of Esther herself (Esther 4:16). In 1485 Rita Besante, a new-
Christian in Teruel (northeastern Spain) confessed that she had kept "the
three Fasts of Queen Esther," and three years later a Spanish *converso* testified to the Inquisition that his grandmother had observed "a fast that
they call the day of Saint Haman [*sic!*]"—adding that she and her fellow
Jews believed that whoever kept that fast "will not die during the coming
year, because on a day like that God is sitting at your right hand." In 1524
an edict promulgated in the Canary Islands against "the deadly law of the
Jews, as of the Moors," had included among prohibited practices "keeping the Jewish fasts . . . and especially the fast of Queen Esther, and the
chief fast" of Yom Kippur. In fact, a statistical study of the 86 Judaizers
sentenced in the 1593 auto-da-fé at Granada revealed that 33 percent of
the men and 25 percent of the women observed Yom Kippur, whereas
only 20 percent of the men but 25 percent of the women observed the
Fast (or Fasts) of Esther.[31] Female identification with the biblical heroine
would seem to explain why as many Granadine *conversas* observed the
Fast of Esther as observed the solemn day of Yom Kippur.

Similarly, a young new-Christian residing in Pisa testified to the
Milanese Inquisition in 1625 that her mother, who had first been
denounced to the Inquisition seven years earlier by her teenage son (who
wanted to become a Capuchin monk), observed three fasts during the
year: those of Yom Kippur, the Ninth of Ab, and Esther.[32] In colonial
Mexico of the sixteenth and seventeenth centuries the Fast was also
observed by new-Christians, especially females. Noteworthy is the case of
the celebrated Carvajal family, which emigrated to Mexico in 1580, and
whose most prominent member (Luis the elder) became governor of
Nuevo León. His niece Isabel Rodríguez Carvajal had a reputation as a
"great faster," as was discovered by her brother Gaspar (a Dominican priest)
in February of 1586, when he came to visit his family in Pánuco and

---

[30] Roth, *Marranos*, 100, 150, 171, 180–83, 188–91, 282 (for the quotation, see 188);
Gitlitz, *Secrecy and Deceit*, 378 and index, s.v. "fasting."

[31] Wolf, *Canary Islands*, 27; Gitlitz, *Secrecy and Deceit*, 43–44, 378–79. The study of the
1593 auto-da-fé (cited by Gitlitz) is that by M. A. Bel Bravo, *El auto de fe de 1593: los
conversos granadinos de origen judío* (Granada, 1988).

[32] Lucia Frattarelli Fischer, "Cristiani nuovi e nuovi ebrei in Toscana fra cinque e seicento,"
135, in Ioly Zorattini, ed., *L'identità dissimulata*; P. C. Ioly Zorattini, "Derekh Teshuva: La
via del retorno," ibid., 233.

found her observing a three-day fast, which "made her so weak she could hardly speak." Isabel, he later reported, came to the table for meals and would put food in her mouth, but she would immediately remove it surreptitiously and throw it under the table. She was arrested by the Mexican Inquisition in 1589. During the previous year two of her other brothers, Luis (the younger) and Balthasar, observed the Fast of Esther in the home of a fellow crypto-Jew. In 1595 a witness reported to the local Inquisition, which had been established in 1571, that he had heard Luis informing a (Judaizing) priest about Yom Kippur and the Fast of Esther. He was publicly burned at the stake a year later.[33]

In 1643, during his lengthy trial before the Mexican Inquisition, Gabriel de Granada spoke of the Jewish education he had received from his mother, Doña Maria, and other female relatives, some of whose Judaizing practices, including the observance of fast days, he had witnessed. His mother, he reported, had taught him

> that there are other fasts of the said law of Moses, and especially those of Queen Esther, which they kept by eating, the previous evening at supper, fish and vegetables and going the three following days without eating or drinking anything, until the night of the last day, and that these fasts were kept by such observers of the said law as pleased.[34]

The women of Gabriel's family, on at least one occasion, took a "tag team" approach to observing the gruelling three days of the fast of Esther, which "were kept one time by his said mother and his grandmother . . . and his two aunts, Margaret and Isabella, and they did not keep the three together without eating during the whole of the three days, but some of them the first day, and others the second and others the third."[35] As late as 1691 the French-born crypto-Jew Fernando de Medina, who was brought to Spain as a boy and later made his way to Mexico, was reported by witnesses to own a prayer book and to have been observed fasting on Yom Kippur and the Fast of Esther.[36]

During the late seventeenth century the latter fast was also alive and well among the *chuetas* (crypto-Jews) of Majorca. When Juanot Cortes, the member of a *chueta* family that included many accused Judaizers, was jailed by the Inquisition in the late 1680s, he allegedly tried to convert his cellmate, a baptized Moor. Cortes, the latter reported, taught him not

---

[33] Arnold Wiznitzer, "Crypto-Jews in Mexico During the Sixteenth Century," *AJHQ* 51 (1961–1962), 202; Cohen, *The Martyr Luis Rodríguez Carvajal*, 114, 128, 208, 316.

[34] Adler, "Trial," 16.

[35] Ibid. See also 69, 72, 121.

[36] Wiznitzer, "Crypto-Jews," 250, 256–58, and Liebman, *New Spain*, 62–63, 95, 261.

only about the precepts of Judaism, but also about observing the Sabbath and such fast days as Yom Kippur and the Fast of Esther, informing him that for those who observed these devotional fasts "God would forgive all their sins."[37] When, earlier in the seventeenth century, Leonor de Piña confessed before the Portuguese Inquisition that she had observed the Fast of Esther for three consecutive days "without eating if it was not dark, or else eating things other than meat," she also explained the biblical origins of the fast, which

> was observed by Queen Esther when, at the order of Haman, the king Ahasuerus decreed to massacre the Jews. Mordecai begged his niece Esther to ask Ahasuerus to revoke the decree. She fasted three days, then went to the king. The latter, though it was ordained that no one ask him anything, kissed his scepter when he saw her, and upon her request, revoked the order against the Jews and executed Haman.[38]

SIN AND SALVATION

Leonor de Piña knew Esther to be Mordecai's "niece," which is how the Latin Vulgate, the version of the Bible used by crypto-Jews, had indeed rendered their relationship ("filiae fratris sui"; Esther 2:7). The ancient Greek Septuagint and the talmudic rabbis (*Megillah* 13a)—followed by a host of Jewish exegetes—had seen the relationship, however, as one of actual marriage. Moreover, as Barry Walfish has recently noted, according to some of the rabbis, "the sexual relationship between Esther and Mordecai continued even after she became queen."[39] This view of Esther as a bed-hopping beauty did not find its way, however, into Louis Ginzberg's rather puritanical *Legends of the Jews*, where her marriage to Ahasuerus was presented, following the *Zohar* (III:275b–76b), as miraculously chaste: "God had sent down a female spirit in the guise

---

[37] Selke, *The Conversos of Majorca*, 177–78. See also Baruch Braunstein, *The Chuetas of Majorca: Conversos and the Inquisition of Majorca* (New York, 1936), 101–2. On the Fast of Esther, see also Cyrus Adler, "Trial of Jorge de Almeida by the Inquisition in Mexico," *PAJHS* 4 (1896): 46; E. N. Adler., "The Inquisition in Peru," *PAJHS* 12 (1904); H. C. Lea, *A History of the Inquisition of Spain*, 4 vols. (New York, 1906), 2:565; Baron, *SRH* 13:36; Charles Amiel, "Crypto-judaïsme et Inquisition: La matière juive dans les édits de la foi des Inquisitions iberiques," *RHR* 210 (1993): 152.

[38] I. S. Révah, "La religion d'Uriel da Costa, Marrane de Porto," *RHR* 161 (1962): 68, quoted (and translated) in Miriam Bodian, *Hebrews of the Portuguese Nation: Conversos and Community in Early Modern Amsterdam* (Bloomington, Ind., 1997), 10.

[39] B. D. Walfish, "Kosher Adultery? The Mordecai-Esther-Ahasuerus Triangle in Midrash and Exegesis," *Prooftexts* 22 (2002): 305–8.

of Esther to take her place with the king."[40] Leonor's recollection that Ahasuerus "kissed his scepter" when he saw Esther approaching (at Mordecai's behest) deviates from the biblical version that has her, perhaps suggestively, touching the tip of the royal scepter.[41] Her recollection may have been inspired by the dramatically expansive treatment of the scene in the Greek Additions to Esther (D:1–16), which she would have known from their Latin translation in the Vulgate (Esther 15:4–19).

After the crypto-Jews, and due probably to their influence, Esther was also regarded as a spiritual hero by adherents of the Sabbatian heresy in the late seventeenth century, though less as a model for themselves than for their "mystical Messiah," Sabbatai Zevi, who in September of 1666 converted, under duress, to Islam.[42] Perhaps most prominent among those believers who regarded the "Messiah," after his apostasy, as having followed in the footsteps of Queen Esther was Abraham (Miguel) Cardoso, who had been born to a Castilian new-Christian family in 1627, and some two decades later—together with his older brother Isaac (Fernando), who like him was also a physician—openly embraced Judaism in Venice.[43] In a letter that he wrote to his brother shortly after the 1666 apostasy, by which time he had settled in Tripoli, Abraham described the perplexing paradox of Sabbatai Zevi's apostasy as akin to Esther's sexual surrender to Ahasuerus.

> Similar to this is what happened to Esther, for through her a great deliverance was accomplished in Israel. And certainly most of the ignorant must have loathed her for having given herself to a gentile idolator in clear violation of the Torah, but the sages who knew this secret and recognized the truth of the matter, did not regard her as a sinner, for it is said in the Talmud "Esther was like the ground of the earth" meaning that had she not given herself willingly she could have been raped.[44]

---

[40] Ginzberg, *Legends*, 4:387–88, 6:460; Moore, *Esther*, 15, 20–21: Fox; *Character and Ideology*, 30, 275–76.

[41] Esther 5:2. On the "overt sexual innuendo" of this scene, see, among others, Celina Spiegel, "The World Remade: The Book of Esther," in *Out of the Garden: Women Writers on the Bible*, ed. Christina Büchman and Celina Spiegel (New York, 1994), 198. It is perhaps worth noting that in John Cleland's pornographic classic *Fanny Hill* (part 10) one of the female characters refers to "that peculiar scepter-member which commands us all."

[42] See Gershom Scholem, "Redemption through Sin," in Scholem, *The Messianic Idea in Judaism and Other Essays in Jewish Spirituality* (New York, 1971), 95, 98; *Sabbatai Sevi: The Mystical Messiah, 1626–1676* (Princeton, 1973), 761, 803–4.

[43] On Abraham's move from Spain to Italy, see Yersushalmi, *From Spanish Court*, 192–206.

[44] For the Hebrew text, see *Iniane Sabbatai Zewi*, ed. A. Freimann (Berlin, 1912), 91; Jacob Sasportas, *Sefer Zizat Novel Zevi*, ed. Isaiah Tishby (Jerusalem, 1954), 295.

Cardoso, alluding to a famous talmudic passage (*Sanhedrin* 74b), requiring a Jew to give his life "for the sanctification of God's name" rather than commit, even under duress, any of three cardinal sins—idolatry, adultery (or incest), and murder—knew that the rabbis, who regarded Esther as Mordecai's wife, justified her sexual behavior on the ground of its having been entirely passive. In his view, Sabbatai Zevi's apostasy was no less excusable, "since the Turk forcibly placed the fez on his head, and did not seek to kill him." Had the Messiah been given a choice between Islam and death, Cardoso suggested, he would have chosen the latter, but following Esther's precedent he found a way to triumph through passivity—for the ultimate benefit, and indeed salvation, of his people.

In the twentieth century, the figure of Esther came to be associated with another controversial apostate, Edith Stein (1891–1942), who was born into an observant Jewish family in Breslau, earned a doctorate in philosophy (with the phenomenologist Edmund Husserl) at the University of Freiburg in 1916, converted to Catholicism in 1922, and twelve years later entered the Carmelite order in Cologne, taking her final vows in 1938. In late October of that year, shortly after the death of her mother, Stein wrote in her diary: "I keep thinking of Queen Esther who was taken away from her people precisely because God wanted her to plead with the King on behalf of her nation. I am a very poor and powerless little Esther, but the King who has chosen me is infinitely great and merciful." On New Year's Eve of 1938 she left the convent in Cologne, so as not to endanger her (Aryan) fellow nuns, and in 1942 she died at Auschwitz. When, in May of 1987, Stein was beatified by Pope John Paul II at an open air ceremony in Cologne's soccer stadium (she was formally canonized as a saint on October 11, 1998) he too compared her with Esther "who with the sacrifice of her own life, contributed in a decisive way to the Salvation of her people."[45]

Vashti and Revolution

If Esther's self-sacrifice allowed her to become a hero to Sabbatians in the late seventeenth century, in the nineteenth century such early feminists as Harriet Beecher Stowe and Lucy Chandler developed, as we have seen, a parallel admiration for her predecessor Vashti, described by the latter as "the first 'woman who dared.'" Modern feminists have gone a step further, often regarding the more passive Esther with disdain. "When

[45] See Sarah Borden, *Edith Stein* (New York, 2004); S. I. Minerbi, "John Paul II and the Jews," March 1, 2000, on the Web site of Israel's Ministry of Foreign Affairs (www.mfa.gov.il). On Stein's Jewishness, see also the articles collected in *The Unnecessary Problem of Edith Stein*, ed. H. J. Cargas (Lanham, Md., 1994).

feminists compare the two women," wrote Alice Laffey in 1988, "they extol Vashti, though they are not at all surprised that the [biblical] literature, produced as it was in a patriarchal culture, honors Esther and relegates Vashti to oblivion." Relatedly, André Lacoque has noted that "with Vashti's humiliation starts the story of salvation, a story worthy of modern liberation theologians."[46]

Particularly striking has been the attempt by Itumeleng Mosala to examine the implications of the book of Esther for South African women in their struggle for liberation. "The anti-patriarchal revolt of Queen Vashti," in her opinion, "represents a form of struggle with which an African biblical feminist hermeneutic must identify. It does not accept the implicit condemnation of Vashti by the text." In recent feminist biblical scholarship Vashti has also been presented as "a prime example of a woman trying to deflect a male gaze," whose "refusal or corporeal resistance amounts to political insurrection."[47]

In *The Nakedness of the Fathers* (1994) the American poet and critic Alicia Ostriker provided a staccato summary of the book of Esther in which Vashti is "demoted for discipline problems" and Esther, the "sexy Jewess," succeeds her by winning the "Miss Persia contest." Ostriker has more recently recalled that upon first reading the Bible as an undergraduate at Brandeis in the 1950s, "Esther, the spoilt beauty queen who saved the Jews only because Mordecai twisted her arm, had no appeal for a bookwormy poet. I preferred proud Vashti."[48] Her contemporary and fellow New York-native Rachel Brownstein has written with great sensitivity— and considerable humor—of her unsuccessful attempt, while teaching Sunday School at the Jewish Center of Tuckahoe (Westchester, N.Y.) during her sophomore year at Barnard, to alter the time-honored convention

---

[46] A. Laffey, *Introduction to the Old Testament: A Feminist Perspective* (Philadelphia, 1988), 214–15; A. Lacoque, *The Feminine Unconventional: Four Subversive Figures in Israel's Tradition* (Minneapolis, 1990), 55.

[47] I. J. Mosala, "The Implications of the Text of Esther for African Women's Struggle for Liberation in South Africa," *Semeia* 59 (1992): 135; Alice Bach, *Women, Seduction, and Betrayal in Biblical Narrative* (Cambridge, 1997), 131; S. W. Crawford, "Esther: Introduction, Commentary, and Reflections," in *The New Interpreter's Bible* (Nashville, 1999), 3:883; C. L. Baskins, "Typology, Sexuality, and the Renaissance Esther," in *Sexuality and Gender in Early Modern Europe*, ed. J. G. Turner (Cambridge, 1993), 39. See also Darr, *Far More Precious than Jewels*, 168–69, 188–89.

[48] A. S. Ostriker, *The Nakedness of the Fathers: Biblical Visions and Revisions* (New Brunswick, N.J., 1994), 219; Ostriker, "Back to the Garden: Reading the Bible as Feminist," in *People of the Book: Thirty Scholars Reflect on their Jewish Identity*, ed. J. Rubin-Dorsky and S. Fisher Fishkin (Madison, 1996), 67. On Ostriker, see the entry by Ruth Whitman, 1017–18, in *Jewish Women in America: An Historical Encyclopedia*, ed. P. E. Hyman and D. D. Moore, 2 vols. (New York, 1997).

whereby at the annual contest for the role of Queen Esther in the Purim play "the prettiest girl in the best costume is awarded the crown," and the role of Vashti is "merely a consolation prize." Brownstein, like Ostriker a professor of English, has effectively used this autobiographical story as a means of undermining the traditionally binary opposition between the two women, "beautiful and unbeautiful, chosen and dismissed." As she now reads the biblical story, Vashti is not merely "the heroine's opposite or foil." Rather, her career, by foreshadowing Esther's, "demonstrates the cruel constraints that limit and shape any woman's chance for success in the world, the humiliations that attend on being obliged to please, the real risks of not playing the game."[49]

The novelist and essayist Norma Rosen, who was born in Borough Park and graduated from Mount Holyoke College in 1946, has recently compared Esther to some of her contemporaries, "so disquieting to preconceptions of what thinking, valorous women ought to look like: the ones who insist on dyeing . . . their hair, who wear sexy clothes, stiletto heels, grow inch-long fingernails lacquered red," but yet at some point "send themselves through law school, medical school, Ph.D. programs, and come out fighting for righteous causes, still wearing three-inch heels." About Esther's predecessor, however, she is less ambivalent:

> When Vashti's incredibly risky refusal of the King makes way for Esther's obsequiousness, we understand that Vashti is haughty in the service of self-respect and the dignity of personhood, made in God's image; Esther is self-sacrificing in the most demeaning way in the service of the Jewish people.[50]

The Canadian Jewish feminist Michelle Landsberg, who entered college in the late 1950s, recalls having felt (precociously) ambivalent about the book of Esther's eponymous heroine while learning the story of Purim at the (Reform) Holy Blossom Religious School in Toronto:

> Saving the Jewish people was important, but at the same time her whole submissive, secretive, manipulative way of being was the absolute archetype of 1950s womanhood. It repelled me. I thought, "Hey, what's wrong with Vashti? She had dignity. She had self-respect." She said: "I'm not going to dance for you and your pals." There I was, nine or ten years old, and I thought, "I like Vashti but I'm supposed to hate her."[51]

---

[49] R. M. Brownstein, "Chosen Women," in *Out of the Garden,* eds. Büchman and Spiegel, 187.
[50] Norma Rosen, *Biblical Women Unbound: Counter-Tales* (Philadelphia, 1996), 169–72. On Rosen see the entry by S. R. Horowitz in *Jewish Women in America,* 2:1169–70.
[51] See *Half the Kingdom: Seven Jewish Feminists,* ed. Francine Zuckerman (Montreal, 1992), 61–62. See also G. T. Reimer, "Eschewing Esther, Embracing Esther: The Changing Representation of Biblical Heroines," 209–16, in *Talking Back: Images of Jewish Women in American Popular Culture,* ed. Joyce Antler (Waltham, Mass., 1998).

A generation (X) later the American writer Elizabeth Wurtzel, best known for her 1994 memoir *Prozac Nation,* had a similar experience. In Hebrew school she had been taught that Vashti "had pimples, that she was vain, that she was disobedient, that she was wicked, and that she deserved to die." Years later, while attending Purim services in college, in her "boredom with the awkwardness of the reader," Wurtzel "started to study the *Megillah* closely and realized that all the implications of Vashti as virago, termagant, hellion, and whatever else were nowhere in the text." Although she has quarrel with the manner in which Jewish inter-pretation has embellished Esther's image as "the righteous woman," she has urged that the story of Purim be taught to children in such a way that

> Vashti can be seen as brave—or at the very least, not evil—in her defiance of the king. After all, how are girls going to grow up to be strong, self-determined women when one of the first things they learn is that if you get pimples and refuse to pose in the nude in public, you deserve to get killed? What kind of message is that?[52]

WARTS AND ALL

Had Wurtzel, during her collegiate reawakening at Harvard, consulted any of the many editions and translations of the Talmud available at the Widener library (where some of the research for this book was done), or even Louis Ginzberg's *Legends of the Jews,* she would have learned that the sudden physical impairment attributed by the rabbis to Vashti—making it impossible for her to appear naked—was not "pimples," but rather leprosy (*Megillah* 12b). Moreover, a second opinion in the Talmud—missing, however in many editions—had the angel Gabriel pinning a "tail" upon her body, which Ginzberg correctly but coyly Latinized—in a footnote— as *venit Gabriel et fecit ei membrum virile.*[53]

By contrast, the embarrassing fate of Vashti as creatively embellished by the rabbis was well known to the future Zionist leader Shmarya Levin (1867–1935) and his friends when he was growing up in the small town of Svisloch (Swislowitz), in Belorussia. During the month of preparations for the annual Purim play,[54] much speculation was devoted to who would receive which role—all of which, of course, were played by males. For

[52] Elizabeth Wurtzel, "Vashti" (1998), available on the Web magazine *Bold Type* at www. randomhouse.com/boldtype.

[53] Ginzberg, *Legends,* 4:375–76; 6:456.

[54] For extended preparations for the annual Purim play, see also the statutes from eighteenth-century Nikolsburg (Moravia) in Simha Assaf, ed., *Mekorot le-Toledot ha-Hinnukh be-Yisrael,* 4 vols. (Tel-Aviv and Jerusalem, 1925–1942), 1:148.

Esther, the perennial director Bencheh needed only "a good-looking boy and some women's clothes." Playing the briefer role of Vashti, however, was considerably more problematic:

> She appeared on the stage just once. But when she did appear, she had to satisfy the traditional history of Vashti. And tradition says that the incident which set in motion the drama of Purim . . . the refusal of Vashti to appear before the assembled guests of the tipsy monarch had a most ludicrous and pitiful explanation. Far from being a woman of innate modesty and good taste, Vashti the queen was as wicked as her husband was foolish; *but* on the day when she was summoned to display herself . . . something exceedingly immodest grew on her forehead.[55]

Like his younger contemporary, the Lithuanian-born luminary Louis Ginzberg (1873–1953), Levin was loathe, even years later, to state straightforwardly what that "immodest" growth had been. "And the modesty which prevents me from saying what it is that grew out on her forehead," he wrote, "also prevented the historic presentation of the role of Vashti the queen." Yet he also reported that "every boy in Swislowitz knew what had happened to Vashti . . . and what the biblical account does not mention. Who told me, I cannot remember, but it was certainly neither the Rebbi [teacher] or my mother. We just knew." The director Bencheh's creative solution was to have Vashti appear on the stage wearing both a crown and a veil covering half her face: "what was under the veil could be left to the imagination."[56] In the next chapter we shall explore the various ways in which Mordecai was imagined, and, in particular, how his stubborn refusal to bow before Haman—widely acknowledged as the most difficult exegetical crux in the book of Esther—was understood by both Jews and Christians over the centuries.

---

[55] S. Levin, *Childhood in Exile*, trans. Maurice Samuel (New York, 1929), 147.
[56] Ibid., 147–48.

3

Mordecai's Reckless Refusal

And all the king's servants . . . bowed down and did obeisance
to Haman; for the king had so commanded concerning him.
But Mordecai did not bow down or do obeisance.

—ESTHER 3:2

BUT MORDECAI DID NOT BOW

MORDECAI, as many have recognized, was a Jew with "attitude."
His refusal to bow is foreshadowed, as many scholars have noted,
by Vashti's equally reckless refusal to appear when summoned by
King Ahasuerus. In both cases, as the Harvard scholar Jon Levenson has
observed, "a mysterious refusal whose cause can only be guessed occasions a catastrophic rage in the one refused (1:12 and 3:5), as well as a crisis of state and an absurd imperial decree."[1] Similarly, Michael Fox of the
University of Wisconsin has noted that Vashti's "taciturnity resembles
Mordecai's, who also refuses an order from above with no excuses that
might help him avoid the consequences." Fox sees Mordecai's refusal to
bow to the king's new vizier as "the biggest puzzle" in the book of
Esther. He has rightly observed, however, that the author "must have in
mind some reason for such persistent, dangerous, and apparently useless
behavior," adding that "whatever the reason for Mordecai's defiance, it is
behavior that the [biblical] author affirms and admires."[2] The mystery of
Mordecai's refusal to explain his refusal has prompted many attempts
through the centuries to explain his ostensibly rash behavior, whose ominous consequences, some assumed, must surely have occasioned serious
second thoughts on his part.

[1] Levenson, *Esther*, 48, 68.
[2] Fox, *Character and Ideology*, 43, 169, 191–92.

4. "Mordecai's Refusal," as depicted in the 1930s. From *Megillat Esther*, ed.
Joseph Kaplan (Leipzig, 1932). Courtesy of the Jewish National
and University Library, Jerusalem.

This was clearly the assumption of the author of the *Targum Sheni*—a richly expansive and enormously popular Aramaic paraphrase of the book of Esther. The words "on that night the king could not sleep," which open the book's sixth chapter, inspire the early medieval author to describe the sleepless night experienced simultaneously (in his retelling) by a number of the book's protagonists—including, somewhat paradoxically, God Himself.[3] The paradox lay not only in that, in the words of the psalmist, "the guardian of Israel neither slumbers nor sleeps" (Ps. 121:4), but also in the frequently noted absence of any explicit reference to God in any of Esther's 167 verses.[4]

Although it had already been suggested in rabbinic literature that the phrase "on that night the king could not sleep" referred to God's sleeplessness,[5] the *Targum Sheni* greatly expanded this line of interpretation so as to include Esther, Mordecai, and Haman among the sleep-deprived on that fateful night. In the case of Haman there is good exegetical reason for his inclusion, since several verses later (Esther 6:4) he appears at the royal palace during (what would appear to be) the middle of the night in order "to speak to the king about having Mordecai hanged on the gallows that he had prepared for him." With both the king and his prime minister already awake, the *Targum Sheni* merely adds their Jewish counterparts to the nocturnal scene. Esther's slumber, we learn, was disturbed by nervous thoughts about the feast to which she had invited Ahasuerus and Haman (Esther 5:6–8). Mordecai's sleeplessness is not explained (he may have heard Esther tossing and turning in bed), but we are informed of its consequences. Since Mordecai "was awake and he could not sleep . . . [the House of] Israel assembled and sat before him, saying to him: 'You caused all this evil . . . because if you had stood up in respect for the wicked Haman and knelt and prostrated yourself to him,

---

[3] On the character of the *Targum Sheni* (hereafter TS) and its popularity, see Grossfeld, *The Two Esther Targums* (New York, 1991).

[4] For discussions of explanations for God's absence from the book of Esther in classical and medieval Jewish tradition, see Walfish, *Esther in Medieval Garb*, 76–79. For surveys of modern critical treatments of this problem, see Moore, *Esther*, xxxii–iii; Baldwin, *Esther*, 36–42; E. L. Greenstein, "A Jewish Reading of Esther," 232–33, in *Judaic Perspectives on Ancient Israel*, ed. Jacob Neusner, B. A. Levine, and E. S. Frerichs (Philadelphia, 1987); Fox, *Character and Ideology*, 235–47.

[5] See *Megillah* 15a, where the opinion is attributed to R. Tanhum. For midrashic parallels, see *Panim Aherim B*, in S. Buber, ed., *Sifre de-Agadeta 'al Megillat Esther* (Vilna, 1886), 47, where the opinion is attributed to R. Yohanan, and *Pirkei de-Rabbi Eliezer* (chap. 50), where it appears anonymously: "That night the sleep of the King who is King of Kings . . . fled, because he saw that Israel was in great distress. The sleep of the king on earth fled, for he had seen in his dream Haman taking the sword to slay him." I follow Gerald Friedlander's translation (London, 1916), 402, taking into account his own notes regarding readings in the early editions.

all this distress would not have come upon us.'" Mordecai's reply to this accusation, according to the Targum was that "the garment which the wicked Haman was wearing, upon it were embroidered two images, one in front and one in the back, and if you would stand up and bow down to him, it would result in your actually worshipping idols."[6]

This explanation for Mordecai's refusal to bow before Haman is hardly original with the *Targum Sheni*,[7] but what is striking is its context. The explanation does not appear, as we might expect, as an immediate gloss upon the verses reporting Mordecai's refusal to prostrate himself before the king's prime minister (Esther 3:2–5), but rather as part of a nocturnal debate taking place three chapters later between Mordecai and the people of Israel—or rather, their celestial representative. Moreover, the Targum presents "the House of Israel"—perhaps representing Mordecai's conscience— as retrospectively rather critical of the latter's reckless behavior. But why, from the Targum's perspective, should Mordecai have been plagued by his conscience on that sleepless night? Presumably he was wondering whether his never-revealed reasons for refusing to bow down to Haman, no matter how strongly felt, were sufficient grounds for endangering the lives of his co-religionists throughout the empire of Ahasuerus. Would such thoughts not cause any good Jew insomnia, let alone the only figure in the entire Hebrew Bible actually referred to (seven times) as "the Jew"?

"LOOK WHAT MORDECAI DID TO US"

Mordecai's stubborn refusal to bow before Haman elicited no small amount of criticism, sometimes subtle and sometimes overt, on the part of his co-religionists living under the rule of (those they often considered to be) later Hamans. The northern French exegete R. Joseph Kara (b. ca. 1060), when commenting on the description of Mordecai in the very last verse of the book of Esther (10:3) as "popular with the multitude [literally, the majority] of his brethren," explained that he was popular with *most* but not *all* of his brethren, for there were those "who used to malign him by saying: 'Look what Mordecai did to us, for he provoked Haman (*she-nitgar be-Haman*) and on his account we would have been sold to be destroyed, slain, and annihilated were it not for God.'"[8] Several decades later, the

---

[6] *TS* on 6:4. I follow the translation of Grossfeld, *The Two Esther Targums*, 168.

[7] See Ilja Katzenellenbogen, *Das Buch Esther in der Aggada* (Würzbeg, 1933), 12, and sources cited there, to which should be added *Pirkei de-Rabbi Eliezer*, chap. 50.

[8] See Kara on 10:3 at end of *Mikraot Gedolot* (Jerusalem and Tel Aviv, 1959), vol. 2, quoted also by Walfish, *Esther in Medieval Garb*, 178, from whose translation mine differs somewhat. Walfish claims that Kara was "the first to raise the issue." On Kara, see Grossman, *France*, 290–325. For a possible later echo of Kara's interpretation of Esther 10:3, see Solomon Alkabetz, *Menot ha-Levi* (reprinted Jerusalem, 1983), 222a.

Spanish exegete Abraham ibn Ezra, while accepting the (rabbinic) view that Haman had worn a garment bearing an idolatrous image,[9] wondered nevertheless why Mordecai insisted on endangering both his own life and the lives of other Jews by flagrantly refusing to bow before him, rather than discreetly leaving the vicinity when he saw Haman approaching.[10]

In the sixteenth century two Middle Eastern rabbis, R. Moses Alashkar and R. David ibn Abi Zimra ("Radbaz") independently addressed queries by fellow Jews who had expressed serious doubts about the wisdom of Mordecai's behavior. The former had been asked by one of his rabbinic colleagues how Abraham had been able to bow before the angels who approached his tent (Gen. 18:2), if, as the rabbis claimed, he thought them to be Arabs who worshiped the dust of their feet. Should he not have abstained from bowing to them while their "idolatry" was still on their persons, just as Mordecai had refused to bow before Haman?

In his lengthy reply Alashkar (d. 1542) cited the talmudic dispute (*Sanhedrin* 61b) between two leading sages in third-century Babylonia regarding one who engages in idolatry through "love or fear" of man, but does not actually accept the idol's divinity: "Abbaye said, he is liable to punishment; but Rava said he is free from a penalty." The former cited the case of Haman, who was worshipped out of fear, and before whom Mordecai nevertheless refused to bow, but Rava regarded the example of Haman as equivocal. Alashkar's understanding of the latter's position was that Haman was both regarded as a deity and also wore an idolatrous image on his chest.[11] Early in the eleventh century R. Hananel of Kairowan (in North Africa) understood Rava's position somewhat differently: "If one encounters a man who is worshipped as a god, such as Jesus, this is prohibited . . . but Haman was bowed down to . . . out of fear . . . and Mordecai's conduct was [thus] supererogatory."[12]

Alashkar's younger contemporary Radbaz (d. 1573) had been asked by a colleague to express his opinion "as to why Mordecai exposed himself and all Israel to great danger, and why did he not avoid controversy and go elsewhere, seeing how well things were going for Haman." His first reply was that Mordecai had decided that he was willing to die as a martyr, but did not quite realize that he was also endangering his co-religionists. His second was that Mordecai saw prophetically that Israel would

---

[9] Note also Bickerman, *Four Strange Books*, 179.

[10] For the two slightly different versions of ibn Ezra's question and answer on this matter, see Walfish, *Esther in Medieval Garb*, 158–59, 178–79. See also Walfish, "The Two Commentaries of Abraham ibn Ezra on the Book of Esther," *JQR*, n.s. 79 (1988–1989): 323–43.

[11] Alashkar, *Responsa* (Jerusalem, 1959), no. 76.

[12] *Otzar ha-Geonim le-Massekhet Sanhedrin*, ed. H. Z. Taubes (Jerusalem, 1967), and see also *Tosafot* on *Sabbath* 72b and *Sanhedrin* 61b.

ultimately benefit through his action, and felt that he had to allow Providence to take its course.[13]

Radbaz's first reply, which used the term *kedushat ha-shem* (the sanctification of God's name), implied that bowing before Haman could have been considered an idolatrous act, reflecting the rabbinic tradition according to which Haman had worn an idolatrous image on his chest. Abraham Saba, like Alashkar an exile from Spain, also referred, in his commentary on Esther, to the rabbinic tradition concerning the idolatrous image worn by Haman, adding, however, in a more contemporary vein, that this was "like the Edomite (Christian) kings who have their officials wear the abominable cross on their clothing, so that whoever sees them would bow down."[14] Whether or not this interpretation of courtly dress codes was correct, Jews in late medieval Europe were often faced with situations in which they were required, by law or convention, to show public respect to the symbols, and even sometimes sacred objects, of the Christian religion they considered idolatrous. Should they have refused, under any circumstance, to do so?

In fifteenth-century Northern Europe two of the leading Ashkenazic rabbis, Jacob Weil and Israel Isserlein, both ruled rather leniently in the matter of Christians wearing the sign of the cross. Not only did neither rabbi recommend that Mordecai's example be emulated—neither even mentioned it. Weil ruled that it was permissible to bare one's head in the presence of a monk whose habit bore the sign of the cross. Isserlein (whose responsum was later cited by Alashkar) was more cautious, suggesting that it was best to avoid situations in which a potential transgression of such severity (i.e., idolatry) was involved. He recalled that in his youth a certain priest from Vienna would fold his robe over the sign of the cross when he expected to be visited by Jews for business purposes, so that they would be able to show him proper respect. Nonetheless, Isserlein also respectfully cited a more lenient ruling (by R. Isaac of Oppenheim), according to which the act of bowing before a priest wearing the sign of the cross was an acknowledgment of his exalted position but not necessarily of the truth of his religion.[15]

---

[13] David ibn Abi Zimra, *Responsa* (Warsaw, 1882), 1:284.

[14] A. Saba, *Eshkol ha-Kofer 'al Megillat Esther*, ed. Eliezer Segal (Drohobycz, 1903), 60–61. See also Walfish, *Esther in Medieval Garb*, 161.

[15] *Leket Yosher*, ed. J. Freimann (Berlin, 1903–1904) 2:14; Issserlein, *Terumat ha-Deshen* (Warsaw, 1882), no. 196. An acknowledged precedent for the latter's ruling was the view "found" by the German scholar Eliezer b. Joel ("Raviyah") in the thirteenth century that crosses hanging from the necks of Christians were not considered idolatrous, since they were worn as signs of having returned from Crusade. See *Sefer Raviyah . . . le-Massekhet 'Avodah Zara*, ed. D. Deblitzky (Benei Berak, 1976), 24–25.

Both in Christian Europe of the fifteenth century and the more religiously diverse Ottoman Empire of the sixteenth, rabbis, as well as members of their communities, were still grappling with the thorny question of whether to confront, dodge, or simply disregard the visible signs of an alien religion. The potentially disruptive challenge to the modus vivendi presented by Mordecai's precedent rarely shaped normative conduct, except, as we shall see in subsequent chapters, on the very day on which his story was read—the holiday of Purim.

An Ancient Enmity

Haman's ostensible connection with idolatry was not the only explanation offered in rabbinic literature for Mordecai's refusal to do him obeisance. Another, which focussed on the hereditary enmity between Israel and Amalek—to which Mordecai, as a Benjaminite descendant of King Saul (Esther 2:5) had a particular connection—was developed with particular ingenuity in one of the versions of the medieval midrash on Esther known as *Panim Aherim*. In its paraphrase of the story, Mordecai, upon being challenged concerning his refusal to bow before Haman, explained that his being a Jew prevented him from doing so. When Haman responded: "But do we not know that your forefathers bowed before mine?" citing Genesis 33, where Jacob and the members of his family all bowed before Esau, Mordecai cleverly replied: "Benjamin my father was in his mother's womb then, and did not bow, and I am his direct descendant [cf. Esther 2:5] . . . and just as my father did not bow [before Esau], so too, shall I not bow before you."[16]

The genealogical link between Esau and Haman upon which the dialogue hinges ran through the notorious figure of Esau's grandson Amalek, whose descendants, as noted earlier, were the first to attack the Jews on their way out of Egypt, and whose very memory they were later commanded to "blot out from under heaven" (Deut. 25:19). Haman, as we recall, is described in the book of Esther as an "Agagite," and Agag was the Amalekite king whom Saul vanquished in battle but nonetheless spared from destruction (1 Sam. 15:8–9). Saul, like Mordecai after him, was a descendant of Kish (1 Sam. 9:1), and, ultimately, of Benjamin, the son of Jacob. Thus, three sets of rivalries emerge in this midrashic reconstruction of the ongoing struggle between the two warring dynasties: Jacob versus Esau, Saul versus Agag, and Mordecai versus

---

[16] *Panim Aherim B*, in Buber, ed., *Sifre de-Aggadeta al Megillat Esther*, 66. See also Ginzberg, *Legends*, 4:396, 6:463; Grossfeld, *The Two Esther Targums*, 143 n.16, and the parallels cited there.

Haman—reminiscent of such modern blood feuds as those between generations of Hatfields (of Logan County, West Virginia) and McCoys (of neighboring Pike County, Kentucky).

Jewish exegesis throughout the ages tended to focus more on Haman's alleged connection with idolatry than on his Amalekite affiliation, despite the much stronger textual basis for the latter. This was presumably because idolatry was one of the three cardinal sins which were to be avoided even at the expense of one's life, whereas bowing before an Amalekite merely violated the spirit of the (positive) commandment to "blot out the memory" of Amalek. Many Christian (primarily Protestant) commentators since the sixteenth century, however, as well as academic scholars in recent decades, have found the "Amalekite" explanation for Mordecai's behavior particularly compelling.

"This deede of Mardocheus seemeth to be rash, wayward, and full of pride and disdaine," wrote the sixteenth-century Lutheran scholar Johannes Brenz (Brentius). "For albeit divine honour . . . be not given unto Princes, yet after their maner they are to be . . . reverenced. For so Jacob worshipped and reverenced his brother Esau." According to Brenz, however, Mordecai's contempt for Haman was "not a worke of the flesh, but of the spirit," and was rooted not only in the latter's Amalekite origins, but in Mordecai's own descent from King Saul, "who was cast from royall majestie in Israel because he had spared the Amalekite king Agag contrary unto the commandement of God." Mordecai, in this view, was "wary" about repeating his ancestor's grave offence (1 Sam. 15), and consequently, with "noble courage" made it clear that "with his reverence he woulde not blesse him, whom God had accursed, and whom God alreadie had appointed unto everlasting punishment."[17]

Similarly the Anglican divine Joseph Hall (1574–1656), in his influential (and frequently reprinted) *Contemplations on the Historical Passages of the Old and New Testament*, originally issued between 1612 and 1626, noted that "the Amalekites, of whose royal line Haman was descended, were the nation, with which God had sworn perpetual hostility, and whose memory he had straitly charged his people to root out from under heaven." Of Mordecai himself, Hall, who later served as bishop of Exeter and of Norwich, wrote admiringly: "He may break, but he will not bow."[18] In the nineteenth century Alexander Davidson of Aberdeen also admired Mordecai's flintiness. "While all others fell down before the [king's] favourite, kissing the dust beneath his feet," wrote the Scottish

[17] Johannes Brenz, *A Right Godly and learned discourse upon the booke of Ester*, trans. John Stockwood (London, 1584), 71–75. On Brenz (1499–1570), see J. M. Estes, *Christian Magistrate and State Church: The Reforming Career of Johannes Brenz* (Toronto, 1982).

[18] Joseph Hall, *Contemplations on the Historical Passages of the Old and New Testament*, 4 vols. (London, 1820), 3:210–11.

preacher, "Mordecai sat immoveable, and no doubt eyed with disdain, both him who received and those who paid the reverence." Davidson, like Brenz and Hall before him, saw it likely that Mordecai's refusal to bow was rooted in Haman's "being an Amalekite—a nation which lay under the malediction of Jehovah, and whose very name was hateful to the Jews."[19] And in 1901 the Congregational minister Lyman Abbott (then of Brooklyn) saw "race animosity" as inflaming the personal hostility between Mordecai and Haman: "The Jew despises the cunning but treacherous Amalekite; the Amalekite hates the rigorous virtue and inflexible pride of the Jew."[20]

Among modern exegetes mention may be made of the British scholar D. J. Clines who acknowledges that the reason for Mordecai's refusal "is obscure," but asserts that the only plausible explanation can be "that as a Jew he would not give honour to a representative of a race anciently hostile to his own."[21] Clines may be contrasted with his countryman, Laurence Browne, who as recently as 1962 (while serving as Vicar of Highbrook in Sussex), was able to assert that the reason for Mordecai's refusal, "though not explicitly stated," was quite evident "from the whole tone of the book." The explanation for Rev. Browne was quite simple: "Haman, the enemy of the Jews, was typical of all Gentiles, only fit for destruction."[22]

GODLINESS AND COURAGE: MORDECAI AS PROTESTANT HERO

Even earlier Protestants who saw Mordecai as a hero recognized that there were reasons to question his judgment. Brenz, as noted above, had written that "this deede of Mardocheus seemeth to be rash, wayward, and full of pride and disdaine." His French Huguenot contemporary Pierre Merlin wrote similarly that "some will say, that this is not to be accounted constancie, but contumacie, or at least rashness and impudencie, to caste himselfe into so evident a danger, to provoke the Kings wrath against him, and to stirre up the rage of so mighty a man against himselfe, yea, and his whole Nation." Merlin, who had been preacher to King Henry III before seeking refuge on the island of Guernsey, felt rather that Mordecai was to be admired for eschewing the simple solution of avoiding Haman's presence and choosing, rather, to advertise his refusal to "honour him whom God had cursed." He suggested to his readers that "this example of rare constancie is necessarie for us at this day" in response to the

---

[19] Alexander Davidson, *Lectures, Expository and Practical, on the Book of Esther* (Edinburgh, 1859), 100.

[20] Abbott, *Life and Literature*, 185.

[21] Clines, *Ezra, Nehemiah, Esther*, 294.

[22] Browne, "Esther," 383.

"flattering speeches, or threatening words" of those "who would have us acknowledge that Antichrist of *Rome* [the pope], and . . . fall before his feete." Merlin's militant message to them was: "Go on brethren, let us call to mind this constancie of Mardocheus: who although hee . . . were urged by the Courtiers to do as they did . . . yet he remaineth without feare . . . and yieldeth not unto them."[23]

In 1626 George Hakewill published a pamphlet comparing England's deliverance from the Gunpowder Plot—the abortive conspiracy on the part of several English Catholics to blow up both Parliament and King James I in November of 1605—with the deliverance of the Jews cele- brated on Purim. Hakewill asserted that Haman had merely pretended to be incensed at Mordecai's refusal to observe the King's rules but what really "stuck in his stomake was Mordecaies stiffenes, he would not creep and crooch unto him as others did."[24] Yet many who admired Mordecai's resolute refusal also acknowledged, as had Brenz and Merlin, that there was good reason to suspect that his motivation may have been less than pure. Such suspicion would have been buttressed, moreover, by the "Prayer of Mordecai," in the (originally Greek) apocryphal Additions to Esther, where he justifies himself to God in the following manner: "You know, Lord, that it was not because of insolence or arrogance or vanity that I . . . did not bow before the arrogant Haman; for I would have been quite willing to have kissed the soles of his feet for Israel's sake. But I did it in order that I might not put the glory of man above the glory of God" (C:5–7).

Influenced evidently by this passage, the English nonconformist divine Matthew Henry (1662–1714) noted that some of Mordecai's contempo- raries had doubtlessly attributed his refusal to bow before the new prime minister to "pride and envy," supposing that "because of . . . his alliance to Esther" he felt himself more deserving than Haman for the post, "or to a factious, seditious spirit." Henry himself had little doubt, however, that Mordecai's "refusal was pious, conscientious, and pleasing to God." For this he provided two reasons: First, that "the religion of a Jew forbade him to give such extravagant honor . . . to any mortal man," but also, that Mordecai "thought it a piece of injustice to his nation, to give such

---

[23] Pierre Merlin, *A Most Plaine and Profitable Exposition of the Booke of Ester* (London, 1599), 154–56. Merlin's work, as his anonymous translator noted, had originally been composed in Latin.

[24] George Hakewill. *A Comparisone Betweene the Dayes of Purim and that of the Powder Treason . . .* (Oxford, 1626), 11. On the link established in England between the Gunpowder Plot and the story of Purim, see Stanley, *Lectures*, 3:178, and Bickerman, *Four Strange Books*, 213.

honour to an Amalekite, one of that . . . nation, with whom God had sworn he would have perpetual war." Henry, like many other nonconformist Protestants, felt that there was a valuable lesson to be learned from Mordecai's stubborn, if risky, refusal: "And let those who are governed by principles of conscience be steady and resolute, however censured or threatened."[25]

Similarly, George Lawson (1749–1820), who served as minister in Selkirk (Scotland) for nearly half a century, asserted that "we may safely say that Mordecai did not decline the required homage to Haman . . . from motives of envy." Rather, he "chose to run every hazard, rather than prostitute to a creature [Haman] those honours which belonged exclusively to God his Maker." Lawson compared Mordecai's brave steadfastness both to that of the early Christian martyrs and of the more recent ones (in Europe) among his fellow Protestants:

> Confessors of the truth who exposed themselves to reproach and punishment for their fidelity to God, have been the wonder of the world in every age; especially when their opposition to the public laws seemed to turn upon small matters. The [Roman] heathens who saw the Christians expose themselves to a cruel death, because they would not throw a few grains of incense into the fire, nor worship the Genius of Caesar, believed that they had lost their reason. The like notions were formed concerning Protestant and Presbyterian martyrs by their [Catholic] enemies.[26]

In 1840 John Hughes delivered a sermon in St. Michael's Chapel, Aberystwyth (Wales), in which he acknowledged that "at first sight we may be fully disposed to censure Mordecai—and to accuse him of pride, or sullenness, or malice, or jealousy." Like his Scottish contemporary Lawson, however, Rev. Hughes felt that "instead of blaming Mordecai . . . we ought to admire his piety in refusing . . . idolatrous homage" to a fellow human being.[27] Even some who found Mordecai's behavior quite inscrutable nonetheless expressed admiration for its indisputable fortitude. Lawson's fellow Scotsman Thomas MaCrie, in his *Lectures on the Book of Esther* (1838), saw an important lesson to be learned from Mordecai's refusal. "Though we should not be able to ascertain the true reason which

---

[25] M. Henry, *An Exposition* . . . 7th ed., 2 vols. (Edinburgh, 1767) 2:527. The first edition was published in 1706. See also W. Harris, *A Practical Illustration of the Book of Esther* (London, 1737), 10–11.

[26] George Lawson, *Practical Expositions of the Whole Books of Ruth and Esther* (Philadelphia, 1870), 197–98, 201.

[27] John Hughes, *Esther and Her People* (London, 1842), 53–54.

actuated Mordecai, we may still learn from this portion of history, that no danger to which we may be exposed ought to induce us to violate our consciences, by honoring those whom we may and ought to despise; or by giving external tokens of feelings alien to our hearts."[28]

The character of Mordecai was especially revered by two redoubtable Englishwomen, the daughter and granddaughter respectively of "General" William (1829–1912) and Catherine Booth who had founded the Salvation Army in the late 1870s. In *The Conflict between Two Laws* (1894), which focused on the book of Esther, Catherine Booth-Clibborn, like many Protestant writers before her, explained Mordecai's refusal to bow before Haman on the grounds of the latter's having been "an Amalekite . . . an enemy of God's people." She also stressed the strength of Mordecai's character: "Principle was involved. He could not violate his conscience. . . . The fact that all the people bowed did not affect Mordecai. He stood alone." She piously encouraged her readers to follow Mordecai's example, and to refuse to "bow down to the gods of this world" or to "put the laws of rulers and earthly governors before the laws of Christ and His Kingdom."[29]

Booth-Clibborn's slim book eventually enjoyed considerable popularity. A second edition was published in 1923, and a third, under the title *The Woman Who Saved a Nation*, was published a year later. Late in the twentieth century her daughter Evelyn Booth-Clibborn, in the last year of her long life, also published an inspirational work on the same theme: *For Such a Time as This: The Message of Esther*. Like her mother, Evelyn saw Mordecai's refusal to bow before the Amalekite Haman as reflecting "both his godliness and courage." God was "the final authority for his conduct, whatever the cost to himself." In this she saw him as a model for all Christians: "That is what we need so desperately, men and women who are loyal to their convictions, who believe in the supreme authority of God and are willing to obey His authority at whatever cost to themselves."[30]

MORDECAI AND HIS MODERN CRITICS

Yet during the nineteenth and twentieth centuries there were also Protestants in the Anglo-American world who did not quite see Mordecai "the Jew" as a paragon of piety. Harriet Beecher Stowe, who greatly admired the figure of Esther, saw Mordecai in a less positive light. "Safe in his near

---

[28] Thomas MaCrie, *Lectures on the Book of Esther* (London, 1838), 69.

[29] Catherine Booth-Clibborn, *The Conflict between Two Laws* (Glasgow, 1894), 10–12.

[30] Eveleyn Booth-Clibborn, *For Such a Time as This: The Message of Esther* (Chichester, 1990), 30.

relationship to the Queen," she observed in 1873, "Mordecai appears to have felt himself quite free to indulge in the expensive and dangerous luxury of quiet contempt for the all-powerful favorite of the King."[31] Mordecai's close relationship with the Queen evidently reminded some nineteenth century writers of another Jewish statesman who enjoyed a close relationship with his queen, Benjamin Disraeli (1804–1881). One of the contributors to the enormously popular *Commentary on the Whole Bible*, edited by Bishop C. J. Ellicott (1819–1905), seems to have had the Jewish-born Disraeli in mind when he described Mordecai as "an ambitious, worldly man who, though numbers of his tribe [of Benjamin!] had returned to the land of their fathers, preferred to remain behind on alien soil." Why, he asked rhetorically, should such a person "endure hardships, when there is a chance of his adopted daughter's beauty catching the eye of the sensual king, when through her he may vanquish his rival [Haman] and become the chief's minister?"[32]

Disraeli, "an ambitious, worldly man" who entered Parliament in 1837 and twice served as prime minister under Queen Victoria—whom he was instrumental in making Empress of India—managed to "vanquish" such rivals as his fellow Conservative Sir Robert Peel and Liberal leader William Gladstone, often with the aid of such women as his (married) mistress Lady Henrietta Sykes and his wealthy wife, the former Mary Anne Lewis.[33] In 1868 Disraeli was explicitly referred to as a "Jew-Boy" in the *Manchester City News*, and compared with his biblical co-religionists "Joseph, Mordecai, and Daniel." A decade later the dandified and—in the eyes of some—provocatively effeminate statesman was compared, in a letter to the *Nonconformist*, to Esther rather than to Mordecai. Like the former, it was argued, "Benjamin—but not by his beauty—has become a great conjuror in the court of a nominal empress, Victoria."[34]

Early in the twentieth century John Edgar McFadyen, who as mentioned earlier was an Oxford-educated professor of Old Testament at Knox College in Toronto, claimed that a main object of the book of Esther was "to glorify the Jewish people." Mordecai's refusal to bow before Haman was explained by McFadyen as implicitly justified in the book by the providential notion that "the Jews are born to dominion, and

[31] Stowe, *Woman*, 199.

[32] C. J. Ellicott, *Commentary on the Whole Bible* (reprinted, Grand Rapids, Mich., 1954).

[33] See Robert Blake, *Disraeli* (London, 1966); Jane Ridley, *The Young Disraeli: 1804–1846* (London, 1995).

[34] For the first, see *Friday Nights: A Jewish Chronicle Anthology, 1841–1971*, ed. William Frankel (London, 1973), 129; for the second, see A. S. Wohl, "'Ben Ju-Ju':Representations of Disraeli's Jewishness in the Victorian Political Cartoon," in *Disraeli's Jewishness*, ed. T. M. Endelman and Tony Kushner (London, 2002), 158, n. 27.

all who oppose or oppress them must fall."[35] In the volume on Esther he contributed to the *International Critical Commentary* McFadyen's contemporary Lewis Paton, who taught at the Hartford Theological Seminary, found Mordecai's behavior "quite inexplicable" and "unreasonable," and suggested that it was his "arrogant refusal to bow down to Haman" that led to the latter's genocidal plot to kill the Jews.[36] Shortly afterward Hinckley Mitchell of Tufts College described Mordecai as "a sycophant who sacrifices his adopted daughter to royal lust for the sake of improving his position at court."[37]

As an admirable exception to this trend we may cite Archibald Duff, who in his 1919 contribution to A. S. Peake's popular *Commentary on the Bible* wrote that Mordecai "has often been condemned" for his "stiff refusal" to bow before Haman, which "is called Jewish narrowness," rather than being recognized as "stern honesty." Duff's own stern honesty had also moved him to comment, as noted earlier, that "the literature on the book [of Esther] . . . is marred by anti-Semitic prejudice which passes too unfavourable a judgement on the Jews."[38]

"The Oak That Resists the Storm," or "The Reed That Bends before the Breeze"

But in recent decades not only anti-Semites, it must be acknowledged, have been critical of Mordecai's conduct. The American scholar Michael Fox, author of one of the most important monographs on the book of Esther, has had the honesty to distinguish between his own personal values and his reading of the biblical text. As a scholar he agrees with those who see "tribal enmity" as the true explanation for Mordecai's refusal to bow before Haman. For the biblical author Mordecai's "first loyalty is to the ancient demands of his people's history," and he "dare not compromise their national honor, even when this stubbornness might imperil their existence." But, as a Jew, Fox acknowledges that he "cannot affirm Mordecai's behavior in the way the author does." In his view, rather than refusing to bow before Haman, Mordecai "should have quit his job when Haman took office."[39]

Harvey Cox, who was raised as a Baptist in rural Pennsylvania, cannot tell us what he feels as a Jew, but he does have a good sense of what Jews

[35] McFadyen, *Introduction*, 314.
[36] Paton, *Esther*, 196–97, 213.
[37] Mitchell, *Ethics*, 373–74.
[38] Duff, "Esther," 336–37.
[39] Fox, *Character and Ideology*, 11, 44, 192–93.

feel—having been married to an observant Jewish woman for over fifteen years and having seen their son through his bar mitzvah. Cox, who has taught for decades at Harvard Divinity School, explains how celebrating Purim annually with his wife and son has given him an opportunity to rethink his own relationship to the character of Mordecai and to the latter's refusal to bow before Haman.

> I have always found this part of the story intriguing. Maybe it is because my ancestors, the ones who immigrated to Pennsylvania from England, were Quakers, who often got themselves into difficulty for refusing to remove their hats in the presence of nobles and kings. Consequently I have always felt some kinship with Mordecai and with the long history of Jewish refusal to display unseemly obeisance to worldly authority.[40]

It is curious, but perhaps not so surprising that Cox feels a stronger kinship than Fox for what he calls "the long history of Jewish refusal to display unseemly obeisance to worldly authority." Is there indeed such a "long history"? If so, it is hardly continuous. The tension in the historical experience of the Jews between stubborn (and sometimes reckless) resistance and prudent malleability was the subject of considerable discussion in the late nineteenth and early twentieth centuries. In his *Israel among the Nations*, the French original of which appeared in 1893, Anatole Leroy-Beaulieu identified "stubbornness" as the dominant trait, the distinguishing quality, of the ancient Hebrew, adding that it was Mordecai, "the haughty zealot, who refused to bend the knee before Haman." Although Leroy-Beaulieu also recognized that Jews had sometimes been compelled to "bend the knee," he asserted that this was "always" done merely as an external gesture: "The Jew was always refractory; even when he yielded to force—and his impotence often compelled him to do so— he submitted outwardly only. The Jews have retained this stubborn spirit; it is part of their very being; it has even been intensified by their age-long ordeal. . . . They have become accustomed to resist."[41]

Leroy-Beaulieu felt, on the one hand, that in his own day the Jewish race still had "as strong a will as ever," yet he also claimed that its inflexibility had disappeared over time by force of circumstances: "After having been the oak that resists the storm, Israel was compelled to become the reed that bends before the breeze." The modern Jew had become a person of paradox: "He is, at once, the most self-willed and the most yielding of men, the most stubborn and the most tractable."[42]

---

[40] Harvey Cox, *Common Prayers: Faith, Family, and a Christian's Journey through the Jewish Year* (Boston and New York, 2001), 103.

[41] Leroy-Beaulieu, *Israel among the Nations*, 192.

[42] Ibid., 192–93.

These last words were later quoted approvingly in Werner Sombart's substantially less philo-Semitic study of *The Jews and Modern Capitalism*, the German original of which appeared in 1911. Sombart saw the Jew's unique adaptability as "perhaps the most valuable of his characteristics." This quality of the Jews, he claimed, "enabled them to submit for the time being, if circumstances so demanded, to the laws of necessity, only to hark back to their wonted ways when better days came." Consequently, the Jew was rarely what he appeared to be: "He is German where he wants to be German, and Italian if that suits him better."[43] Was such a person to be trusted?

Significantly, both Leroy-Beaulieu and Sombart commented on the fascinating figure of Disraeli in their discussions of the Jewish character. "To force their way into the select circle of society is the dream of thousands of his coreligionists," wrote the former, "and this dream, Disraeli the *Sephardi* of Venice [*sic*] . . . realized in the most exclusive of societies." And Sombart used him as a prime example of the Jew's "peculiar capacity" for adaptation:

> If the Jew is anything, it is not because he must [be] but because he determines to be so. Any convictions he may have do not spring from his inmost soul; they are formulated by his intellect. . . . He lacks depth of feeling and strength of instinct. . . . That Lord Beaconsfield was a Conservative was due to some accident or other, or some political conjuncture; but [Freiherr vom] Stein and [Otto von] Bismarck and [Thomas] Carlyle were Conservatives because they could not help it; it was in their blood.[44]

According to Leroy-Beaulieu, moreover, there had been both moral and physiological consequences to the Jew's peculiar pliancy:

> For this flexibility of his whole being the Jew has had to pay dear; constant bending has given him a stoop. Not infrequently his figure has become deformed . . . by it; it has left him with something like a curvature of the spine. His soul has lost stature and his heart has shrunk, like his body. In many cases moral abasement has kept pace with physical degeneration. Constrained to accommodate himself to all sorts of situations, he has, of necessity, grown used to objectionable compromises.[45]

---

[43] Werner Sombart, *The Jews and Modern Capitalism*, trans. Mordecai Epstein (1913), with a new introduction by S. Z. Klausner (New Brunswick, N. J., 1982), 269, 271. On Sombart and the Jews, see Klausner's introduction and most recently N. Z. Davis, "Religion and Capitalism Once Again? Jewish Merchant Culture in the Seventeenth Century," in *The Fate of Culture: Geertz and Beyond*, ed. S. B. Ortner (Berkeley, 1999), 56–60.

[44] Leroy-Beaulieu, *Israel among the Nations*, 243; Sombart *The Jews and Modern Capitalism*, 271.

[45] Leroy-Beaulieu, *Israel among the Nations*, 193.

In short, for both Leroy-Beaulieu and Sombart, proud and stubborn Mordecai, who would not stoop or compromise, was a figure of the distant Jewish past. More typical of the modern Jew was the baptized Lord Beaconsfield, Benjamin Disraeli, who was supremely capable of "objectionable compromises."

Yet in the years between the publication of Leroy-Beaulieu's *Israel Among the Nations* (1893) and Sombart's *The Jews and Modern Capitalism* (1911), a new movement emerged among the Jews of Europe that sought both to create a new kind of Jew and to bring him back to his ancient land. Max Nordau, who in 1898 had been one of the speakers at the Second Zionist Congress in Basel, soon afterward published an essay under the title "Muskeljudentum" ("Muscular Judaism" or "Jewry of Muscle") in which he called upon his co-religionists to "take up our oldest traditions" and "once more become deep-chested, sturdy, sharp-eyed men."[46] He presumably meant that Jews should seek to overcome the curvature of the spine that had deformed them, in the opinion of Leroy-Beaulieu and others, both physically and psychologically.

In 1904 Theodore Herzl visited Pope Pius X at the Vatican, hoping to solicit his support for a Jewish state in Palestine. "He received me standing and held out his hand, which I did not kiss," Herzl later wrote in his diary. "I believe that this spoiled my chances with him," he added, "for everyone who visits him kneels and at least kisses his hand. This hand kiss had worried me a great deal and I was glad when it was out of the way."[47] Like Mordecai, Herzl did not give a reason for his rude refusal, nor did he regret it despite (what he perceived to be) its negative consequences.

Such Mordecai-like refusal was not then unique to adherents of the Zionist movement. When in 1898 Kaiser Wilhem II of Germany made his famous visit to Jerusalem, all of the city's leading clergymen were invited to attend the lavish reception in his honor. Two ultra-Orthodox rabbis, however, refused to attend, one of whom was the fervent anti-Zionist Joseph Hayyim Sonnenfeld. When asked years later why he had declined, despite the rare opportunity to recite the ritual blessing uttered upon seeing a royal personage, Rabbi Sonnenfeld reportedly replied: "I had heard from my late teacher, R. Judah Leib Diskin, of a tradition attributed to R. Elijah, the Gaon of Vilna, that the German nation descended from Amalek . . . and how could I bless with the divine name a monarch who ruled over a people whose memory we have been commanded to

---

[46] Nordau's essay originally appeared in the *Jüdisches Turnzeitung*, and is translated in *The Jew in the Modern World: A Documentary History*, ed. Paul Mendes-Flohr and Jehudah Reinharz (New York, 1995), 547–48.

[47] *The Diaries of Theodor Herzl*, ed. and trans. Marvin Loewenthal (New York, 1956), 427. See also Tom Segev, "Ha-Neshika she-lo Hayeta," *Haaretz* March 21, 2000, 26–27.

destroy?"[48] Sonnenfeld could hardly have been unaware of the link between his refusal to honor the German emperor and Mordecai's earlier refusal to bow before an Amalekite.

In the years after Hitler's ascent to power, as we shall see further in the next chapter, the antagonism between Haman and Mordecai became a favorite metaphor for the adversarial relationship between the Jews and those evil forces emanating from Germany that threatened the entire world. In 1934 the young Anglo-Jewish historian Cecil Roth (to whom we shall often return) depicted the Jew as the world's "Eternal Protestant" who had always refused to respect falsehood. "The Jew," asserted the Oxford-educated Roth, "is still the Mordecai, who refuses to bow down or to do reverence; still the Eternal Protestant."[49]

Ironically, however, in using such an expression Roth inadvertently confirmed Sombart's assertion concerning the peculiar (and to his mind pernicious) pliancy of the Jew's identity, allowing him to be German "where he wants to be German, and Italian if that suits him better." The reaction of Roth (who had recently written *A History of the Marranos* [1932]) to the rise of Hitler was to proclaim that his persecuted co-religionists were actually Protestants! But, then again, even proud Mordecai had advised Esther to prudently hide her identity. He himself would not bow, but he realized that others sometimes had to.

[48] S. Z. Sonnenfeld, *Ha-Ish 'al ha-Homa* (Jerusalem, 1973), 2:108–9.
[49] Cecil Roth, *Personalities and Events in Jewish History* (Philadelphia, 1953), 70, 76. The article, under the title "The Eternal Protestant," originally appeared in *Opinion* (September 1934).

4

The Eternal Haman

Hamans and Mordecais

W
E MEET the Hamans today as we met them a thousand years ago," wrote the Yiddish journalist and Socialist educator Abraham Sachs toward the end of World War I, at a time when hundreds of thousands of Jews in his native Eastern Europe were suffering dislocation, humiliation, and bloodshed at the hands of German, Austrian, Polish, and Russian forces.[1] The Lithuanian-born Sachs who, after studying in Germany, had emigrated to the United States in 1908, added:

> We meet them in all lands where the Mordecais are found—Jews who worship their own God, observe their own customs, and follow their own mode of life. . . . The Jew, however, does not lose courage. He feels sure that in the end the obstinate Mordecai will overcome the Hamans who will meet their downfall, and the Jews will rejoice again. . . . The Jew laughs. He makes fun of the Hamans who seek to wipe out the people of Israel.[2]

These words were later echoed (if not quite plagiarized) during the dark days of the Holocaust by the Brooklyn rabbi and educator Hyman Goldin. "Haman, the hater of the Jews, and Mordecai, the Jew, who insists on worshipping God in his own way, are not mere figures in history," wrote Goldin in 1941, noting also that Hamans were to be found "in every land where there are Mordecais." Like Sachs, moreover,

---

[1] S. W. Baron, *The Russian Jew under Tsars and Soviets* (2nd ed. New York, 1987), 181–86; L. P. Gartner, *History of the Jews in Modern Times* (New York, 2001), 270, 282–86.

[2] A. S. Sachs, *Worlds That Passed,* trans. Harold Berman (Philadelphia, 1928), 228. The essay on Purim had already appeared in his Yiddish book *Horeve Velten* (New York, 1917), 245–53. On Sachs (1879–1931), whose other publications included *Basic Principles of Scientific Socialism* (1925), see the entry in *Who's Who in American Jewry* (2nd ed., New York, 1928), 599–600.

5. The "Triumph of Mordecai" scene, which depicts one of the major reversals
in the book of Esther, was made famous in European art by Paolo Veronese and
Rembrandt. Twentieth-century Jewish artists adapted it to reflect new realities.
From *The Book of Esther*, illustrated by Arthur Szyk (Arthur Szyk Society, 1974).
Courtesy of the Arthur Szyk Society.

he added reassuringly: "The Jew laughs; he does not lose courage. . . . He is convinced that in the end the obstinate Mordecais will overcome the heartless Hamans who will meet their downfall, as Haman did of old."[3]

Both Goldin, who was born in 1881, and Sachs, who was born two years earlier, knew from their childhoods in Eastern Europe that enemies of the Jews had customarily been referred to by the epithet "Haman." Mary Antin, who like Goldin had been born in the fateful year of Czar Alexander II's assassination, and had also emigrated to America, recalled that when she was growing up in Polotsk (Belorussia) the Jews had referred to Alexander III, whose first years of rule witnessed several outbreaks of anti-Jewish violence and who authorized numerous measures limiting Jewish rights, as a latter-day Haman.[4]

Similarly, Shmarya Levin recalled that in the fall of 1881, the wandering preachers (*magidim*) began using biblical euphemisms in order to prudently pour out "the unexpressed rage of the Jews upon their implacable enemies." The new czar (Alexander III) was often referred to as Pharaoh, and various ministers were referred to by the code-name of Haman: "What need to say "Ignatiev" or "Pobedonostev" (the two bitterest persecutors of the time) when the Bible had so thoughtfully given us a Haman as a symbol, and the sages had so thoughtfully provided us with countless legends about him?"[5]

Sachs also recalled that during the Purim festivities of his youth it had been customary "to add Jew-baiters, past and present, to the Haman family." Not only would Haman's name be used, but also the names of his ten sons: "If we imagined a certain enemy of the Jews, big, burly and stout, he would be named Parshandata [the eldest]. If he was a puny, wizened sort of shrimp, he was crowned with the name Vayzatha [the youngest]. For each Jew-baiter a suitable name was found."[6]

[3] H. E. Goldin, *Purim: A Day of Joy and Laughter* (New York, 1941), 9. See also B. M. Edidin, *Jewish Holidays and Festivals* (New York, 1940), 130.

[4] See Mary Antin, *The Promised Land*, ed. W. Sollors (New York, 1997), 17. On the events of 1881, see Aronson, *Troubled Waters*; Aronson, "The Anti-Jewish Pogroms in Russia in 1881," 44–61, in Klier and Lambroza, eds. *Pogroms*.

[5] S. Levin, *Childhood in Exile*, trans. Maurice Samuel (London, 1929), 276–77; Levin, *Youth in Revolt*, trans. M. Samuel (London, 1930), 29–30, 35. N. P. Ignatiev was first Russian minister of state domains and then became minister of the interior. K. P. Pobedonostev was an influential advisor to Alexander III, whose tutor he had been, and director general of the Holy Synod—that is, secular head of the Russian Orthodox Church. See Aronson, *Troubled Waters*, infra.

[6] Sachs, *Worlds that Passed*, 232.

Staging Haman and "Backstage Discourse"

In the Lithuanian town in which Sachs grew up, the role of Haman in the annual *Purimshpiel* was traditionally given to Sheikeh, the butcher's son, who "attired himself in a pair of worn out soldiers' boots with clinking spurs, a three-cornered hat, and huge turned-up mustachios." The choice of soldiers' boots clearly reflects the traditional depiction of the "evil son" in illustrated Passover *Haggadot* as a military figure.[7] Sheikeh was paid for his efforts, but as Sachs dryly noted, "had to endure a lot for his few pennies." What he had to endure was the pent-up rage of the entire community against the "Hamans" from whom they suffered all year. "Each and every one of us would take it out on Haman, one with a good dig, another with a wallop; this one would pinch him, another would spit at him; everybody considered it a mizvah to inflict all kinds of torture on Haman."[8]

By contrast, in the Swislowitz of Shmaryah Levin's childhood, Bencheh, the organizer of the annual Purim plays, always reserved the coveted role of Haman for himself. "True, the role of the tyrant and Jew-hater . . . is not a grateful one," wrote Levin, but Bencheh "was an artist, and he chose a role that had plenty of action. Besides, the more hateful the role, the more room there was for skill and subtlety." And how did Bencheh outfit himself for the role of Haman? "By devious ways . . . he obtained a cast-off uniform of the district commissioner himself." He also managed to obtain "an ancient sword discarded by the town sergeant."[9] Although much effort was devoted to getting the necessary items for Haman's costume, little effort was invested in acquiring the clothing for Mordecai's. At the beginning of the play he was simply an old Jew, and toward the end, as Levin explained, "Mordecai did become an important figure; he was elevated to Haman's place." But after the latter was hanged "his clothes could be used for Mordecai—an economic stroke and a fine symbolic act in one."[10] Mordecai in Haman's clothing!

Levin also described "the deafening roar" that broke through the local synagogue on Purim night when the word "Haman" was read from the *Megillah*—"a tumult of several hundred rattlers whirled vigorously by as many youthful hands." His sensitive reconstruction of this childhood

---

[7] For the tradition of such depictions from the Prague Haggadah of 1526 through Jacob Steinhardt's illustrated edition of 1923, see Y. H. Yerushalmi, *Haggadah and History* (Philadelphia, 1975), pls. 11, 60, 134.

[8] Sachs, *Worlds that Passed*, 231.

[9] Levin, *Childhood in Exile*, 147, 149.

[10] Ibid., 146.

experience tells us a great deal about the inner experience of Purim for many of his contemporaries:

> Children as we were, we knew well that Haman was not in our synagogue. . . . But we understood the symbolism instinctively. There were Hamans every-where, great enemies and little enemies of the Jews. And we took revenge for the evil they had done us and the evil they contemplated. . . . We felt that these blows of ours, delivered in the air, were not without effect. In one way or another the Hamans of the world felt the noisy onslaught in their bones. And we were filled with contentment. We had done something to get even with the enemies of the Jewish people.[11]

Although Levin and his young friends felt that they had "done some-thing to get even with the enemies" of their people, they had not *really* "done something" to those hated enemies. They had, at the most, acted out a fantasy—and a rather benign one at that. And although Bencheh the bachelor wore the cast-off uniform of the district commissioner when playing the role of Haman in the local *Purimshpiel*, it is not likely that the commissioner himself knew of it. Here we touch, not for the last time, upon what James Scott has called "the dialectic of disguise and surveil-lance that pervades relations between the weak and the strong," a dialec-tic which sheds valuable light on many aspects of Jewish life in both medieval and modern Europe. The process of domination, Scott has argued, generates both a "hegemonic public conduct" of consent and "a backstage discourse consisting of what cannot be spoken in the face of power."[12]

The "deafening roar" heard by Levin and his Eastern European Jewish contemporaries resurfaced, as a rather desperate form of "backstage dis-course," among hitherto smugly assimilated German Jews during the years following Hitler's rise to power. Joachim Prinz, who served then as rabbi of a Reform congregation in Berlin, later recalled that after 1933, "people came by the thousands to the synagogue to listen to the story of Haman and Esther," which "became the story of our own lives." To the Jews of Berlin, especially after the enactment of the Nuremberg Laws, the *Megillah*, read in Hebrew and then translated, "suddenly made sense," for "it was quite clear that Haman meant Hitler." On Purim during the Nazi years those ordinarily supremely seemly Jews allowed themselves to let loose. "Never had I heard such applause in a synagogue when the names of Haman's ten sons were read, describing their hanging from the

---

[11] Ibid., 153–54.
[12] Scott, *Domination*, xii, 4.

gallows," recalled Rabbi Prinz. "Every time we read 'Haman' the people heard Hitler, and the noise was deafening."[13]

For centuries it had been customary among the Jews of Central and Eastern Europe to vent their hostility toward the symbols of their powerful adversaries primarily through the dramatic depiction of Haman on the stage. The classic depiction of the Jews' archenemy in the often raucous *Purimspiels* of the sixteenth through eighteenth centuries featured an ecclesiastical cross worn prominently on his garments. It was also referred to explicitly in the dramatic text itself as an explanation for Mordecai's refusal to bow before the king's new prime minister. As Chone Shmeruk noted, this overtly "Christianized" image of Haman may be found not only in the standard printed editions of the *Ahashveroshpiel*—five of which appeared between 1697 and 1720—but already in a Yiddish poem, based on the book of Esther (and intended evidently for dramatic recitation on Purim), composed in sixteenth-century Venice by Gumprecht of Szycebrszyn.[14] The printed editions, in fact, considerably obscure—out of self-censorship—many of the references to Haman's Christian identity present in earlier versions, which seem to reflect oral traditions. But what was missing in the text could be supplied by other means.

In the Jewish communities of Poland and Ukraine it was common, in the early eighteenth century, to hire a Christian to play the role of Haman in the annual *Purimspiel*. In 1722 the bishop of Lutsk published a pastoral letter stating that "when the act of Haman is commemorated, we forbid Catholics under penalty to be hired to perform this function," a practice which a church synod in Lutsk again banned four years later. A similar decree issued by the bishop of Przemśyl in 1743 mentioned that Jews had recently hired a Christian to play the role of Haman on Purim, and warned the local Jewish community that if they did so again a considerable fine would be incurred and the rabbi would serve a year in prison. Yet even at the end of the nineteenth century, according to Jewish memoirists, it was still common for Haman to be played by a young or poor Christian, preferably Yiddish-speaking.[15]

---

[13] J. Prinz, "A Rabbi under the Hitler Regime," in *Gegenwart in Rückblick*, ed. H. A. Strauss and K. R. Grossman (Heidelberg, 1970), 235.

[14] C. Shmeruk, *Yiddish Biblical Plays 1697–1750* (in Hebrew) (Jerusalem, 1979), 103. Gumprecht's text was first published by Moritz Stern, *Lieder des venezianischen Lehrers Gumprecht von Szczebrszyn um 1555* (Berlin, 1922). See especially 25, lines 707–20. On the history of these Purim plays, see more recently Jean Baumgarten, "Le 'Purim shpil' et la tradition carnavalesque juive," *Pardes* 15 (1992): 37–62; Evi Butzer, *Die Anfänge der jiddischen purim shpiln . . .* (Hamburg, 2003), 34–167.

[15] Shmeruk, *Yiddish Biblical Plays*, 20–35; Hanna Wegrzynek, "Sixteenth-Century Accounts of Purim Festivies," 89–90, in *Polin: Studies in Polish Jewry* 15 (2002); G. D. Hundert, *Jews in Poland-Lithuania in the Eighteenth Century: A Genealogy of Modernity* (Cambridge, 2004), 63–64.

As we have seen Haman was associated with Christianity and its adherents for a number of reasons. Not only was his form of death remarkably similar to that of Jesus, but he is repeatedly referred to in the book of Esther as an "Agagite," linking him genealogically with the Amalekites and ultimately with Esau, the grandfather of Amalek through his first-born son, Eliphaz. And "Esau" together with "Edom" became, in the early middle ages, the standard Hebrew term for Christendom.[16]

In an eleventh-century hymn composed for recitation on the Fast of Esther, *Bi-Mtei Mispar* ("We are but few in number . . ."), the Ashkenazic author—either R. Meshullam b. Kalonymos or R. Meshullam b. Moses—referred unabashedly to the fact that "the foe and his children were hanged on the gallows; they were strung together like . . . fishes on a hook."[17] *Hutlu zeluvim*, the words chosen by the author to describe the fate of Haman and his sons, could also be translated as "were crucified." This was not the only medieval Ashkenazic liturgical poem in which Haman's gallows were cleverly conflated with the cross of Jesus.[18] These poems, still recited today, served for centuries as "backstage discourse," allowing the Jews who recited them to conflate in their minds the dramatic downfall of Haman, Amalek, and Christianity—without imprudently arousing the ire of their oppressors.

HAMANS OVER THE CENTURIES

These oppressors, as some Christians themselves realized, were often referred to as "Haman." Late in the twelfth century R. Ephraim of Bonn, in his account of the Second Crusade, compared the Cistercian monk Radulf, who "arose against the nation of God to destroy, slay, and annihilate them," with Haman.[19] Four centuries later the Lutheran scholar Johannes Brenz observed that the Jews of his time "marvellously please themselves" in reading the book of Esther, adding that if any magistrate treated them poorly or drove them from his borders, "they give him the

---

[16] Samuel Krauss, "Die hebräischen Benennungen der modernen Völker," 380–85, in *Jewish Studies in Memory of G. A. Kohut*, ed. S. W. Baron and Alexander Marx (New York, 1935); G. D. Cohen, "Esau as Symbol in Early Medieval Thought," *Jewish Medieval and Renaissance Studies*, ed. Alexander Altmann (Cambridge, Mass., 1967), 28–29 (G. D. Cohen, *Studies in the Variety of Rabbinic Cultures* [New York, 1991], 248–49).

[17] *The Authorised Selichot for the Whole Year*, trans and ed. Abraham Rosenfeld (4th ed., London, 1969), 360.

[18] Horowitz, "And It Was Reversed," 142.

[19] Haberman, *Gezerot*, 115; Eidelberg, *The Jews and the Crusaders*, 121. On the tendency in medieval historiography to refer to "the latest oppressor" as Haman, see Yerushalmi, *Zakhor*, 36.

name of Aman." Brenz also claimed that it was the Jews' greatest hope "to be revenged of their enemies, that is, of the Christians among whom they live," in like manner to the vengeance on their enemies taken during the days of Mordecai and Esther. This, he asserted, following the (unacknowledged) lead of Luther himself, transformed the modern Jews into "the cousins and kindred of Aman the Amaleckite," for "they hate the true Israelites, which are the Christians, with the same fierce hatred that Haman had for their ancestors."[20]

Whether or not the Jews of Brenz's day dubbed *every* hostile magistrate as "Haman," as he claimed, there is certainly ample evidence that this epithet was commonly used. Earlier in the sixteenth century R. Elijah Capsali of Crete, in his poignant account (to which we shall return in the last chapter) of the tribulations and ultimate salvation of the Jews of Cairo during the 1524 rebellion of Ahmed Shaitan, referred to the latter repeatedly as "Haman."[21] In Italy, where Capsali had studied in his youth, the Jews later found a way of linking the widely hated Pope Paul IV (the former Cardinal Gian Pietro Carafa, who ascended to the papacy in 1555), with Haman: They conveniently discovered that the Hebrew spelling of "Theatino," the epithet by which Paul IV was known on account of his having cofounded the Theatine order (officially known as the Congregation of Divine Providence) when he was bishop of Chieti (*Theate*), was numerically equivalent, according to the laws of *gematria*, to the letters of Haman's name.[22]

In early seventeenth-century Germany Samuel Friedrich Brenz (no relation to Johannes), who had converted to Christianity with his wife and two sons in 1610, asserted that his former co-religionists commonly used the epithet "Haman" with regard to Christians.[23] Although many of Brenz's claims in his *Abgestreiter judischer Schlangenbalg* were challenged

[20] J. Brenz, *A Right Godly and learned discourse upon the booke of Ester* (London, 1584), 165–66. For Luther's equation of the Jews with Amalek, see Brevard Childs, *The Book of Exodus: A Critical, Theological Commentary* (Philadelphia, 1974), 317.

[21] Elijah Capsali, *Hasdei ha-Shem* 2:154, 156, in *Seder Eliyahu Zuta*. Similarly, in the account of the events of 1524 inserted by Joseph ibn Verga in his father's *Shevet Yehudah*, Ahmad Shaitan is referred to as an "Agagite." See ibn Verga, *Shevet Yehudah*, 145.

[22] Joseph Ha-Kohen, '*Emek ha-Bakha*, ed. M. Letteris (Vienna, 1852), 116–17; David Kaufmann, "Délivrance des juifs de Rome en l'annee 1555," *REJ* 4 (1882): 93. On the anti-Jewish policies of Carafa/Paul IV, see K. R. Stow, *Catholic Thought and Papal Jewry Policy 1555–1593* (New York, 1977). On his role in founding the Theatine order, see Peter Partner, *Renaissance Rome, 1500–1559: A Portrait of a Society* (Berkeley, 1976), 210–11.

[23] Brenz, *Abgestreiter judischer Schlangenbalg*, in Johannes Wülfer, *Theriaca Judaica* (Nuremberg, 1681), chap. 3, p. 12. Brenz was also quoted by Eisenmenger, *Entdecktes*, 2:721, and from there by Schudt, *JM*, 2:308 (chap. 35). On S. F. Brenz, see Schreckenberg *Adversus-Judaeos III*, 654–57; Carlebach, *Divided Souls*, 213–14.

by contemporaries, this one seems to have been well founded.[24] In late August of 1614, the very year in which Brenz's book first appeared, the ghetto of Frankfurt was plundered and its Jews were driven out by an angry mob of artisans led by Vincenz Fettmilch, whose followers had already seized the city hall some months earlier. In early 1616 the old city council returned to power, publicly executed Fettmilch and six of his followers, and permitted Frankfurt's Jews to return to their quarter, an event they commemorated with a local Purim. R. Elhanan b. Abraham, who composed a poem of thanksgiving chronicling the dramatic events of 1612–1616, asserted that Fettmilch had taunted the local Jews by referring to himself as their Haman—allegedly adding that they had no Mordecai to save them.[25]

Later in the seventeenth century Raphael Levy of Metz, who was imprisoned and then burned at the stake in 1670 for allegedly murdering a Christian child, had referred to the local public prosecutor as "Haman" in one of his letters from prison.[26] When Glückel of Hameln arrived in Metz, home of her second husband, three decades later, the anniversary of Levy's execution was still being observed as a fast day. In her autobiography she later described the circumstances that caused the delay of the marriage of her son Moses to the daughter of Samson Baiersdorf, court Jew to the Margrave of Bayreuth, when the latter's new counselor "played the Haman" and sought to destroy Samson. In the end, however, "God cast down the wicked Haman and turned all his evil into good, so that the wicked were overthrown and Samson Baiersdorf rose higher every day."[27]

[24] In 1615 Solomon Zvi Oppenhausen published his *Jüdischer Theriak* in response to Brenz's work. Both were later reprinted by Wülfer in his 1681 work mentioned in note 23, above. As Schudt later noted, Brenz's claim concerning the use of Haman as an epithet had not been rebutted by Oppenhausen.

[25] The poem was republished in Bernfeld, *Sefer ha-Dema'ot*, 3:48–89. For a critical edition and translation see now Ulmer, *Turmoil, Trauma and Triumph*. For Fettmilch's self-reference to Haman, see Bernfeld, 66; Ulmer, 57–58, 134–35. Among the scholars who have accepted the poem's assertion regarding this self-reference as factual, see A. Freimann and F. Kracauer, *Frankfort*, trans. B. S. Levin (Philadelphia, 1929), 100; Roth, *Book of Days*, 60; Doniach, *Purim*, 188–89. On the Fettmilch uprising, see most recently Friedrichs, "Politics or Pogrom?"; Ulmer, *Turmoil*, introduction.

[26] A. N. Amelot de la Houssaye, *Abrégé du procès fait aux juifs de Metz* (Paris, 1670), quoted by E. Drumont, *La France juive*, 2 vols. (Paris, 1886), 394–95. On the prosecution and execution of Raphael Levy, see also Arthur Hertzberg, *The French Enlightenment and the Jews: The Origins of Modern Antisemitism* (New York, 1968), 20, 34.

[27] *The Life of Glückel of Hameln, 1646–1724, Written by Herself*, trans. and ed. Beth-Zion Abrahams (London, 1962), 148; N. Z. Davis, *Women on the Margins: Three Seventeenth-Century Lives* (Cambridge, Mass., 1995), 13–17.

In the late nineteenth century, as we have seen, the epithet "Haman" was used by Russian Jews both for Czar Alexander III and his leading advisors, and in the twentieth century it was conferred, by Jews the world over and with remarkable staying power, upon the heinous figure of Adolf Hitler.

HAMAN, HITLER, AND THE HOLOCAUST

Already in 1934 the American author of *Mr. Haman Objects*, a Purim play for children, had one of his characters declare: "When Hitler, our modern Haman, studies this scroll [of Esther], he will learn what happened to the decrees and commands of oppressors."[28] The following year Britain's chief rabbi Joseph Hertz, in his annual address to Anglo-Jewish preachers, raised the question as to why Haman was described as "the enemy of *all* the Jews" (Esther 9:24) when he planned the destruction only of those in the Persian Empire. Hertz replied: "Because his proposal encouraged the Hamans in all other lands, near and far, to preach his doctrine. Even so is it in our day. There are elements in most countries that are impatiently awaiting the hour when they can follow Germany's example."[29] And in a Yiddish essay that appeared during the summer of 1939, the great Jewish historian Simon Dubnow described the world in which he and his fellow Jews had been plunged as "the epoch of Haman."[30]

Yet there were those who were able to contemplate the link between Haman and Hitler with greater equanimity. Reflecting, in November of 1943, on the fate of his former co-religionists, amidst the splendid seclusion of his magnificent villa, "I Tatti," outside of Florence, Bernard Berenson wrote in his diary: "Like the ants, the Jews never lose faith in life. . . . Hamans and Hitlers everywhere; they live on, and enjoy life."[31] Had Berenson, who had entered the world as Bernhard Valvrojenski, paid a return visit to his native Lithuania or any other parts of Nazi-occupied Europe, he would not have found many Jews who were busy enjoying

---

[28] S. M. Segal, *Mr. Haman Objects* (New York, 1934), 20.

[29] Hertz, *Sermons*, 2:211–12.

[30] The essay was originally published in *Oyfn Shaydveg*. See the recent French translation in Nathan Weinstock, "Simon Doubnov [Dubnow] (1860–1941); Que faire quand sonne l'heure d' Haman?" *Revue d'Histoire de la Shoah* 174 (2002): 9–17, esp. 12–13.

[31] B. Berenson, *Rumor and Reflection* (New York, 1952), 156.

life—even during the traditionally Bacchanalian season of Purim. The Nazis, in fact, in keeping with what came to be known as the "Goebbels calendar," seem to have taken a perverse pleasure in suffusing Jewish holidays with suffering and slaughter. On Purim eve 1943, several months before Berenson penned his lines about "Hamans and Hitlers," more than a hundred Jewish doctors and their families were taken to the cemetery in Czestochowa and shot. On the following day (March 21) the Jewish doctors of Radom were taken to nearby Szydlowiec, ostensibly in order to be transported to Palestine, but found newly dug graves awaiting them. In that same year the Nazis played a particularly cruel Purim prank on the Jews residing in the ghetto of Piotrkow. Claiming that there would be an exchange of Jews for Germans living in the Palestine colony of Sarona (near Tel-Aviv), the Nazis asked for ten volunteers with university degrees who were willing to emigrate. Rather than being taken to Palestine, however, they were taken to a nearby Jewish cemetery to be shot. Since there were only eight volunteers, however, the cemetery's Jewish watchman and his wife were conscripted to complete the quorum of ten—corresponding, of course, to the number of Haman's sons who were hanged.[32]

Less than a year later, in a speech delivered on January 30, 1944, Hitler predicted that if the Nazis were defeated the Jews would one day celebrate "a second triumphant Purim."[33] He evidently did not know that the Jews of Casablanca had already instituted a local Purim—a subject to which we shall return—to commemorate their having escaped Nazi terror when American forces liberated their city during the winter of 1942. For the first celebration, which took place a year later, a special "scroll" was written, called *Megillat Hitler*. It was modeled linguistically on the Scroll of Esther, and its evil protagonist was described as a descendant of both Haman and Amalek.[34] Albert Memmi, who was born and raised in nearby Tunis, later recalled that during the Purims of his youth the Jews would "bear aloft the traditional effigy of the Persian minister decked out with the little moustache of the Nazi dictator."[35]

Understandably, images of Hitler were given particular prominence in the first Purim celebrations held by survivors of the Holocaust in the

---

[32] Martin Gilbert, *The Holocaust* (New York, 1986), 552–53. For the events of Purim 1942, see ibid., 297–99. On the "Goebbels calendar," see also 617–18, 739.

[33] *New York Times*, January 31, 1944, quoted in Goodman, *Purim Anthology*, 4.

[34] *Sefer ha-Mo'adim*, ed. Y. T. Lewinski, 6:309, 320; Michal Sharf, *Megillat Hitler be-Zefon Afrika* (Lod, 1988).

[35] A. Memmi, *Portrait of a Jew*, trans. Elisabeth Abbott (London, 1963), 19.

Displaced Persons camps of Europe. In March of 1946 survivors in the DP camp of Landsberg, Bavaria, organized a week-long Carnival in honor of the holiday. One of the featured events of the first day was the symbolic burning of *Mein Kampf*, which had been written in the local prison in 1924.[36] At the entrance to the Landsberg Jewish Center, the camp's newspaper reported: "Hitler hangs in many variants and in many poses; a big Hitler, a fat Hitler, a small Hitler, with medals and without medals. Jews hung him by his head, by his feet, or by his belly." Dr. Leo Srole, the UN-appointed welfare director for Landsberg, and one of the organizers of the 1946 Purim carnival later recalled: "It was (a day) of such elation, I had never seen anything like it . . . Hitler and Haman now had their due."[37] In that same year the American writer Alexander Kohanski published a rhymed version of the book of Esther, clearly intended primarily for children. He too linked Haman and Hitler.

> This fellow, this Haman, like Hitler today,
> He said to the sov'reign, Ah'suerus the king:
> "With shekels your coffers I'll fill in a day;
> Just seal my decree with Your Majesty's ring."[38]

In 1961 the American rabbi Charles Wengrov, in his introduction to the book of Esther, wrote: "Over and over again the Hamans rise up and try to destroy the Jewish people. They never succeed. Within our scarred memory a Hitler arose. . . . He too failed, and is no more."[39] Thirteen years later Robert Gordis, a leading Conservative rabbi and biblical scholar, referred in his commentary on Esther to Hitler as "Haman's spiritual descendant."[40] More recently the two were paired by the Canadian biblical scholar Peter Craigie, in his posthumously published introduction to the Old Testament. "From Haman in Persia to Hitler in Europe," wrote Craigie, who was an Anglican, "there have arisen over the centuries those who have threatened the Jewish people."[41]

Even more recently, the American poet Anthony Hecht—who died as this book was going to press, and who, as a twenty-year-old in the Ninety-seventh Infantry Division, helped liberate the Flossenburg concentration

---

[36] Toby Blum-Dobkin, "The Landsberg Carnival: Purim in a Displaced Persons Center," in *Purim: The Face and the Mask* (New York, 1979), 53–54, 57.

[37] Ibid., 55, 57.

[38] A. S. Kohanski, *Queen Esther: The Purim Megillah in Legend* (Lewiston, Maine, 1946).

[39] *The Book of Esther* (New York, 1961), 3.

[40] Robert Gordis, *Megillat Esther: The Masoretic Hebrew Text with Introduction, New Translation, and Commentary* (1974), 62–63.

[41] P. C. Craigie, *The Old Testament: Its Background, Growth, and Content* (Nashville, 1986), 243.

camp in Germany—in his poem "Haman" conflated the evil biblical character with his modern counterpart:

> I shall have camps, *Arbeit Macht Frei*, the lure
> Of hope, the chastening penalty of torture,
> And other entertainments of despair,
> The which I hanker after like a lecher.[42]

Hecht's younger contemporary Leslie Epstein, in his darkly humorous
novel *Ice, Fire, Water*, placed its protagonist Leib Goldkorn, a New York
composer working on a opera called "Esther: A Jewish Girl at the Persian
Court," in Paris on the day of his thirty-seventh birthday (November 9,
1938) as news arrived of the *Kristallnacht* in Germany. On the one hand
Goldkorn identified with Mordecai, "a stranger in a strange land." On the
other he was also "filled with joy," quickly seeing an opportunity to score
an artistic triumph while changing the course of history: "Surely the subtle French, so wise in the ways of the world," Goldkorn thinks to himself,
"would understand the association of Haman with Hitler. Both begin
with the letter H. *Formez vos bataillons!*" Among the lines he plans for his
triumphant chorus are:

> Drink wine, eat sweets, and roast marshmallows
> All Haman's sons will be hanged on the gallows.[43]

HANGING HAMAN AND HIS SONS

Well before the twentieth century, however, enemies of the Jews were
associated with the Agagite villain of the book of Esther. As we have seen,
in the twelfth century the Cistercian monk Radulf was conflated with the
character of Haman, and in the sixteenth century this was done with
regard to Cardinal Carafa, who became Pope Paul IV. Although medieval
Judaism clearly privileged the word over the image,[44] one image that
achieved considerable (and understandable) popularity among the Jews of
late medieval Europe was that of Haman hanging from a tree with five of
his sons on either side. This, as scholars have noted, was the most common

---

[42] Anthony Hecht, *The Darkness and the Light: Poems* (New York, 2001), 17.
[43] Leslie Epstein, *Ice, Fire, Water: A Leib Goldkorn Cocktail* (New York, 1999), 24–25, 39.
[44] See Elliott Horowitz, "The People of the Image," *The New Republic* (September, 2000):
41–49; Horowitz, "Odd Couples: The Eagle and the Hare, the Lion and the Unicorn,"
JSQ 11 (2004): 243–48.

6. The hanging of Haman and his sons, all of whom are blindfolded in this illustration, was the most popular Purim-related image among the Jews of late medieval Europe. From the "De Castro Pentateuch," 1344, Germany, fol. 361r. Courtesy of the Israel Museum, Jerusalem. Photo: David Harris.

illustration in the monumental illuminated Ashkenazi *mahzorim* produced in the thirteenth and fourteenth centuries.[45] Six of the seven illuminated prayer-books produced in German-speaking Europe during this
period include such scenes,[46] as do at least four biblical manuscripts.[47] The
"Leipzig Mahzor," executed in the Upper Rhineland during the early
fourteenth century, includes a full-size depiction of the hanging of
Haman and his sons in which all eleven figures are wearing blindfolds.[48]
A similar scene is found in the 1344 "De Castro Pentateuch," also illustrated in Germany.[49]

Such blindfolds may be found on the figure of the hanging Haman in
such late medieval Christian manuscripts as the "Arsenal Bible" (in Paris),
which was executed in Crusader-controlled Acre during the third quarter
of the thirteenth century.[50] Although many illuminated Latin manuscripts
(such as the Catalan "Roda Bible" and the "Florence Cathedral Bible")
include scenes of the execution of Haman, none has yet been identified
that also depicts the hanging of his sons.[51] For Christians, the hanging (or
crucifixion) of Haman could have moralistic or theological significance,[52]

---

[45] See Jacob Leveen, *The Hebrew Bible in Art* (London, 1944), 94; Bezalel Narkiss, "Introduction to the Mahzor Lipsiae," in *Machsor Lipsiae*, 2 vols. (Vaduz, Liechtenstein, 1964),
1:104; Narkiss and Aliza Cohen-Mushlin, "The Illumination of the Worms Mahzor," in *The
Worms Mahzor*, 2 vols. (Vaduz, Liechtenstein, 1985), 1:82.

[46] These are: The 1258 Michael Mahzor (in Oxford), the Laud Mahzor (also in Oxford), the
1272 Worms Mahzor (in Jerusalem), the first volume of the Double Mahzor (in Dresden),
the Leipzig Mahzor, and the 1348 Darmstadt Mahzor. See Gabrielle Sed-Rajna, *Le Mahzor
enluminé: Les voies de formation d'un programme iconographique* (Leiden, 1983), 64–65,
67–68, 70, 76, and figs. 25–28; M. Metzger and T. Metzger, *Jewish Life in the Middle Ages*
(New York, 1982), 295n112.

[47] See Sed-Rajna, *Le Mahzor enluminé*, 42, and figs. 54–55; Leveen, *The Hebrew Bible in
Art*, 87–88; Metzger and Metzger, *Jewish Life*, 295 n112.

[48] See Narkiss, "Introduction," 106; Joseph Gutmann, *Hebrew Manuscript Painting* (New
York, 1978), 86–87, pl. 24.

[49] The manuscript was formerly part of the Sassoon collection in England and is now in the Israel
Museum (MS 180/94). It is reproduced in Sed-Rajna, *Le Mahzor enluminé*, pl. 28, fig. 55.

[50] Hugo Buchtal, *Miniature Painting in the Latin Kingdom of Jerusalem* (Oxford, 1957),
pl. 74. See also A. Katzenellenbogen, *Allegories of the Virtues and Vices in Medieval Art:
From Early Christian Times to the Thirteenth Century* (London, 1939), pl. 32.

[51] See Louis Réau, *Iconographie de l'art chrétien*, 2 vols. (Paris, 1956), 1:340–41; Walter
Cahn, *Romanesque Bible Illumination* (Ithaca, 1982), 78, 154; Cahn, *Romanesque Manuscripts: The Twelfth Century*, 2 vols. (London, 1996), 1: no. 2:163; nos. 58, 69, 79; Narkiss
and Cohen-Mushlin, "The Illumination," 82.

[52] See Edgar Wind, "The Crucifixion of Haman," *Journal of the Warburg Institute* 1 (1937):
245–48; Bickerman, *Four Strange Books*, 211–12.

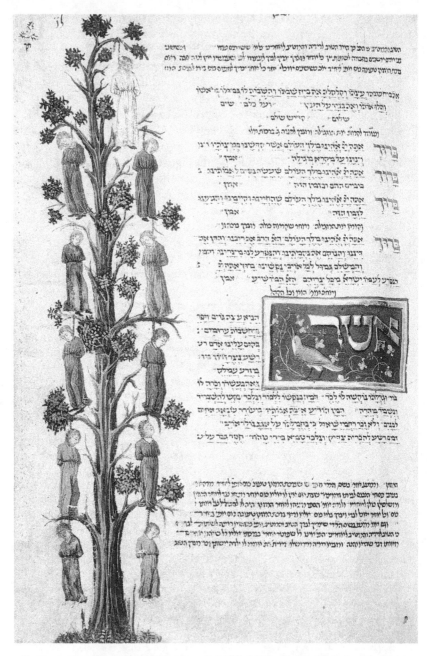

7. From the "Rothschild Miscellany," 1450–1480, Northern Italy, fol. 114 v. Courtesy of the Israel Museum, Jerusalem. Photo: David Harris. Another illustration in the same late fifteenth-century Italian manuscript depicts the hanging of Haman alone.

but the hanging of his sons—who had no overt connection with their father's evil designs—was more difficult to explain, and had no visceral appeal. Jews, however, were able to see Haman's sons, by definition, as Amalekites, who were thus deserving of decimation by divine decree.[53]

Whether the artists who executed the illustrations in the late medieval Ashkenazic *mahzorim* were Jewish or Christian,[54] they were working for Jewish patrons who clearly had an interest in seeing Haman and his sons hanging together in the pages of their Hebrew bibles or prayer books.[55] The late fifteenth-century "Rothschild Miscellany" executed in northern Italy, which continued this tradition, was evidently the first illuminated Hebrew codex to include two separate scenes of the hanging of Haman (in the Passover Haggadah section) and of his sons (among the daily prayers).[56]

These images continued to exercise a strong appeal even among the cultivated Jews of Renaissance Italy, reappearing in the illustrated Esther scrolls executed by Abraham b. Moses Pescarol in early seventeenth-century Ferrara. Pescarol, who was a member of a well-known Ashkenazi family, produced three illustrated scrolls, two of which contain colophons (dating from 1616 and 1618, respectively), and one which is undated, but presumably also from the second decade of the seventeenth century—the period following the ghettoization of Ferrara's Jews after the city's annexation by the Papal States in 1598. From northern Italy the custom of illustrating actual Esther scrolls with favorite scenes from the book spread elsewhere in Europe—to Holland, Germany, Moravia, Poland, and Slovakia. These illustrated scrolls continued to frequently depict the hanging not only of Haman, but also of his sons.[57] Such hanging scenes were also used, during

[53] For this explanation of their hanging, see P. R. Davies, "Haman the Victim," in Davies, ed., *First Person: Essays in Biblical Autobiography* (Sheffield, 2001), 154.

[54] On this thorny question, see Narkiss, "Introduction," 104; Narkiss, "Description and Iconographical Study," in *The Worms Mahzor*, 1:87–89; Horowitz, "The People of the Image," 44–45.

[55] On the popularity of this scene, see also Mendel Metzger, "The John Rylands Megillah and Some Other Illustrated Megilloth of the XVth to XVIIth Centuries," *BJRL* 45 (1962): 151–52.

[56] Leveen, *The Hebrew Bible*, 97–98; Heinrich Strauss, *Die Kunst der Juden im Wandel der Zeit und Umwelt* (Tübingen, 1972), 61–62, fig. 24.

[57] See Mendel Metzger, "A Study of Some Unknown Hand-Painted Megilloth of the Seventeenth and Eighteenth Centuries," *BJRL* 46 (1963–1964): 84–126; Metzger, "The Earliest Engraved Italian Megilloth," *BJRL* 48 (1966): 381–442; Victor Klagsbald, *Catalogue raisonné de la collection juive du musée de Cluny* (Paris, 1981), nos. 71–73, 75, 77; Chaya Benjamin, *The Stieglitz Collection: Masterpieces of Jewish Art* (Jerusalem, 1987), nos. 186, 188; Abraham Kanof, *Jewish Ceremonial Art and Religious Observance* (New York, n.d.), 176–77, nos. 181–82; *Catalogue of the Permanent and Loan Collections of the Jewish Museum of London*, ed. R. D. Barnett (London, 1974), nos. 285–86, 295, 302, 336 (dated

8. Abraham Pescarol, an Ashkenazic Jew in early seventeenth-century Italy, chose in this illustrated *Megillah* to depict both the hanging of Haman and the hanging of his sons. Both images from the Pescarol *Megillah*. Courtesy of The Jewish National and University Library, Jerusalem.

the eighteenth and nineteenth centuries, to decorate liturgical manuscripts, silver cases for holding the Esther scroll, and pewter plates used for delivering the customary gifts of food (*mishloah manot*).[58]

It had also been customary, at least in Poland, to fashion wooden noise-makers (*groggers*) in the form of a gallows, complete with human figures

---

1775); M. E. Keen, *Jewish Ritual Art in the Victoria and Albert Museum* (London, 1991), no. 35. (I have examined all of the London scrolls cited). For the nineteenth century, see also Erno Namenyi, "Ein Ungarisch-Jüdischer Kupferstecher der Biedermeierzeit (Marcus Donath)," 252–57, figs. 1–2, in *Jubilee Volume in Honour of . . . Bernhard Heller*, ed. Alexander Scheiber (Budapest, 1941); Ilona Benoschofsky and A. Scheiber, *The Jewish Museum of Budapest*, trans. J. H. Wiesenberg (Budapest, 1987), no. 203.

58 Barnett, *Catalogue*, 54 (no. 277); Kanof, *Jewish Ceremonial Art*, 181, no. 188 (1768); Benjamin, *The Stieglitz Collection*, nos. 190–91; Isaiah Shachar, *Jewish Tradition in Art: The*

9. The tradition of graphically depicting the sons of Haman hanging continued in eighteenth-century Moravia. From an illustrated *Megillah*, 1715, Moravia. Courtesy of the Library of The Jewish Theological Seminary of American, New York.

representing Haman and his sons. A late example—with two heads that were hit alternately by a hammer, one of Haman and one of Hitler—was created in 1933.[59] This, however, was less a case of continuity than a response to recent events. For by the early twentieth century European Jews were clearly less eager to display images of Haman and his hanging than they had been in previous generations.

BETWEEN GALICIA AND GEORGIA

The first years of the twentieth century witnessed a wave of bloody pogroms in Eastern Europe, beginning with that of Kishinev in 1903 and escalating to more than six hundred during the years 1905–1906, which

10. The hanging of Haman, but only some of his sons, is depicted on this pewter
plate for delivering *mishloah manot* on Purim. Nineteenth century, Germany.
Feuchtwanger Collection, 135/12. Courtesy of the Israel Museum, Jerusalem.

claimed more than three thousand Jewish lives.[60] Yet the illustrated
editions of Esther produced in Europe during the first decades of the twentieth century shied away from depicting scenes of Jewish vengeance.[61]
Although the extensively illustrated edition of Esther published in Paris in

[60] Gartner, *History*, 245–47; Shlomo Lambroza, "The Pogroms of 1903–1906," in Klier
and Lambroza, *Pogroms*, 195–247.
[61] The 1904 edition with German translation published in Rödelheim included four illustrations and the 1908 edition published there included three; "the triumph of Mordecai" and
"Esther accusing Haman" appeared in both, but neither included a single gallows scene nor
a scene of the Jews taking revenge against their enemies.

1925 by Arthur Szyk did include a scene of the Jews revenging themselves against their enemies,[62] neither the hanging of Haman nor his sons was depicted by the Polish-born Szyk.

By contrast, Abel Pann's 1926 album of twenty-four drawings graphically depicting Jewish suffering in Eastern Europe, which he had executed in 1917, included an image of three Jews hanging with telegraph wire wound around their necks. Pann (né Pfefferman, 1883–1963), it has been shown, drew heavily on the American journalist Abraham Cahan's (Yiddish) reports from the killing fields of Galicia published in New York's *Forverts* (*Forward*) in 1915.[63] In that same year, it may be noted, the American Jew Leo Frank was lynched in Atlanta after being accused of murdering a fourteen-year-old-girl.[64] It would appear that when Jewish bodies were hanging, whether in Galicia or in Georgia, it was harder for Jews to view gallows scenes of Haman and his sons with unalloyed gratification.

Although Arthur Szyk included no such scenes in his 1925 edition of Esther, he did include, as mentioned above, a scene illustrating the Jewish revenge described in chapter nine of that book. This may well have been a response to the successive waves of anti-Jewish violence that had erupted in Poland, Ukraine, and Belorussia in the aftermath of World War I. Szyk's native Lodz, in fact, had been one of the nearly four hundred localities in which Jews were brutally assaulted. In Lwow, the capital of the short-lived republic in western Ukraine, there was a major pogrom in 1918 from which the Galician-born writer Uri Zvi Greenberg (who, like Szyk, identified strongly with Revisionist Zionism) and his family narrowly escaped, giving rise to Greenberg's later reference, in a 1931 poem, to "the kingdom of Amalek on the Dniester."[65] Other responses in Hebrew literature to the Ukrainian pogroms of 1917–1920, "the bloodiest mass killings of Jews in history until then," were Saul Tchernikhovsky's sonnet cycle "On the Blood" (1923) and Isaac Lamdan's epic poem "Massadah" (1927).[66]

---

[62] Szyk, *Le livre d'Esther* (Paris, 1925), pl. 17.

[63] Pann, *Der Trauenungen* (Jerusalem, 1926); Gid'on Ofrat, *Haaretz*, November 21, 2003, 4.

[64] See Leonard Dinnerstein, *The Leo Frank Case* (New York, 1968), and most recently Stephen Oney, *And the Dead Shall Rise: The Murder of Mary Phagan and the Lynching of Leo Frank* (New York, 2004).

[65] Gartner, *History*, 282–83; Ezra Mendelsohn, *The Jews of East Central Europe between the World Wars* (Bloomington, Ind., 1983), 40–41; U.Z. Greenberg, *Rehovot ha-Nahar* (Jerusalem and Tel-Aviv, 1951), 11; Dan Miron, *Prolegomena to U.Z. Greenberg* (in Hebrew) (Jerusalem, 2002), 24–25.

[66] Gartner, *History*, 286.

Yet Jewish artists working during the interwar years rarely depicted the hanging of Haman,[67] and none, it seems, were willing to depict the hanging of his sons. In 1932 Nahum Gutmann, who had emigrated to Palestine twenty-five years earlier from his native Romania, published an illustrated edition of Esther which included no hanging scenes. On the page listing the names of Haman's ten sons their fate was hinted at, however, by a finger pointing accusingly at each one.[68] In the same year Josef Kaplan, who had been born in Swislowitz a year after Shmarya Levin, included two execution scenes in the edition of Esther he published in Leipzig. Neither of these, however, showed actual bodies hanging. In one scene Haman was merely being led to the gallows; in another his ten sons were depicted in size order facing the tree that would soon serve as their gallows—but not hanging from it.[69] Kaplan, who was himself responsible for the graphics (but not the line-drawings) in his 1932 edition, also provided some iconological commentary. He explained his decision to surround many of the pages (including the frontispiece) with intertwined thorns in light of the artistic convention of using the thorn as a symbol of suffering—as though it were entirely unrelated to the crown of thorns worn by Jesus! And the "garland" (*zer*) of thorns surrounded by twelve stars which graced the frontispiece was similarly linked by Kaplan to the five times the number twelve is mentioned in the book of Esther—as though neither the thorns nor the numbers twelve (apostles) or five (wounds) had anything to do with the figure of Jesus whom Jews had for centuries slyly conflated with that of Haman.

Not surprisingly the number three also figured prominently in Kaplan's graphic design, though here too there was some scriptural basis in the book of Esther. In the ninth chapter it is stated three times that the Jews "laid no hand on the plunder." These words appear emphatically in bold three times on one of the pages of Kaplan's edition, where they are juxtaposed with three linked swords, in order to stress, he explained, the ethical manner in which the Jews pursued their war. On the final page Kaplan placed these words on each of the three sides of a *hamantasch* ("Haman's ear")—the traditional Purim pastry.[70]

As Kaplan probably realized, the biblical author's stress on the Jews having "laid no hand on the plunder" was clearly intended as a pointed

[67] For a rare (and rather restrained) instance, see *Megillath Esther: die Purimgeschichte für Kinder* (Hamburg, 1931), 15.

[68] N. Gutmann, *Megillat Esther* (Tel-Aviv, 1932), 27.

[69] *Megillat Esther*, ed. Josef Kaplan (Leipzig, 1932), 52, 61.

[70] Ibid., 64. On Kaplan see Salomon Wininger, *Grosse jüdische National-Biographie*, 7 vols. (Czernowitz, 1925–1936) 3:398, 7:152–53.

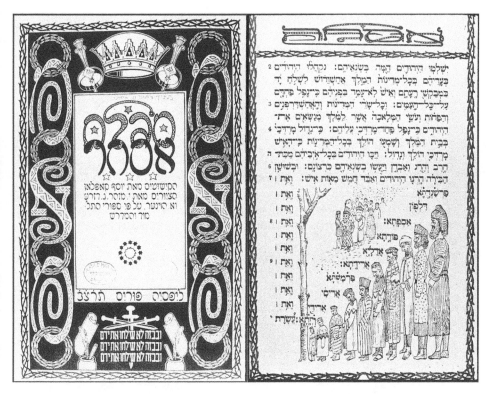

11. From *Megillat Esther*, ed. Josef Kaplan (Leipzig, 1932). Courtesy of The Jewish National and University Library, Jerusalem.

contrast with Saul's battle against the Amalekites, when, contrary to the instructions he had received from the prophet Samuel, "the people took of the spoil, sheep, and oxen" (1 Sam. 15:21). Moreover, whereas Saul himself had been personally derelict in allowing Agag, the Amalekite king, to survive, his descendant Mordecai and the Jews of his day had compensated for the king's misplaced mercy by killing both Haman and his sons. Could this mean that Israel's battle with its archenemy Amalek was actually over? Clearly for Kaplan, who could not bring himself to depict the hanging of Haman or his sons, but nonetheless framed the pages of his edition of Esther with intertwined thorns, the battle with Amalek was not yet over.

In 1936 the German-Jewish artist Otto Geismar published an illustrated edition of the book of Esther in which he too pointedly avoided depicting the actual hanging of Haman's sons. Beneath their names Geismar included a scene which showed only the base of a gallows, next to which several people were depicted looking upward, allowing the reader to imagine—but not to see—the ten figures dangling.[71] By contrast when the German-born artist Jacob Pins, who came to Palestine in 1936, executed, during the early 1940s, a series of woodcuts based on the book Esther, he included scenes of Haman and his sons hanging. These illustrations, however, were never published in book form.[72] And although one of the twelve illustrations executed by the Polish-born artist Nota Koslowsky for a bilingual edition of Esther that appeared in New York during World War II showed Haman contemplating the gallows he had prepared for Mordecai, none depicted actual scenes of punishment or revenge. The omission is particularly striking, since that 1944 edition, published and distributed to raise funds for a Jerusalem orphanage, included prayers to be recited for American servicemen and for Allied victory over "those evil ones who wish to destroy the enlightened and democratic world."[73]

Illustrated editions of Esther published in Europe and America during the years immediately following World War II continued to shy away from depicting the sons of Haman hanging, although it became more common to depict their father himself hanging from a gallows. The last of the sixteen illustrations by Gregor Rabinovitch in a bilingual (German and Hebrew) edition published in 1948 depicted the Jews celebrating, with Haman hanging in the background. The only illustration accompanying the names of his sons, however, was a hand clutching a raised dagger.[74] A year later Saul Raskin, who was born in Russia in 1878 and came to the United States in 1904, published a rather whimsically illustrated edition of the "Five Scrolls," including that of Esther. Raskin depicted Haman and his ten sons facing the gallows in size order, but avoided any actual hanging scenes.[75]

In 1950, however, Arthur Szyk, who had since 1946 been living in suburban Connecticut, completed a second illustrated edition of the book of Esther which appeared posthumously. Its provocative illustrations were quite different from those he had published in Paris twenty-five years earlier. Rather than limiting himself to the archaizing Orientalist style he had

[71] See also Rachel Wischnitzer, "The Esther Story in Art," in Goodman, *Purim Anthology*, 243.

[72] See *Pins: Woodcuts, 1942–1985* (Jerusalem, 1985), figs. 3.10, 3.22.

[73] *The Book of Esther*, with a translation and introduction by Sidney B. Hoenig (New York, 1944).

[74] *Megillath Esther* (Geneva, 1948).

[75] Saul Raskin, *Five Megilloth* (New York, 1949), 83.

12. From *The Book of Esther*, illustrated by Arthur Szyk (1974). Courtesy
of the Arthur Szyk Society. In his second illustrated edition of Esther,
completed in 1950 but published after his death, Arthur Szyk, who was
born in Poland and lost many relatives in the Holocaust, consistently
depicted Haman as a Nazi member of the SS. In this bold illustration,
Szyk includes himself contemplating the hanging Haman from his work
desk, holding in one hand a *hamantasch*, the traditional Purim pastry,
upon which he is munching, while with his other hand he transcribes the
blessing recited upon conclusion of the *Megillah* reading.

used earlier, Szyk brought the book of Esther "up to date" by liberally sprinkling swastikas and SS emblems in several of the illustrations depicting Haman, especially in that of his execution. But even Szyk, whose mother had been killed at Maidanek, avoided depicting the sons of Haman hanging.[76]

Why this reticence? Although in 1945 Benito Mussolini was hanged publicly (upside down) in Milan, together with his mistress, American Jews of the postwar years may have continued to identify the image of dead young men hanging primarily with the brutal lynching of blacks in the American South.[77] The painful memory of these lynchings was perpetuated through the powerful song "Strange Fruit," which was (and is still) associated primarily with the great jazz singer Billie Holiday, but was actually composed by Abel Meeropol, a Jewish schoolteacher in New York City. Its opening lines read:

> Southern trees bear a strange fruit,
> Blood on the leaves and blood at the root,
> Black body swinging in the Southern breeze,
> Strange fruit hanging from the poplar trees.

"Strange Fruit" was first performed by Holiday in 1939 at Café Society, the Greenwich Village nightclub owned by Barney Josephson, and she continued to mesmerize audiences with it until her death in 1959.[78] Although The *Sabbath and Festival Prayer Book* published jointly in 1946 by the (Conservative) Rabbinical Assembly of America and the United Synagogue did not shy away from literally translating the last words of the *Al ha-Nisim* prayer for Purim, which read "and they hanged him and his sons upon the gallows," by 1961 the *Weekday Prayer Book* published by the former rendered those same words euphemistically: "On the gallows he made for Mordecai, Haman, together with his sons, suffered death." The tamer translation, which studiously avoided the question of agency, continued to be used in the 1970s and 1980s.[79]

---

[76] *The Book of Esther* (Tel-Aviv, 1974). On Szyk and his biography, see most recently Luckert, *Art and Politics.*

[77] Between 1889 and 1940 nearly four thousand people were lynched in the United States. Ninety percent of the cases were in the South, and eighty percent of the victims were black.

[78] See David Margolick, *Strange Fruit: Billie Holiday, Café Society, and an Early Cry for Civil Rights* (Philadelphia, 2000), 15–131.

[79] See E. L. Friedland, "O God of Vengeance, Appear!" *Judaism* 37 (1988): 73–74.

5

Amalek

THE MEMORY OF VIOLENCE AND THE VIOLENCE OF MEMORY

"MEMORY IS AN AGGRESSIVE ACT"

IN the opening chapter of his *Against the Apocalypse* (1984) the literary scholar David Roskies included a fascinating autobiographical vignette about bringing a fountain pen as a gift to one of his mother's Israeli friends.

> Regina, who studied with Eisenstein in Moscow and is [or was] the first professor of film history at an Israeli university, tested the pen just as her father had taught her to do in Bialystok before World War I: She wrote the word "Amalek" and then crossed it out. Here was a lapsed daughter of her people, heeding the ancient call of Deuteronomy. . . . A quarter century of Yiddish secular life in Vilna followed by another quarter century of professional success in communist Poland had done nothing to dim what Regina had learned about memory from an ultraorthodox father in Bialystok. Memory is an aggressive act.[1]

More recently, in his autobiographical account of his lifelong, though highly ambivalent, involvement with Zionism and the land of Israel, the late novelist Mordecai Richler, like Roskies, a native of Montreal, cited a curious custom that had been followed by his grandfather, Rabbi Yudl Rosenberg (1859–1935), a popular and prolific writer who was also a Torah scribe. Before beginning a new scroll, reported Richler, his grandfather, who had left his native Poland in 1913, "would have been obliged to test his quill and ink by writing the name 'Amalek' and crossing it out," symbolically blotting out Amalek in observance of the divine command in Deuteronomy 25. For the benefit of his readers Richler explained that "Amalek was the grandson of Esau and ancestor of the Amalekites,

---

[1] Roskies, *Against the Apocalypse*, 10.

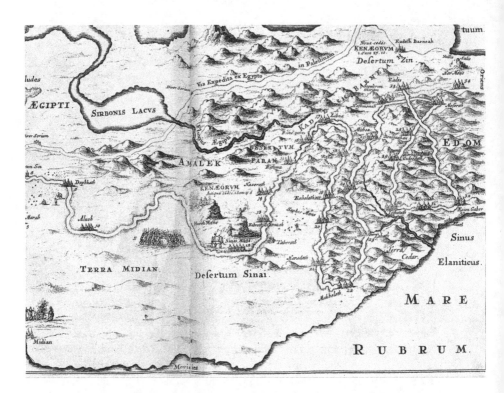

13. The numbers on Fuller's map indicate the stops made by the Israelites
on their way from Egypt to Canaan. To the right of no. 11 is the battle
at Rephidim. Moses may be seen with his arms upraised. Map of "Desert
of Paran," from Thomas Fuller, *Pisgah-Sight of Palestine and the Confines
Thereof with the History of the Old and New Testament* (London, 1650).
Collection of the author. Photo: Jordan Penkower.

nomads in the land between Egypt and Canaan, many of whose descendants," he added, "can no doubt now be found organizing for Hamas in the Palestinian camps of Khan Yunis, Rafa, Jabalia, and Gaza Town."[2]

Such sentiments, as we have seen, are now commonly found among Jewish settlers on the West Bank and their supporters. Yet for centuries Amalek, in keeping with biblical genealogy, was associated in Jewish discourse with Esau/Edom, and more broadly with the world of Christendom. In the later middle ages, as the German Hebraist Johannes Eisenmenger keenly demonstrated, European Jewish authors had even begun to actually conflate Esau/Edom with Amalek, referring to Christendom (often in an eschatological context) as "the kingdom of Edom and Amalek."[3] This, of course, as the erudite Eisenmenger, who was no friend of the Jews, stressed, said a good deal about their attitudes toward their Christian neighbors.

By Eisenmenger's own day, they had found "nonviolent" ways of combating their archenemy Amalek. In 1705 his contemporary, the Lithuanian-born rabbi and ethical writer R. Zvi Hirsch Koidonover published his immensely popular *Kav ha-Yashar*. In that work Koidonover cited the custom of "our teacher Rabbi Heschel," by which he meant the kabbalist (and former silversmith) Joshua Heschel Zoref, who was born in Vilna in 1633 and in the late seventeenth century became, according to Gershom Scholem, "the most important figure" of the Sabbatian movement in Lithuania. Zoref, whenever he was testing a new writing quill, "would write the name of Amalek, or of Haman and [his wife] Zeresh, and then cross them out" in order to perform the commandment of blotting out the memory of Amalek.[4] Koidonover's *Kav ha-Yashar* was republished in

---

[2] Mordecai Richler, *This Year in Jerusalem* (London, 1996), 204. (For a modern photographic depiction of the scribal practice referred to by Richler, see Paul Cowan, *A Torah Is Written* [Philadelphia, 1986]). On Rosenberg, see most recently (and comprehensively) S. Z. Leiman, "The Adventure of the Maharal in London: R. Yudl Rosenberg and the Golem of Prague," *Tradition* 36 (2002): 26–58, with ample bibliography. On the practice of writing and crossing out '*Amalek*, see also Zalman Schachter-Shalomi, *Wrapped in a Holy Flame* (San Francisco, 2003), 82. For a different way of "blotting out the memory of Amalek" by means of writing, see, Margaliot, *Sefer Hasidim*, 534–35.

[3] Eisenmenger, *Entdecktes* 1:658–59. Although the earliest sources cited by Eisenmenger were the Torah commentaries of R. Bahya b. Asher (Spain) and R. Menahem Recanati (Italy), Ephraim Gottlieb has shown that both drew upon a passage by the Provençal kabbalist R. Asher b. David, a student of R. Isaac the Blind. See Efraim Gottlieb, *The Kabbalah in the Writings of R. Bahya ben Asher ibn Halawa* (in Hebrew) (Jerusalem, 1970), 90.

[4] See Horowitz, "From the Generation of Moses," 451. On Zoref, see also Gershom Scholem, *Kabbalah* (New York, 1974), 276–77, 452–53. On *Kav ha-Yashar*, see now Jean Baumgarten, "Between Translation and Commentary," *Journal of Modern Jewish Studies* 3 (2004): 269–87.

the original Hebrew no less than thirty times before the end of the nineteenth century, not to mention seven Yiddish editions and three in Ladino. It is not surprising that R. Heschel's mode of blotting out the memory of Amalek spread widely as well, as is evident from Mordecai Richler's anecdote about his grandfather.

As David Roskies aptly remarked, "memory is an aggressive act," particularly among people with limited access to other forms of aggression. The memory of Amalek, one of the most powerful in Jewish tradition, has taken on, as we shall see, different forms over the centuries. Amalek, as noted earlier, is first mentioned in the Bible as the grandson of Esau (Gen. 36:12). But it was at Rephidim that the Amalekites were seared into the consciousness of the Israelites as the first enemy they encountered, after their exodus from Egypt (Exod. 17:8–17). Although by the battle's end the militarily inexperienced Israelites, led by Joshua, somehow "mowed down Amalek and his people with the edge of the sword," enough Amalekites survived for God to vow that He would continue to wage war with Amalek "from generation to generation." In the book of Deuteronomy (25:17–19), however, the battle at Rephidim was presented rather as a defeat for the "faint and weary" Israelities, who were "cut off in the rear"—a suggestive phrase to which we shall return. There, moreover, God did not vow to wage continuous war against the Amalekites, but instead, commanded the Israelities themselves "to blot out the remembrance of Amalek." Recently, it may be added, a Scottish Bible scholar has suggested—with a clear eye on the contemporary Middle East—that the Amalekite attack at Rephidim should properly be seen as a "defence of their home territory," and warned against readily accepting "the Deuteronomist's claim that the victim is the aggressor."[5]

This command "to blot out the remembrance of Amalek" resurfaced, as we have noted, in the first book of Samuel (15:2–3), when Saul was commanded in God's name by the eponymous prophet to "go and smite Amalek, and utterly destroy all that they have." Although Saul and his army did indeed defeat the Amalekites, they spared both King Agag, who was taken captive, and "the best of the sheep and of the oxen and of the fatlings" (1 Sam. 15:7–9). Samuel, after powerfully expressing God's displeasure at this partial fulfilment of His command, dramatically executed the Amalekite king in the presence of his belatedly repentant Israelite counterpart (1 Sam. 15:22–33). The Hebrew verb used was the

---

[5] A. G. Hunter, "(De)nominating Amalek: Racist Stereotyping in the Bible and the Justification of Discrimination," in *Sanctified Aggression: Legacies of Biblical and Post-Biblical Vocabularies of Violence*, ed. Jonneke Bekkenkamp and Yvonne Sherwood (London, 2003), 99.

hapax legomenon, "shsf," which allowed for considerable creativity in rendering the precise form of execution. According to one modern translation (JPS), Samuel "cut Agag down," according to another (RSV), he "hewed Agag in pieces."[6]

In his *Legends of the Jews* Louis Ginzberg noted rather vaguely that "Samuel inflicted a most cruel death upon Agag," but elaborated in his notes, where he presented two of the opinions found in rabbinic literature as to how the execution was carried out: "According to some," he reported, "Samuel cut Agag's body into pieces," but according to others, "he bound him on four poles, and killed him by pulling the poles apart."[7] The latter interpretation, as Ginzberg aptly noted, implicitly solved the problem presented by the fact that Samuel was a Nazirite, and thus prohibited from contact with any dead body. But in line with his aforementioned reticence in matters relating to the reproductive organs, the learned Lithuanian-born scholar neglected, even in his notes, to mention that according to another rabbinic tradition Agag was castrated by Samuel.[8]

This allowed a certain closure through what some rabbinic sages saw as symmetrical retribution: Amalek had attacked Israel "below the belt" and that is where Agag was painfully hit as well. How he managed, despite his castration and/or death, to beget the progeny through whom "Haman the Agagite" was later descended is a question which the ever-inquisitive rabbis addressed as well. In their view, as Ginzberg gingerly put it, "in the short span of time that elapsed between the war [with Israel] and his execution, Agag became the ancestor of Haman."[9]

REAR ATTACK AT REPHIDIM

The rabbis had also engaged in some rather imaginative speculation on the precise nature of the heinous deeds perpetrated at Rephidim, deeds that were deemed evil enough in the eyes of God for Him to command that the memory of the perpetrators be annihilated. In the book of Deuteronomy the Amalekites are described as having "cut off at your rear [*va-yezanev*

---

[6] For the latter translation, see also William Gesenius, *A Hebrew and English Lexicon of the Old Testament*, trans. E. Robinson, ed. F. Brown, S. R. Driver, and C. A. Briggs (Oxford, 1907), 1043. On the biblical account, see, among others, Diana Edelman, "Saul's Battle Against Amaleq (I Sam. 15)," *JSOT* 35 (1986): 71–84.

[7] Ginzberg, *Legends*, 4:68, 6:233.

[8] See, for example, Braude, *PR*, 239–40; Braude and Kapstein, *PRK*, 49–50. For references to the Hebrew editions of these and the other midrashim cited below, see Horowitz, "From the Generation of Moses."

[9] Ginzberg, *Legends*, 4:68, 6:233–34.

be-kha] all who lagged behind you (RSV), or, in Driver's more quaint translation (in the *International Critical Commentary*), "all that were fagged
behind thee." This "rear attack" was interpreted with characteristic creativity by the rabbinic sages.

Some, for example, linked the root "znv" with the Hebrew word for
"tail" (*zanav*), which was also used in rabbinic Hebrew as a euphemism
for "penis," as in the aforementioned legend explaining Vashti's enigmatic
refusal to appear before Ahasuerus. In one version of this phallic interpretation of the attack at Rephidim, the Amalekites sodomized the Jews
from behind, befouling them with their semen—an image that may also
been seen a metaphor for the brutal conquest of Palestine by the Romans,
who were sometimes referred to as Amalekites. As scholars have stressed,
military invasion is often represented "through highly charged, often
erotic, language as an act of anal penetration that may be construed as . . .
a humiliating sexual violation."[10] The relaxed attitude toward homosex-
ual acts in imperial Roman society, especially those involving active penetration, is well known,[11] and was probably known to the rabbis of Roman
Palestine as well.

According to another midrash, which would appear to conflate castration anxiety transposed into the distant past with recent memories of the
Roman ban on circumcision, the evil Amalekites cut off the Jews' circumcised organs and insolently flung them upward toward Heaven.[12]
Ginzberg, in his *Legends of the Jews*, omitted the former tradition and represented the latter only rather coyly: "Not only did Amalek kill them,"
wrote Ginzberg, "but he also mutilated their corpses . . . by cutting off *a
certain part of the body*, and throwing it upward" (emphasis added). His
timidity in this matter should be seen in light not only of the volume's
date of publication (1911), but also, perhaps, of its having been dedicated
to his mother! Ginzberg did, however, offer the valuable observation that
"in the legend Amalek's sneering at the Abrahamic covenant characterizes
the attitude of the Romans (especially during the Hadrianic persecutions)
towards this very important ceremony [of circumcision]."[13]

[10] Jonathan Goldberg, *Sodometries: Renaissance Texts, Modern Sexualities* (Stanford, 1992);
V. A. Lankewish "Assault from Behind: Sodomy, Foreign Invasion and Masculine Identity in
the Roman d'Anéas," 212–20, in *Text and Territory: Geographical Imagination in the European
Middle Ages*, ed. Sylvia Tomasch and Sealy Gilles (Philadelphia, 1998), quotation is from 213.
[11] See, for example, Paul Veyne, "Homosexuality in Ancient Rome," in *Western Sexuality*,
ed. Philippe Ariès and André Béjin, trans. A. Forster (Oxford, 1985), 26–35; Eva Cantarella,
Bisexuality in the Ancient World, trans. C. Ó Cuilleanáin (New Haven, 1992), chaps. 5–7.
[12] See Buber, *Tanhuma*, 41–42; Braude, *PR*, 238–39; Braude and Kapstein, *PRK*, 51–52
(and Nemoy's note there).
[13] Ginzberg *Legends*, 3:57, 6:24.

The Romans, it may be added, had often linked circumcision with mutilation and castration, which had been explicitly banned by several emperors.[14] Scholars are divided as to whether the Hadrianic ban on circumcision was universal or applied to Jews only, and also as to whether it was actually a cause or a consequence of the Bar Kokhba revolt. Peter Schäfer has recently suggested that Hadrian, the most "Greek" of the Roman emperors, was probably motivated less by moral objections to circumcision than aesthetic ones.[15] Whichever was the case, it is clear that in the revolt's aftermath the Amalekites, with a little help from the biblical text, were reimagined by the rabbis as remarkably like the sinfully sodomical and circumcision-obsessed Romans.

Both traditions—that which regarded the Amalekites as having sodomized the Israelites and that which regarded them as having performed the Amalekite equivalent of scalping—found ample expression in the liturgy for *Shabbat Zakhor*, the Sabbath before Purim. Both were also represented in Rashi's classic commentary on the Pentateuch (Deut. 25:18), which was for centuries the single most popularly studied work among European Jewry.

Remembering Rephidim: Josephus, the Rabbis, and Rome

It was clear, then, that the memory of Amalek was to be blotted out on account of the heinous deeds perpetrated at Rephidim. But who and where were the Amalekites? Just as early Christian authors, notably Irenaeus and Hippolytus, grappled with the question of the Antichrist's ethnic identity, deciding ultimately that he would be a Jew from the tribe of Dan,[16] so too did Jews sometimes ponder (with understandable ambivalence) the precise location of Amalek's pedigreed descendants. Perhaps the first to do so was Josephus Flavius in the first century, who in his *Biblical Antiquities* linked the ancient Amalekites with the nomadic Arabs of eastern Idumea. This has been explained by Johann Maier as an attempt "to avoid the impression of an existing linkage between Esau's

---

[14] The author of the *Historia Augusta*, in seeking to explain the outbreak of the Bar Kokhba revolt (against Hadrianic Rome during the years 132–135 CE) asserted that "the Jews began war, because they were forbidden to mutilate their genitals." See Peter Schäfer, *Judeophobia: Attitudes toward the Jews in the Ancient World* (Cambridge, Mass., 1997), 103–4.

[15] Ibid., 104–5. For Roman opposition to circumcision during the reign of Hadrian, and scholarly debates concerning its precise extent and motivation, see Feldman, *Studies in Hellenistic Judaism*, 572–73; Schäfer, *Judeophobia*, 103–5, and the literature cited there.

[16] See C. E. Hill, "Antichrist from the Tribe of Dan," *Journal of Theological Studies*, n.s. 46 (1995): 99–117. I thank Steven Wasserstrom for bringing this article to my attention.

grandson Amalek and Rome," and to identify the Amalekites with an
actual enemy of the latter, thus transferring "the emotional aspects of the
hostility between Israel and Amalek to the relationship between Romans
and Arabs." Amalek, according to Maier, was thus presented by Josephus,
primarily for political reasons, as "an enemy common to Rome and
Israel."[17]

Josephus devoted considerable attention to the inaugural encounter
between Israel and Amalek, constructing a version of the story quite different from the biblical original, one in which, as Louis Feldman has
stressed, Moses "plays a much more active role" than in the original.
Rather than delegating the military leadership to Joshua, he is transformed
into a "conquering general."[18] Maier, however, has seen the account of
Israel's battle with Amalek as "a skillful celebration of Jewish heroism in a
Hellenistic manner," in which Josephus sought to conceal from his non-
Jewish readers "the militant, eschatological-messianic implications" of the
original biblical text.[19] Christopher Begg, like Feldman, has observed that
Moses is transformed by Josephus into "a kind of Jewish Titus," noting
also that by amplifying the threat posed by the numerically and materially
superior Amalekites, he also magnifies Israel's subsequent military triumph. Begg has also followed Feldman's lead in suggesting that Josephus
may have been anticipating the later rabbinic use of Amalek as a "cipher for
Rome," thus lending a "polemical dimension" to his account of Israel's
victory at Rephidim. Unlike Maier, he sees Josephus as writing primarily
for Jewish readers, for whom his account of Amalek's defeat "would . . .
hold out, in necessarily coded language, the prospect of Rome's eventual
defeat and despoliation at their hands."[20] Whether Josephus is to be read
as anticipating the rabbis in their use of Amalek as an anti-Roman cipher,
or rather as communicating a message of reconciliation to his Roman readers, his was only the first of several Jewish rereadings of the encounter
between Israel and Amalek at Rephidim, and its implications.

After that battle, according to the book of Exodus (17:16), God
declared (Exod. 17:16) that He would wage war with Amalek "from

[17] Johann Maier, "Amalek in the Writings of Josephus," in *Josephus and the History of the Greco-Roman Period: Essays in Memory of Morton Smith*, ed. F. Parente and J. Sievers (Leiden, 1994), 117–18, 124–26.

[18] L. H. Feldman, *Jew and Gentile in the Ancient World: Attitudes and Interactions from Alexander to Justinian* (Princeton, 1993), 271–72. See also Feldman, *"Remember Amalek": Vengeance, Zealotry, and Group Destruction in the Bible According to Philo, Pseudo-Philo, and Josephus* (Cincinnati, 2004).

[19] Maier, "Amalek in the Writings of Josephus," 118.

[20] Christopher Begg, "Israel's Battle with Amalek according to Josephus," *JSQ*, 4 (1997): 203–5, 214–15.

generation to generation." The sense of continuous contest with Amalek that persisted during the period of Roman rule may be seen from an early and widely circulated midrash in which the words "from generation to generation" are glossed by three rabbinic sages: R. Eliezer, R. Joshua, and R. Jose (b. Halafta), all three seeking to identify the primary period of God's pursuit of the Amalekites:

> R. Eliezer said that the period was from the generation of Moses to the generation of Samuel. R. Joshua said it was from the generation of Samuel to the generation of Mordecai and Esther. And R. Jose said it was to be from the generation of Mordecai and Esther through the generation of the king Messiah, which is to endure as long as three generations.[21]

Here reference is made to four major moments in Israel's ongoing struggle with Amalek—three in the past (the generation of Moses, the generation of Samuel, and the generation of Mordecai and Esther), and one in the future (the generation of the Messiah). Rather than offering mutually exclusive interpretations of the words "from generation to generation," the three rabbis seem to differ rather in emphasis. Most striking, therefore, is the position of R. Jose which implicitly links the verse with contemporary history; framing the Jewish struggle with Rome—regarded as the latest incarnation of Amalek—between the defeat of Israel's mythic archenemy during the days of Mordecai and Esther and its future defeat at the hands of the messianic king.

R. Jose b. Halafta, a native of Sepphoris and one of the leaders of Palestinian Jewry during the period following the Bar Kochba Revolt, was a student of R. Akiva—a leading figure in that revolt, and probably the first rabbinic sage to equate Rome with Esau and Edom.[22] R. Jose, who is on record as having referred to Rome as the "evil empire,"[23] presumably saw considerable contemporary relevance in the subject of God's war against Amalek, a term which had also in his time become a code-word for Rome.[24] By placing the stress of the verse upon God's pursuit of Amalek "from the generation of Mordecai and Esther through the generation of the king Messiah" he was thus providing a measure of solace to those who

---

[21] Buber, *Tanhuma*, Ki-Tetze, 22b–23a;. Braude and Kapstein, *PRK*, 55 (I have altered the translation slightly).

[22] See L. H. Feldman, "Some Observations on Rabbinic Reaction to Roman Rule in Third Century Palestine," *HUCA* 63 (1992): 47 (Feldman, *Studies in Hellenistic Judaism* [Leiden, 1996], 446).

[23] See *Shabbat*, 15a, *Avodah Zara*, 8b.

[24] W. Bacher, *Die Agada der Tannaiten* 1 (2nd ed., 1930), 146n3; Ginzberg, *Legends*, 5:272n19.

may have feared that in its Roman imperial incarnation, Amalek was no longer under divine surveillance.

"Towards Him before We Prostrate/Insolently Did He Expectorate"

The rabbinic traditions concerning the Amalekite attack at Rephidim were imaginatively expressed and reworked in the liturgical poetry of R. Eleazar Kallir, who resided in Byzantine Palestine, and who was evidently the first Jewish author to use Amalek as a cipher for Christendom.[25] His poems for *Shabbat Zakhor*, like most of his compositions, "are intimately attached to the conception and language of the midrash" and are, on account of their neologisms and other obscurities, notoriously difficult to translate.[26] Like his other compositions, moreover, they were absorbed into the liturgical traditions of virtually all Jewries living under Christendom.[27]

Perhaps the most famous (or infamous) of these poems is the tongue-twister known as *Atz Kotzetz ben-Kotzetz*, on account of its alliterative opening words alluding to Haman's haste to harm the Jews, which became synonymous in modern literary Hebrew with the baroque excesses of laboriously learned liturgical poetry.[28] At the beginning of Kallir's poem Haman's plot is described as having been intended "to cut down my cut [circumcised] ones." As the poem progressively moves back in time Amalek is described as having, at Rephidim, "unleashed his hand upon the shapely of thigh" and "attacked from the rear all who passed by"—apparently an allusion to the rabbinic legend of the Amalekites as sodomizers. The reference to the Jews as "shapely of thigh" (cf. Song of Sol. 7:2) seems to be one of Kallir's characteristic linguistic innovations, and appears to be a euphemistic reference to their circumcised organs.[29] Some lines later Amalek is described by the poet as having angrily wielded his gleaming sword against Israel in such a way that "their circumcisions

[25] Leopold Zunz, *Die synagogale poesie des Mittelalters* (rev. ed., Frankfurt, 1920), 455.

[26] Ismar Elbogen, *Jewish Liturgy: A Comprehensive History*, trans. and rev. R. P. Scheindlin (Philadelphia, 1993), 244–46. On Kallir, see there generally 241–47.

[27] On Kallir's enormous popularity and stature among the Jews of medieval France, see Grossman *France*, 331–40, 534.

[28] See Yosef Yahalom in *Haaretz*, March 14, 2003.

[29] See Ben Yehuda, *Dictionary*, s.v. *yarekh*, where the phrase *hamukei yarekh* is attributed only to Kallir. On *yarekh* in rabbinic Hebrew as a euphemism for the sexual organ, and the circumcised phallus in particular, see, for example, Targum Pseudo-Jonathan and Rashi on Gen. 24:2; 47:29.

he slew/which then heavenward he threw/and towards Him before we prostrate/insolently did he expectorate."[30] Clearly for Kallir, who wrote under an acute sense of domination by Rome/Christendom, the circumcised penis, allusions to which recur frequently in his poems for *Shabbat Zakhor*,[31] figured prominently in the ongoing war between Israel and Amalek.

In another poem in his series of yozerot for *Shabbat Zakhor*, Kallir reaches back to the misdeeds of Amalek's ancestor (Esau) but turns at the end from mere remembrance to petition, calling upon God to remember that Amalek is His enemy as well as Israel's, and to take divine vengeance upon their common foe. Using the female name '*Adina* for Rome/Christendom Kallir implores God, toward the poem's end, to obliterate her memory "from every nook and every corner/and return the kingdom to its rightful owner,"[32]—a request, apparently, for Jerusalem to be seized from the Byzantine Christians and restored to Jewish rule.

The final poem in the series, beginning, "Keep not thou silence, Oh God" (Ps. 83:2), focuses on the theme of Amalek as the mutual enemy of God and the Jewish people, with such biblical phrases as "remember what Amalek did to you" bounced back to their original Author—somewhat irreverently, but following midrashic precedent. The list of Amalek's misdeeds is extended beyond the Bible, also following midrashic precedent, to include those perpetrated during the period of Roman rule in Palestine.[33] Claiming that "more than they have done to us they have done to You," Kallir goes on to list, side by side, parallel features of Amalek's attack upon the Israelites in the desert and the Roman destruction of Jerusalem in such a way as to lend greater weight to the latter. The clear message to God from the Jewish people is for Him to avenge Himself against their mutual enemy.

Kallir's liturgical poems for *Shabbat Zakhor*, like much of his literary oeuvre, were closely scrutinized during the eleventh and early twelfth centuries by some of Western Europe's leading sages, who accorded them status equal to that of the classics of rabbinical literature, and composed learned commentaries upon them. These commentaries, still primarily in manuscript,[34] at once reflect the enormous influence of Kallir's poetry

---

[30] For the Hebrew text, see S. Baer, '*Avodat Yisrael* (Roedelheim, 1868), 664–65; Lewinski, *Sefer ha-Moadim*, 6:16.

[31] In addition to his *yozerot*, see his *shiv'atot*, published by Shulamit Elitzur, *Be-Todah uve-Shir* (Jerusalem, 1991), 51–78.

[32] Baer, '*Avodat Yisrael*, 663. On '*Adina* as a common code-word for Rome, see Zunz, *Die synagogale poesie*, 456–57.

[33] See Ginzberg, *Legends*, 3:62, 6:25, and the sources cited there.

[34] See especially Grossman, *France*, 507–38, with ample bibliography.

among the Jews of pre-Crusade Europe, and served also to perpetuate that influence. The annual recitation, over the centuries, of his Amalek cycle of *piyyutim* on the Sabbath before Purim in Jewish communities situated throughout the lands of Edom/Rome/Christendom undoubtedly left its mark upon the ways in which those Jews experienced Christian rule and related to their Christian neighbors.

One last theme worth addressing, therefore, is the manner in which the memory of the outcome of the battle at Rephidim was manipulated. Quite understandably for his place and time, Kallir chose in his liturgical poems for *Shabbat Zakhor* to privilege, with unapologetic lachrymosity, the memory of Amalek's attack(s) upon Israel over the memory of how Israel managed, in the end, to achieve victory. The Bible itself (or its redactors) had done much the same in the transition from the book of Exodus, where Israel's dramatic victory is described, to Deuteronomy, where mention is made only of humiliating defeat.[35] Nonethless, Kallir did not entirely sidestep the subject of victory. Among the various explanations offered in rabbinic legend as to how Israel vanquished Amalek, Kallir preferred that (by R. Joshua ben Levi) which attributed Israel's success to the magic of Moses, or rather to his turning the astral magic of the Amalekites against them.[36]

This explanation was not as far from the straightforward biblical account as one might think, for before we learn that Israel "weakened Amalek,"[37] we are told that "whenever Moses held up his hand, Israel prevailed; but whenever he let down his hand, Amalek prevailed" (Exod. 17:11). This seems to suggest, as many biblical scholars have noted, that a mysterious force emanating from Moses (perhaps by means of his rod) is focused in the direction of the Israelites, a force that could understandably be regarded by R. Joshua b. Levi, and after him by R. Eleazar Kallir, as magical, just as it was so understood (independently) by modern scholars.[38]

---

[35] See Brevard Childs, *The Book of Exodus: A Critical Theological Commentary* (Philadelphia, 1974), 313.

[36] See Jerusalem Talmud, *Rosh ha-Shanah*, 3:8 (59a), and Ginzberg, *Legends*, 6:24. As paraphrased by Ginzberg, Amalek, "who was a great magician, selected, for the attack on Israel, those of his warriors whose birthday was on the day of the battle. . . . Moses, however, confounded the course of the heavenly bodies . . . and thus frustrated Amalek's device."

[37] I follow the literal translation suggested by S.R. Driver, *Exodus* (1911), 159. For other translations of the verb *va-yahalosh*, note "discomfited" (King James), "mowed down" (RSV) or "overwhelmed" (JPS).

[38] See Martin Noth, *Exodus: A Commentary*, trans. J. S. Bowden (Philadelphia, 1962), 142; Childs, *The Book of Exodus*, 315; and more recently, N. M. Sarna, *Exodus* (Philadelphia, 1991), 95, who suggests that "Moses' action might . . . be interpreted as a sort of mysterious focusing of supernal power on Israel."

But there were, of course, less magical forces to which Israel's victory over Amalek had been attributed. To quote one of the most famous passages in the Mishnah: "But could the hands of Moses promote the battle or hinder the battle! It is to teach you that when the Israelites directed their thoughts on high and kept their hearts in subjection to their father in heaven, they prevailed, otherwise they suffered defeat."[39]

Here victory is understood in terms of Israel's having gained God's favor through subjecting their hearts to Him. Amalek is "weakened" neither by Israel nor by Moses, but by God Himself. The Mishnah's reply to its own rhetorical question reflects both an attempt to provide an alternative to the magical view of Moses (suggested by the biblical text itself) but also, it would appear, to the sense of powerlessness experienced by the Jews of Palestine in the wake of their repeated defeats at the hands of Rome—making it difficult to imagine that they had managed to defeat the ancient Amalekites "by the sword."

The Mishnah's interpretation, which also appeared in the *Mekhilta*, was later included by Rashi in his popular commentary on the Torah.[40] By his time it was perhaps even more difficult for the Jews to imagine that it was by military valor that their ancestors, descendants of Jacob ("the tent dweller"), had been victorious over the Amalekites, descendants of Esau ("the skilful hunter"), at Rephidim. Yet it is important to note that neither rabbinic nor medieval Judaism spoke in one voice on this matter. Side by side with the Mishnah's "spiritual" description of the means by which Israel gained victory, Rashi saw fit to mention another, albeit less known, rabbinic tradition concerning the manner in which Amalek was "weakened," one which asserted that Joshua "went down and cut off the heads of the mighty men that were with Amalek."[41] Parallel to the Amalekites cutting off the circumcised organs of the Israelites, Rashi, following also Targum Pseudo-Jonathan, had the latter cutting off the heads of the mightiest Amalekites, sparing only their weakest warriors. This image—of the weak, under exceptional circumstances, triumphing dramatically over their mighty enemies—also found its place within the medieval Jewish mentality. It was an image with special resonance for the holiday of Purim, upon which the verses from Exodus describing the bloody battle at Rephidim were read in the synagogues.

---

[39] *Rosh ha-Shana* 3:8. I follow the translation by Herbert Danby, *The Mishna* (Oxford, 1933) with only slight changes. See the parallel passage in the *Mekhilta*, ed. H. S. Horovitz and I. A. Rabin (2nd ed., Jerusalem, 1960), 179–80.

[40] See Rashi on Exod. 17:11.

[41] *Mekhilta*, 181.

REPHIDIM AND THE RHETORIC OF CHRISTIANITY

Their Christian neighbors, of course, had their own understanding of what had transpired at Rephidim. As early as the *Epistle of Barnabas,* usually dated to the early second century, the image of Moses with his hands upraised was seen as prefiguring the salvational cross of Jesus: "The Spirit, speaking to the heart of Moses, [tells him] to make a representation of the cross and of him who was to suffer upon it. . . . So Moses placed one shield upon the other in the midst of the fight, and standing there . . . kept stretching out his hands, and so Israel began to be victorious."[42] Even medieval Jews, at least in northern France, seem to have known of this Christian interpretation. As the American art historian Meyer Schapiro noted, an illustrated Hebrew manuscript produced in Paris around 1278 shows Moses, with Aaron and Hur at his sides, strangely holding both hands "close to his breast." This was, as Schapiro observed "a common posture of prayer in Christian art," but not one that would have required, or was indeed conducive to, external support. He therefore suggested that the illustration in the Hebrew manuscript "was apparently designed to avoid the repugnant symbolism of the outstretched hands."[43]

Schapiro, as he himself acknowledged, was not the first scholar to detect evidence of a Jewish polemical reaction to this Christian reading of the outstretched hands of Moses. Louis Ginzberg, whom he knew personally, had cited the aforementioned rabbinic passage: "But could the hands of Moses promote the battle or hinder the battle?" asked the rabbis, replying that the true message was that "when the Israelites directed their thoughts on high and kept their hearts in subjection to their father in heaven, they prevailed, otherwise they suffered defeat."[44] Yet this passage, which, as noted previously, appears in both the *Mekhilta* and the Mishnah, probably predates the Christian prefigurative interpretation, which is first mentioned only in the *Espistle of Barnabas.*

Rephidim continued to reverberate in Christian rhetoric through the middle ages and early modern times. Pope Urban II, in (one of the versions

---

[42] *Epistle of Barnabas* 12:2–3, quoted in James Kugel, *Traditions of the Bible* (Cambridge, Mass., 1996), 623. On its date, see E. Ferguson, s.v. "Barnabas, Epistle of," *Encyclopedia of Early Christianity* (2nd ed., New York, 1997), 167–68, and the literature cited there. On the Christological interpretation of the hands of Moses at Rephidim, see also Childs, *The Book of Exodus,* 316; Schreckenberg, *Adversus-Judaeos* 1:65, 175, 189, 219, 319, 391.

[43] Meyer Schapiro, *Words, Script, and Pictures: Semiotics of Visual Language* (New York, 1966), 46–47.

[44] See *Mekhilta,* 179–80; G. F. Moore, *Judaism in the First Centuries of the Christian Era* (Cambridge, Mass., 1927), 2:06; Ginzberg, *Legends,* 6:25.

of) his famous 1095 speech to the Crusaders at Clermont, drew upon the image of Moses at prayer: "It is our duty to pray, yours to fight against the Amalekites. With Moses we shall extend unwearied hands in prayer . . . while you go forth . . . like dauntless warriors, against Amalek."[45] Urban was not the first Christian to refer to the Arabs as Amalekites. The Byzantine chronicler Theophanes, who died early in the ninth century, referred to the Muslim conquerors of Palestine (in the seventh century) as "the desolate Amalek."[46]

In the desolate wilderness of seventeenth-century Massachusetts, the Puritan preacher Cotton Mather found contemporary relevance for the battle of Rephidim as well. Mather, who had been active in efforts to convert the local Indians not merely to Christianity but, as one of his biographers has noted, to "New England Protestantism," did not shirk from calling for the extermination of those infidel Indians who would not convert to his religion. In a 1689 sermon he exhorted troops: "*Turn not back till they are consumed: Wound them that they shall not be able to Arise.*" In his dramatically concluding words, Mather compared himself to Moses at Rephidim; "And for a close, let me mind you, that while you *Fight*, we'll *pray*. . . . We will keep in the *Mount* with *our hands lifted up*, while you are in the *Field* with your *Lives* in your Hands against the *Amalek* that is now annoying this *Israel* in the Wilderness."[47] During the French and Indian Wars of the eighteenth century, religious hostility toward the Indians was intensified since, as Roland Bainton noted, "these 'Amalekites' came to be allied with the minions of Antichrist, the French papists." Then too some preachers asserted that, like their biblical namesakes, they were to be completely destroyed.[48]

Later in the century, after Horatio Nelson's stunning victory over the French Navy at the Battle of the Nile (1798), Rev. Abraham Jobson, "chaplain to the Lord Bishop of London," was able to preach a thanksgiving sermon under the title, "The Conduct of Moses, when Israel

---

[45] Quoted from Baldric, archbishop of Dols, *Historia Hierosolimitana* by A. Krey, *The First Crusade* (Princeton, 1921), 36. See also Schapiro, *Words, Script, and Pictures*, 35; D. C. Munro, "The Speech of Urban II at Clermont," *AHR* 11 (1906): 233.

[46] *The Chronicle of Theophanes*, trans. and ed. H. Turtledove (Philadelphia, 1982), 34; R. L. Wilken, *The Land Called Holy: Palestine in Christian History and Thought* (New Haven, 1992), 235.

[47] Cotton Mather, *Souldiers Counselled and Comforted* . . . (Boston, 1689), 28, 37; R. H. Bainton, *Christian Attitudes Toward War and Peace* (New York and Nashville, 1960), 167–68; Kenneth Silverman, *The Life and Times of Cotton Mather* (New York, 1985), 238–39.

[48] Bainton, *Christian Attitudes*, 168–69.

fought with Amalek, compared with that of Admiral Lord Nelson in the Battle of the Nile." Jobson noted triumphantly that the "sandy deserts, where the Israelites cried out for water, and where Moses stood with his rod lifted up to heaven" were "comparatively near the spot" where 1,500 of Napoleon's soldiers had died of thirst and where the splendid victory [of the Nile], for which we this day bless God, was obtained." In July of 1797, just over a year before the Battle of the Nile (after which he became "Baron Nelson of the Nile and Burnham Thorpe"), Nelson's right arm had been amputated after a firefight with the Spanish Navy, and his single remaining arm was dramatically utilized by Jobson, who noted in his sermon that Rephidim was not far from the spot "where Admiral Nelson, like another Moses, lifted his one hand to Heaven." He also compared the piety of the two leaders: "The Man of God, who lifted up his hands to Heaven, while Israel fought with Amalek, finds an equal in piety with our Admiral. The religion of Nelson is as highly singular as is his bravery."[49] Nelson had indeed written shortly after the battle to Sir William Hamilton, the British consul at Naples (whose wife Lady Emma soon became his mistress, and, later, his wife), that "Almighty God had made me the happy instrument in destroying the enemy's fleet."[50]

AMALEKITES = ARMENIANS

For Jews too the memory of Amalek remained alive in sometimes surprising ways, one of which was the curiously long-lived link between the Armenians and Amalek that began in the tenth century and continued well into the nineteenth, leaving the imprint of its legacy, as mentioned in the introduction, also upon life in contemporary Jerusalem. The use of '*Amalek* as the Hebrew word for "Armenian" is first attested in the tenth-century chronicle *Yosippon* (composed in Byzantine southern Italy),[51] and was quite common among Mediterranean Jews between the fifteenth and seventeenth centuries. When late in the fifteenth century R. Obadiah of Bertinoro, a native of Umbria who had emigrated to Jerusalem, described the city's sects in a letter to his father, he listed "the Latins, Greeks, Jacobites, Amalekites, and Abyssinians [Ethiopians]," each of whom, he added, "declares the faith of the others to be false, just as the Samaritans and

---

[49] A. Jobson, *The Conduct of Moses* . . . (Cambridge, 1798), 6–9.

[50] See Terry Coleman, *The Nelson Touch* (Oxford, 2002), 149–63; Edgar Vincent, *Nelson: Love and Fame* (New Haven, 2003), 259–73.

[51] *The Josippon*, edited, with introduction, commentary, and notes by David Flusser (in Hebrew), 2 vols. (Jerusalem, 1978–1980), 487.

Karaites do with respect to the Rabbanites."[52] Early in the seventeenth century another Italian Jew writing home from Jerusalem mentioned the two dominant groups of "the uncircumcised" Christians in Jerusalem: the "Franks [Latin Catholics] from the cities of Italy," and the "Amalekites."[53]

Byzantine Jews may have initially adopted the epithet "Amalekite" with regard to the Armenian Christians in order to distinguish them from members of the Greek Church, whose rites and customs were quite different. Armenians, like Latins, crossed themselves from left to right, and used unleavened bread in the Eucharist, a practice which "called forth many bitter denunciations by Greek clergymen" and in the eleventh century was condemned as heretical by the patriarch of Constantinople. During that same period Armenia was enjoying an unprecedented period of "power, prosperity, and cultural achievement" after King Ashot the Iron (914–928) managed to rid it of the Muslim marauders that had plagued it for centuries. Under his able successors Abas I, Ashot the Merciful, and Smbat the Conqueror, the Armenians, an originally proud and warlike people who "often had to bow to an alien yoke," were finally recognized, for over a century, "as the masters of the greater part of their native land."[54] The anonymous author of the Hebrew *Yosippon* was a contemporary of these tenth-century Armenian kings.

The usage of the term "Amalek" that he employed, and that continued for centuries, was a weak one in that it served primarily to maintain the sense that there were still Amalekites somewhere within the domain of Christendom rather than to express particular antipathy toward Armenians. Similarly, in his eighteenth-century autobiography Ber Birkenthal of Bolechow (in Galicia) referred, without rancor, to "an Amalekite wine-trader from Kamieniec."[55] Yet Birkenthal's contemporary Abraham Levie, a Dutch Jew who had been born in Germany, used the term "Armenian"

---

[52] *Jewish Travellers in the Middle Ages*, ed. E. N. Adler (New York, 1987) (originally published as *Jewish Travellers* [London, 1930]), 242. For the Hebrew text, which I have translated more literally than Adler, see Abraham Ya'ari, *Iggerot Eretz Yisrael* (Ramat Gan, 1971), 136, and the critical edition of M. E. Artom and Abraham David, *From Italy to Jerusalem* (in Hebrew) (Ramat Gan, 1997), 81.

[53] See Horowitz, "From the Generation of Moses," 431, and the literature cited there. (In n. 21, however, R. Obadiah's letter is carelessly misattributed.)

[54] See Steven Runciman, *The Eastern Schism* (Oxford, 1955), 40–41; D. M. Lang, *Armenia: Cradle of Civilisation* (London, 1970), 39, 176–77, 190; J. H. Forse, "Armenians and the First Crusade," *JMH* 17 (1991): 18–19.

[55] B. D. Weinryb, *The Jews of Poland* (Philadelphia, 1973), 123; *The Memoirs of Ber of Bolechow, (1723–1805)* trans. and ed. M. Vishnitzer (London, 1922), 55–56. In his translation Vishnitzer correctly rendered "Amalekite" as Armenian, as did Adler (see note 51, above) before him.

quite pejoratively when referring, in his Yiddish travelogue of 1764, to a (probably Catholic) priest on the island of Elba who had tried to turn him over to the Spanish Inquisition.[56]

In the nineteenth century the term "Amalekite" was almost always used negatively with regard to Armenians, possibly as a result of the economic competition that often prevailed between them and the Jews, both of whom were known for their sly business practices. Robert Curzon, who had briefly been a member of Parliament before traveling to the Middle East in 1833, provided readers of his *Visits to Monasteries in the Levant* with an estimate of the "peculiar qualities" of Egypt's "various nations," which, he added, "may be relied upon so far that it was composed by a person who had acquired a practical knowledge of their capacities by having been cheated more than once by the countrymen of each of the nations." According to the table provided by Curzon, it took the wits of:

> 4 Turks to overreach one Frank.
> 2 Franks to cheat one Greek.
> 2 Greeks to cheat one Jew.
> 6 Jews to cheat one Armenian.[57]

In 1839, as mentioned in the introduction, the British missionary Joseph Wolff found it "remarkable that the Armenians, who are detested by the Jews as the supposed descendants of the *Amalekites*, are the only Christian church who have interested themselves for the protection and conversion of the Jews." Three years later, as also mentioned there, the Scottish missionaries Bonar and McCheyne suggested that "the peculiar hatred which the Jews bear to the Armenians may arise from a charge often brought against them, namely that Haman was an Armenian, and that the Armenians are the *Amalekites* of the Bible."[58] Late in the nineteenth century Joseph Judah Chorny reported hearing from the Jews of Georgia, among whom he had traveled, of their ancestral tradition that the Armenians were descendants of the Amalekites, and another Jewish traveler reported a bizarre practice in eastern Galicia, whereby the Armenians who did business with the local Jews would mourn Haman's death every Purim, and light candles in his memory.[59] If there was any truth to

---

[56] *Travels among Jews and Gentiles: Abraham Levie's Travelogue, Amsterdam 1764*, ed. Shlomo Berger (Leiden, 2002), 132. Berger, however, failed to understand Levie's use of the term. See ibid., 30, 184.

[57] Robert Curzon, *Visits to Monasteries in the Levant* (reprint: London, 1983 [1849]), 100.

[58] Joseph Wolff, *Journal of the Rev. Joseph Wolff* (London, 1839), 255; Bonar and McCheyne, *Narrative*, 706.

[59] See M. Kossover in *Yiddishe Shprakh* 18 (1958): 17–19; Horowitz, "From the Generation of Moses," 450–51.

the latter report, it is likely that Armenians were paid to do so by the local Jews, as a form of Purim entertainment, just as elsewhere in Eastern Europe Jews would often hire Christians to play the role of Haman in their Purimshpiel.

During the final decade of the nineteenth century the Latvian-born scholar and polemicist Ephraim Deinard published a (privately printed) pamphlet against the use on the holiday of Sukkot of *etrogim* (citrons) from Greece, especially those grown on the island of Corfu, where, in 1891, a blood libel had caused most of the seven thousand local Jews to flee for their lives. The *etrogim* of Corfu had been a controversial subject throughout the nineteenth century, primarily because of problematic rabbinic supervision, and the controversy had been rekindled in 1875 after dealers raised their prices. Deinard's pamphlet, which carried the provocative title *Milhama la-Shem be-'Amalek* (God's War with Amalek), was perhaps the most rabid contribution to the renewed debate. Among the reasons he gave for boycotting the *etrogim* of Greece was that its denizens were descendants of Amalek.[60] His strange confidence in making this assertion would seem to have drawn on the tradition maintained for centuries that the Armenians (including members of their large Diaspora) were Amalekites. Both the Armenians and the Greeks were minorities within the world of Christendom with a prominence nonetheless in the holy city of Jerusalem. The venerable tradition of regarding the former as Amalekites evidently allowed Deinard to extend the category to the latter as well.

AMALEK/ESAU/CHRISTENDOM

For centuries the Jews of Europe, who commonly referred to Christendom as the realm of "Esau" or "Edom,"[61] seem to have had an acute sense of dwelling also in the pernicious presence of his grandson Amalek. The two were often conflated in medieval sources—most famously, perhaps, in Rashi's widely read Torah commentary, which drew heavily on rabbinic exegesis. In the *Tanhuma* and other midrashim, the view, based on a perceived link between Exodus 17:6 and Psalms 9:6–8, had been attributed to R. Levi that "when Amalek's seed will be removed from the world, [God's] throne and name will [again] be whole."[62] In the paraphrase that appeared in his

---

[60] E. Deinard, *Milhama la-Shem be-'Amalek* (New York, 1892), iv, viii. On the earlier controversy regarding the *etrogim* of Corfu, see Joseph Salmon, "The Controversy over Etrogim from Corfu and Palestine, 1875–1891" (in Hebrew), *Zion* 65 (2000): 75–106.
[61] See Berger, *Jewish-Christian Debate*, 246.
[62] See Buber, *Tanhuma*, 23a, and the parallels cited there.

commentary, however, Rashi (or one of his copyists) transformed Amalek into Esau, stating that "God had sworn that neither His name nor His throne would be whole until *Esau's* name was utterly destroyed."[63]

Rashi was not the only medieval author in whose work this particular conflation appeared. It may also be found in the late twelfth-(or early thirteenth-) century *Sefer ha-Manhig* by the Provençal scholar R. Abraham Ha-Yarhi of Lunel, to whom we shall return.[64] Several generations later the teaching that neither God's name nor His throne would be complete until Esau is destroyed was quoted by Don Isaac Abrabanel (in his commentary on Obadiah) as if it were part of an ancient midrash.[65] Thus through the writings of three popular authors—one Ashkenazic, one Provençal, and one Iberian—the notion was both preserved and promoted that God would remain restless until Esau (which for medieval Jews meant Christendom), rather than merely Amalek, was utterly defeated and destroyed.

A different means of conflating the identities of Esau and Amalek appears in the Torah commentary of Moses Nahmanides, composed in thirteenth-century Christian Catalonia. Although Esau, who had long been dead at the time of the battle of Rephidim, is of course nowhere mentioned in the account of Israel's engagement with Amalek, Nahmanides acutely felt his powerful presence between the lines. The apprehensiveness of Moses in the face of the battle, prompting him to take such unusual measures as ascending to the top of a hill with God's rod in hand (Exod. 17:9) was seen by Nahmanides as relating to Amalek's direct descent from Esau, who had received from his father, Isaac, the blessing, "By your sword you shall live" (Gen. 27:40). And Amalek's future defeat, according to Nahmanides, would augur the long-awaited end of Israel's

---

[63] See H. D. Chavel, *Perushei Rashi ʿal ha-Torah* (Jerusalem, 1982), 233, who confirms this reading, different from that of later editions, on the basis of the *editio princeps* of 1475 and MS. Oxford-Bodleian 2440. On the other hand, such MSS. of Rashi's commentary as Vienna 23, Vienna 24, Parma 181, and Paris 155 all read "Amalek" rather than "Esau." See also the MS. readings cited by J. F. Breithaupt, *R. Salomonis Jarchi, Commentarius Hebraicus in Pentateuchem Mosis* (Gotha, 1710), 533. (I am indebted to Jordan Penkower for this reference). For a possible talmudic influence on Rashi (or his copyist) in conflating Amalek and Esau, see *Bava Batra* 21a–b.

[64] *Sefer ha-Manhig*, ed. Y. Raphael, 2 vols. (Jerusalem, 1978), 1:56.

[65] See Abrabanel's commentary on Obadiah 1:21. Abrabanel, while quoting an actual midrash from *Bereshit Rabbah*, included Rashi's teaching about Esau as if it were part of the same passage. His words were noted by Eisenmenger, *Entdecktes Judenthum*, 1:655; Jacques Basnage, *L'histoire et la réligion des juifs depuis Jésus Christ jusqu'à present* (Rotterdam, 1706–1707), 3:7–16.

exile under Edom/Esau/Christendom. The use of the first person plural lent a particular poignancy to his remarks:

> For both Israel's first and final wars are with this clan, as Amalek is a descendant of Esau. It is Amalek who declared war against us "at the beginning of nations" (Num. 24:20), and Esau's descendants who have caused us to suffer our last exile and destruction, as our sages have taught that we are today in the exile of Edom. When he shall be vanquished, and he together with the nations that are with him shall be weakened, we shall be redeemed [from that exile] forever, as it is stated: "And the saviors shall come up on mount Zion to judge the mount of Esau; and the kingdom shall be the Lord's." (Obad. 1:21)[66]

Although Nahmanides could rely on such sources as the Targum of Onkelos (on Num. 24:20) to bolster his claim that Amalek had been Israel's first enemy, his eschatological assertion that Amalek would also be Israel's last was considerably bolder, and was evidently rooted in his novel reading of the concluding verse of Obadiah in a manner that consciously conflated Esau and Amalek. In asserting that when Edom/Esau "together with the nations that are with him shall be weakened, we shall be redeemed ... forever," Nahmanides presumably meant European Christendom under the spiritual rule of Rome, whose defeat, then, he saw as a prerequisite to Israel's ultimate redemption.

The potentially explosive import of these remarks was undermined, perhaps intentionally, by Nahmanides' comments on the concluding words of Exodus 17: "the Lord will be at war with Amalek from generation to generation." Rather than seeing in these words an exhortation to fight God's battle against the Amalekites in each generation (hence, by implication, also against those residing in medieval Europe), Nahmanides favored an interpretation which limited the obligation to do war with Amalek only to those periods when a Jewish monarch ruled over his people, as in the days of Saul or David. This interpretation, which does not appear in classical rabbinic sources, had earlier been put forward by R. Joseph Kara, Rashi's younger contemporary, and then later in the twelfth century by another French exegete, R. Joseph Bekhor Shor of Orléans.[67] Since neither of the French exegetes nor Nahmanides in thirteenth-century Spain realistically expected that a Jewish monarch would soon be returning to sit on David's throne, this was a convenient means of postponing any actual battle with Amalek into the distant future

---

[66] See Nahmanides on Exod.17:9, 16 (translation mine). See also his *Sefer ha-Geulah*, in *Kitvei Ramban*, ed. C. B. Chavel, 2 vols. (Jerusalem, 1963), 1:284–85.

[67] *Sefer Tosafot ha-Shalem: Otzar Perushei Ba'alei ha-Tosafot* (Jerusalem, 1988), 7:312; *R. Yosef Bekhor Shor 'al ha-Torah*, ed. Y. Nevo (Jerusalem, 1994), 128, 365.

while preserving the notion that there were still Amalekites to be found among the descendants of Esau in Christian Europe.

R. Eliezer of Metz, who like Bekhor Shor had been a student of the eminent tosafist (and grandson of Rashi) R. Jacob Tam, went a step further in removing actual war with Amalek from the realities of medieval Jewish life, asserting in his *Sefer Yereim* that the biblical commandment to destroy Amalek (Deut. 25:19) applied "only to the king and not to the remainder of Israel."[68] This assertion, like the comments of the biblical exegetes discussed above, could allow the Jews of Europe to see (and refer to) their Christian neighbors as Amalekites without being obligated thereby to wage a holy but hopeless war against them.

The Jews of Christian Europe knew, of course, that they could never hope to vanquish the Amalekites of their day on the battlefield, but some found ways to carry the holy war against them to a more convenient site, where they would enjoy "the home-court advantage"—the synagogue. Beginning with the Jews of Franco-Germany around the time of Rashi, the solemn *Kaddish* prayer, one of the central texts of the synagogue service, was conscripted into battle against the ancient archenemy of the Jews and their God. In the *Sefer ha-Pardes,* which was composed by Rashi's students, the opening words of the *Kaddish* (which expressed the hope that the name of God be enhanced and hallowed) are explained in the following manner: "And thus we pray *yitgadal ve-yitkadash,* meaning: Let it be the will of He through whose word the world was created that He redeem us from among the nations and destroy the memory of Amalek and His name will be hallowed to be complete."[69] Thus, in a classical case of intertextual interpretation, God's name in the *Kaddish* was linked with the popular midrash (paraphrased by Rashi) that His "throne and name will [again] be whole" only after Amalek is destroyed. Similarly, in a passage from the *Mahzor Vitry* (also produced by Rashi's students), which has only recently come to light, the opening words of the *Kaddish* are explained in terms of the sundered name of God, who "swore by His right hand and by His throne that His name would not be complete . . . until He avenged Himself against Amalek."[70]

Although the Tosafists dismissed this rather bellicose interpretation on philological grounds,[71] it nonetheless made its way southwest to the Jewish communities of Provence and Christian Spain, who also saw themselves

---

[68] *Sefer Yereim*, ed. A. A. Schiff (Vilna, 1901), 500 (par. 435).

[69] *Sefer ha-Pardes*, ed. H. Y. Ehrenreich (Budapest, 1924), 325–26.

[70] The passage was deleted from the London manuscript upon which the printed edition (of 1923) is based, but versions of it may be found in two other manuscripts. See also Leon Wieseltier, *Kaddish* (New York, 1998), 427–31.

[71] *Berakhot*, 3a.

living among the descendants of Esau. In his aforementioned *Sefer ha-Manhig* (which was written in Toledo), R. Abraham ha-Yarhi stated emphatically that the *Kaddish* was "primarily about redemption," and he glossed its opening words as a fervent prayer that God's name become whole, in keeping with His oath (allegedly hinted at in Exod. 17:16) "that neither my throne nor my name will be complete until revenge is taken upon Esau."[72] As noted above, R. Abraham was one of the first medieval Jewish authors to conflate Esau and Amalek, so that, according to his interpretation, the *Kaddish* effectively became a petition for the downfall of Esau/Edom/Christendom.

In the fourteenth century two influential Spanish authors, R. David Abudarham and R. Jacob b. Asher, included similar interpretations of the *Kaddish* in their works. The former saw the words *yehei shmei rabba mevorakh . . .*, with which the congregation responded to the opening words of the *Kaddish*, as a prayer on their part for God's name to become complete again, "and this will be at the time of redemption, when he avenges Himself against Amalek, who is a descendant of Esau."[73] By stressing Amalek's ancestry, Abudarham, like R. Abraham ha-Yarhi before him, evidently sought to signal to his co-religionists that the *Kaddish* should be seen (and experienced) as part of the cosmic struggle between their God and the evil empire of Esau/Edom. After the "Amalek-oriented" interpretation of the *Kaddish* spread from Franco-Germany to the Hispano-Provençal world, there were thousands of Jews across late medieval Europe who prayed several times daily for God to avenge Himself against the archenemy whose continued existence kept His name sundered—and thus painfully postponed their own redemption.

MAIMONIDES AND HIS INFLUENCE

For Jews living in the Muslim world, far away from the descendants of Esau, the situation was somewhat different. Moses Maimonides (1135–1204), who was born in Andalusia but composed most of his works in Egypt, included in his *Book of the Commandments* three that were connected with Amalek: two positive (188–89) and one negative (59).[74] The first of the two positive commandments was potentially the most unsettling for medieval

---

[72] *Sefer ha-Manhig*, 1:56.

[73] *Abudarham ha-Shalem* (Jerusalem, 1963), 66; *Tur Orah Hayyim*, no. 56. On the move westward of the Amalek-oriented interpretation of the *Kaddish*, see Daniel Sperber, *Minhagei Yisrael* (Jerusalem, 1989), 1:71–77.

[74] These are paralleled by three passages in the Laws of Kings at the end of his *Mishneh Torah* (Melakhim 1:1, 5:5, 6:4).

Jews: "By this injunction," wrote Maimonides, "we are commanded that among the descendants of Esau we are to exterminate only the seed of Amalek, male and female, young and old."[75]

The commandment's problematic character is reflected in Maimonides' double-edged interpolation concerning the descendants of Esau. One the one hand, it highlighted the connection between Amalek, Esau, and, by implication, the realms of Christendom. On the other, it sought to stress that the commandment of extermination applied only to a small minority of Edomites, thus minimizing—though not necessarily neutralizing—its practical import.[76] Later, in his more overtly philosophical *Guide of the Perplexed*, Maimonides used the principle of *lex talionis* to explain why the Amalekites deserved such severe punishment, asserting that "it was commanded that Amalek, who hastened to use the sword, should be exterminated by the sword."[77]

He also returned there to the matter of Amalek's descent from Esau, arguing that the Torah had devoted an entire chapter (Genesis 36) to the latter's genealogy so that it would be possible to determine which descendants of Esau were Amalekites (through his grandson) and which were not. Maimonides stressed, furthermore, that ten verses in that chapter were devoted to the genealogy of Se'ir the Horite, who was not even a descendant of Esau, but whose progeny resided in the same lands as the Edomites and intermarried with them. Consequently, he asserted, "those whom you see today in Se'ir and the kingdom of Amalek are not all of them children of Amalek, but some of them are descendants of this or that individual and are only called after Amalek because the latter's mother [Timna, daughter of Se'ir] belonged to them."[78]

In his great code, the *Mishneh Torah*, composed between the two aforementioned works, Maimonides presented the commandment of destroying Amalek (Laws of Kings 5:5), without alluding, however, to the genealogical ties between the latter and the descendants of Esau. He did

---

[75] I follow the translation in C. B. Chavel, *The Commandments: Sefer Ha-Mitzvoth of Maimonides*, 1:202. On the position of Maimonides regarding Amalek, see Avi Sagi, "The Punishment of Amalek in Jewish Tradition: Coping with the Moral Problem," *HTR 87* (1994): 323–46, and more recently (and cogently), Josef Stern, "Maimonides on Amaleq: Self-Corrective Mechanisms, and the War against Idolatry," in *Judaism and Modernity: The Religious Philosophy of David Hartman*, ed. J. W. Malino (Aldershot, 2004), 359–92. I thank Prof. Stern for sharing his paper with me in advance of its publication.

[76] For a later echo of this position, see *Ibn Kammuna's Examination of the Three Faiths*, ed. and trans. Moshe Perlmann (Berkeley, 1971), 58.

[77] Moses Maimonides, *Guide of the Perplexed*, trans. and ed. Shlomo Pines (Chicago, 1963), 3:41.

[78] Ibid., 3:50.

make it quite clear, however, that there still were authentic Amalekites to be found in the world—in contrast to the descendants of the "seven nations," who were in theory also to be destroyed (Laws of Kings 5:4) but whose memory, he asserted, "had long perished." Unlike R. Joseph Bekhor Shor and R. Eliezer of Metz in Christian Europe, Maimonides did not suggest that the commandment to "destroy the memory of Amalek" was limited to particular circumstances.

His straightforward formulation, however, proved too practicable for comfort among thirteenth-century students of his code residing across the Mediterranean, in the evil empire of Edom. R. Moses of Coucy (in northern France) whose *Sefer Mitzvot Gadol* closely followed the *Mishneh Torah* of Maimonides, felt the need to add, after listing the commandment to destroy the memory of Amalek, that "this commandment applies only during the days of the messianic king, after the conquest of the land." Later in the thirteenth century another French scholar, R. Isaac of Corbeil, went a step further, omitting entirely from his *Sefer Mitzvot Katan* (*Semak*), a code also closely modeled on that of Maimonides, the obligation of destroying Amalek. Instead, he listed only the more passive commandments connected with memory rather than violence—the negative commandment of not forgetting Amalek and the positive one of remembering Amalek.[79] Through this discreet omission he contributed to the obliteration among Ashkenazic Jewry of the command to obliterate Amalek's memory.

Yet it would certainly be wrong to assert that R. Isaac, who wrote less than a century after such events as the public burnings of Jews in Blois, the burning of the Talmud in Paris, and numerous local expulsions throughout France, had no interest in revenge against the descendants of Amalek. Revenge, in fact, was a major theme in the liturgical poetry written in commemoration of the mass martyrdom at Blois (1171) and recited on the fast day which had been decreed (by R. Jacob Tam) to memorialize the event. These included such lines as: "Fight against my foes and make their blood flow/Oh God of vengeance, thyself show" and "Jacob's voice is crying out loud/for the blood shed by Esau to be avenged."[80]

In a similar spirit R. Isaac explicated in his *Sefer Mitzvot Katan* the negative commandment of not forgetting what he called "the affair of Amalek." It meant, he explained, not forgetting "that God saved us from him, and therefore His fear should be upon us always lest we sin, and by

---

[79] *Sefer Mitzvot Katan*, nos. 23, 147.
[80] The lines are from the poem by Hillel b. Jacob of Bonn, "Emunei Shlomei Yisrael," in Haberman, *Gezerot*, 140. See also the lines of Hillel's famous brother Ephraim, ibid., 136. On the burnings at Blois and their commemoration, see Yerushalmi, *Zakhor*, 48–49, 51–52, and the literature cited there.

this He shall give us strength to take revenge against him [Amalek], *amen amen selah*." The same author who was apparently the first to omit from his code the commandment to destroy Amalek, nonetheless expressed unconcealed desire for revenge against Amalek's descendants, highlighted by the concluding flourish *amen amen selah*. Revenge was thus transformed by R. Isaac from a positive commandment to a reward for fearing God, a reward whose indefinite postponement was more easily explained to his contemporaries (and to himself) than that of performing a divine commandment. R. Isaac's personal desire for revenge against Amalek was undoubtedly greater than that of Maimonides, and yet, paradoxically, in its century of travel between Cairo and Corbeil the injunction to annihilate Amalek was effectively effaced.

It must be acknowledged, however, that in his *Guide*, as opposed to the two earlier (and less philosophical) works, Maimonides too found a way of neutralizing the practical import of the biblical commandment. To quote Josef Stern: "Scripture's description of the historical facts related to the genealogy of Amalek renders it impossible," according to Maimonides, "for us to put its own legislation into practice."[81] Nonetheless, it should be stressed that these comments of Maimonides merely pointed to the practical problems that prevented implementing the commandment to annihilate Amalek, but did not defer the commandment, as did Franco-German halakhists, to some point in the imaginably distant future. Furthermore, these comments appeared only in the *Guide*, a philosophical work, whereas readers of the more practically authoritative *Mishneh Torah* were given no indication that the commandment of destroying Amalek could (or should) not be performed in their own day.

In his treatment of the biblical commandment to remember Amalek, Maimonides took a more far-reaching position not only than the rabbis of medieval Europe, but even than those of the Talmud. "By this injunction," he wrote in his *Book of the Commandments*, "we are commanded to remember what Amalek did to us in attacking us unprovoked [and to hate him always]. We are to speak of this at all times, and to arouse the people to make war upon him and bid them to hate him, and that hatred of him be not weakened or lessened with the passage of time."[82] It is quite striking that hatred toward Amalek appears three times (apparently for emphasis) in Maimonides' definition of the commandment, although it is surprisingly absent from both of the midrashic prooftexts (*Sifre* and *Sifra*) he cites.[83] From his *Sefer ha-Mitzvot* this link between remembering

[81] Stern, "Maimonides on Amaleq."

[82] Chavel, *The Commandments*, 1:203. The interpolated words are taken from the first edition of *Sefer ha-Mitzvot* as cited by Heller in his edition (of 1946), 82n4.

[83] For a possible explanation of how this hate-oriented definition came about, see Horowitz, "From the Generation of Moses," 448.

Amalek and hating Amalek finds its way quite naturally into the *Mishneh Torah* (Laws of Kings 5:5), albeit not in the modern (mis)translation of Hershman, where we read: "It is a positive commandment always to bear in mind his evil deeds . . . so that we keep fresh the memory of the hatred manifested by him."[84] A more correct translation (especially in light of the parallel passage in the *Book of the Commandments*) would read: "It is a positive commandment always to bear in mind his evil deeds . . . in order to arouse our enmity towards him."

Maimonides was probably using "hatred" in its medieval sense, that is, less in the sense of an emotion (such as anger) than as "an enduring public relationship between two adversaries" often expressed through "a consistent and formulaic set of behavioral patterns." A fourteenth-century preacher's handbook that circulated in England but drew upon such older sources as Saint Augustine and Gregory the Great distinguished in the following manner between hatred and revenge: "For many people today cannot take their revenge with material weapons and therefore retain hatred through hardened anger (*iram induratam*) in their hearts."[85] Maimonides, perhaps because he recognized that revenge against Amalek was not a practical possibility, seems to have transformed the commandment to remember Amalek into a commandment to maintain "hardened anger" toward his descendants.

When the Maimonidean version of this commandment traveled from Cairo to Corbeil, and thus from the world of Ishmael to that of Esau/Amalek, it too underwent significant change. Not only was the element of enmity edited out by R. Isaac in his *Sefer Mitzvot Katan*, but no less significantly, the commandment to remember Amalek was transformed from one binding "always" to one to be performed annually on the Sabbath before Purim, through the public reading of the last three verses in Deuteronomy 25.[86] By both reducing its emotional intensity and linking its observance to a particular time and a particular text R. Isaac effectively shrunk the commandment by several sizes. The medieval Franco-German Jews who regarded his code as authoritative no longer needed to contemplate the daunting task of annihilating Amalek, nor did they need to remember him with enmity. In fact, they barely needed to remember him at all. Their relationship with Amalek's memory could safely be confined to one morning each year.

By both localizing and ritualizing the injunction to remember Amalek, R. Isaac was also removing it, in effect, from the various spheres of actual

---

[84] *The Code of Maimonides . . . The Book of Judges*, trans. A. M. Hershman (New Haven, 1949), 217.

[85] See D. L. Smail, "Hatred as a Social Institution in Late-Medieval Society," *Speculum* 76 (2001): 90–91, 108.

[86] *Sefer Mitzvot Katan*, nos. 23, 146.

encounter between Jew and Christian in medieval Europe: the street, the market, or even the home. Maimonides, who did not earn (or buy) his bread among the medieval descendants of Amalek, could without much difficulty deem it necessary "always to bear in mind his evil deeds." For those in Christian Europe, however, even those who harbored the ideal of martyrdom in their minds, it was hardly a viable modus vivendi.

Early in the fourteenth century the Spanish halakhist R. Jacob b. Asher of Toledo composed his famous *Turim*, which later served as the model for R. Joseph Caro's better known *Shulkhan 'Arukh*. Both works limited themselves, unlike the code of Maimonides, to the rules and regulations governing Jewish religious life in the Exilic era, omitting those which applied to the Temple cult, as well as others, such as the Laws of Kings, which would remain inapplicable until the messianic era. Although the commandment of remembering Amalek appears in the *Turim*, the ostensibly twin commandment of destroying Amalek is absent from that work, reflecting its postponement to the messianic era by Franco-German authors of the twelfth and thirteenth centuries. Not surprisingly, the commandment of annihilating Amalek was also omitted by R. Joseph Caro from the *Shulkhan 'Arukh*, which over the past four centuries has been the most single influential code of Jewish law.[87]

AMALEK ALLEGORIZED

Another medieval mechanism for dealing with the ostensible obligation of waging continuous war against the Amalekites was to allegorize the notion of Amalek, transforming it into the "evil inclination," which, if Jews did not necessarily have a better chance of defeating, they would presumably incur fewer losses fighting. This allegorized notion of Amalek seems to have surfaced first in southwest France, in a twelfth-century liturgical poem by R. Zerahia of Lunel, and became popular in both philosophical and kabbalistic circles during the succeeding centuries.[88] In a letter to R. Abba Mari of Lunel, his ally in the early fourteenth-century controversy over rationalism that sharply divided the Jewish scholars of Spain and southern France, R. Solomon ibn Adret of Barcelona complained of those "who had not failed to transform a single verse" into allegory: "Abraham and Sarah

---

[87] See Isadore Twersky, "The Shulhan Arukh: Enduring Code of Jewish Law," 322–43, in *The Jewish Expression*, ed. Judah Goldin (New Haven, 1976) (originally appeared in *Judaism* 16 [1967]).

[88] See *Shirat ha-Maor* (in Hebrew), ed. Isaac Meiseles (Jerusalem, 1984), 41–42; Horowitz, "From the Generation of Moses," 444–45.

have become matter and form, and Amalek the evil inclination."[89] One of those who had indeed used the war with Amalek as an allegory for battling the evil inclination was their opponent in the "Maimonidean controversy" of 1305–1306, R. Menahem ha-Meiri of Perpignan.[90]

But the allegorization of Amalek was by no means limited to the medieval rationalists. Meiri's contemporary, the Spanish kabbalist R. Joseph Gikatilla (1248–c. 1325) linked Amalek with the "primordial serpent" of the Creation story, and in the *Zohar* Amalek was also used, like Samael, as a synonym for Satan. The author of the *Tikkunei ha-Zohar* went a step further, placing Amalek prominently in the satanic string of synonyms that included the evil inclination, the serpent, Samael, Goliath, and the angel of death.[91] In these sources, however, we find a tendency to conflate the various elements of evil, so that together with the allegorization of Amalek we also have the demonization of Christendom. Among the Iberian exiles of the late fifteenth century this line of thinking was continued by R. Abraham Saba, and in the sixteenth century it appears in the sermons of R. Solomon le-Vet Levi, a native of Salonika.[92]

And yet in Christendom itself the notion of an "inner Amalek" eventually emerged. In eighteenth-century England John Wesley (1703–1791), the founder of the Methodist movement, and his brother Charles (1707–1788), wrote a number of hymns based on scriptural passages, one of which began: "Jesus, we dare believe in Thee, Against this Amalek within, He soon extirpated shall be." Another included the line: "Too well that Amalek I know, Who still maintains the war within."[93] In the following century the British clergyman Joseph Exell wrote in his *Homiletical Commentary on the Book of Exodus* (1879) that "every pure soul has its Amalek. It has to contend with the Amalek of an evil heart; with the Amalek of a wicked world, and with the Amalek of fallen angels."[94]

"The Amalek of a wicked world" had also been the subject of a synagogue sermon delivered in Philadelphia fifteen years earlier, while the

---

[89] See *Minhat Kenaot* (Pressburg, 1838), 41; *Teshuvot ha-Rashba*, ed. H. Z. Dimitrovsky, 2 vols. (Jerusalem, 1990), 1:344.

[90] Moshe Halbertal, *Between Torah and Wisdom* (in Hebrew) (Jerusalem, 2000), 36.

[91] See Horowitz, "From the Generation of Moses," 445, and the sources cited there.

[92] Abraham Saba, *Zeror ha-Mor*, ed. B. Weicholder (Benei Berak, 1990), 2:500; Alan Cooper, "Amalek in Sixteenth-Century Jewish Commentary: On the Internalization of the Biblical Enemy" (in Hebrew), in *The Bible in Light of Its Interpreters: Sarah Kamin Memorial Volume* (in Hebrew), ed. Sara Japhet (Jerusalem, 1994), 493, Horowitz, "From the Generation of Moses," 442–43, 445.

[93] John and Charles Wesley, *Short Hymns on Select Passages of the Holy Scriptures*, in *The Poetical Works* (1868), vol. 9, nos. 164, 271.

[94] J. S. Exell, *Homiletical Commentary on the Book of Exodus* (London, 1879), 319.

American Civil War was still raging, by the Bavarian-born Reform rabbi David Einhorn (1809–1879), who had come to the United States in 1855 to lead Baltimore's Congregation Har Sinai. Einhorn was forced, however, to leave town six years later when his denunciations of slavery put him in danger, and he moved north to Philadelphia's Knesseth Israel congregation, where in March of 1864, on the Sabbath before Purim, he delivered a sermon under the title "War with Amalek!" At the outset of his sermon, for which he chose as his scriptural passage Exodus 17:16 ("God is at war with Amalek from generation to generation"), Einhorn explained that as a consequence of his "arch-enmity against God and His people," Amalek had "assumed the type of the evil principle among Israel." He then went on to present a decidedly "Social-Gospel" conception of that evil principle: "It is Amalek's seed," Einhorn declared, "wherever the evil and wicked rule; wherever . . . rude violence with cheaply bought courage makes war upon defenceless innocence, and wherever a majority in the service of falsehood directs its blows with ruthless fists against the very face of a weak minority."[95]

In his *Shabbat Zakhor* sermon Einhorn presented three ways in which God's war with Amalek "should be carried out in our country and under existing circumstances." The first was a "war against the *Enslavement of Race*, which has brought the Republic to the verge of destruction, against an Amalek-seed [the Confederacy] which is turned into a blood-drenched dragon seed." Einhorn asked rhetorically whether it was "anything else but a deed of Amalek, rebellion against God, to enslave beings created in His image, and to degrade them to a state of beasts having no will of their own?" And he bravely replied that "God commands no war against the black color, but against the dark deeds of Amalek."[96]

Einhorn stressed that it was also necessary "to struggle against Amalek" in two other respects, "the enslavement of the conscience" and "the enslavement of the spirit." The first referred to recent attempts to introduce an amendment to the Constitution "recognizing the American nation as a Christian nation," which Einhorn linked with anti-Semitic aspersions upon the Jews, which accused them of being merely "a nation of traders." In response to these new threats to American Jewry he ringingly asserted:

> Well then, let us make war upon this Amalek; let us meet this newly-budding religious animosity with all honorable weapons at our command! Let us seek to crush, at its very birth, the many-headed serpent which designs to clutch

[95] *American Sermons: The Pilgrims to Martin Luther King Jr.*, ed. Michael Warner (New York, 1999), 665.
[96] Ibid., 665–68.

the [American] Eagle in its coils and to kill him in the very hour of a hot and exhausting struggle, as Amalek attacked weary and exhausted Israel after his departure from Egypt![97]

Einhorn did not fail to remind his audience, in conclusion, that "we must not, above all, forget to make war upon the Amalek in our own midst, upon the *Enslavement of the Spirit,*" by which he meant the "crude worldliness" that had, he believed, become so predominant among his co-religionists.

> How many of us have become utterly indifferent to Israel's sublime mission, to carry the divine truths into all parts of the earth, and to glorify the name of God in the eyes of all the nations! How many among us, driven on by a restless lust of earthly gain, have lost all sense for man's higher destination, all desire for spiritual elevation![98]

Like Pope Urban II at Clermont and Cotton Mather in seventeenth-century Massachusetts, Rabbi Einhorn roused his troops "to disperse now as in times of yore . . . the enemies of our race and God," and to "advance toward the exalted goal, to blot out the remembrance of Amalek," which for him meant, however, "the reign of falsehood and darkness."[99] The medieval Jewish rationalists had allegorized Amalek as the evil lurking within, and in this they were followed by the Wesley brothers in eighteenth-century England. In the nineteenth century, however, the allegorization of Amalek was taken a step further by Exell in England and Einhorn in Philadelphia to encompass also those realms where, as the latter memorably put it, "rude violence with cheaply bought courage makes war upon defenceless innocence." In modern Israel, it may be added, the social activist Anat Gov has put forward a similar definition of Amalek: "It's not the Arabs," she has said. "It's those that attacked the Jews from the back, the old and the crippled that were dragging behind. Amalek is the principle of evil, hurting the old and the disabled."[100]

AMALEK IN THE TWENTIETH CENTURY

Similarly, in his 1913 installation sermon as chief rabbi of the British Empire at London's Great Synagogue Joseph Hertz declared his readiness to fight "those Amaleks whose onslaught is ever directed against the innocent, the weak, the helpless," and, implicitly comparing himself to Moses

---

[97] Ibid., 668–71.
[98] Ibid., 671–72.
[99] Ibid., 673.
[100] Quoted by Rochelle Furstenberg, "The World's Her Stage," *Jerusalem Post Magazine,* November 5, 1999.

at Rephidim, asked the community for support if his hands became weary: "In my fight against ignorance and irreligion, crime or race hatred, those Amaleks whose onslaught is ever directed against the innocent, the weak, the helpless, my hands may become heavy and weary. It is essential that a united Jewry be ever ready loyally to support my hands and steady them."[101] Hertz (1872–1946) was born in East Central Europe but grew up in the United States. He had attended New York's City College, where he was president of the Browning Society and received a gold medal for English composition, and in 1894 was the first rabbinical graduate of the Jewish Theological Seminary of America.[102] Although there has been some recent debate as to whether Hertz should be considered, by today's standards, "liberal Orthodox" or "traditionalist Conservative," in the late nineteenth and early twentieth centuries this distinction was not really operative.[103]

In 1918, as World War I was drawing to its end, Hertz returned, in a sermon for the Jewish New Year, to the subject of Moses at Rephidim, citing the aforementioned view of the Mishnah (*Rosh ha-Shanah* 3:8) that the hands of Moses did not "make the battle or break the battle," but rather that "as long as the children of Israel looked to Heaven for aid, and subjected their hearts to their Father in Heaven, they were strong; but as soon as they ceased to do so, they failed." Speaking again in London's Great Synagogue the chief rabbi applauded those of his countrymen who had courageously shown "the readiness for utmost sacrifice," but also expressed the fear that the whirlwinds of war might fan ignoble passions in some of them: "As the conflict ebbs and flows, a tidal wave of hysteria often sweeps over the masses; race prejudice blinds their vision. . . . A veritable epidemic of moral incendiarism is promoted by the unscrupulous; and the wildest aspersions, often as unfounded as they are cruel, are hurled wholesale against groups and communities."[104]

Hertz exhorted his audience always to continue looking heavenward, and stressed that patriotism should not become an excuse for "senseless malice against the weak and defenceless," nor should the "ways of Amalek" be emulated: "Blessed is the people that in its conflict with Amalek does not copy the ways of Amalek, but can, like Moses, lift pure hands Heavenwards. The hands of such a nation shall remain steady till

---

[101] Hertz, *Sermons*, 1:13.

[102] See S. D. Temkin, "Orthodoxy in Moderation: A Sketch of Joseph Herman Hertz," *Judaism* 24 (1975): 278–80.

[103] See H. W. Meirovich, *A Vindication of Judaism: The Polemics of the Hertz Pentateuch* (New York, 1998), and the extensive review by D. H. Ellenson in *Modern Judaism* 21 (2001): 67–77.

[104] Hertz, *Sermons*, 1:31.

the day's work is done, till the fight against Amalek is at end, till the Dominion of Arrogance has passed away from earth."[105]

In his influential and widely read commentary on *The Pentateuch and the Haftorahs*, the first edition of which appeared between 1929 and 1936, Hertz continued to connect Amalek with adverse moral character-istics. In the second volume (on Exodus), published in 1930, he asserted that "Amalek has disappeared from under heaven, but his spirit still walks the earth," adding that in the Lord's battle "against the Amalekites in the realm of the Spirit, the only successful weapons are courage and convic-tion, truth and righteousness."[106] In the third volume, which appeared two years later, Hertz offered some thoughts on the "additional reading" (from Deut. 25) for the Sabbath before Purim. He unflinchingly acknowledged that "the moral difficulty" in connection with the com-mand to blot out the memory of Amalek was "very real," but sought to resolve it by asserting that the commandment's true charge "is to blot out from the human heart the cruel, cowardly Amalek spirit, and to heal the wounds caused by 'man's inhumanity to man.'"[107]

One young person who was comforted, if not quite convinced, by this interpretation was the future Anglo-Jewish writer and editor John Gross. In his recent autobiography *A Double Thread*, Gross described the frantic preparations for his bar mitzvah in 1948, which, as his teacher only belat-edly recognized, fell on the Sabbath before Purim, when "the readings, commemorating the war between the Israelites and the Amalekites, were exceptionally ferocious." Gross, who went on to study at Oxford and eventually became editor of the *Times Literary Supplement*, recalled being disturbed by the injunction to destroy Amalek, but also the comfort of finding "no less an authority than the formidable Chief Rabbi of my childhood . . . explaining that it should be understood as a call 'to blot out from the human heart the cruel Amalek spirit.'" Although he was "far from convinced that this had been the intention of whoever wrote the [biblical] passage," he had no doubt "that Hertz's comment represented his own deepest conviction—that this was the moral development we were supposed to have reached."[108]

---

[105] Ibid., 33.

[106] J. H. Hertz, *The Pentateuch and the Haftorahs: Hebrew Text, English Translation with Commentary: Exodus* (London, 1930), 190.

[107] Idem, *The Pentateuch and the Haftorahs: Hebrew Text, English Translation with Com-mentary: Leviticus* (London, 1932), 441. The quotation is from the Scottish poet Robert Burns.

[108] J. Gross, *A Double Thread: Growing Up English and Jewish in London* (Chicago, 2002), 23, 30. Gross evidently quoted from the one-volume (posthumous) second edition of Hertz's work, in which the latter's comments on the readings for *Shabbat Zakhor* were somewhat

Although in his 1930 volume on Exodus Hertz was able to write that "Amalek has disappeared from under heaven, but his spirit still walks the earth," he made no such assertion two years later in his comments on the readings for the "Sabbath of Remembrance." By 1932, it seems, developments in Germany had made Hertz less confident that it was only the spirit of Amalek that still stalked the earth. In his annual sermon, in May of that year, to the conference of Anglo-Jewish preachers, the chief rabbi noted "with amazed alarm the growth of Hitlerism in Germany," observing rather presciently that "an insane hatred has taken possession of large sections of the German people."[109]

Although Hertz seems to have consciously avoided using the term "Amalek" to describe Nazi Germany or other anti-Semitic regimes in Europe, at least until the outbreak of World War II, such language became quite common during the 1930s. In 1931, it will be recalled, the Galician-born poet Uri Zvi Greenberg referred to "the kingdom of Amalek on the Dniester," an allusion to the short-lived republic in western Ukraine whose capital had been Lvov (Lemberg), and where in late 1918 Greenberg and his family had narrowly escaped death in a pogrom—one that Hertz himself singled out for its brutality in his impassioned sermon delivered at a 1919 "Service of Prayer and Mourning for the Victims of the Pogroms in Poland," held at Queen's Hall.[110]

By 1936, however, Greenberg was less concerned with the horrors of the past than with those waiting in the wings, eerily foreseeing "Amalekite eagles taking flight from the Rhine/Heading towards the tall roof of Westminster."[111] Although as a Revisionist Zionist he was fervently opposed to the British mandatory presence in Palestine, after the rise of Nazism Greenberg associated the territory of Amalek with the banks of the Rhine rather than with those of the Thames. A year earlier the noted historian Simon Dubnow (1860–1941), writing from his exile in Riga (Latvia) to his disciple Simon Rawidowicz, had bemoaned the recently promulgated Nuremberg Laws, and then exclaimed, "We are at war with Amalek."[112]

---

abridged. See J. H. Hertz, *The Pentateuch and the Haftorahs: Hebrew Text, English Translation and Commentary* (2nd ed, London, 1960), 995.

[109] Hertz, *Sermons*, 2:188.

[110] Ibid., 1:43–49; U. Z. Greenberg, *Rehovot ha-Nahar* (Jerusalem and Tel-Aviv, 1951), 11. This explanation now seems to me more correct than the one I offered in "From the Generation of Moses," 429. On Greenberg's traumatic experiences in 1918, see Miron, *Prolegomena to U.Z. Greenberg*, 24–25.

[111] Miron, *Prolegomena*, 143.

[112] *Simon Dubnov in Memoriam: Essays and Letters* (in Hebrew), ed. Simon Rawidowicz (London and Jerusalem, 1954), 447.

By that time some ultra-Orthodox European rabbis were using the epithet Amalek with reference to their co-religionists who adhered to modern ideologies (Communism or Zionism), which they regarded as antithetical to authentic Judaism. In his polemical pamphlet *Omer Ani Ma'asai la-Melekh* ("I Address My Verses to the King" [Ps. 45:2]), first published in mid-1930s, R. Elhanan Wasserman (1875–1941), one of the most prominent figures in the world of Eastern European *yeshivot* and a leader of the ultra-Orthodox *Agudat Yisrael* movement, asserted that Amalekites could be found among those Jews who had "cast off the burden of the Torah," both in the Diaspora and the Holy Land. He also cited his late teacher R. Israel Meir ha-Kohen (also known as "the Hafetz Hayyim," 1838–1933), who had been certain that the Soviet Jewish Communists (known as the *Yevsektzia*) were "descendants of Amalek."[113] In fact, presumably unbeknownst to Rabbi Wasserman, as early as 1928 his rhetorically robust British colleague Joseph Hertz referred to the latter as "Jewish Hamans."[114] Wasserman may well have known, however, that his (*ne plus*) ultra-Orthodox Hungarian colleague, R. Hayyim Eleazar Spira of Munkacz (1872–1937), included among the Amalekites not only the Zionists, but even the, to his mind, dangerously modern members of *Agudat Yisrael*.[115]

In 1932, while these internecine conflicts were brewing side by side with Europe's gathering storm, the Polish-born artist Arthur Szyk, who was then living in Paris, began work on an illustrated Passover Haggadah. In that Haggadah, first published in 1939, Szyk chose to give prominent expression to the theme of Amalek, although it had no overt connection to Passover and was nowhere mentioned in the text he was illustrating. Szyk, moreover, had originally planned to paint swastikas on the Egyptians, as a means of rather heavy-handedly suggesting continuity between ancient oppressors and modern ones, and to dedicate his work to the Jews of Germany. Printers, however, first in Czechoslovakia and then in England (where he completed the Haggadah), were worried about the political implications, and forced him to remove most of the swastikas, only one of which one remained in the final version.[116]

Any doubts as to whom Szyk was referring in the many allusions to Amalek he included in his Haggadah were dispelled by a letter he published

---

[113] See Horowitz, "From the Generation of Moses," 428–29, and the sources cited there. On Wasserman, see now Gershon Greenberg, "Elhanan Wasserman's Response to the Growing Catastrophe in Europe," *JJTP* 10 (2000): 171–204.

[114] Hertz, *Sermons*, 1:113.

[115] See E. J. Schochet, *Amalek: The Enemy Within* (Los Angeles, 1991), 106. See also M. K. Silber, "The Emergence of Ultra-Orthodoxy: The Invention of a Tradition," in *The Uses of Tradition: Jewish Continuity in the Modern Era*, ed. Jack Werthcimer (Cambridge, 1992), 80.

[116] Luckert, *Art and Politics*, 23, 28.

14. Although the text (Psalms 136) makes no mention of Amalek, Szyk, responding to the rise of Nazism in Germany, chose to depict Joshua at the battle of Rephidim. A page from his Passover Haggadah, executed during the 1930s. Courtesy of the Arthur Szyk Society.

in January of 1940 in which he asserted that "Polish Jews have always called the Germans Amalek."[117] In his introduction to the 1939 edition, the Anglo-Jewish scholar Cecil Roth observed that "Szyk . . . thinks of the conflict between Israel and his persecutors, the motif of the entire

[117] Ibid., 42.

Haggadah, largely in terms of the struggle between Israel and the eternal Amalek." Roth himself clearly agreed that the Jews of his day were facing, in Nazi Germany, a new incarnation of their eternal nemesis. "So long as . . . Amaleks live in our own day," he wrote, "there must be perpetual vigilance, perpetual remembrance."[118] Like his Eastern European–born contemporaries, the poet Uri Zvi Greenberg, the historian Simon Dubnow, and the artist Arthur Szyk, the Oxford-educated Roth had no doubt in 1939 that there were indeed live Amalekites "in our own day."

By 1941, even Chief Rabbi Hertz, who had responsibly resisted using such terminology during the 1930s, spoke of the war against Nazism as a battle with Amalek. In September of that year Hertz delivered a thundering sermon at a public "intercession service" held on the ruins of London's Great Synagogue, which had just been destroyed by German bombs. Drawing upon the previous Sabbath's scriptural reading, which enjoined the Israelites to remember Amalek's "unprovoked treacheries," Hertz declared: "That same judgement must be passed on Amalek's latest spiritual descendant; he fears not God; he closes the gates of mercy on those who cannot resist his might. His resolve is the establishment of a jungle society in which hundreds of millions of robots are to slave for a 'master people' with a heart of stone."[119]

In his 1941 sermon, delivered three months before the United States entered World War II, Hertz stressed that God's war with Amalek was not to be left in divine hands, but was to be "carried out by . . . men and nations filled with an endless loathing of Amalek and all his works and ways." He also praised those Jews around the world who had shown support for "our beloved country in her struggle to blot out the memory of Amalek from under the heavens of the Lord."[120] Roth, who like his chief rabbi, was a staunch Zionist, had expressed the confident hope, in his introduction to Szyk's Haggadah, that with the establishment of a state in Palestine the Jews would finally be able to put Amalek's menacing memory behind them: "Only when at last the Lord God of Israel gives His people peace," he wrote, "only when they are reconstituted again as a normal people, with a nucleus tilling soil on its own land . . . only then may we forget."[121]

As the demonstrations in Israel during the German reparation debates of the early 1950s clearly indicated, however, the powerful memory of Amalek was not buried together with the bodies of the soldiers who fell in the 1948

---

[118] *The Haggadah: Executed by Arthur Szyk*, ed. C. Roth (reprinted Jerusalem and Tel-Aviv, 1960), introduction (unpaginated).

[119] J. H. Hertz, *Early and Late: Addresses, Messages, and Papers* (Hindhead, 1943), 67–68.

[120] Ibid., 69.

[121] Roth, ed., *The Haggadah: Executed by Arthur Szyk*, introduction.

War of Independence. In those heated debates and sometimes violent demonstrations, the memory of Amalek was often invoked, and the complexity of the moral issues was intensified by the ponderous biblical overtones of which most participants in the controversy were keenly aware. On the morning of January 7, 1952, the day set for the Knesset's debate on reparations, the front page of *Herut*, the newspaper published by Menahem Begin's opposition party, featured a banner with the legend (from Deut. 25), "Remember what Amalek did unto thee." At the mass demonstration held later that day at Jerusalem's Zion Square many wore yellow stars of David, bearing the same biblical legend beneath the German word *Jude*.[122]

Years later the Holocaust historian Raul Hilberg wrote of his life's work on the morbid mechanics of the Final Solution: "I insist on delving into forbidden territory and presenting Amalek with all his features, as an aggregate of German functionaries."[123] And in 1978 the American-Jewish writer Herman Wouk chose as his epigram for *War and Remembrance*, a novel about the Holocaust and World War II (completed on Purim 5738 [March 23, 1978]), a quotation from the end of Exodus 17: "Write this for a remembrance in a book . . . that the Lord has a war with Amalek from generation to generation."[124]

By that time, however, Amalek, in the minds of many Jews, had lost its exclusive association with Nazi Germany, and had been extended to include the Soviet Union and the Arab enemies of Israel. Already in 1948, in his inspirational remarks to Yeshiva students going to fight in Israel's War of Independence, R. David Cohen (1887–1972), the "Nazirite" disciple of the grand theologian of Zionism (and chief rabbi of Palestine) R. Abraham Isaac Kook, described the days in which they were living as "the birth pangs of the Messiah and the kingdom of Israel, a time in which our surrounding enemies have risen up to destroy us—Tyre, Damascus, Amon, Moab, and Egypt, all lead by Amalek and Edom."[125]

Eight years later, in a sermon delivered at Yeshiva University in New York on Israel Independence Day, R. Joseph Soloveitchik (1903–1993), who was widely recognized as the spiritual leader of postwar American Orthodoxy, advanced the notion that an Amalekite was anyone, of any background, who harbored unconditional hatred of the Jewish people.

---

[122] Tom Segev, *The Seventh Million: The Israelis and the Holocaust*, trans. H. Watzman (New York, 1993), 207–16.

[123] R. Hilberg, *The Politics of Memory: The Journey of a Holocaust Historian* (Chicago, 1996), 132.

[124] See also E. S. Shapiro, "Herman Wouk and American Jewish Identity," *AJH* 84 (1996): 343–34. For another literary reflection of the wartime association of the Nazis with Amalek, see Zvi Jagendorf, *Wolfy and the Strudelbakers* (Stockport, 2001), 62.

[125] D. Cohen, *Megillat Milhamah ve-Shalom* (Jerusalem, 1974), 25.

The Lithuanian–born Soloveitchik, who had earned a doctorate in Philosophy at the University of Berlin before emigrating to the United States, asserted in 1956 that "in the thirties and forties this position was occupied by the Nazis, led by Hitler . . . today it is occupied by the hordes of [Gamal Abdel] Nasser and the Mufti [of Jerusalem]."[126]

Soloveitchik's position is to be contrasted with that of his older contemporary, the Prague-born philosopher Samuel Hugo Bergman (1883–1975), who emigrated to Palestine in 1920 and later taught at the Hebrew University of Jerusalem. Bergman, like Soloveitchik, saw religious significance in the state of Israel, but courageously argued, in a 1959 essay, that part of its significance was that Jews were now required to confront the "antihumanistic" aspects of their religious heritage. He cited with approval the view of the Yiddish and Hebrew writer Aaron Zeitlin (1898–1974) that the Jewish state must strive to be the very "opposite of the Amalekite state."[127] It is likely that Britain's Chief Rabbi Hertz, who died shortly before the establishment of the state of Israel, would have agreed.

In recent decades, however, Bergman's conception of Amalek, in his inaugural sermon, as representing "those . . . whose onslaught is ever directed against the innocent, the weak, the helpless," has been far less popular in Jewish religious circles than the conception associated with Rabbi Soloveitchik, which has even been "codified" by Blu Greenberg in her handbook *How to Run a Traditional Jewish Household*. The holiday of Purim, she has written, "is about remembering. . . . Remember the Amalekites . . . remember that evil Haman, remember Hitler. In the midst of my laughter . . . I remember our enemies, past and present. The names change, but not the character or intent. Haman, Antiochus, Hitler. Arafat—all bent on destroying my people."[128] And Shlomo (a.k.a. Steven) Riskin, whose rabbinical career has taken him from the New York's West Side to Efrat on the West Bank, has recently written, on the alleged authority of his "revered rebbe" Soloveitchik, "that the spiritual heirs of Amalek include the Nazis, the Soviet communists, and those Arabs who will not rest until we disappear from the land."[129]

---

[126] See J. B. Soloveitchik's "Kol dodi dofek: It is the Voice of My Beloved that Knocketh," trans. Lawrence Kaplan, 98, in *Theological and Halakhic Reflections on the Holocaust*, ed. B. H. Rosenberg and F. Heuman (Hoboken and New York, 1992). For the Hebrew original see, Soloveitchik *Ish ha-Emunah* (Jerusalem, 1968 [1961]), 101–2. See also Soloveitchik, *Divrei Hashkafa* (2nd ed., Jerusalem, 1995), 22–23, 183.

[127] S. H. Bergman, *Ba-Mish'ol*, ed. Nathan Rottenstreich (Tel-Aviv, 1976), 116–17. On Bergman and the concept of Amalek, see also Tom Segev, *Elvis in Jerusalem: Post-Zionism and the Americanization of Israel*, trans. H. Watzman (New York, 2002), 6.

[128] B. Greenberg, *How to Run a Traditional Jewish Household* (New York, 1983), 396–97.

[129] S. Riskin "Destroying the Concept of Evil," *Jerusalem Post*, March 25, 1997.

Riskin did not say precisely which "land," nor did he explain why the "spiritual heirs of Amalek" would not include Americans or Europeans who might share the sentiments of "those Arabs who will not rest until we disappear from the land." As mentioned in the introduction, just before Purim of 2000, Riskin's senior colleague in the Israeli rabbinate, Ovadiah Yosef, said of then Minister of Education Yossi Sarid that "he is wicked and satanic and must be erased like Amalek."[130] As I argued there, acts of religious violence against Armenians in Jerusalem's Old City should also be seen against the background of the continuing war against Amalek in its various modern manifestations. But Jewish violence against the cross also has its own complicated history, which we shall pursue in the next chapter.

[130] See Kamil, "Ovadia Yosef."

PART TWO

JEWS LIVING DANGEROUSLY

6

"The Fascination of the Abomination"

JEWS (AND JEWISH HISTORIANS)
CONFRONT THE CROSS

NATIONAL HEROES OR DEMENTED ICONOCLASTS?

IN 1941, the *Am Oved* press in Tel-Aviv, founded by the Labor Zionist leader Berl Katznelson, published its first book, *Sefer ha-Gevura*, an anthology of Jewish heroism and martyrdom edited by the young historian Israel Halpern. In the section dealing with Jewish heroism during the period of the Crusades, Halpern included from R. Ephraim of Bonn's chronicle of the Second Crusade the story of Samuel b. Isaac who, when attacked on the road to Mainz, managed to wound "three of the enemy" before he was killed, and that of Gutalda of Aschaffenburg, who refused baptism "and drowned herself in the river."[1] He chose, however, to pass over the story of Kalonymos of Bacharach, which appears in R. Ephraim's chronicle between the two aforementioned tales of heroism. When Kalonymos and his co-religionists, who had fled to the Stahlbeck fortress on the outskirts of Mainz, were forced by the crusaders to decide between conversion and death, he "spat conspicuously upon an image of the Crucified One" before being killed. Halpern also omitted the story, from the same chronicle, of a young woman from Würzberg "who was brought into their place of idolatry in order to be defiled [baptized], but she sanctified the name of God and spat upon the abomination [ti'uv]. They then struck her with stone and fist."[2]

---

[1] *Sefer ha-Gevura*, ed. Israel Halpern (Tel-Aviv, 1941), 64. On this work, see Israel Bartal, "The Ingathering of Traditions," *Prooftexts* 17 (1997): 85–87, and on the early years of *Am Oved*, see Anita Shapira, *Berl: The Biography of a Socialist Zionist*, trans. H. Galai (Cambridge, 1984), 310–17.

[2] Ephraim of Bonn's *Sefer ha-Zekhira* was originally published in 1858. It was republished in Neubauer and Stern *Hebräische Berichte*; Bernfeld, *Sefer ha-Dem'aot*; and Haberman, *Gezerot*. Subsequent references will be to the Haberman volume. Both cases, by contrast, have recently been discussed by Christoph Cluse, "Stories of Breaking and Taking the Cross: A Possible Context for the Oxford Incident of 1268," *RHE* 90 (1995): 438–39.

Why these omissions? Were the former two deeds more heroic or more worthy of emulation (by the standards of 1941 Labor Zionism) than the latter two? Or did Halpern perhaps doubt that these martyrs actually spat upon the cross before meeting their deaths? A decade later the Anglo-Jewish historian Cecil Roth published a monograph on the Jews of medieval Oxford in which he discussed the 1268 incident of a local Jew who snatched and trampled a processional cross on Ascension Day. "It may be that some Jew was pushed accidentally against the Cross or else dragged towards it by the mob, and made the bearer stumble," he wrote, adding that "possibly a demented iconoclast may have taken it into his head to make this foolish gesture."[3] Could only a demented Jew have intentionally seized and destroyed a processional cross in thirteenth-century Europe?

Although Roth's reluctance, in the aftermath of the Holocaust, to acknowledge that Jews may indeed have sometimes been guilty of the anti-Christian actions often attributed to them is understandable, a more open-minded approach is clearly called for. In his now classic study *Exclusiveness and Tolerance*, published only a decade after Roth's monograph, Jacob Katz was able to write with admirable frankness of the repulsion with which the visible signs of Christianity were regarded by medieval European Jews. "Even had their religion not emphatically prohibited visible representation of the Godhead," Katz wrote, "such representations would still have repelled the Jews, who had not shared the intellectual and emotional experiences which made these representations meaningful to Christian worshippers. Throughout the literature of the time we find the rejection of Christianity expressed in the form of the repudiation of one of its visible symbols, more particularly that of the crucified Christ."[4]

This chapter shall attempt to go beyond Katz's pioneering remarks both by examining some of the specific forms which such repudiation took, and also by looking into the (paradoxically) related issue of the cross's attraction to medieval Jews, by whom it could be regarded not only as an idolatrous object, but also one of illicit desire. These two dimensions could dovetail in such brazen actions as urinating or rudely exposing oneself in the presence of the cross; actions which, not surprisingly, were often followed by religious martyrdom. But in a society that regarded martyrdom as its highest ideal, such reckless acts of repudiation were hardly rare. Although often feeling "powerless disgust" (to quote Joseph Conrad's *Heart of Darkness*, from which this chapter's title is also taken) in the presence of the cross, medieval and early modern Jews could sometimes also empower themselves sufficiently to express their disgust

---

[3] Cecil Roth, *The Jews of Medieval Oxford* (Oxford, 1951), 152.

[4] Jacob Katz, *Exclusiveness and Tolerance: Jewish-Gentile Relations in Medieval and Modern Times* (Oxford, 1961), 22–23.

through acts of abuse or violence against it. This was true not only during the Purim "season" but also at other times of the year.

SPRING FEVER

One period particularly prone to anti-Christian expression was the frequent overlap of Holy Week (between Palm Sunday and Easter) and the week-long holiday of Passover, when, as many scholars have noted, "the lines of demarcation between Christian and Jew were most clearly drawn."[5] Another was the briefer period, later in the spring, when Shavuot (The Feast of Weeks, fifty days after Passover) and Ascension Day (forty days after Easter) would often overlap. In Merovingian France ecclesiastical councils such as the Third Council of Orléans (538) and the Council of Mâcon (581) specifically forbade Jews to mix with Christians during the period from Holy Thursday through Easter.[6] A striking instance of the sort of violence that could result when Jews mixed with Christians during that tense period occurred in Clermont-Ferrand (central France) between those two councils. On Easter day of 576, as we learn from the chronicler Gregory of Tours, one of the Jews of Clermont-Ferrand threw rancid oil upon the head of a former co-religionist who had been baptized earlier that day as the latter, robed in white, entered the city with the other participants in the Easter procession. Gregory attributed the Jew's action to the devil's influence,[7] evidently assuming that a sane Jew would not endanger his community through such rash behavior. And indeed, forty days later, according to both Gregory's *History of the Franks* and the epic poem by his friend Fortunatus, the synagogue of Clermont was destroyed by enraged local Christians after the Ascension day procession.[8]

---

[5] See, among others, Cecil Roth, "European Jewry and the Dark Ages," *HUCA* 23 (1950–1951): 151–53; Brian Brennan, "The Conversion of the Jews of Clermont in AD 576," *JTS* 36 (1985): 327 (from whom the quotation is drawn); Nirenberg, *Communities of Violence*, chap. 7. On the critical dialogue between Passover and Easter since the early Christian centuries, see Yisrael Yuval, "The Haggadah of Passover and Easter" (in Hebrew), *Tarbiz* 65 (1995): 5–25, and Yuval, *Two Nations*, 72, 219–66.

[6] Baron, *SRH*, 3:50–51.

[7] See Manya Lifschitz-Golden, *Les Juifs dans la littérature française du moyen âge* (New York, 1935), 167; Trachtenberg, *Devil and the Jews*, 42–3.

[8] "On that blessed day, however, when the Lord ascends to the heavens in glory after redeeming man," wrote Gregory, "when the bishop [Avitus] processed with psalm-singing from the cathedral to the basilica [of St. Illidius], the entire crowd following [the procession] fell upon the synagogue of the Jews and levelled it to the ground, so that the spot resembled a bare field." See Brennan, "Conversion of the Jews," 321–37, and Walter Goffart, "The Conversions of Avitus of Clermont, and Similar Passages in Gregory of Tours," 473–97, in J. Neusner and

Who started? Some four decades ago Bernhard Blumenkranz suggested that on Easter day the former Jew had been provocatively paraded past the homes of Clermont's Jews, but as later scholars have noted, this unfortunately does not appear in Gregory's text. More to the point is Blumenkranz's observation that the rancid oil seems to have been especially chosen to mock the neophyte's anointing earlier that day. This has prompted Walter Goffart to suggest, quite reasonably, that the Jew who threw the oil probably first positioned himself in a suitably strategic position.[9] Neither scholar has noted, however, that in 576 Easter Sunday (April 5) was also the eve of the seventh day (and second holiday) of Passover. It may already have been customary in France for the Jews to have read as the *haftarah* on the intermediate Sabbath of Passover the prophet Ezekiel's vision of the dry bones (the Jewish countervision of the Resurrection) in which God promised: "Behold, I will open your graves, and raise you from your graves, O my people; and I will bring you home into the land of Israel" (Ezek. 37). On the seventh day of the holiday they were to read in their synagogues the story of their ancient enemies, Pharaoh and his soldiers, drowning in the Red Sea.

Even without the scriptural echoes it is clear that the significant overlap in 576 between the (eight-day) week of Passover and the Christian Holy Week could exacerbate the tensions aroused by the Jew's conversion. And it may well be that the choice by Clermont's Christians of Ascension Day as the date for their act of reprisal was motivated by their recognition of the religious (and perhaps even festive) character of the violent act perpetrated on Easter Sunday. Goffart has perceptively noted that in Gregory's account "the connection between the first affront and its sequel is strongly implied; the levelling of the synagogue, too thorough for casual aggression, was the premeditated Christian reply to the Easter insult."[10]

Easter insults, or perceptions thereof, continued throughout medieval times. The Arab-Christian chronicler Yahya ibn Sa'id (Eutychius), for example, claimed that as part of their revolt against Byzantine rule the Jews of early seventh-century Tyre (in present day Lebanon) had hoped to murder all of the city's Christians on Easter night.[11] In early eleventh-century Rome, as we shall see in greater detail below, a number of Jews

---

E. S. Frerichs, eds., *"To See Ourselves as Others See Us": Christians, Jews, and "Others" in Late Antiquity* (Chico, Calif., 1985) (W. Goffart, *Rome's Fall and After* [London, 1989], 293–317), whose translation of the passage from Gregory's *History* I have followed. For a different translation, see *The History of the Franks*, trans. Lewis Thorpe (Harmondsworth, 1974), 266.

[9] B. Blumenkranz, *Juifs et Chrétiens dans le monde occidental, 430–1096* (Paris and The Hague, 1960), 140; Goffart, "The Conversions of Avitus," 491.

[10] Goffart, "The Conversions of Avitus," 491.

[11] Angelo Pernice, *L'imperatore Eraclio: Saggio di storia byzantina* (Florence, 1905), 60; D. M. Olster, *The Politics of Usurpation in the Seventh Century: Rhetoric and Revolution in Byzantium* (Amsterdam, 1993), 103.

were beheaded after a co-religionist informed papal authorities, sometime between Good Friday and Easter Sunday, that a crucifix had been mocked in the synagogue. Later in that century, as we shall also see, Archbishop Eberhard of Trier threatened the town's Jews with expulsion in 1066 if they would not convert by the Saturday before Easter, which in that year was also the intermediate Sabbath of Passover. Rather mysteriously, the bishop is reported to have died on that very day.[12]

In late medieval Spain violence often erupted between Christians and Jews in connection with alleged Jewish violations of limitations imposed upon the latter during Holy Week. In Gerona, for example, the Jewish neighborhood was attacked in 1302 after Jews had reportedly refused to stay indoors during that week. In 1326 the Jews of Saragossa were accused of building a tower onto their homes so that they could observe services in a neighboring church, and of provocatively throwing meat bones from there onto the façade gallery of the church on Good Friday.[13]

DESIRE AND DESTRUCTION

Let us return, however, to the world of medieval Ashkenazic Jewry and to its peculiar fascination with the abomination of the cross, which emerges from the controversial twelfth-century autobiography of Herman-Judah of Cologne, who, according to his Latin account, was baptized circa 1128–1129. In his twentieth year, while he still went under the name Judah, business brought him to Münster, from whose bishop he had an outstanding loan to collect. During his extended stay, he had occasion to enter the local cathedral, less "out of devotion as much as out of curiosity," where he saw "among the artful varieties of carvings and pictures" on its walls "a particularly monstrous idol." Yet this image had a powerful impact upon the young German Jew, for he "discerned one and the same man abased and exalted, despised and lifted up, ignominious and glorious."[14] Although in a subsequent debate with Rupert, abbot of Deutz, Herman-Judah, according to his own testimony, accused Christians of "the impiety of manifest idolatry" on account of the "huge images elaborately wrought with the arts of painters and sculptors" they

---

[12] On the Rome and Trier incidents, see the discussion later in this chapter.

[13] Baer, *Die Juden* I, 1:171, 407; Nirenberg, *Communities of Violence*, 210, 220–21.

[14] I quote from the translation by Karl Morrison in his *Conversion and Text: The Cases of Augustine of Hippo, Herman-Judah, and Constantine of Tsatos* (Charlottesville, 1992), 80. On the scholarly debate as to the authenticity of the work, see ibid., 39–41, and the literature cited there. For more recent discussions of Herman-Judah and his autobiography, see Jeremy Cohen, *Living Letters of the Law: Ideas of the Jew in Medieval Christianity* (Berkeley, 1999), 291–305, and the essays by Jonathan Elukin and W. C. Jordan in M. A. Signer and J. Van Engen, eds., *Jews and Christians in Twelfth-Century Europe* (Notre Dame, 2001).

had placed in their churches as "objects of adoration,"[15] he was already of two minds on the subject of the "monstrous idol" he had seen in the Münster cathedral—unable to decide whether it was more worthy of adoration or abomination.

Later in the twelfth century, during the Second Crusade, as mentioned earlier, three Jews fled with their families to the Stahlbeck fortress outside of Mainz, which they were obliged to leave on the eve of Shavuot. "The errant ones [Crusaders] rose up against them and pursued them," wrote R. Ephraim of Bonn, "demanding that they defile themselves [become baptized]. But they refused, for they deeply loved their Creator, even unto death. Mr. Kalonymos spat conspicuously upon an image of the Crucified One, and they slew him on the spot."[16] Was this daring act on the part of Kalonymos, we may ask, wholly spontaneous, or had he perhaps thought to himself, like a medieval Samson, while passing various Christian images in the streets and thoroughfares, "May it be God's will that I shall be privileged to spit before the Gentiles upon one of these abominations ere I die?" Or was he prompted, perhaps, by the heightened religious tension which must have pervaded the community of Mainz during the days between the third of Sivan, which marked the anniversary of the slaughter of Mainz Jewry during the First Crusade in 1096,[17] and the sixth of that month, which marked the giving of the Law to Moses at Sinai? Rather than attempting to choose one of these possibilities over the others, I would prefer to point to the complex web of memory confronting a twelfth-century Rhenish Jew as he confronted the cross on the eve of Shavuot and contemplated martyrdom.

Side by side with the story of Mr. Kalonymos the martyr, we may place another which also took place on Shavuot eve, not in twelfth-century Germany, but in thirteenth-century England, where, we learn from an anonymous Hebrew account, "there was a learned, wealthy, and diligent student of the Talmud, the late R. Yom Tov, who hanged himself on the eve of Shavuot." The latter's father, Rabbi Moses the Pious, "did not leave his room, nor did he shed a tear, but studied in his library as if no evil had befallen him, asserting that his son had caused his own death."[18] The anonymous author reports that "on that night he [the deceased] appeared to me in a dream, and he looked well, better than he had in life. And he also

---

[15] Morrison, *Conversion and Text*, 82.

[16] Haberman, *Gezerot*, 118; Eidelberg, *The Jews and the Crusaders*, 125. Here and elsewhere I follow Eidelberg's translation with minor changes.

[17] Haberman, *Gezerot*, 30; Eidelberg, *The Jews and the Crusaders*, 29.

[18] On not mourning suicides, see Maimonides, *Mishneh Torah* Laws of Mourning, 2:8.

appeared to others that night, reporting that he had seen a great light."
Later in his account the chronicler provides some background information
concerning the late R. Yom Tov: "And he was somewhat afflicted by a
demon (*vegam mikzat shed haya bo*) ... and he would say (it is not clear
whether the following words were said in life or after death) that the demon
would place before him the sign of the cross and press him to commit idolatry." The anonymous author concluded with the following advice: "It is
better for man to perform penance in this world through self-affliction and
flagellation"—apparently intending thereby to transform R. Yom Tov's
death from one of depressive suicide to one of heroic martyrdom.[19]

This short but striking passage was discussed by the late Israeli historian
Haim Hillel Ben-Sasson, who saw in it testimony that "the cross had
penetrated, ineluctably, the mental world of a learned and God-fearing
medieval English Jew."[20] One could, of course, argue with the assertion
that the cross's penetration was ineluctable, but Ben-Sasson's words
remind us that the cross could arouse not only passionate revulsion
among medieval European Jews but also passionate attraction, and just as
the former response could lead Mr. Kalonymos to his tragic death, so
could the latter response lead R. Yom Tov to a similar end—and both on
the eve of Shavuot.

All three stories—those of Herman-Judah, Kalonymos, and R. Yom-
Tov—when taken together, allow us to grasp the complicated nature of
the medieval Jew's attitude toward the cross, a matter which also comes
across from the rich lexicon devised by medieval Jews so as to avoid calling it by its true name. Within this lexicon I would like to focus on the
twin (masculine and feminine) words *ti'uv* and *to'evah*, both meaning
"abomination." Thus Ephraim of Bonn, when describing acts of martyrdom in Würzberg during the Second Crusade, mentions the case of a
young maiden "who was brought into their place of idolatry in order to
be defiled [baptized], but she sanctified the name of God and spat upon
the abomination [*ti'uv*]."[21] Similarly, when R. Eleazar Rokeah came to
describe the background to the suffering of the Jews of Mainz during the
Third Crusade he mentions hearing before Hannukah [of 1187] that the
Muslims had taken Acre and the areas outside of Jerusalem, "and that
they had captured the abomination [*to'evah*] upon which Jesus had been
crucified ... and had taken the abomination with them to the land of

[19] E. Kupfer, "A Contribution to the Chronicles of the Family of R. Moses ben R. Yom-
Tov, 'the Noble' of London," (in Hebrew), *Tarbiz* 40 (1971): 384–87.
[20] H. H. Ben-Sasson, "Assimilation in Jewish History" (in Hebrew) *Molad* 7 (1976): 305
(Ben-Sasson, *Continuity and Variety* [in Hebrew], ed. J. Hacker [Tel-Aviv, 1984], 61–62).
[21] Haberman, *Gezerot*, 119; Eidelberg, *The Jews and the Crusaders*, 127.

Ishmael." The same author utilized similar language to describe the arrival of the returning Crusaders at the gates of his own city: "And the uncircumcised had marked themselves with the signs of their abomination [*ba-ti'uv shelahem*] by the hundreds and thousands."[22]

One could add dozens if not hundreds of examples, but I would like to pause for a moment to examine the particular resonances of the word "abomination" when used by medieval Jews in reference to the Christian cross. One the one hand, it alluded to such biblical verses as Deuteronomy 7:26, "And you shall not bring an *abomination* into your house, and become accursed like it," where the reference is to artifacts of idolatry, but also, on the other, to verses where the context is one of prohibited intimacy. These include Leviticus 18:22, "You shall not lie with a male as with a woman; it is an *abomination*," and Ezekiel 22:11, "One commits *abomination* with his neighbor's wife."

It is not surprising that medieval Ashkenazic Jews, as the American scholar Ivan Marcus has noted, could conceive of conversion to Christianity as a form of adultery.[23] Along the same lines I would argue that the the abominated cross was regarded by medieval Jews not only as an idolatrous object but also as a potential object of illicit desire. Recognizing that Jewish violence against the cross could stem not only from undiluted hostility but also from anxiety engendered by an object of illicit desire, we are in a better position to take Christian reports of Jewish cross-desecration seriously rather than dismissing them as anti-Semitic inventions. There is also no paucity of references to such conduct in Jewish sources (some of which have already been mentioned), but these have all too often either been quietly passed over by Jewish historians or tendentiously misrepresented.

Early in the eleventh century R. Joseph Tov-Elem of Limoges sent a responsum to the Jews of Sens, upon whom the neighboring community of Troyes had imposed a tax for the redemption of captives. "But when the missive arrived in Sens," wrote R. Joseph, "the Jews there declared themselves free of any obligation, giving as grounds the great troubles which surrounded them. . . . The messenger from Troyes found them greatly troubled by the calamity which had befallen them as a result of the shattering of an 'abomination' [*to'eva*] in their locality."[24] R. Joseph would appear to be matter-of-factly passing on the information that the

22 Haberman, *Gezerot*, 162–63.
23 I. G. Marcus, "Une communauté pieuse et la doute: Qiddouch ha-Chem . . . chez les juifs d'Europe du Nord et l'histoire de rabbi Amnon de Mayence," *AHSS* 49, no. 5 (1994): 1043.
24 Irving Agus, "Democracy in the Communities of the Early Middle Ages," *JQR* 43 (1952): 166–67, Agus, ed., *Responsa of the Tosephists* (in Hebrew), (New York, 1954), no. 1.

Jews of Sens had smashed a crucifix and were now paying the price.[25] Yet the Israeli scholar Abraham Grossman, in a recent discussion of this responsum, has chosen to speak rather of an "*accusation* against the Jews of Sens,"[26] suggesting that, in his view, they probably were not guilty of smashing the item disdainfully referred to by R. Joseph as an "abomination." In this connection it may be apt to redeem from obscurity the bold observation about medieval European Jews made (in a footnote) by Solomon Grayzel in 1933: "It is clear . . . [that they] were indiscreet, but one must remember that they had not yet learned the self-effacement which the subsequent centuries were to teach them."[27]

THE CROSS AS ABOMINATION

Before proceeding to other instances of indiscreet behavior vis-à-vis the cross, let me return to the term "abomination" and the history of its use by Jews as a means of referring cacophemistically (my neologism) to the cross.[28] The earliest instance I have been able to find occurs in the late midrashic work known as *Pirkei de-Rabbi Eliezer* (The Chapters of Rabbi Eliezer), which, as noted earlier, was evidently composed in eighth-century Palestine. As we have seen, the work's author implicitly attempts, in retelling the story of Purim, to solve one of the thorniest problems in the exegesis of the book of Esther: Why did Mordecai refuse to bow down to Haman? According to *PRE*, Haman "had an 'image' [*tzelem*] embroidered on his garment, and anyone who bowed down to Haman bowed also to the 'abomination' [*to'eva*] which he had made. Mordecai saw this and did not consent to bow down to his 'disgusting thing' [*shikutzo*], as it is said, 'But Mordecai bowed not, nor did him reverence.'"[29] The author of this late midrash transforms Haman into a Christian bishop who proudly wears upon his chest the sign of the cross, referred to by the uncomplimentary trinity of Hebrew terms—*tzelem*,

[25] A local source of tension between Jews and Christians in Sens may have been the claim of the latter that a relic of the rod of Moses was to be found in St. Stephen's Church, to which pilgrims flocked from all over Europe. See H. Fichtenau, *Living in the Tenth Century: Mentalities and Social Orders*, trans. P. Geary (Chicago, 1991), 11.

[26] Grossman, *France*, 20. Cf. Haym Soloveitchik, *The Use of Responsa as Historical Source: A Methodological Introduction* (in Hebrew) (Jerusalem, 1990), chap. 8.

[27] Grayzel, *Church and the Jews*, 29n42.

[28] It is not discussed in the otherwise helpful study by Anna Sapir Abulafia, "Invectives against Christianity in the Hebrew Chronicles of the First Crusade," 66–72, in P. W. Edbury, ed., *Crusade and Settlement* (Cardiff, 1985).

[29] *Pirkei de Rabbi Eliezer*, chap. 50. See Gerald Friedlander's translation (London, 1916), 399, which is less literal than the one I have provided.

to'eva, shikutz. And although the midrashic author apparently resided in Umayyad Palestine, he nonetheless felt the need to link the ancient arch-enemy of the Jewish people with the central symbol of Christianity.

This is actually less anomalous than might first appear, for we know that in religious disputations which took place in the Near East between Jews and Christians during the seventh and eighth centuries, the former, per-haps emboldened by the hostility to religious images of the ruling Muslims, were particularly vehement in their criticisms of the cross and its veneration. As the American scholar Sidney Griffith has written: "It is clear that beginning already with the Persian Conquest . . . and continu-ing into the Islamic period, there was a renewed polemic between Christians and Jews, and for the first time it included arguments about the Christian practice of venerating the cross and the images of Christ and the saints."[30]

This may be seen from such Christian apologetical works as *The Tro-phies of Damascus* late in the seventh century and the *Disputation of Sergius the Stylite against a Jew* in the middle of the eighth. Sergius, who like the author of the *Trophies* composed his work in the form of a dia-logue, devoted an entire chapter to the subject of the cross. The Jewish disputant is portrayed as an unrelenting "nudnik" continually insisting that veneration of the cross constitutes a transgression of the Second Commandment, "But you," he says to the Christian, "behold, you have filled the earth with crosses of every material found by you—of wood and stone, of bronze and iron, and the rest . . . in what way are they less than idols?"[31] These aggressive comments, the likes of which appear also in the writings of Leontius of Neapolis (in Cyprus), dovetail with the placing of a pectoral cross on Haman's garment by the contemporary author of *Pirkei de-Rabbi Eliezer*, and the use in reference to it of such uncompli-mentary epithets as *shikutz* and *to'eva.*

But Jews did not engage only in discourse about Christianity and its symbols. Words had, since late antiquity, carried over into deeds, as in the practice, prohibited by the Theodosian law of 408, of burning a crucified figure on Purim. Centuries later, Jewish converts to Christianity in the Byzantine Empire were required not only to generally renounce every Hebrew law, custom, and ceremony, but to specifically "curse those who keep the festival of the so-called Mordecai . . . nailing Haman to wood, and then mixing him with the emblem of the cross and burning them together." Such a prebaptismal oath, dating from some time between the

---

[30] Sidney Griffith, "Theodore Abu Qurrah's Arabic Tract on the Christian Practice of Venerating Images," *JAOS* 10 (1985): 59.

[31] A. P. Hayman, trans., *The Disputation of Sergius the Stylite against a Jew*, 2 vols. (Louvain, 1973), 1:24, 30, 32.

eighth and early eleventh centuries, has come down to us from the Byzantine East.[32]

In this connection we may also note the letter sent by Doge Pietro II Candiano of Venice to the German Emperor Henry I and to Archbishop Hildebert of Mainz, apparently after the Erfurt conference of 932. The doge mentioned reports he had received of a religious disputation that had taken place in Jerusalem between Jews and Christians which concluded with a great miracle at the Church of the Holy Sepulchre, after which many Jews of Jerusalem converted to Christianity. He concluded his letter to the emperor and archbishop with a particular request: that this story be told to the Jews under their jurisdiction and that they be forced to accept Christianity. Should any Jew fail to do so, "let it be commanded throughout their kingdom that his polluted hands shall not be permitted to touch the sign of the cross on any item of metal or cloth, or any other merchandise."[33]

Although many (though not all) scholars have doubted the report concerning the disputation in Jerusalem and its alleged consequences, none has (to my knowledge) challenged the authenticity of the doge's letter. Yet the full import of its attempt to distance Jews from the sign of the cross has not been appreciated. Salo Baron confidently asserted, some forty years ago, that it was economically motivated: "Though couched in terms of extreme Christian sensitivity," he wrote, "the doge's recommendation could not conceal his intention to place insuperable obstacles in the way of Jewish traders handling merchandise, which *often* bore the sign of the cross in its commercial markings."[34] No evidence was provided, however, that tenth-century commercial markings frequently included the sign of the cross, nor did either explain why it was "obvious" that the doge's pious language derived not from concern that crosses on commercial merchandise might be desecrated by Jews but rather from the desire to avoid Jewish competition in trade. It is perhaps worth noting the later opinion of *Sefer Hasidim,* the bible of Ashkenazic pietism (many of whose

---

[32] See Horowitz, "Rite to Be Reckless," 28–29.

[33] For the Latin text with German translation, see Julius Aronius, *Regesten zur Geschichte der Juden im fränkischen und deutschen Reiche* (Berlin, 1902), 53–54. For a recent discussion of the letter and its background, see Zvi Baras, "Jewish-Christian Religious Disputation in Jerusalem (932)" (in Hebrew), *Cathedra* 63 (1992): 31–51, who provides a Hebrew translation (33–34).

[34] Baron, *SRH,* 4:25. Similarly, Cecil Roth, writing (evidently under Baron's influence) a decade later, claimed that "the economic jealousy behind this ostensibly pious ejaculation is obvious." See Roth, "Italy," in Roth, ed., *The World History of the Jewish People: The Dark Ages* (Tel-Aviv, 1966), 116. Though Roth does not cite Baron, the latter's influence is evident in the difference between his 1966 treatment of the doge's letter and his earlier discussion of the same document in his *Venice,* 7–8.

traditions derived from medieval Italy), that if a Jew acquired a "a dish, or cup, or any utensil upon which the sign of the cross [*sheti va-'erev*] had been placed, he should not use it until [the cross is] removed."[35]

Baron's reluctance to entertain the possibilty that the doge was actually worried about Jews desecrating the sign of the cross goes hand in hand with his skepticism concerning the report by the Christian chronicler Yahya ibn Sa'id (Eutychius) that in 937 (five years after the doge's letter) Jews had participated, together with Muslims, in the burning of St. Mary's Church in Ascalon (Ashkelon).[36] The same chronicler reported that some thirty years later the Jews of Jerusalem had participated in the anti-Christian riots which broke out between Ascension Day and Pentecost, during which three of the city's churches were badly damaged and the patriarch, John VII, was cruelly murdered. According to the testimony of ibn Sa'id/Eutychius, "the Jews exceeded the Muslims in acts of destruction and ruin."[37] If these reports of Jewish violence against churches in tenth-century Palestine do indeed reflect wider eastern Mediterranean realities (and there is reason to believe that they do), the Venetian doge's concerns about Jews desecrating objects carrying the sign of the cross may well have been quite genuine.

AFTER THE TURN OF THE MILLENIUM

It is after the year 1000 that reports of Jewish violence against the cross begin to appear on the European continent itself, beginning, in fact, in Rome—the very capital of Western Christendom—during the spiritually tense years between the millennium after Christ's birth and the millennium after his death. This was also a period during which the image of the crucifix became much more prominent and widespread in Western Christian piety on both popular and elite levels,[38] a development which was undoubtedly noted by European Jews. Early in the eleventh century, during the papacy of Benedict VIII (1012–1024), a number of Roman

---

[35] Wistinetzki, *Sefer Hasidim*, 176, no. 663.

[36] According to Baron (*SRH*, 3: 137), "this tale is too strictly in line with the Church's traditional accusations of Jewish involvement in anti-Christian persecutions to merit full credence."

[37] See S. D. Goitein, "Jerusalem in the Arab Period (638–1099)" (in Hebrew) in *Yerushalayim* 1(1953):94; Goitein, *Palestinian Jewry in Early Islamic and Crusader Times* (in Hebrew), ed. J. Hacker (Jerusalem, 1980), 17.

[38] E. Delaruelle, "La crucifix dans la piété populaire er dans l'art, du VIe au XIe siécle," in Delaruelle, *La piété populaire au moyen âge* (Torino, 1975), 27–42; Richard Landes, *Relics, Apocalypse, and the Deceits of History: Ademar of Chabannes, 989–1034* (Cambridge, Mass., 1995), 301–2.

Jews were executed on what Cecil Roth called the "improbable charge of mocking a crucifix."[39] According to the contemporary chronicler Ademar of Chabannes (d. 1034), this occurred after an earthquake accompanied by a severe storm erupted on Good Friday, prompting a Roman Jew to inform the papal palace that some of his co-religionists had mocked a crucifix in their synagogue. After those found guilty were beheaded, the earthquake ceased.[40] Ademar claims that these events took place "circa 1020," although a later chronicle (by Cesare Baronius, 1538–1607) gives the date as 1017.[41] Baronius also added the important information that the storm lasted through Vespers on the following Saturday. A century ago, Vogelstein and Rieger, in their monumental history of the Jews of Rome, suggested 1021 as the most likely date, based on external testimony that an earthquake had actually occurred in that year. They implicitly accepted the testimony of Baronius, however, that the earthquake lasted through the Saturday before Easter, although they expressed serious doubt (echoed by Roth half a century later) that the Jews of Rome might have actually engaged in such "absurd conduct" as mocking a crucifix, endangering thereby the entire community.[42]

Yet conduct which appeared absurd to German Jews late in the nineteenth century might well have appeared less so to Roman Jews of the early eleventh. Vogelstein and Rieger apparently failed to note that in 1021 Easter Sunday and (the first day of) Passover fell on the very same

---

[39] Roth, *Italy*, 72.

[40] For Ademar's account of the events in Rome, see *Monumenta Germaniae Historica: Scriptores* (Hannover, 1841), 4:139, and the summary in Schreckenberg, *Adversus-Judaeos*, 2:541–42. Kenneth Stow has strangely attributed to Ademar the report that "Pope Benedict VIII burned twenty Roman Jews at the stake for desecrating a holy image and causing an outbreak of plague." See his *Alienated Minority: The Jews of Medieval Latin Europe* (Cambridge, Mass., 1992), 95. Yet the chronicle clearly refers to an earthquake ("terrae motu") and to the Jews as having been beheaded ("decollatis"), although no number is given. On Ademar's chronicle, see also Landes, *Relics, Apocalypse*, who has little, however, to say about the Rome incident. It is also curiously omitted in Joseph Shatzmiller, "Desecrating the Cross: A Rare Medieval Accusation" (in Hebrew), *Studies in the History of the Jewish People and the Land of Israel* 5 (1980): 159–73.

[41] See Cesare Baronius, *Annales Ecclesiastici*, ed. A. Theiner, (Bari, 1849), 16:42. Both Schreckenberg and Stow assert that no other source corroborates Ademar's account. Neither seems to be familiar with the discussion in Vogelstein and Rieger (see note 42, below), where Baronius is cited. Among scholars who evidently made use of Baronius's account, we may also note Schudt, *JM* II, book 6, 17:12, and Zunz, *Synagogale Poesie*, 19.

[42] Hermann Vogelstein and Paul Rieger, *Geschichte der Juden in Rom*, 2 vols. (Berlin, 1895–1896), 1:212–13. Roth, who gives the date of the incident as "1020 or 1021," had clearly seen their discussion. Note also Gerd Tellenbach, *The Church in Western Europe from the Tenth to the Early Twelfth Century*, trans T. T. Reuter (Cambridge, 1993), 98.

day (April 2), and that Good Friday was therefore both the day of the burning of *hametz* and the eve of what came to be known (evidently due to Christian influence) as "the Great Sabbath."[43] If the Jews of Rome had indeed mocked the crucifix on that Friday, it may well have been by burning some wood in the shape of a cross together with the remnants of their leavened bread. And if one of them had indeed informed the papal authorities of the sacrilege, it may well have been after hearing, on that "Great Sabbath" (and Easter eve), the prophetic reading from Malachi which spoke of "the coming of the awesome, fearful, day of the Lord (3:23),"[44]—words eminently capable of arousing apocalyptic feelings and also, perhaps, feelings of guilt and contrition, especially when accompanied by heavy gusts and an earthquake's aftershocks.

In both the other years mentioned as possible dates for the Roman incident, 1017 and 1020, Good Friday fell on the eve of the intermediate Sabbath of Passover, the Sabbath upon which Ezekiel's vision of the dry bones returning to life (chap. 37) was read in the synagogue, a custom explained in a contemporary responsum as being rooted in the belief that the resurrection of the dead would take place in the month of Nisan.[45] Reminding Jews in this way of the difference between their resurrection narrative and that of the Christians undoubtedly added to the already tense and emotionally charged atmosphere prevailing for centuries during the days from Holy Thursday through Easter Sunday.

Some four decades later a similar accusation was made against the Jews of Aterno, near Pescara.[46] This accusation occurred during the lifetime of R. Joseph Tov-Elem, who, as noted above, mentioned matter-of-factly the "smashing of an abomination" by the Jews of Sens. It is noteworthy, then, that shortly after the turn of the millenium and well before the First Crusade, Jewish violence against the crucifix, as a response, in part, to the new prominence of the latter, begins to appear in Western Europe. If the experience of the First Crusade did not initiate such violence, it seems, however, to have raised it to new heights.

---

[43] On Christian influence upon the shaping of the "Great Sabbath" and on the (paradoxically) anti-Christian character of its liturgy and readings, see Yuval, *Two Nations*, 114, 226–41.

[44] On the anti-Christian character, real or perceived, of the burning of *hametz*, and the beginnings of the custom to read Malachi 3 on the Sabbath before Passover, see Yuval, *Two Nations*, 236–46.

[45] See the responsum attributed to R. Hai Gaon (d. 1038) in B. M. Lewin ed., *Otzar ha-Geonim: Megillah* (Jerusalem, 1932), 63–64, and the sources cited there.

[46] Peter Browe, "Die Hostienschändungen der Juden im Mittelalter," *RQCAK* 36 (1926): 170; Roth, *Italy*, 72.

THRUSTING THE ROD

R. Solomon b. Samson, one of the Hebrew chroniclers of the First Crusade, reported that on the first day of Passover, 1096, crusaders from France led by Peter the Hermit arrived in Trier and soon after began to desecrate the community's Torah scrolls. The Jews "undertook penitence and charity, and fasted six weeks from day to day [during the daytime hours], from Passover to Shavuot."[47] Acts of martyrdom, some quite dramatic, began only after the Christian Pentecost, when the local bishop began to demonstrate a less protective attitude toward the town's Jews. Tensions between Christians and Jews in Trier (which had acquired the status of a "second Rome") had emerged as early as 1066. In that year, according to the *Gesta Trevorum*, Archbishop Eberhard threatened the town's Jews with expulsion if they would not convert by the Saturday before Easter. The Jews, it was claimed, burned a wax figure of the bishop which they had arranged (through bribery) to have baptized, and thus allegedly caused his death on that very Saturday.[48]

The most dramatic incident in Trier narrated by R. Solomon b. Samson is the martyrdom of Asher b. Joseph the *Gabbai*, who was put to death first before the gate of the bishop's palace "so as to instill fear and terror in the rest." On the way to his death Asher invited other members of the community to join him in welcoming the Divine Presence; an invitation to which only the youth Meir b. Samuel responded affirmatively. "When they emerged from the gate of the palace, the crucified one was brought before them so that they would bow before him. *They cast a branch at the abomination*, and the two pious men were slain in sanctification of the [Divine] Name."[49]

How did the two pious Jews of Trier provoke their slayers? The Hebrew phrase *hitilu zemorah*, was translated rather literally by Shlomo Eidelberg as "they cast a branch,"[50] but I would prefer the no less literal "they thrust a rod." The Hebrew phrase, as scholars have noted, clearly alludes to a cryptic verse in Ezekiel (8:17): "Then he said to me, 'Have you seen this, O son

---

[47] Eidelberg, *The Jews and the Crusaders*, 62–63. See also Robert Chazan, *European Jewry and the First Crusade* (Berkeley, 1987), 287–88.

[48] On Trier as a "secunda Roma," and on the processional consequences thereof, see Fichtenau, *Living in the Tenth Century*, 9, 11, 13, 49, 54–55. On the alleged events of 1066, see, among others, Aronius, *Regesten*, 76, no. 160; Adolf Kober, "Trier," in *Germania Judaica* (Tübingen, 1963), 1:376.

[49] Haberman, *Gezerot*, 55; Eidelberg, *Jews and the Crusaders*, 65; Chazan, *European Jewry*, 291. I have adopted elements of both translations.

[50] Contrast the less literal translations of S. Baer (in Neubauer and Stern, *Hebräische. Berichte*, 135) and Chazan, *European Jewry* ("they mocked the image").

of man? Is it too slight a thing for the house of Judah to commit the *abomination* which they commit here, that they fill the land with violence . . . Lo,
they put the *branch* to their nose.'" Thus it appears in the RSV, closely following King James. In the new JPS translation (*Tanakh*, 1988) the last
words are rendered "*thrust* the branch to their nostrils," which fits better
with the phallic connotations of "rod" (like *Rute* in German), well illustrated
in one of Ezra Pound's *Cantos*: "his rod hath made god in my belly."[51]

I am not suggesting (as did Graetz) that *zemorah* necessarily means
"phallus" in the abovementioned verse from Ezekiel,[52] but rather that its
most likely use among medieval Ashkenazic authors would have been in
the phallic sense. This usage was prominent in midrashic literature,[53] especially in the legends, discussed in the previous chapter, concerning Amalek's
attack upon the Israelites at Rephidim, in some versions of which the
circumcised organs of the latter were cut off and insolently thrown heavenward.[54] These legends, as we have seen, became the basis for some of
the liturgical poems composed by R. Eleazar ha-Kallir, in early medieval
Palestine, for recitation on the Sabbath before Purim. In these poems
Kallir uses the term *zemorah* when referring to the circumcised penises
victimized by the Amalekites, a matter not always understood by his modern translators.[55] Among medieval Ashkenazic Jews, however, Kallir's
poems were not only widely recited, but also carefully studied; achieving,
as Abraham Grossman has noted, a canonical status akin to that of rabbinic literature.[56] In the commentary composed by R. Eliezer b. Nathan
(R. Solomon b. Samson's younger contemporary and fellow chronicler of
the First Crusade), two possible explanations were offered for this
usage.[57] There can be little doubt, therefore, that R. Solomon b. Samson

---

[51] See R. W. Burchfield, *A Supplement to the Oxford English Dictionary* (Oxford, 1982),
3:1320; Eric Partridge, *A Dictionary of Slang and Unconventional Language* (8th ed.,
1984), 983.

[52] Heinrich Graetz, "Die euphemistische Bedeutung des Wortes [*zemora*] im Hebräischen,"
MGWJ 25 (1876): 507–8. See also Alexander Kohut, *Aruch Completum* (Vienna, 1926),
3:300–301.

[53] In addition to Kohut, *Aruch Completum*, see Jacob Levy, *Wörterbuch über die Talmudim
und Mirashim* (Berlin and Vienna, 1924), 1:544.

[54] See, for example, *Pesikta de-Rav Kahana*, ed. Bernard Mandelbaum (2nd ed., New York,
1987), 49 (and n. 4 there); Braude and Kapstein, *PRK*, 52–53.

[55] Note, for example, that by Joseph Marcus, *Yozerot for Shabbat Shekalim, Zakhor* . . . (New
York, 1965), 9.

[56] See the important comments of Grossman, *France*, 331, 534, and the literature cited
there.

[57] (1) The root *zmr*, used as a verb in the sense of pruning (Lev. 25), suggests circumcision;
(2) the shape of the phallus is similar to that of a branch (or rod). R. Eliezer's commentary
is quoted by Buber, *Tanhuma*, 2:42.

was familiar with the liturgical poems of Kallir in which *zemorah* was used as a term for the circumcised phallus, and that its usage in his chronicle conformed to that of the revered poet.

When we are informed, then, that two Jews in Trier "thrust a rod" upon the crucifix when it was offered to them, what R. Solomon b. Samson seems to be saying is that they urinated upon it. These Jews are not the only martyrs of 1096 to whom R. Solomon b. Samson attributes such brazen conduct. Earlier in his chronicle he recounts the death (some months later) of Natronai b. Isaac, one of the martyrs of Xanten: "Some priests of his acquaintance had come to him throughout the previous day attempting to persuade him to defile himself in their evil waters, for he was a handsome man, pleasant to sight. He threw a branch in their mouths (*zarak zemorah be-fihem*) and said: 'God forbid that I should deny God-on-High . . .' He slaughtered his brother and then himself."[58]

What sort of branch (or rod) did Natronai throw in the mouths of the priests before his martyrdom? Shlomo Eidelberg, in his annotated translation, states that "the reference is to an act of disdain toward the offered baptismal rites," but refrains from suggesting precisely what sort of act.[59] In contrast to those prudent historians who have not been willing to go out on a limb, I would suggest that Natronai is described by our chronicler as having disdainfully linked his (exposed) phallus with the baptismal waters, either by actually urinating or by merely indicating his readiness to do so. When R. Solomon b. Samson says that Natronai "threw a rod" in the mouths of the priests, he may have meant to say that he used his "rod" to shut their mouths. The rude behavior attributed to him by R. Solomon b. Samson is rather like that attributed to President Lyndon Johnson by Arthur Goldberg, who reported that "during a private conversation with some reporters who pressed him to explain why we were in Vietnam, Johnson lost his patience . . . unzipped his fly, drew out his substantial organ and declared: 'This is why!'"[60]

R. Solomon b. Samson described two separate acts of First Crusade martyrdom, one in Xanten and the other in Trier, as having involved the provocative use of the Jewish phallus in order to express disdain for Christianity's hallowed symbols. That the male organ in particular was chosen for this purpose (whether by the martyrs themselves or their later chronicler) is not especially surprising, for in medieval Europe it symbolized, in its circumcised form, the quintessential difference between

[58] Haberman, *Gezerot*, 49; Eidelberg, *Jews and the Crusaders*, 57–58.
[59] Eidelberg, *Jews and the Crusaders*, 155; Robert Chazan says even less; see his *European Jewry*, 283.
[60] Robert Dallek, *Flawed Giant: Lyndon Johnson and His Times, 1961–1973* (New York, 1998), 491.

Christian and Jew.[61] During the First Crusade and its aftermath the internal sign which the Jew bore on his lower body seems to have been consciously pitted against the external sign (of the cross) which the crusader wore on his upper body, to which the Hebrew chroniclers referred by the same word (*ot*) used in the Bible (Gen. 9:12, 17) for the sign of circumcision.[62] Whether or not R. Solomon's b. Samson's descriptions of these brazen acts which preceded martyrdom are accurate in all of their details, what is hardly less important is that he recorded narrative traditions which were circulating in his day,[63] and which he regarded as worthy of transmission to future generations.

The act—or at least seriously contemplated possibility—of urinating on (or near) a cross as an expression of disdain for Christianity survived in Ashkenazic culture well past the era of the First Crusade, as may be seen from the thirteenth-century *Sefer Hasidim*. In the midst of discussing such questions as whether it is permissible to have the windows of one's home face a cross (*to'eva*), the rather cryptic story is told of one who wanted to relieve himself and was warned that he might be put to death. When he responded that his death would be considered martyrdom, he was told: "you will receive no reward for causing your own death, for it is a sin, and furthermore do not endanger your family and fellow townsmen."[64] Now, most people relieving themselves put neither their lives nor those of their family in jeopardy, unless they do so on, or in the proximity of, an object or site venerated by others. It would seem, therefore, that the author(s) of *Sefer Hasidim* (or a later copyist) prudently left out the precise details, expecting that contemporary readers of the work would be able to figure them out for themselves. Just as there was danger in urinating on a cross, so too was there danger in writing about it too explicitly.

One author who did not shy away from doing so, however, was R. Joseph Official in thirteenth-century France. In his polemical work

---

[61] For twelfth-century Jewish perspectives on circumcision as a sign of Jewish distinction, see, for example, R. Joseph Bekhor Shor's *Torah Commentary* (in Hebrew), ed. Yehoshafat Nevo (Jerusalem, 1994), 29 (Gen. 17:2, 11), and the famous poem of Judah Halevi, *Yom la-Yabasha*, 2:404–5, no. 165, in Dov Yarden, ed., *Shirei ha-Kodesh* . . . (Jerusalem, 1980). For translations (one in rhyme) see *Selected Poems of Jehudah Halevi*, trans. Nina Salaman (Philadelphia, 1924), 139–40, 170–71.

[62] See Haberman, *Gezerot*, 24, 72; Eidelberg, *Jews and the Crusaders*, 21, 79.

[63] For recent debate on the issues of "facticity" and "narrative" see Jeremy Cohen, "The 'Persecutions of 1096'—From Martyrdom to Martyrology: The Sociocultural Context of the Hebrew Crusade Chronicles" (in Hebrew) *Zion* 59 (1994): 169–208; Ivan Marcus, "The Representations of Reality in the Narratives of 1096," *Jewish History* 13 (1999): 37–48.

[64] Wistinetzki, *Sefer Hasidim*, 333–34, nos. 1353–65. As Yisrael Yuval has brought to my attention, the very next passage (no. 1366) discusses the question of relieving oneself in a Karaite synagogue, suggesting that the prospective martyr had a similar place in mind.

Yosef ha-Mekaneh he relates an astonishing anecdote concerning his father R. Nathan, who once accompanied the archbishop of Sens on a journey by horseback. When the latter stopped along the way and dismounted in order to urinate in front of a bush, R. Nathan also dismounted and (allegedly) began to urinate upon a cross. When the bishop expressed disapproval of his Jewish companion's action, R. Nathan replied that it was also wrong to urinate in front of a bush, through which God had once revealed himself to Moses.[65] Although it is clear that R. Joseph's story cannot be accepted as accurate in all of its details, it is also clear that he took seriously the possibility, as did R. Solomon b. Samson and the author(s) of *Sefer Hasidim*, that a medieval European Jew might defiantly desecrate, and even urinate upon, a cross. It is therefore a possibility which modern historians should take quite seriously as well.

THE DEACON AND THE JEWESS

From Germany and France let us return to England. In the same century in which the authors of *Sefer Hasidim* and *Yosef ha-Mekaneh* wrote of Jews urinating on the cross, Matthew Paris (d. 1259) described similar conduct in his *Historia Anglorum*. I refer to the 1222 incident later given the rather picturesque title "The Deacon and the Jewess" by the legendary legal historian F. W. Maitland in his eponymous article, first published in 1886.[66] Matthew Paris, who died in 1259, claims to have heard this version from an eyewitness, Master John of Basingstoke. According to Matthew (in Maitland's translation):

> An English deacon loved a Jewess with unlawful love, and ardently desired her embraces. "I will do what you ask," said she "if you will turn apostate, *be circumcised*, and hold fast the Jewish faith." When he had done what she bade him he gained her unlawful love. But this could not long be concealed

[65] See Rosenthal, *Joseph Hamekane*, 14. Note, relatedly, the passage in the thirteenth-century *Nizzahon Vetus* in which the author suggests that a Christological reading of Genesis 47:31 might be countered with the claim, based on Genesis 48:2, that Jacob had put a cross "under his anus"—a reading which would seem to reflect the author's fantasies. See Berger, *Jewish-Christian Debate*, 59.

[66] The article was originally published in the *Law Quarterly Review* 2 (1886), and reprinted first in Maitland's *Roman Canon Law in the Church of England* (London, 1898) and then in the *The Collected Papers of Frederic William Maitland*, ed. H.A.L. Fisher (Cambridge, 1911), 385–406. See also *TJHSE* 6 (1908–1912): 260–76 , where it was again republished with an important introduction by Israel Abrahams (254–59), who called it "delightful in form as well as original in substance."

and was reported to [Archbishop] Stephen [Langton] of Canterbury. Before him the deacon was accused . . . he was convicted and then confessed all these matters, and that he had taken part in a sacrifice which the Jews made of a crucified boy. *And when it was seen that the deacon was circumcised*, and that no argument would bring him to his senses, he solemnly apostasised before the archbishop and the assembled prelates in this manner:—a cross with the Crucified was brought before him and he defiled the cross ["et minxit super crucem"] saying, "I renounce the new-fangled law and the comments of Jesus the false prophet" and he reviled and slandered Mary . . . and made against her a charge not to be repeated." . . . Thereupon the archbishop, weeping bitterly at hearing such blasphemies, deprived him of his orders.[67] (emphasis added)

In this particular version of the story, the ex-deacon was grabbed, as he exited the church, by a certain Fawkes of Bréauté, and shortly thereafter decapitated. So scrupulous a historian as Maitland could hardly accept every detail of this story at face value. "Eye-witness and archdeacon though Master John of Basingstoke may have been," he wrote, "we cannot believe all that he had said." Among other problems in the account, Maitland saw it as unlikely that "the assembled prelates gave the apostate an opportunity of manifesting his change of faith in a fashion at once very solemn and very gross."[68] It is clear, however, that had Maitland been familiar with the medieval Hebrew sources discussed above, he would have been less skeptical about the possibility that the deacon had learned how to die defiantly the Jewish way, having perhaps even heard stories of the brave martyrs in Xanten and Trier.

Maitland found the former deacon's action so "gross" that he could not even bring himself to translate it precisely, rendering it euphemistically as "defiled the cross" and discreetly inserting in a footnote the Latin original: "et minxit super crucem." Curiously, whereas Matthew Paris and his informant had no problem reporting that the circumcised deacon had urinated on a crucifix, the latter's indecorous charge concerning Mary was not deemed worthy of repeating, even euphemistically. Maitland by contrast, writing during the last decades of Queen Victoria's reign, was more squeamish about the deacon's "very gross" act than about his blasphemous words.

Nonetheless he was willing to provide considerably more information about that act than was, several decades later, the Anglo-Jewish historian Cecil Roth. In his *History of the Jews in England* (published in 1941) Roth

---

[67] Maitland, "The Deacon and the Jewess; or, Apostasy at Common Law," in *The Collected Papers*, 1:399.
[68] Ibid., 400.

briefly narrated the story of thirteenth-century deacon "who had been induced through the study of Hebrew to adopt Judaism and had married a Jewess," mentioning the former's blasphemy but not his defilement of a crucifix. A decade later, in his monograph on *The Jews of Medieval Oxford*, Roth was a bit more generous with details concerning the former deacon's last moments, acknowledging that he had defiled a crucifix, but still not revealing the precise nature of the defilement.[69] Yet it is hardly clear that the charges against Jesus and Mary quite reliably, in Roth's view, attributed to the ex-deacon possess greater facticity than Matthew's report that he also urinated on a crucifix. Historians may sometimes think themselves scrupulous when they are simply being squeamish.

Returning then to our less squeamish medieval chroniclers, we have R. Solomon b. Samson in twelfth-century Germany speaking of two Jews in Trier urinating on a cross offered to them at the moment of martyrdom, and Matthew Paris reporting a case of similar behavior in thirteenth-century England. Both chroniclers are writing at a distance of two or three decades from their subjects, and both explicitly state that they have their information at second hand. Their accounts may be seen as corroborating each other, if perhaps less on a factual level than on a mental one. To both Jews and Christians of their time (unlike some historians of recent generations) it was not difficult to imagine a Jew, whether naturally born or converted, urinating on a cross if given the opportunity to do so. Unlike ritual murder or host-desecration this form of hostile conduct, it may be added, was not reported exclusively by Christian sources.

ASCENSION DAY, 1268

The tragic story of the former deacon who dramatically denied the cross may be linked, somewhat paradoxically, with that of his countryman and contemporary, Yom Tov b. Moses, who met his death on account of his attraction to the very same sign. Both point to the centrality of the cross as symbolizing the tense (and yet sometimes porous) lines of demarcation between the worlds of Judaism and Christianity. And both may be linked with a third, well-documented story from thirteenth-century England: the snatching and trampling of a processional cross by a Jew of Oxford as an ecclesiastical procession passed through the center of the town's Jewry on Ascension Day, 1268.

---

[69] Cecil Roth, *A History of the Jews in England* (London, 1941), 41; Roth, *Medieval Oxford*, 20. See also in a similar vein, G. Dahan, *Les intellectuels chrétiens et les juifs au moyen âge* (Paris, 1990), 190.

"A certain Jew of the most consummate impudence," as the historian Tovey wrote in the eighteenth century, "violently snatched it from the bearer, and trod it under his feet, in token of his contempt for Christ."[70] News of this event came to King Henry III, who intervened personally in the matter, demanding that the Jews of Oxford be thrown into jail until they had made reparation, and that they not be permitted to administer their property until they had given adequate security for the replacement they would provide. This, it was determined, would consist of a stately marble crucifix limned in gold, with a figure of the crucified Jesus on one side and the Virgin on the other, which was to be erected at the place where the crime had been committed. At the top of the cross was to be an inscription containing the cause of its erection. Likewise, they were to present a portable crucifix of silver, of the size that was usually carried before archbishops, to be given to the chancellor and the scholars of the university for use on such occasions when they went in procession.[71]

The 1268 cross-snatching by an Oxford Jew, which Tovey, himself a fellow of Merton College, called a "most astonishing crime," was discussed with evident discomfort by a twentieth-century Jewish resident of Oxford, Cecil Roth, who attempted to put an acceptable "spin" on the incident. "It may be that some Jew was pushed accidentally against the Cross or else dragged towards it by the mob, and made the bearer stumble," he wrote, "or possibly a demented iconoclast may have taken it into his head to make this foolish gesture." But Roth was not the only Jewish historian to seek an explanation in the realm of psychopathology. As late as 1980, Joseph Shatzmiller, who had been a student of Ben-Sasson, suggested that the Oxford Jew had attacked the cross "in a moment of temporary madness."[72]

More recently Christoph Cluse, while describing Roth's attempt at explanation as "fully valid," especially since it was offered "so soon after the Holocaust" (in 1951!), has advanced the "daring" (in his view) hypothesis that an Oxford Jew did intentionally snatch and smash a processional cross on Ascension Day, 1268. He has also gone beyond the event to examine its "narrative," which, he suggests, emerged "in an

[70] D' Blossiers Tovey, *Anglia Judaica: Or, the History and Antiquities of the Jews in England* (London, 1738), 168. See also Roth, *Medieval Oxford*, 151–53; Trachtenberg, *Devil and the Jews*, 118; Robert Stacey, "The Conversion of Jews to Christianity in Thirteenth-Century England," *Speculum* 67 (1992): 264–65.

[71] D' Blossiers Tovey, *Anglia Judaica*, 168; Roth, *Medieval Oxford*, 152. For the Latin original of the king's letter, see *Close Rolls of the Reign of Henry III . . . A.D. 1268–1272* (London, 1938), 14–15. The (admittedly loose) translation I have offered draws on both Tovey and Roth.

[72] Roth, *Medieval Oxford*, 152; Shatzmiller, "Desecrating the Cross," 161.

atmosphere dominated by the preaching of the crusade and [Lord] Edward's preparations for taking the Cross on St. John's Day (June 24), 1268," an atmosphere of religious tension in which the story "made sense" to both "Jews and Christians alike." In addition to pointing to previous accusations of cross-desecration which bear some degree of verisimilitude, Cluse has made the important observation that in the year 1268 Ascension Day fell on the third of Sivan, the first of the three "days of limitation" before Shavuot, and the anniversary (as noted above) of the massacre of Mainz Jewry in 1096.[73]

It would, of course, be "very speculative," as Cluse himself has admitted, "to think that the Oxford Jew who broke a processional cross on Ascension Day 1268" was influenced by the memory of that distant event. But one should note nonetheless the heightened tensions which must have frequently prevailed between Christians and Jews in the years after 1096 when the commemorations of three momentous events overlapped or occurred in close proximity: The ascent of Moses "up to God" (Exod: 19:3) in order to receive the Torah; the ascent of Jesus "into heaven" (Acts 1:9–10) after his resurrection; and the ascent "to God, all together," as R. Solomon b. Samson wrote of the martyrs of Mainz.[74] And just as the overlap between Passover and Holy Week frequently gave rise to religious tensions between Jews and Christians resulting in crime (on the part of the former) and punishment (on the part of the latter, as in Clermont and Rome), so too could the clash between the dates commemorating the ascent of Moses on Mount Sinai (for forty days) and the ascension of Jesus on the Mount of Olives (after forty days) create a similarly explosive environment.[75] This, of course, would only be magnified for those who recalled the martyrs of Mainz in 1096.

As Shatzmiller aptly noted, the anonymous assailant of the processional cross in Oxford was a contemporary of the unfortunate R. Yom Tov who took his life on the eve of Shavuot after "a demon showed him an image of the cross and pressed him to worship it." To these two "mad Englishmen" of the thirteenth century I have added a third—the deacon who "loved a Jewess with unlawful love," and embraced her religion with such ardor that he was willing (according to Matthew Paris) to urinate (with his newly circumcised phallus) upon the crucifix he once revered above all else. In doing so, he followed, whether knowingly or not, the tradition of rude and reckless denial of Christianity associated in European Jewish memory with the martyrs of the Crusades. It was a tradition, however, for

[73] Cluse, "Stories of Breaking and Taking the Cross," 403–5, 428, 430–31.

[74] See Haberman, *Gezerot,* 29–30; Eidelberg, *The Jews and the Crusaders,* 29.

[75] On the link between the biblical accounts of the ascension of Moses and the ascension of Jesus, see Georg Kretschmar, "Himmelfahrt und Pfingsten," *ZK* 66 (1954–1955): 217–18.

which Israel Halpern found no place in his 1941 anthology of Jewish valor, just as Cecil Roth, in his history of English Jewry published the very same year, found no place for the former deacon's defilement of a cross. In this chapter I have attempted to return these "demented iconoclasts" to the realm of Jewish historical memory, and to explain how their actions could have made sense to them and to their Christian contemporaries.

FROM CROSS TO HOST

Late in the thirteenth century a new accusation against the Jews emerged in Western Europe—that of host-desecration. At the Fourth Lateran Council of 1215 the doctrine of transubstantiation had been established as an article of faith, setting the stage for Christian anxieties about pernicious Jewish designs upon the consecrated eucharistic wafer. The commune of Avignon decreed in 1243, for example, that Jews over the age of nine should not be permitted to remain in the streets when the consecrated host was carried in procession, and similar legislation was passed at the church synod of Vienna in 1267.[76] As Miri Rubin has recently noted, "the first fully documented case of a complete host desecration accusation, from discovery to punishment," occurred in Paris during Holy Week of 1290, a year in which Easter and Passover overlapped. A Jewish pawnbroker was accused of having procured a host by promising a female Christian debtor the return of her pawn and cancellation of her debt if she brought him the host sanctified at Easter communion. During the following decade such accusations spread from northern France to German-speaking lands, culminating in the bloody Rindfleisch massacres of 1298, which centered upon the region of Franconia. Further to the east, in the Austrian town of Pulkau (twenty-five miles north of Vienna) 150 Jews lost their lives as a result of a host-desecration accusation in 1338, another year in which Passover and Easter overlapped.[77]

Could there have been any material basis for such accusations? Just as Cecil Roth, writing shortly after the Holocaust, referred dismissively to "the improbable charge of mocking a crucifix" leveled against the Jews of eleventh-century Rome, so too the American rabbi and historian Joshua Trachtenberg, in *The Devil and the Jews* (1943), described the host-desecration accusation as both "one of the commonest charges against the Jews, and the one that must seem to us most unreasonable." Trachtenberg

---

[76] See Trachtenberg, *Devil and the Jews*, 113; Miri Rubin, *Gentile Tales: The Narrative Assault on Late Medieval Jews* (New Haven, 1999), 29–30.

[77] Browe, "Hostienschändungen," 174–79; Trachtenberg, *Devil and the Jews*, 114–17; Rubin, *Gentile Tales*, 40–54, 65–68.

pointed to "the absurdity of attributing to Jews an acceptance and utiliza-
tion" of so "un-Jewish" a dogma as that of transubstantiation.[78] Yet in recent
decades Jewish historians have been more open to the possibility that such
acts of desecration, not necessarily always premeditated, could indeed have
taken place from time to time. As another historian and rabbi, David Berger,
has written: "I have little doubt that if . . . a Jew had found himself in possession of this idolatrous object symbolizing the faith of his oppressors, it
would not have fared very well in his hands."[79]

A good example of the mundane circumstances under which Jews might
come in to contact with the consecrated host and choose to desecrate it
occurred in England less than two decades after the Oxford incident of
1268. In 1285 a group of Jews and Christians were arrested in Norwich on
the charge of having broken into two nearby churches one night, during
which they allegedly "stole chalices, vestments, books, and other ecclesiastical ornaments, and vilely broke a pyx in which Christ's body [corpus
Christi] had been placed, and crushed the Lord's body beneath their
feet."[80] One could easily imagine that if Jews were indeed among those who
broke into the church for purposes of theft, one of their company might
have been moved to destroy the host-containing pyx as an act of private
revenge against what Berger has aptly called "the faith of his oppressors."

In 1275 the Bishop of Worcester issued a mandate to the deans of West-
bury and Bristol, ordering them to refrain from contact with the Jews of
Bristol, who had uttered insults while a local chaplain had carried a sanctified host through the Jewish quarter on his way to a gravely sick woman.
In Vienna six years later King Rudolph of Austria sat in judgment concerning the case of a Jew who allegedly had "wounded a priest walking
with Christ's body [a sanctified host] with a lump of mud or a stone."[81]
Was such behavior highly unlikely? I believe not. Nor should we dismiss
the story in early fourteenth-century Koblenz of a nominally Christian
woman who removed a host from St. Paul's church and sold it to the Jews
(apparently at her own initiative) so that they could mock it. Reportedly,
when the woman witnessed the abuse she ran into the street shouting:
"Christ's body is being horribly tortured by the Jews."[82]

---

[78] Trachtenberg, *Devil and the Jews*, 109–10.

[79] David Berger, *From Crusade to Blood Libels to Expulsions: Some New Approaches to Medieval
Antisemitism* (Second Annual Lecture of the V. J. Selmanowitz Chair of Jewish History,
Touro College Graduate School of Jewish Studies, New York, 1997), 15. Berger points to
similar comments by Marc Saperstein. Prior to both, however, see Baron, *SRH*, 11:165.

[80] Z. E. Rokéah "The Jewish Church-Robbers and Host Desecrators of Norwich (ca. 1285)"
REJ 141 (1982): 348; Rubin, *Gentile Tales*, 34.

[81] Rubin, *Gentile Tales*, 31.

[82] Ibid., 75.

The theme of a processional host being attacked by Jews resurfaces in late fourteenth-century Prague, during Holy Week of 1389. According to one (Christian) account, a local Jew threw a stone at the monstrance carried by a priest not far from the Jewish quarter. According to another, a priest bringing the Eucharist to a sick person on Easter Sunday was verbally and physically attacked by Jews, causing the monstrance to fall and the consecrated hosts to disperse on the ground. In retaliation a number of local Jews were killed and burned on the last day of Passover: a poem of lament in their memory was composed by R. Avigdor Kara.[83] This case, like the alleged attacks (verbal or physical) upon processional hosts in thirteenth-century Bristol and Vienna, is not fundamentally different from the attack on a processional cross at Oxford in 1268. Although Cecil Roth had suggested, concerning the latter, "that . . . possibly a demented iconoclast may have taken it into his head to make this foolish gesture," it is clear that for medieval Jews, attacking a consecrated host during Holy Week or smashing a processional cross on Ascension Day may have been a reckless act, but it was far from a "foolish gesture." As Emily Dickinson wrote: "Much madness is divinest sense/to a discerning Eye."

MAD AND BAD MARRANOS

The Oxford incident, moreover, was not the only one of its type. In the following century the Italian jurist Peter de Ancharano (1330–1410) offered an opinion concerning "a Jew who hurled mud at a crucifix being carried in procession."[84] And in the Piedmontese town of Savigliano there were, during the early 1430s, four apparently related instances of Jews insulting Christians and/or their religion. A woman named Reyna (or Reyneta) was fined six dinars for "obliterating with charcoal a cross painted on the wall of her house"—apparently the one she shared with her husband Bonafey, who was fined a far greater sum for insulting a Christian. Two other Jewish residents of Savigliano were fined for similar actions, one for beating a Christian with a cane, and another for accusing a Dominican friar of keeping women in his home.[85]

[83] Browe, "Hostienschändungen," 187; Bernfeld, *Sefer ha-Demaot*, 2:159–64; Trachtenberg, *Devil and the Jews*, 114; Rubin, *Gentile Tales*, 135–40. For a translation of Kara's lament, see Rubin, *Gentile Tales*, 196–98.

[84] James Muldoon, *Popes, Lawyers, and Infidels: The Church and the Non-Christian World, 1250–1550* (Philadelphia, 1979), 23.

[85] Segre, *Piedmont*, 1:76–77. For the relationship between Reyna and Bonafey, see ibid., 94.

During the fifteenth century acts of cross-desecration seem to have been quite common among crypto-Jews in Spain, most of whom, as nominal Catholics, kept crucifixes in their homes. Actual testimonies, however, appear only after the establishment of the Inquisition in 1478. Before the end of the fifteenth century accusations of various forms of cross-desecration were made against new-Christians residing in the provinces of Cuenca, Ciudad Real, Saragossa, Soria, and Valencia, often on the basis of testimony by relatives or members of their households. It must be acknowledged, however, that not all historians have been willing to regard these testimonies as reliable historical evidence.[86] In 1487 witnesses testified to the Inquisition of Valencia that local *conversos* had scourged a crucifix, and two years later local inquisitors asked a female defendant if she had ever performed such a blasphemous act or knew of anyone who had. In his classic (though controversial) *History of the Jews in Christian Spain* the Jerusalem historian Yitzhak Baer saw this as "an amazing question." True, he conceded, "Jews and *conversos* were capable of at times breaking crucifixes or trampling them underfoot, but scourging," he felt "is unthinkable."[87] But perhaps even evil inquisitors can be forgiven for thinking the unthinkable when they merely reacted to testimony that was presented to them—and to their colleagues elsewhere. As Baer himself noted, after the inquisitor Pedro de Arbues was murdered in September of 1485, the men implicated by the Inquisition of Saragossa were said "to have scourged a crucifix, to the accompaniment of Hebrew prayers and sermons, in imitation of the torments of Jesus on the cross." Yet the German-born Baer was certain that "these tales were manifest tissues of lies invented by antisemites."[88]

This approach was continued by his student Haim Beinart in his study of the *conversos* of Ciudad Real, one of whom, Juan Díaz—a draper whose commitment to Judaism is perhaps best exemplified by his having circumcised himself when already an old man—was posthumously tried by

---

[86] For Cuenca, see W. A. Christian, Jr., *Local Religion in Sixteenth-Century Spain* (Princeton, 1981), 192, and for the other instances see below. On the debate concerning the reliability of Inquisition sources, see Yerushalmi, *From Spanish Court*, 21–24, and the literature cited there. As we shall see, however, some scholars who have eagerly accepted the testimony of these sources concerning other "Judaizing" practices have rather selectively rejected their testimony concerning cross-desecration.

[87] Baer, *Christian Spain*, 2:362–63. Regarding Valencia, note also that in 1540 a large number of prominent new-Christians were punished "on the charge of holding conventicles in which Jewish fasts were observed and a crucifix was scourged." H. C. Lea, *A History of the Inquisitiion of Spain*, (New York, 1906), 2:584. According to Lea, however, they later "asserted that their confessions had been extorted by fear."

[88] Baer, *Christian Spain*, 2:379–80.

the local Inquisition in 1484. Among the "Judaizing" acts attributed to
him by some of the witnesses was that he would scourge a cross on Fridays, before the beginning of the Sabbath. Beinart, who eventually published the files of Ciudad Real's Inquisition, saw them as a valuable source
for reconstructing what Cecil Roth pioneeringly called "the religion of
the Marranos."[89] But whereas Beinart, like Roth before him, was happy
to accept as historical evidence the testimony of witnesses reporting that
new-Christians had performed circumcision, abstained from pork, or
observed (some form of) the Sabbath, he followed his teacher Baer in
refusing to consider acts of violence toward Christian images as part of
Marrano religion. Rather than accept the testimony of Díaz's fellow new-
Christians that he had regularly (and ritually) scourged the crucifix which,
as a nominal Catholic, he kept in his home, Beinart suggested that it was
because of the pious draper's deep attachment to "all things Jewish" that
"witnesses maligned him by inventing a tale" that he would scourge a crucifix each week "just before the commencement of the Sabbath."[90]

Both of these Hebrew University historians seem to have believed that
crypto-Jews who sought valiantly to distance themselves from Christianity
could not possibly have made ritual use of a crucifix in one of their own rituals, or have had any reason to reconstruct Christ's Passion as part of their
own religious observance. But aside from their well-established syncretism
(as in their aforementioned veneration of Saint Esther), is it not possible that
these *conversos* might not wish to neutralize the "black magic" of the crucifixes they had in their homes, especially before the onset of the holy Sabbath?

For Beinart, and evidently also for Baer, the fifteenth-century Spanish
testimonies regarding the scourging of crucifixes were inseparable from
the infamous auto-da-fé in Madrid a century and a half later, in which six
condemned Judaizers were burned at the stake. The main accusation
against the Portuguese new Christians who had been arrested in 1630 and
were marched, amid great pomp, to Madrid's Plaza Mayor on July 4,
1632, was that they would gather weekly in the home of Miguel
Rodríguez and flagellate an image of the crucified Christ. Shortly after the
six were burned (nine other accused Judaizers were penanced) the house
in which they had resided was torn down, and on its site the Capuchin
Convento de la Paciencia was erected in 1639.[91]

---

[89] Roth, *Marranos*, 168–94.

[90] H. Beinart, *Conversos on Trial by the Inquisition* (in Hebrew) (Tel-Aviv, 1965), 178, 231
(English trans., *Conversos on Trial: The Inquisition in Ciudad Real* [Jerusalem, 1981], 220,
292); Beinart, ed., *Records of the Trials of the Spanish Inquisition in Ciudad Real* (Jerusalem,
1974), 1:85–86.

[91] Yerushalmi, *From Spanish Court*, 105–8; Beinart, *Conversos on Trial*, 118, 231–32
(English trans., 141, 292).

Yosef Yerushalmi has discovered that four of the condemned did eventually confess to scourging an image of Christ,[92] but whether or not there was any basis to later accusations, the fifteenth-century evidence must be examined on its own terms. Nonetheless, Baer's candid admission that—in contrast to scourging, which he considered "unthinkable"—Jews and *conversos* "were capable of . . . breaking crucifixes or trampling them underfoot," is worthy of attention. In his *History of the Jews in Christian Spain* he also discussed the 1266 accusation against two prominent Aragonese Jews, that they and other members of their family had desecrated a crucifix. Although James I dismissed the charges against them, Baer did not insist that the accusation was obviously libelous, and even allowed for the possibility that the king was merely defending his valuable aides.[93]

The late fifteenth-century testimonies regarding cross-desecration by Iberian new-Christians should also be seen in light of the evidence concerning such behavior during the sixteenth and seventeenth centuries, both in Europe and the New World. In 1550, for example, a young Castilian immigrant to Venice testified to the local Inquisition that a family of Portuguese immigrants residing in the Santa Croce neighborhood (outside the Ghetto) had, for eight consecutive days soon after Passover, flogged a marble crucifix in the yard below their house.[94] Fourteen years earlier the Mexican farmer Gonzalo Gómez was accused of hanging strings of chili peppers to dry on the arms of a cross he had placed for that purpose on the roof of one of his huts, and also of breaking the arms of three crosses on Good Friday.[95]

As the American scholar David Gitlitz has recently observed, allegations of such behavior appear "with such frequency in the literature, in so many widely-separated locales, and with such varied evidence, much of it eyewitness," that they cannot be dismissed as mere libels. Gitlitz has argued

---

[92] One woman confessed "after a prolonged period of physical and mental agony," but two confessed "in the torture chamber, just before the torment was to begin," and Miguel Rodríguez, who originally admitted only to Judaizing since the age of fourteen, confessed several months later to flagellating an image of Christ as well. See Yerushalmi, *From Spanish Court*, 113. In 1634 there was another such accusation near Salamanca, and in 1639 another in Madrid. See Christian, *Local Religion*, 193.

[93] Baer, *Christian Spain*, 1:158. The two Jews were the bailiff Judah de la Cavalleria and his son-in-law, who was royal secretary for Arabic correspondence.

[94] The Castilian boy (Juan Aloncigaria) also testified that a certain Alfonso Alvares, who was possibly the head of the Portuguese family, had thrown into the fire a crucifix drawn on paper which he (Juan) had kept on the wall in his room. See P. C. Ioly Zorattini, ed., *Processi del S. Ufficio di Venezia contro ebrei e giudaizzanti, 1548–60* (Florence, 1980), 93–94; Brian Pullan, *The Jews of Europe and the Inquisition of Venice, 1550–1670* (Oxford, 1983), 131.

[95] Liebman, *New Spain*, 53.

that the reports of cross-desecration by crypto-Jews need to be taken seriously as expressions of their "negative feelings" toward the religion they pretended to observe, expressions that "ran the gamut from disbelief and scorn to the physical mistreatment of . . . images." The crucifix, in particular, he has stressed, "was targeted by crypto-Jews with great cynicism and hostility, both as an object of Christian idolatry and as emblem of that aspect of Christianity they found hardest to accept: the divinity of Christ." He has also recognized that their acts of violence toward the cross reflected considerable ambivalence: "Paradoxically, for crypto-Jews to vent their rage on the crucifix indicates that they too held some measure of belief in its sacred power."[96]

And, as in the medieval Ashkenazic world, both sexual and scatological motifs are sometimes evident in such acts of desecration. Among the Castilian Inquisitorial documents published by Baer in 1936 (and more recently discussed by Gretchen Starr-Lebeau) was the testimony of Inés González that her mother, Mari Sánchez, widow of a butcher in the town of Guadalupe, had taken a "drawing of the crucifixion of Our Lord" that her late husband had brought home "and threw it in a latrine." Mari herself confirmed the testimony, but explained in her defense that two cypto-Jewish men (whom she named) had been in her house at the time, and they said to her: "What is the devil doing here? Throw it in the latrine."[97] In 1491 a female witness in the Spanish province of Soria testified that she had often seen a crucifix in the bed of a certain Doña Aldonza, "and it was not put there for honest reasons." A century later Diego Castanho of Bahia, in eastern Brazil, was accused of having had "carnal relations with a black slave who was lying on a crucifix." Another new Christian in Bahia, Joam Nuñes, was reported to have kept a crucifix in his lavatory— a fact allegedly "known to everyone in Olinda."[98]

It is within this context that we should see the confession, during the 1520s, of a female new-Christian living in San Juan, Puerto Rico, that she and her brother, Gonzálo de Morales, used to flog a crucifix, and that he had even urinated upon it—testimony which Gonzálo himself later confirmed (and was burnt for).[99] In a programmatic essay published some

---

[96] Gitlitz, *Secrecy and Deceit*, 162.

[97] Baer, *Die Jüden*, 2:447–48; G. Starr-Lebeau, "Mari Sánchez and Inés González: Conflict and Cooperation among Crypto-Jews," 34–36, in *Women in the Inquisition: Spain and the New World*, ed. M. E. Giles (Baltimore, 1999); Starr-Lebeau, *In the Shadow of the Virgin: Inquisitors, Friars, and Conversos in Guadalupe, Spain* (Princeton, 2003), 183, 194.

[98] Arnold Wiznitzer, *Jews in Colonial Brazil* (New York, 1960), 21; Gitlitz, *Secrecy and Deceit*, 162–63.

[99] G. R. Conway, "Hernando Alonso, a Jewish Conquistador with Cortes in Mexico," *PAJHS* 31 (1928): 20; Wiznitzer, "Crypto-Jews," 172.

three decades ago, the American scholar Martin Cohen asserted that such "disrespectful treatment of a crucifix . . . was obviously not part of the [Mexican] Judaizers' religious rituals, though some . . . were guilty of it."[100] By contrast, Cohen's contemporary and countryman Seymour Liebman not only saw "the beating of images of Christ and breaking images of saints" as "the most common manner of exhibiting contempt and soul-burning hatred of Christianity" among crypto-Jews, but later asserted that "in some places" these acts "were part of a ritual."[101]

This position—to which I need not confess my partiality—was also adopted by Gitlitz, who observed, moreover, that accusations of striking and defiling crucifixes increased in the seventeenth century, especially in the New World. In 1643, for example, Gabriel de Granada testified before the Mexican Inquisition that his aunt and other female members of his family "used some nights to flog a small wooden crucifix" they had removed from the wall. Later in that decade two sons of Duarte de León Jaramillo testified before the Mexican Inquisition that their father would sometimes bring an eighteen-inch crucifix from the family's living quarters to his store, where he would place it on the counter and flog it face down for an hour with straps, saying that "its law was not good." As late as 1696 a Mexican new-Christian who was convicted of Judaizing and sentenced to public scourging and six years of servitude in the Philippine galleys testified that he and four others used to beat an ivory crucifix on Fridays, each administering precisely thirteen lashes.[102] Considering that Friday was, as they all knew, the day of the crucifixion and that the Sabbath, during which crypto-Jews were at their most Jewish, began on Friday evening, it is not hard to imagine such scourging—which, as we have seen, is first reported in late fifteenth-century Spain—as a "transitional rite" between the "Catholic" days of the week and the "Jewish" Sabbath.

In 1653 similar testimony was given by Francisco Vicente, a young "colored" native of Havana who had recently come to La Palma (in the Canary Islands) from London, as had his former employer, the new Christian merchant Diego Rodríguez Arias. In London, Francisco reported, it had been the latter's custom on Friday and Saturday nights to take a "half a yard long" crucifix "from the box where he kept his sword and clothes and thrash it with a leather whip for about half an hour each time," during which he would murmur some words to himself. In the same year it was reported by a nephew of the licentiate (priest) Diego de Artiaga, a resident of the Canary Islands, that every night he would perform "heretical

---

[100] M. A. Cohen, "Some Misconceptions about the Crypto-Jews in Colonial Mexico," *AJHQ* 61 (1972): 288.

[101] Liebman, *New Spain*, 53, 84–85; Liebman, *New World Jewry*, 102.

[102] Adler, "Trial," 62; Liebman, *New Spain*, 84–85; Gitlitz, *Secrecy and Deceit*, 164.

practices" and beat a crucifix. Sixteen years earlier, in 1637, de Artiaga—who was believed to be "a descendant of Jews"—had been denounced to the local Inquisition for such suspicious actions as "averting his eyes from the Host while carrying it in procession." It was also reported that "a crucifix belonging to him was found all broken without head or feet."[103]

These remarkable testimonies, together with many other documents from the Canariote Inquisition (which had been established in 1504), were published by Lucien Wolf in his *Jews in the Canary Islands* (1926). From those documents we learn also of such crypto-Jews as the shoemaker Alvaro Gonçales, a native of Castil Blanco in Portugal, who had converted there with his family to Catholicism in 1496, but shortly afterwards (apparently in order to better observe Jewish practices) fled to Gibraltar. From there Alvaro migrated with his family to the island of San Miguel, in the Azores, where he was soon arrested, apparently for making a "gesture of contempt" in church as the priest elevated the host. Together with some other imprisoned new-Christians he escaped from jail in San Miguel and made his way to the Canaries, arriving in La Palma in 1504. Two years later a resident of the island informed the local Inquisition that it was "commonly reported" that when Alvaro was living in the Azores, "he and other converts threw down and spat upon a crucifix." Whether or not this report was accurate, there is little doubt that he was an active Judaizer in La Palma. In 1519 it was reported to the local Inquisition that "meat was seen cooking in his oven on a fish day," and at his lengthy trial, which began in 1524, he was denounced for a wide range of activities including immoral conduct with a Moorish slave girl, preparing his meat according to Jewish law, circumcising his sons, observing the Sabbath, and maintaining a synagogue in his home. It was also reported that Alvaro spoke mockingly of Christians, "alluding to them as dogs," and that he had said that "the crucifix was nothing but a piece of wood."[104]

Alvaro, except for his alleged immoral conduct with a slave girl, was a character much like the pious draper Juan Díaz, who was posthumously tried by the Inquisition of Ciudad Real in 1484, where he was accused, among other things, of keeping Jewish books in his home, observing Jewish fasts, and scourging a cross on Fridays. As we have seen, Haim Beinart, who regarded Díaz as a model *converso* on account of his deep commitment to all things Jewish, rejected the possibility that scourging the cross might have been part of this Marrano's religion. In this he followed not only his teacher Yitzhak Baer, but also Cecil Roth. The latter, in his *History of the Marranos* (1932), which included an important chapter on

---

[103] Wolf, *Canary Islands*, 129, 136–37, 144. For an earlier instance of a priest having been accused of stabbing a crucifix (Cuenca, 1517), see Christian, *Local Religion*, 192.

[104] Wolf, *Canary Islands*, xvi–xvii, 14, 18, 24, 42–50. See also 109 (1580).

Marrano religion, drew upon Wolf's work on the Canary Islands, but made no reference to the report that Alvaro Gonçales, when living in the Azores, had thrown down and spat upon a crucifix, or that Diego Rodríguez Arias, when living in London, used to thrash a crucifix on Friday and Saturday nights. Yet there is no more reason to reject reports of crucifix-desecration than to reject reports that new Christians fasted three days in honor of Queen Esther. Neither practice was inherited from rabbinic Judaism but both were part and parcel of what Roth memorably described as "the religion of the Marranos."

Epilogue: "See the Sign We Hateful Hold"

> On their raiment, wrought with gold,
> See the sign we hateful hold.

These lines were written not by a European Jew of the Middle Ages, but rather, by a nineteenth-century English scholar and cleric, Edward Plumptre (d. 1891), who, in a remarkable feat of empathy, spoke through the former's voice while describing the experience of Jewish martyrdom during the Crusades.[105] When speaking in his own voice of the cross of Christ, in one of his numerous essays, Plumptre had asserted that "a man may put forth his own hand and eat of the fruit thereof, and live for ever."[106] Yet he was also able to understand that many a medieval Jew regarded the sign of the cross with unmitigated hatred.

By mere coincidence, a century after Plumptre's death, the editors of the interfaith journal *Sidic* (Service International de Documentation Judéo-Chrétienne) published a special issue on "The Cross in Jewish-Christian Historical Perspective." The primary motivation for its publication was the international controversy that erupted when, in the autumn of 1988, a tall cross was erected inside the compound of the Carmelite nuns (of which order Edith Stein had been a member) facing the former concentration camp at Auschwitz. The twenty-six-foot cross, incidentally, had been originally erected for an open-air mass that Pope John Paul had performed at Auschwitz in 1979. The editors of *Sidic*, in their introduction to the special issue, noted that the cross, though "a sign of

---

[105] E. H. Plumptre in Joseph Friedlander, compiler, and G. A. Kohut ed., *The Standard Book of Jewish Verse* (New York, 1917), 217–18. On Plumptre, who began his career as chaplain at King's College, London, and rose eventually to be dean of Wells, see the entry in EB 21:856.

[106] "The Tree of Life," in E. H. Plumptre, *Biblical Studies* (London and New York, n.d.), 64. The essay was written before 1869.

redemption and love for the Christian" was often "an object of horror and threat for the Jew."[107]

The persistence of the latter aspect was strikingly illustrated in some of the contributions. The American Catholic priest Edward Flannery related his own personal experience, in the mid-1960s, of having walked on New York's Park Avenue "in the company of a young Jewish couple" during the Christmas season. Behind them a huge illuminated cross shone from one of the office buildings. "Glancing over her shoulder, the young lady—ordinarily well disposed toward Christians—declared: 'That cross makes me shudder.'" When asked by Father Flannery what she meant, she explained, "It's like an evil presence."[108] Another contributor, Michael Chilton, reported that as a community rabbi in England he often came across elderly Jews who had decided to join his synagogue in order ensure that they have a Jewish funeral. "When discussing the matter with them," he wrote, "I frequently find that they are quite terrified by the possibility that a Christian funeral will be arranged for them. When asked what it is about a Christian funeral that disturbs them, they often reply 'The Cross.'"[109]

Later in the 1990s Polish authorities again confronted the thorny question of crosses at Auschwitz, after more than a hundred crosses (some large and some small) were added by Catholic activists as part of an overall effort to erect a total of 152—to commemorate the 152 Catholics executed there in 1941. For many Poles, of course, the crosses at Auschwitz symbolized not only Christian faith but also decades of staunch resistance to German Nazism and Soviet atheism. Jewish sentiments, on the other hand, were expressed by a letter sent by the Simon Wiesenthal Center to Poland's ambassador in Washington complaining that his government had "ceded its international responsibility . . . to a group of Polish radicals who intend to impose Christian symbols on Jewish suffering."[110]

Yet in the heat of the fierce debates about the Auschwitz crosses, it was somehow forgotten that since the late nineteenth century such prominent Jewish artists in Europe and the United States as Samuel Hirschenberg, Joseph Budko, Marc Chagall, and Barnett Newman had appropriated both the cross and the crucifixion as symbols of Jewish suffering. Chagall

[107] *SIDIC*, 24:1 (1991) (English trans. 25–26). On the Auschwitz controversy itself, see also *Memory Offended: The Auschwitz Convent Controversy*, ed. Carol Rittner and J. K. Roth (New York, 1991).

[108] E. H. Flannery, "The Cross in Jewish-Christian Relations," *SIDIC* 24, no. 1 (1991): 5. Flannery had first narrated the incident, somewhat differently, in the introduction to his *The Anguish of the Jews* (New York, 1965), xi.

[109] Michael Hilton, "The Shadow of the Cross," *SIDIC* 24, no. 1 (1991): 2.

[110] *International Herald Tribune*, August 15–16, 1998; *Jewish Chronicle* August 21, 1998.

in particular had done so repeatedly—in such works as *White Crucifixion* (1938), *Descent from the Cross* (1941), and *The Crucified* (1944). His *Yellow Christ* (also known as *Crucifixion*), painted shortly after his arrival in New York, even served as the frontispiece for the *Menorah Journal* issue for October–December, 1943.[111]

Not only did Jewish artists develop an attraction to the use of the cross, so did such early twentieth-century Jewish writers as Sholem Asch, Lamed Shapiro, and Uri Zvi Greenberg, and, in recent decades, Elie Wiesel (*Night*) and Chaim Potok (*My Name is Asher Lev*).[112] In 1909 Asch and Shapiro each published stories with explicit Christian imagery in the same Yiddish periodical, *Dos naye lebn*. These stories, as Matthew Hoffman has recently observed, "represented a pioneering development in modern Yiddish literature" in their use of the figure of Jesus (Asch) and the sign of the cross (Shapiro) as their central images.[113] They may well have influenced the Galician-born Greenberg, who in 1922—shortly after witnessing the bloody pogroms in Poland and the Ukraine—published a Yiddish "concrete" poem in the form of a cross, which carried the provocative title: "Uri-Zvi Before the Cross/INRI." The latter four letters were printed in their original Latin form, representing the well-known acronym for "Jesus of Nazareth King of the Jews." In the poem Greenberg addressed "Brother Jesus" and drew his attention to the killing fields of Galicia, which had become a new Golgotha: "At your feet: A heap of cut-off Jewheads. Torn *talises* [prayer shawls]. Pierced parchments. Blood-stained white sheets. . . . Ancient Jewpain. Golgotha, brother, don't you see. . . . And in Rome they sing psalms in the churches."[114]

Another native of Galicia who developed a deep attachment to the cross and eventually made his way to Rome, serving as its chief rabbi before switching sides to sing psalms in its churches, was Israel Zoller, who was born in Brody in 1881 and grew up in Stanislav, later studying in Vienna and Florence. In 1939, as Israel Zolli, he was appointed chief rabbi of

[111] See Z. Amishai Maisels, "The Jewish Jesus," *JJA* 9 (1982): 84–104; Benjamin Harshav, "The Role of Language in Modern Art: On Texts and Subtexts in Chagall's Paintings," *MODERNISM/modernity* 1 (1994): 51–87; R. I. Cohen, "Entre errance et histoire: interpretations juives du mythe de Gottlieb à Kitaj," in *Le juif errant: un témoin du temps*, ed. J. Braillon-Philippe and L. Goldstenne (Paris, 2001), 51–71; Matthew Baigell, *Jewish Artists in New York: The Holocaust Years* (New Brunswick, N.J., 2002), 66–87.
[112] Michael Brown, "On Crucifying the Jews," *Judaism* 27 (1978): 476–88; Roskies, *Against the Apocalypse*, 266–74. On Wiesel, see also Naomi Seidman, "Elie Wiesel and the Scandal of Jewish Rage," *JSS*, n.s. 3 (1997): 11–16.
[113] Matthew Hoffman, "Us and the Cross: Russian-Jewish Intellectuals Take a Stand on the Crucifix Question," *JJS* 53 (2002): 354.
[114] See Harshav, "The Role of Language in Modern Art," 67–69, whose translation I follow. For a photograph of the poem itself, see ibid., 68.

Rome, after having served in the rabbinate at Trieste and as a professor at the University of Padua. In February of 1945 much of the world was shocked when Zolli and his wife converted to Christianity and the former rabbi took as his baptismal name Eugenio Maria, in homage to Pope Pius XII (the former Eugenio Pacelli).[115] In his 1954 autobiography Zolli fondly recalled the afternoons he spent as a schoolboy in Stanislav (where my own paternal ancestors then lived), studying with his friend Stanislaus in the latter's home, where on one of the white walls hung "a crucifix of plain wood, with the branch of an olive tree over it." The crucifix, rather than making the young Israel uncomfortable, had, he later recalled, quite the opposite effect.

> We boys never became boisterous or disorderly during our study or in the intervals. It seemed that in that white room, and in the presence of the cru- cifix, one could not help being serene, gentle, and good. Sometimes—I do not know why—I would raise my eyes to that crucifix and gaze for a long time at the figure hanging there. This contemplation, if I may call it that without exaggeration, was done not without a stirring of my spirit.[116]

Writing in the Warsaw Ghetto, some three years before Zolli's conver- sion, the historian Emmanuel Ringelblum, also a native of Galicia, described a group of young female Jewish partisans who managed to move between the Ghetto and the outside world, armed with false Aryan papers. "One of them," he remarked, "even wears a cross all the time, and feels its absence when she is in the ghetto."[117] *Israel Zolli*, his younger Galician contemporary Uri Zvi Greenberg, and the even younger female partisan described by Ringelblum, all born and raised as Jews in East- Central Europe, each represent the transgressive craving for the cross that was often, as we have seen, the flip-side of the dark desire to desecrate it.

---

[115] See the two articles by W. P. Sillanpoa and R. G. Weisbord, "The Baptized Rabbi of Rome: The Zolli Case," *Judaism* 38 (1989): 74–91; "The Zolli Conversion: Background and Motives," *Judaism* 38 (1989): 203–15.

[116] Eugenio Zolli, *Before the Dawn: Autobiographical Reflections* (New York, 1954), 24. Zolli also recalled that "this crucified one" awakened in him "a sense of great compassion." This recollection was later challenged by Sillanpoa and Weisbord ("The Zolli Conversion," 207) on the rather simplistic grounds that "an association between the figure of Christ and the quality of mercy was most unlikely for a Jew—even a young Jew—in that era [since] for almost two millenia Jews had been persecuted in Christ's name." They clearly ignored the examples of Asch, Shapiro, and Greenberg, as well as the artists Hirschenberg, Budko, and Chagall—all born in late nineteenth-century Europe.

[117] E. Ringelblum, *Diary and Notes from the Warsaw Ghetto* (in Hebrew), 2 vols. (Jerusalem, 1993–1994), 1:365. Contrast the sanitized version in *Notes from the Warsaw Ghetto: The Journal of Emmanual Ringelbaum*, ed. and trans. Jacob Sloan (New York, 1958), 273.

The perplexingly paradoxical identification with the cross on the part of even traditional Jews continued in the years after the Holocaust. The Lithuanian-born Louis Ginzberg, who was a professor at New York's Jewish Theological Seminary, was able in 1949 to cheerfully appropriate the cross as a symbol of Jewish suffering. In response to a comment by his physician, a southern (Christian) gentleman, that he would have to carry the cross (of his ailment) until nature took its course—a comment for which the former quickly apologized—Ginzberg replied: "We Jews dance with the cross—carrying it for thousands of years would have exhausted us completely."[118]

Ginzberg, like Chagall, may have enjoyed playfully appropriating the cross as a symbol of Jewish suffering, but actual crosses generally proved more problematic for most members of their generation. Arthur Miller, who was born in New York City in 1915, recalled that his maternal grandfather once instructed him "never to walk under a large lighted cross overhanging the sidewalk outside a Lenox Avenue church; if by accident I did, I must spit when I realized what I had done, in order to cleanse myself."[119] Expectoration as a form of protecting oneself from demons or to counteract magic is, of course, an ancient and widespread practice,[120] but the instructions given by Miller's grandfather also echo the responses of some medieval European Jews when forced to decide between conversion and death: Kalonymos of Bacharach "spat conspicuously upon an image of the Crucified One" before being killed, and his young female contemporary from Würzberg "was brought into their place of idolatry in order to be defiled [baptized], but she sanctified the name of God and spat upon the abomination." For medieval Jews and for many of their modern descendants, the cross, as we have seen, elicited not only fear but also disgust. But the abominated object, as we have also seen, could also hold a certain fascination—what Joseph Conrad, in his *Heart of Darkness*, called "the fascination of the abomination—you know, imagine the growing regrets, the longing to escape, the powerless disgust, the surrender, the hate." And the medieval Jew's heart of darkness sometimes prompted him to surrender to his hate and thrust a rod at the abomination.

---

[118] Quoted from a 1949 letter in Eli Ginzberg, *Keeper of the Law: A Personal Memoir* (Philadelphia, 1966), 267.

[119] Arthur Miller, *Timebends: A Life* (New York, 1987), 25. See also Harry Golden, 308, in *Autobiographies of American Jews*, ed. H. Ribalow (Philadelphia, 1965).

[120] See W. Crooke, "Saliva," 11:100–104, in James Hastings, ed., *Encyclopaedia of Religion and Ethics* (Edinburgh, 1920); Joshua Trachtenberg, *Jewish Magic and Superstition: A Study in Folk Religion* (New York, 1939), 107, 120–21, 159, 162, and the sources cited there, to which may be added Margaliot, *Sefer Hasidim*, 209, no. 235.

15. Daniel Mendoza (1763–1836), on the left, was a Sephardic Jew, who was English boxing champion between 1791 and 95. The print, which was drawn by C. R. Ryley and engraved by I. Grozer, depicts the third fight between Mendoza and Richard Humphreys, which took place on September 29, 1790. Humphreys had been victorious in the first bout (January 1788), but Mendoza won the second (May 1789) and third fights. This is one of twenty-one prints on the subject listed by Alfred Rubens, *Anglo-Jewish Portraits* (London, 1935). Eighteenth-century stipple engraving. Collection of the author.
Photo: Jordan Penkower.

7
Mild Men or Wild Men?

HISTORICAL REFLECTIONS ON
JEWS AND VIOLENCE

The Jews are the mildest of men, passionately hostile to violence.
That obstinate sweetness which they conserve in the midst of the
most atrocious persecution, that sense of justice and of reason
which they put up as their sole defense against a hostile, brutal,
and unjust society, is perhaps the best part of the message they
bring to us and the true mark of their greatness.

—JEAN-PAUL SARTRE, *Anti-Semite and Jew*

The image of the Jew as an easy mark, as one who backs off,
as one who allows himself to be pushed back, as a "patsy,"
is the image that must be changed. . . . Not only does that image
cause immediate harm to Jews but it is a self-perpetuating thing.
Because a Jew runs away and because he allows himself
to be stepped upon, he guarantees that another Jew in the future
will be attacked because of the image which he has perpetuated.

—MEIR KAHANE, *Never Again!*

NEW JEWS AND OLD JEWS

BOTH of these striking passages, the one written just after the Holocaust by a Parisian philosopher and the other written in the aftermath of Israel's Six Day War by a Brooklyn-born rabbi, react to a particular image of the Jew—one which was seen in a clearly positive light by the former and a decidedly negative one by the latter. Both Sartre and Kahane, each in his own way, were more concerned with politics than with history, and consequently gave little thought to where this image came from and how it came to be constructed. Sartre later admitted to having written *Anti-Semite and Jew* "without reading one Jewish book,"[1] and Kahane, who had read a good many, nonetheless oversimplified considerably when he asserted that "the tough, free, young *sabra* [native-born Israeli] is hardly a 'New Jew'; he is rather, the resurrection of the 'Old Jew.'"[2]

Was there indeed an "Old Jew" who would not run away from his enemies and was not averse to fighting back? If so, when and under what circumstances did he disappear? Was the Sartrian image of the mild Jew "passionately hostile to violence" shared by Jews and non-Jews alike? These are larger and more complicated questions than can be answered here, but I do not intend to be so cowardly as to dodge them entirely. The present chapter shall investigate how the submissively pacific image of the Jew which both Sartre and Kahane, in their different ways, have evoked came to be constructed, and how it has affected modern historical treatments of premodern Jewish violence.

FEAR AND TREMBLING

During the early 1840s the Scottish missionaries A. A. Bonar and R. M. McCheyne, whom we met previously, traveled to Palestine and continued as far as Poland in order to assess the potentials and pitfalls of Protestant conversion efforts. Of the Jews of Safed they wrote: "It was easy to read their deep anxiety in the very expression of their countenances: they were truly in the state foretold by Moses more than 3,000 years ago." The prooftext cited by the two Presbyterians was from the book of Deuteronomy (28:65–66): "The Lord shall give thee a trembling heart . . . and sorrow of mind: and thy life shall hang in doubt before thee; and thou shalt fear day and night, and shalt have none assurance of thy life."

When visiting a synagogue in Tarnopol (Ternopil, western Ukraine) some months later the two missionaries were also quite confident about

---

[1] See S. R. Suleiman, "The Jew in Sartre's *Reflexions sur la question juive*: An Exercise in Historical Reading," in *The Jew in the Text: Modernity and the Construction of Identity*, ed. Linda Nochlin and Tamar Garb (London, 1995), 216, quoting from Sartre's interview with Benny Lévy, "The Last Words of Jean-Paul Sartre," trans. Rachel Phillips Belash, *Dissent* (Fall, 1980): 418–19. For the opening quotation, see Jean-Paul Sartre, *Anti-Semite and Jew*, trans. G. J. Becker (New York, 1948), 117. The French original, under the title *Reflexions sur la question juive*, appeared two years earlier.

[2] Meir Kahane, *Never Again!: A Program for Survival* (Los Angeles, 1971), 140–42, 151. See also J. L. Dolgin, *Jewish Identity and the JDL* (Princeton, 1977), 78–79.

the message to be read on the countenances of the local Jews: "Our entrance caused considerable commotion to the worshippers," whose faces, they wrote, "assumed an aspect of terror . . . and they whispered anxiously to another." Explaining that the Jews' alarm was based on their fear that the two Christians "were officers of the Austrian government come to spy their doings," the authors piously added: "How truly these words [from Leviticus 26] have come to pass, 'I will send a faintness into their hearts in the land of their enemies; and the sound of a shaken leaf shall chase them; and they shall flee as fleeing from a sword; and they shall fall when none pursueth.' "3

When Bonar published his popular commentary on Leviticus some years later it is not surprising that he had the following to say about the book's twenty-sixth chapter: "The unwarlike, timid, feeble state of the Jews in every land fulfills verses 36, 37. . . . The Jews never can resist and never try to resist their foes: they suffer and complain and their cries spread over the earth."4 He had apparently forgotten something he had been told during his travels by a former Jew who had served as a missionary in Hamburg. After sending a circular to the local Jews, he reported, "many soon threatened to kill him."5

The verses from Leviticus and Deuteronomy cited by Bonar and McCheyne, together with others from the Old Testament, had been used for centuries by Christian authors to explain what they perceived to be, despite considerable evidence to the contrary, the innate timorousness of the Jews. In his popular *Historia orientalis*, written early in the thirteenth century, Jacques de Vitry sought to explain how the Jews had become "weak and unwarlike even as women [*quasi mulieres*]." After slaying their true brother Abel [Christ], he asserted, "they were made wanderers and fugitives over the earth, cursed like Cain, with a trembling head, that is, a quaking heart [*cor pavidum*], fearing both day and night, and not believing in their lives [*vite sue non credentes*]."6 Here the learned bishop of Acre cleverly conflated two biblical traditions, one reaching back to the book of Genesis, as interpreted by Saint Augustine, and the other rooted in the aforementioned verses from Leviticus and Deuteronomy.

---

3 Bonar and McCheyne, *Narrative of a Mission*, 365–66, 591.

4 A. A. Bonar, *A Commentary on Leviticus* (Reprint, London, 1972), 489. The first edition appeared in 1846 and a fourth in 1861.

5 Bonar and McCheyne, *Narrative of a Mission*, 668. See there also 660 on the report of another former Jew who had been a missionary in Amsterdam.

6 *Historia orientalis* (Douai, 1597), 82, quoted from I. M. Resnick, "Medieval Roots of the Myth of Jewish Male Menses," *HTR* 93 (2000): 259. The next several paragraphs draw upon Horowitz, "A Dangerous Encounter," 342–48.

In the twelfth book of his *Reply to Faustus the Manichean*, composed around 400 CE, Augustine, drawing upon the Old Latin version of the Bible, heavily dependent upon the Greek Septuagint rather than the Vulgate of his contemporary Saint Jerome, described Cain as "groaning and trembling [*gemens et tremens*] . . . on the earth" as part of his punishment for the murder of his brother.[7] Although Augustine was not the first of the church fathers to interpret Cain's punishment in this manner, he was the first to cast Cain's punishment in typological terms as foreshadowing Jewish life in the centuries after Christ's crucifixion: "Now behold," he wrote, "who cannot see, who cannot recognize how, throughout the world, wherever that people has been scattered, it wails in sorrow for its lost kingdom and trembles in fear of the innumerable Christian peoples."[8]

Later interpreters, beginning evidently with the Venerable Bede (d. ca. 735) in England, were to see Cain's "groaning and trembling" not only as his punishment, but as his distinctive sign, or mark. From Bede this interpretation spread, during the early middle ages, to such Continental authors as Rabanus Maurus (d. 856) in Germany and Remigius of Auxerre (d. ca. 908). Although some later medieval Christian commentators saw Cain's sign as a "trembling of the limbs" characteristic of a madman, Peter Comestor (d. 1179), in his highly influential *Historia scholastica*, described the sign as a "trembling of the head," and from there it seems to have come to Jacques de Vitry.[9]

In early fifteenth-century Spain the roving Dominican preacher Vincent Ferrer used the Catalan term *jueu* (Jew) in his sermons in the pejorative sense, as David Nirenberg has noted, of "a coward who refuses to take vengeance."[10] His younger contemporary Alfonso Tostado, who served as bishop of Avila in the years immediately before his death in 1455, posed the following question in his discussion of Leviticus 26: was the timorousness which Jews now possess beyond all other peoples a consequence of their continuous servitude, or of a curse inflicted by God

---

[7] The Vulgate, by contrast, rendered the Hebrew *n'a va-nad* (Gen. 4:14) as "vagus et profugus." See Ruth Mellinkoff, *The Mark of Cain* (Berkeley, 1981), 18, 40–41; D. K. Delaney, "The Sevenfold Vengeance of Cain: Genesis 4 in Early Jewish and Christian Interpretation," (Ph.D. diss., University of Virginia, 1996), 161–71.

[8] I follow the translation of Jeremy Cohen, *Living Letters of the Law: Ideas of the Jew in Medieval Christianity* (Berkeley, 1999), 28. For a slightly different rendering, see *Disputation and Dialogue: Readings in the Jewish Christian Encounter*, ed. Frank Talmage (New York, 1975), 28–32. For further literature on medieval exegesis of Cain's punishment, see Cohen, *Living Letters*, 28n7.

[9] Mellinkoff, *The Mark of Cain*, 46–50.

[10] Nirenberg, *Communities of Violence*, 35n59.

[*vel ex maledictione inflicta a Deo*]? His unequivocal response, antici-pated by Jacques de Vitry and later echoed by many Christian exegetes, was that a divine curse was indeed responsible for this Jewish character-istic. This, Tostado illustrated, as a medieval Spanish priest well might have, through a comparison of Jews and "Saracens" living under Christ-ian domination. The former, he claimed, were always fearing that their situation would become even worse.[11] In his exegetical comments on Deuteronomy 28 Tostado returned to the theme of Jewish timorousness. There he provided, however, an additional, more naturalistic explanation to this Jewish characteristic—namely that "even from their infancy they have learned to fear a Christian. For the Christians will persecute them, snatch from them, and strike them even in their childhood."[12]

Tostado's Bible commentaries were first published in 1596 as part of the thirteen-volume Venice edition of his *Opera omnia*. His remarks on Jewish tremulousness, which reflected those of other Spanish authors,[13] were quoted approvingly by the French Jesuit Jean de Lorin (d. 1634) and the English Hebraist Andrew Willet (d. 1621) in their respective commentaries on the book of Leviticus.[14] They also provide a literary con-text for the comments on Jewish timorousness that the Spanish exile Solomon ibn Verga, in his *Shevet Yehudah*, placed in the mouth of a medieval Spanish priest.

In the seventh chapter of that semifictional work, ibn Verga presented a wide-ranging, though largely imagined, dialogue between an enlight-ened Spanish king (Alfonso) and a learned priest (Tomás) on the practices and proclivities of the Jews. The dialogue is set in the wake of a public sermon preached by the local bishop in which the accusation had been made that Jews require Christian blood in order to celebrate the Passover holiday. The king himself was inclined to dismiss the claim as "absolutely removed from reason," but asked Tomás to provide him with substantive

[11] Alphonsi Tostati, *Commentaria in Leviticum* (Venice, 1596), 318d–19a.

[12] Tostati, *Commentaria in Deuteronium* (Venice, 1596), 153 a–b ("Et adhuc facit nimis nutritio a puero, quia a tenera etate timere discunt, cum Christiani eos adhucteneros perse-qui incipiant, diripere, et percutere").

[13] See Eleazar Gutwirth, "Gender, History, and the Judaeo-Christian Polemic," in *Contra Iudaeos: Ancient and Medieval Polemics between Christians and Jews*, ed. Ora Limor and G. G. Stroumsa (Tübingen, 1996), 265–66. Tostado should be added to the list of Spanish authors cited there.

[14] See Joannis Lorini, *Commentarii in Leviticum* (1619), 951d–54d. On Lorin, who con-cluded his career teaching in Rome, see Henri Fouqueray, S. J., *Histoire de la Compagnie de Jésus en France . . . 1528–1762* (Paris, 1925), 4:271. For Willet (1562–1621), a graduate of Christ's College (Cambridge), see his *Hexapla in Leviticum* (London, 1631), 704.

arguments to that effect, both in order to set his mind at rest, and in order to respond to popular demands that the Jews be punished.[15]

Among the various arguments placed by ibn Verga in the priest's mouth, one is particularly striking. It would be highly unlikely, asserted Tomás, that a Jew would have the courage to murder someone in his own locality for the purpose of using his blood, knowing that if he were caught, which was most likely, he would be chopped to pieces. "And what shall we say of their faintness of heart," he continued, "for if there be a hundred Jews on the street and a small Christian child approaches, saying 'let us attack the Jews,' all of them will flee."

Although scholars have tended to see this passage as reflecting the (rather pathetic) self-image of a late medieval Spanish Jew, my own inclination is to see it as a reflection of how a learned Spanish Jew saw himself reflected in the writings and teachings of the Christian tradition. This, I think, becomes especially clear in the continuation of the passage: "And if your judges lawfully sentence someone to death," said Tomás to the King, "all the Jews will flee [from the place of execution] for their nature does not tolerate seeing even their enemies being killed. And this is because God has cursed them, as it is written (Lev. 26:36), 'I will cast faintness into their hearts in the land of their enemies. The sound of a driven leaf shall put them to flight.'"[16]

Ibn Verga's priest here clearly alluded to the verse from the book of Leviticus quoted above. His "enigmatic work," as Yosef Yerushalmi has aptly called it,[17] was published no less than seventeen times, in various languages (including Yiddish and Latin), between the mid-sixteenth and early nineteenth century,[18] and one wonders how its thousands of readers, both Jewish and non-Jewish, responded to the priest's description of Jewish timorousness. Did it ring true, or did it seem outdated? Did they see it as reflecting the views of a Spanish priest or of a Jewish historian?

[15] Ibn Verga, *Shevet Yehudah*, 26. See the translation of most of this passage in Y. H. Yerushalmi, *The Lisbon Massacre of 1506 and the Royal Image in the* Shebet Yehudah (Cincinnati, 1976), 40.

[16] *Shevet Yehudah*, 28–29 (my translation). For the view that this passage reflects the self-image of late medieval Spanish Jewry, see, among others, Américo Castro, *The Spaniards: An Introduction to Their History*, trans. W. F. King and S. Margaretten (Berkeley, 1971), 577–78.

[17] Yerushalmi, *Lisbon Massacre*, 3.

[18] Yerushalmi, *Zakhor*, 68. See also the list of editions compiled by Moritz Steinschneider, *Die Geschichtsliteratur der Juden* (Frankfurt a. M., 1905), 78–79. On the Yiddish, see Michael Stanislawski, "The Yiddish *Shevet Yehudah*: A Study in the 'Ashkenization' of a Spanish-Jewish Classic," 134–59, in *Jewish History and Jewish Memory: Essays in Honor of Yosef Hayim Yerushalmi*, ed. Elisheva Carlebach, J. M. Efron, and D. N. Myers (Hannover and London, 1998).

Readers of the popular Latin translation by the Lutheran Orientalist George Gentius (a.k.a. Georg Gentze, 1618–1687), a project he undertook at the request of the Amsterdam rabbi Manasseh ben Israel, would have encountered therein at least one expression not quite suggested by the original Hebrew. Whereas ibn Verga's Tomás referred to *morekh levavam*, the Jews' alleged faintness of heart (alluding to Leviticus 26:36), Gentius's translation, which first appeared in 1651 and was twice republished within three decades, had him speaking of *effeminita Judaeorum socordia*,—the effeminate weak-mindedness of the Jews.[19] Moreover, in rendering the biblical verse which Tomás used as his prooftext Gentius did not follow the Vulgate, but rather, the late sixteenth-century Latin translation of the Old Testament and Apocrypha by Tremellius and Junius, which "acquired great fame among Protestants, particularly those of the Reformed Church."[20] Thus rather than the Vulgate's *dabo pavorem in cordibus eorum*, rendered loosely as "I shall put fear into their hearts," Gentius (and before him, Junius-Tremellius) had God vowing to the Jews that in the lands of their enemies he would introduce "softness" into their souls (*inducam mollitiem in animus illorum*).[21]

This translation, as the English bishop Simon Patrick pointed out late in the seventeenth century, had much to commend it on literal grounds,[22] but in early modern Europe it could also both reflect and confirm the widespread notion that Jewish men were less virile than others. A common meaning of *mollities* in medieval Latin was "homosexuality," which helps

---

[19] *Historia Judaica: Res Judaeorum*, trans. Georgio Gentio (Amsterdam, 1651), 25–26. Another edition with the same title appeared there in 1654, and a third, under the more accurate title *Tribus Judae* (but with the Hebrew title misspelled) was published in 1680–1681. See M. Wiener, *Das Buch Schevet Jehuda* (Hannover, 1856), xix–xxii, who also discusses some of the translation's inaccuracies. On the German-born and Dutch-educated Gentius, who had earlier translated *Hilkhot De'ot* from the code of Maimonides (Amsterdam, 1640), see A. L. Katchen, *Christian Hebraists and Dutch Rabbis* (Cambridge, Mass., 1984), esp. 247–69.

[20] See Basil Hall, "Biblical Scholarship: Editions and Commentaries," in *The Cambridge History of the Bible: III "The West from the Reformation to the Present Day"* (Cambridge, 1963), 71–73.

[21] Gentius must have been quoting from memory since he substituted the word *eorum* for *illorum*. The Junius-Tremellius translation was also followed by the German theologian Joannes Piscator in his 1615 Latin commentary on Leviticus.

[22] See Simon Patrick, *A Commentary upon the Third Book of Moses, Called Leviticus* (London, 1698), 556, who noted that "the Hebrew word we translate faintness signifies softness," and more recently B. A. Levine, *The JPS Torah Commentary: Leviticus* (Philadelphia, 1989), 190, who points out that the Hebrew *morekh* occurs only in this verse "and is probably derived from the root r-k-k, 'to be soft.'"

to explain how it came also to serve as a term for masturbation.[23] The priest's words in their popular Latin translation could thus suggest certain things about the alleged effeminacy of the Jews that were not quite present in the original Hebrew of *Shevet Yehudah*, and that Manasseh ben Israel, who was busy at the time with foreign matters,[24] may not have noticed. Someone as conversant as he with Iberian literature would probably not have been greatly surprised, nevertheless, to find Jewish cowardice linked with Jewish effeminacy. Cervantes (d. 1616) had a character in one of his dramas refer to the Jews disparagingly as *gente afeminada* and it has been noted that "the terms *cobarde* and *afeminado* are frequent epithets associated with the Jew in literary works of the Golden Age."[25] Salo Baron also drew attention to the "growingly accepted view" in late medieval and early modern Europe that Jews were "effeminate and cowardly."[26]

The effeminacy of the Jews was linked in Christian Europe not only with their alleged cowardliness but also with a rather grotesque physical symptom: the malady, or curse, of menstruation, which was said to characterize Jews of both genders. As Irvin Resnick has recently noted, this claim seems to have surfaced first in Jacques de Vitry's thirteenth-century *Historia orientalis*.[27] From there it spread widely. Early in the fourteenth century the Italian astrologer Cecco d'Ascoli wrote that "after the death of Christ all Jewish men, like women, suffer menstruation." Late in the fifteenth century the Jews of Tyrnau (Trnava, in western Slovakia), who were accused of ritual murder, were said to have explained that both Jewish men and women had found Christian blood an effective means of alleviating their menstrual cramps.[28] In 1648 the English scholar Thomas

---

[23] *Lexicon Latinitatis Medii Aevi* (Turnholt, 1975), 596. On "mollitia" or "mollities" as masturbation, see John Boswell, *Christianity, Social Tolerance, and Homosexuality* (Chicago, 1980), 107n55, 180n38, J. C. Brown, *Immodest Acts: The Life of a Lesbian Nun in Renaissance Italy* (New York, 1986), 17.

[24] Katchen, *Christian Hebraists*, 261. On Manasseh having entrusted the translation to Gentius, see also ibid., 152, 247.

[25] William Byron, *Cervantes: A Biography* (Garden City, 1978), 27; Edward Glaser, "Two Anti-Semitic Word Plays in the Guzmán de Alfarache," *MLN* 69 (1954), 345. See also Castro, *The Spaniards*, 580, 594, and the sources cited by Gutwirth, "Gender, History," 265–66.

[26] Baron, *SRH* 11, 154. See also James Shapiro, *Shakespeare and the Jews* (New York, 1996), 241.

[27] Resnick, "Medieval Roots of the Myth," 241–63. Note also I. G. Marcus, "Images of the Jews in the Exempla of Caesarius of Heisterbach," in *From Witness to Witchcraft: Jews and Judaism in Medieval Christian Thought*, ed. Jeremy Cohen (Wiesbaden, 1996), 250, and Elliott Horowitz, "Jews, Stereotypes of," in *Encyclopedia of Medieval Folklore*, 2 vols. (Santa Barbara, 2000), 1:554.

[28] Peter Biller, "Views of Jews from Paris around 1300: Christian or 'Scientific'?" *SCH* 29 (1992): 198–99; Trachtenberg, *Devil and the Jews*, 50, 148–49.

Calvert cited the claim of the thirteenth-century Dominican Thomas de Cantimpré that "Jews, men as well as females, are punished *curso menstruo sanguinis*, with a very frequent blood flux." Although Calvert later added, "I leave it to the learned to judge and determine by writers or travellers, whether this be true or no,"[29] some of his contemporaries were somewhat less agnostic.

Yosef Yerushalmi has noted that Juan de Quiñones de Benavente composed an entire treatise (never published) in the seventeenth century attempting to prove that Jewish men menstruate, a charge which he has seen as suggesting implicitly that "Jewish males . . . are, in effect, no longer men but women, and the crime of deicide has been punished by castration."[30] Other scholars, such as Sander Gilman, have linked the charge of male menstruation with the truncated (and thus ostensibly less virile) phallus of the circumcised Jew.[31] I would stress, however, that the link between cowardice and effeminacy in both the Latin and Iberian literary traditions may well have contributed to the popularity of this myth, which effectively conflated the "curse" of Jewish timorousness with the "curse" of female menstruation. The myth of Jewish male menstruation, once it emerged in European discourse, helped to frame the Jew's biblical "faint-heartedness" in terms of his alleged effeminacy.

If readers of *Shevet Yehudah* in Gentius's Latin translation would probably not have seen Tomás's words about "*effeminita Judaeorum socordia*" as reflecting the self-perception of the book's Hispano-Jewish author, what about other readers of the work? Yerushalmi has asserted that "some of the most original and daring views" expressed by ibn Verga "are purposely veiled by being embedded in fictitious dialogues,"[32] but he did not explicitly cite Tomás's comments on Jewish faintness of heart as one of these instances. Two earlier scholars, Isidore Loeb and Fritz (Yitzhak) Baer, however, implicitly regarded the priest as ibn Verga's own spokesman on this subject.[33] This seems to me simplistic, for although his

---

[29] T. Calvert, "A Large Diatriba of the Jews' Estate," prefacing his translation of *The Blessed Jew of Marocco; or, a Blackmoor Made White* (York, 1648), 19–20, 31. See Shapiro, *Shakespeare*, 37–38; and D. S. Katz, "Shylock's Gender: Jewish Male Menstruation in Early Modern England," *RES*, n.s. 50 (1999): 440–62.

[30] Yerushalmi, *From Spanish Court*, 128. See also ibid., 123, 126–33.

[31] See Sander Gilman, *Freud, Race, and Gender* (Princeton, 1993), 25, 38–39, and Daniel Boyarin, *Unheroic Conduct: The Rise of Heterosexuality and the Invention of the Jewish Man* (Berkeley, 1997), 210–11, and the sources cited there.

[32] Yerushalmi, *The Lisbon Massacre*, 4.

[33] I. Loeb, "Le folklore juif dans la chronique du Schebet Iehudah d'ibn Verga," *REJ* 24 (1892), 14n2; F. Baer, *Untersuchungen über Quellen und Komposition des Schebet Yehuda* (Berlin, 1923), 83.

words were written in Hebrew for a Jewish audience, they were placed in the mouth of a Catholic priest speaking to a king, and therefore reflect the manner in which Jews understood themselves to be perceived, rather than their own self-image, which may have been quite different. We should also bear in mind the observations of James Scott regarding the ubiquitous "dissembling of the weak in the face of power." As Scott has written, "The more menacing the power, the thicker the mask."[34]

"A NATION OF A MOST DEBASED AND WEAK SPIRIT"

Not long after ibn Verga composed his "enigmatic work" the no less enigmatic Jewish adventurer David Reubeni, who claimed to have a Jewish army at his disposal, arrived in Venice from Alexandria in 1523 and continued on to Rome, where he was received by Pope Clement VII, whom he sought to draw into an alliance against the Turks. In his "diary" (of which he may not have been the actual author), Reubeni contrasted the Jews of Palestine and Egypt, whom he regarded as fainthearted and unsuitable for battle, with those of Rome and Italy in general, where one could find strong and intrepid Jews who were ready for war and "whose hearts are like those of lions in every respect."[35]

One suspects, however, that the Italian Jews themselves were considerably less eager to advertise their "lion-hearted" character. This would appear to explain the "dissembling" we find a century later in Simone Luzzatto's *Discorso circa il stato de gl'hebrei*, written in the Venetian Ghetto. As part of Luzzatto's attempt to delineate the mercantile benefits offered by the Jews to the Venetian state, he took pains to categorically deny any interest on their part in possessing political power. Although the Jews of the various countries of the world, he claimed, were quite different from each other, one generalization could be made about them: They were "a nation of a most debased and weak spirit [*d'animo molto invilito e fiacco*], incapable under present circumstances of any political rule."[36] Whether or not the Jews were indeed capable of political rule, Luzzatto may have been consciously exaggerating when he described their spirit as

---

[34] Scott, *Domination*, 1–5.

[35] *Sippur David Reuveni*, ed. A. Z. Aescoly (Jerusalem, 1940), 43, and Cecil Roth, *The Jews in the Renaissance* (Philadelphia, 1959), 26.

[36] Simone Luzzatto, *Discorso circa il stato de gl' hebrei, et in particolar dimoranti nell'indita città di Venetia* (Venice, 1638), 37a. See the Hebrew translation by Dante Lattes in *Maamar 'al Yehudei Venezia*, ed. A. Z. Aescoly (Jerusalem, 1950), 106, (and the introductions by R. B. Bachi and M. A. Shulvass), as well as Benjamin Ravid, *Economics and Toleration in Seventeenth-Century Venice* (Jerusalem, 1978).

being "most debased and weak," although he probably expected his Christian readers to believe him.

One Christian reader who took the claim even further was Melchiore Palontrotti, who, as Benjamin Ravid has noted, "accused Luzzatto of artificially making a virtue out of necessity," since the Jew had no choice by nature but to be obedient. In his *Breve riposta*, published in 1641 in response to the *Discorso*, Palontrotti countered Luzzatto's claims about Jewish loyalty with the assertion that this ostensibly positive trait was actually rooted in "cowardice and fear, for they even are afraid when there is no [reason for] fear."[37] Palontrotti may have drawn this characterization from some of the medieval Christian authors, such as Alfonso Tostado, who had discussed the Jewish curse of incessant timorousness. But, somewhat ironically, he may also have taken it from ibn Verga's *Shevet Yehudah*, which he seems to have read in the original Hebrew.

Both Luzzatto and Palontrotti seem, however, each for his own reasons, to have been exaggerating the timidity of seventeenth-century Italian Jews. In late February of 1609 the Jews of Rome responded to a parody of a Jewish funeral performed, during Carnival, in the streets of their ghetto by flinging a variety of household objects down upon the participants in the mock-procession, causing a number of injuries. The police arrested 140 Jews.[38] Several years later, in 1621, a Catholic miller whose partner's horse, loaded with flour, had knocked over a Jew on the main street of the Roman ghetto testified: "I saw that a number of Jews . . . had hurled themselves upon my companion and they were punching him and kicking him and had even taken his whip and were beating him with it." According to one Christian witness, the Jew who had been knocked over "began to abuse us, calling us insolent cuckolds and using many injurious words." Another reported that "many Jews were passing up and down before the miller who was being beaten by the Jew, and as they passed they would punch him in the stomach . . . and after doing so they would laugh. Many cheered as though they had won a victory."[39] In 1645 the English traveler John Evelyn found himself attending, while in Rome, one of the obligatory conversionary sermons its Jews were required to attend. He was struck not only by the unconcealed "malice in their countenances" but by the spitting, humming, coughing, and movement which

---

[37] Ravid, *Economics and Toleration*, 4; Ravid, "Contra Judaeos in Seventeenth-Century Italy: Two Responses to the Discorso of Simone Luzzatto by Melchiore Palontrotti and Giulio Morosini," *AJS Review* 7–8 (1982–1983): 314.

[38] Boiteux, "Juifs dans le Carnaval," 757–58.

[39] Simona Feci, "The Death of a Miller: A Trial *contra hebreos* in Baroque Rome," *Jewish History* 7 (1993): 9–12. See also R. C. Davis, *The War of the Fists: Popular Culture and Public Violence in Late Renaissance Venice* (New York and Oxford, 1994), 213n90.

took place during the sermon, such that "it is almost impossible they should heare a word from the preacher."[40] It is not likely that he would have agreed with Simone Luzzatto's assessment that the Jews were "a nation of a most debased and weak spirit."

BRITISH EXEGETES AND TRAVELERS

Yet biblical commentators continued to link Jewish behavior in the present with scriptural prophecies in the past. Late in the seventeenth century Bishop Simon Patrick of Ely (1626–1707) saw the aforementioned verses in Leviticus as pointing to a degree of timorousness that would make life "always uneasie for the Jews," and a degree of cowardice "as should render them vile and despicable." He then continued in a more contemporary vein: "And so they are noted at this day to be mean spirited, and faint hearted: it being scarce ever heard, that a Jew listed himself for a Soldier; or ingaged in the defense of the Country where he lives."[41] Bishop Patrick, who was familiar with *Shevet Yehudah* (probably in its Latin translation) did not cite ibn Verga's work in connection with the verse in Leviticus, but did cite it repeatedly in his commentary on Deuteronomy. One particularly striking example occurs in his comments on 28:28 ("And the Lord shall smite thee with madness . . ."), which he illustrated with the information culled from *Shevet Yehuda* that "in some places of Germany" the Jews were possessed with such madness "that they cut one another's throats, to avoid the Oppression of their Enemies; and burnt themselves and their Neighbors in their Houses." Patrick added: "Such was their extream Rage and furious Revenge, on those Christians who pressed them to change their Religion."[42] He seems to have seen no inconsistency between acknowledging, on the one hand, the extremes of rage and revenge of which the Jews were capable when "pressed . . . to change their Religion," and on the other, of perpetuating the trope, in his commentary on Leviticus, of their being fainthearted and averse to matters military.

   This trope of Jewish passivity and lack of manliness had also featured prominently in seventeenth-century travel writing. George Sandys (1578–1644), a son of the archbishop of York who embarked upon an

---

[40] William Bray, ed., *Memoirs Illustrative of the Life and Writings of John Evelyn*, 2 vols. (London, 1818), 1:124; *The Diary of John Evelyn*, ed. A. Dobson (London, 1908), 83.

[41] Patrick, *A Commentary*, 557. Patrick was bishop of Chichester from 1689, and of Ely from 1691.

[42] Simon Patrick, *A Commentary on the Fifth Book of Moses, called Deuteronomy* (London, 1700), 498–99. For some other citations of *Shevet Yehudah*, see ibid., 496, 504, 506, 525, 534.

extensive voyage through Europe and the Levant in 1610 (after dropping out of Oxford), later wrote of the Jews he encountered: "Many of them have I seen abused, some of them beaten; yet never saw I [a] *Jew* with an angry countenance." And shortly afterward Henry Blount, an Oxford graduate who had traveled through the Levant during the 1630s, reflected in his enormously popular account of that voyage on why the Jews could never "ciment into a temporall Government of their owne." Among the reasons that he gave ("beside the many disadvantages of their *Religion*") was that "the *Jewish* complexion is so prodigiously *timide*, as cannot be capable of Armes; for this reason they are no where made Souldiers, nor slaves."[43]

Four decades later, another Oxford graduate, Lancelot Addison, who had served as chaplain to the British garrison in Tangier during the 1660s, wrote similarly of his experience among the Jews of Morocco. Even when bullied by the Moors, he reported, "they dare not move a finger, or wag a tongue in their own defense and vindication." Addison stressed, however, that the "stoical patience" with which they faced all injuries and insults "cannot be imputed to any Heroick Temper in this People, but rather to their customary suffering, being born and Educated in this kind of Slavery. By reason whereof, they were never acquainted with the Sentiments of an ingenuous and manly Usage." This lack of manliness, Addison asserted, also explained the Jewish aversion to all matters military: "The *Moor* permit not the *Jews* the possession of any warlike Weapons. . . . And herein they do not so much restrain, as gratifie their disposition, for they seem generally enclined to a great averseness to everything that is Military: being as destitute of true Courage, as good Nature."[44] The comments of all three Oxonians nonetheless clashed, as they probably recognized, with the words Shakespeare had placed in the mouth of Shylock: "And if you wrong us, shall we not revenge? If we are like you in the rest, we will resemble you in that."[45]

Nonetheless, the stereotype of Jewish timidity and estrangement from matters military continued to characterize the discourse of both scholars and travelers. The English writer Tobias Smollett, writing from Nice in 1764, reported hearing that two decades earlier, during the War of the

---

[43] G. Sandys, *A Relation of a Journey begun AD 1610* (London, 1621), 146. H[enry] B[lount], *A Voyage into the Levant* (2nd ed., London, 1636), 123. This passage was quoted by Shapiro, *Shakespeare*, 35, 176, and before that by D. S. Katz, *Philo-Semitism and the Readmission of the Jews to England: 1603–1655* (Oxford, 1982), 168.

[44] L. Addison, *The Present State of the Jews* (2nd ed. London, 1676), 8–9. On this passage, and some reactions to it, see also Elliott Horowitz, "'A Different Mode of Civility': Lancelot Addison on the Jews of Barbary," *SCH* 29 (1992): 316–17.

[45] W. Shakespeare, *The Merchant of Venice*, act 3, scene 1.

Austrian Succession, a large number of circumcised bodies had been found among the Spanish troops who had recently attacked nearby Piedmontese battalions. Although the locals had concluded that "a great many Jews engage in the service of his Catholic majesty," Smollett's opinion was that they must be Moors, for, as he wrote, "the Jews are the least of any people that I know addicted to a miltary life."[46]

By the end of the eighteenth century a Jew, Daniel Mendoza, had been England's boxing champion between 1791 and 1795. And Mendoza was hardly the only prominent Jewish pugilist of his generation. "From the 1760s through the 1820s," as Todd Endelman has observed, "at least thirty Jews were active enough in the ring to merit inclusion in the standard accounts of boxing compiled in the nineteenth century." Late in the first decade of that century the authors of the *New Newgate Calendar* complained that the Jews had lately become "the bullies of the people of London."[47]

The newly dominant presence of Jews in the world of British boxing was very much in the mind of the traveler Charles Macfarlane when he visited Istanbul in 1828 and encountered the Jews of the Ottoman Empire, who were allegedly known for their timidity and cowardliness. "Throughout the Ottoman dominions," he wrote, "their pusillanimity is so excessive, that they will flee before the uplifted hand of a child. Yet in England the Jews become bold and expert pugilists, and are as ready to resent an insult as any other of His Majesty's liege subjects."[48] Several years later Julia Pardoe, also writing from Istanbul, was similarly struck by the timidity of Ottoman Jews, and their alleged unwillingness to revenge themselves even upon "puny" enemies:

> There is a subdued and spiritless expression about the Eastern Jew, of which the comparatively tolerant European can picture to himself no possible idea until he has looked upon it. . . . It is impossible to express the contemptuous hatred in which the Osmanlis hold the Jewish people; and the veriest Turkish

---

[46] T. Smollett, *Travels through France and Italy*, ed. Frank Felsenstein (Oxford, 1979), 118–19.

[47] Todd Endelman, *The Jews of Georgian England, 1714–1830* (Philadelphia, 1979), 219–21; S. A. Riess, "A Fighting Chance: The Jewish-American Boxing Experience, 1890–1940," *AJH* 74 (1984–1985), 223–24. The next several paragraphs draw upon Horowitz, "They Fought Because They Were Fighters."

[48] Macfarlane, who clearly did not share the view that pugilism was a "disgraceful practice," saw this alleged difference between English and Ottoman Jews as "striking proof of the effects of oppression in one country, and of liberty, and of the protection of equal laws, in the other." See Charles Macfarlane, *Constantinople in 1828*, (London, 1828), 1:115–16, quoted also by Bernard Lewis, *The Jews of Islam* (Princeton, 1984), 164.

urchin who may encounter one of the fallen nation in his path, has his meed of insult to add to the degradation of the outcast and wandering race of Israel. Nor dare the oppressed party revenge himself even upon this puny enemy, whom his very name suffices to raise up against him.[49]

Early in the twentieth century Elizabeth Butler commented similarly on the Jews of Jerusalem, the male variety of which—"extraordinary figures in long coats and round hats"—appeared "white and unhealthy, many of them red-eyed and all more or less bent, even the youths." In her view, "No greater contrast could be seen than between those poor creatures and the Arabs who jostle them in the alleys, and who are such upstanding athletic men, with clear brown skins, clean-cut features, and heads turbaned majestically. They stride along with a spring in every step."[50]

THE PERILS OF MISSIONIZING

Yet, as other European visitors to Jerusalem realized, those pallid and unhealthy "poor creatures" could, on occasion, act quite brazenly, especially when they felt that their religion was threatened. While Margaret Thomas visited the city circa 1890, a Jewish woman died in the hospital operated by the London Society for Promoting Christianity Amongst the Jews. "The Jews," she reported, "refused to bury her as she died in a Christian house, and the English applied to their consul to know how to act." The English consul approached the city's Turkish governor, who made it clear that "if the Jews did not perform this office, the Turks would." "Accordingly he sent a stretcher and four bearers, together with a number of soldiers, and they carried the body to a waste piece of land on the Jericho road . . . dug a grave and buried it. But the Jews assembled in their thousands and stoned the soldiers, who drove them back with whips." Thomas, who witnessed the scene, added, "Altogether it was a lively scene from where we saw it, and many people were hurt, for stones are very handy in Jerusalem."[51]

Earlier in the century, following the arrival of the Jewish-born Michael Solomon Alexander (né Pollack) as Jerusalem's first Anglican bishop, tensions between Jews, Anglican missionaries, and potential converts from

[49] Miss (Julia) Pardoe, *The City of the Sultan* (London, 1837), 2:361f, quoted by Lewis, *Jews of Islam*, 165.

[50] E. Butler, *Letters from the Holy Land* (London, 1903), 17. On modern travelers and the Jews see now Elliott Horowitz, "As Others See Jews," in *Modern Judaism: An Oxford Guide*, ed. Nicholas de Lange and Miri Freud-Kandel (Oxford, 2005): 415–25.

[51] M. Thomas, *Two Years in Palestine and Syria* (London, 1900), 37–38. See also A. A. Boddy, *Days in Galilee and Scenes in Judaea* (London, 1900), 259.

Judaism began to erupt into violence. In October 1842 three European-born Jews who had expressed interest in conversion were forced to seek shelter, fearing "personal violence in consequence of having declared their belief in Christianity."[52] In addition, the British artist William Bartlett reported that, shortly after his return to Jerusalem in 1853, a clergyman connected with the Anglican mission "in the exercise of a zeal certainly more fervent than prudent . . . had repaired to the Jewish quarter, to preach the Gospel in the open street." Shortly after he began to speak "certain of the Rabbis . . . instigated their followers to drive him from the spot with a storm of stones and dead cats." Bartlett's sober judgment of the missionary's "zealous" action is quite striking: "However disgraceful this violence, it was surely not a little imprudent thus to arouse the fanaticism of the Jews."[53]

The Italian engineer Ermete Pierotti, who spent eight years in Palestine during the mid-nineteenth century, noted that the Protestants of Jerusalem "call the Greeks and the Latins heretics, idolaters, heathen; and they stir up still worse feelings by sermons in which they ridicule their services, their processions, their worship of the Virgin and the Saints." Pierotti offered a similar observation about the city's Jews, who "do not show more moderation when speaking of their oppressors . . . and revenge their injuries when they get a chance."[54] His remarks, together with those of Bartlett and Thomas, confirm that the stereotype of Jewish timidity and timorousness could be undermined and even shattered in certain situations, particularly those in which the honor of the Jewish religion was at stake.

This was true not only in the holy city of Jerusalem, but also in the more profane city (and from 1898, borough) of Brooklyn. Joseph Hoffman Cohn, whose father had converted to Christianity in Edinburgh in 1892 and two years later opened "the first Jewish mission in the history of Brooklyn," wrote of the latter's travails: "On a Saturday afternoon, when he was going home from one of his gospel services in Brownsville, a bunch of Jewish lads chased after him and threw stones. . . . One stone hit him in the cheek . . . and caused the flesh to break and the blood to run."[55]

---

[52] Martin Gilbert, *Jerusalem: Rebirth of a City* (London, 1985), 34–35.

[53] W. H. Bartlett, *Jerusalem Revisited* (London, 1855), 27. The event described by Bartlett may be identical with the one similarly described by Finn in the same year, which took place, not coincidentally, on the day of Purim. See Arnold Blumberg, *The View from Jerusalem, 1849–1858: The Consular Diary of James and Elizabeth Ann Finn* (Rutherford, N.J., 1980), 125.

[54] Ermete Pierotti, *Customs and Traditions of Palestine*, trans. T. G. Bonney (Cambridge and London, 1864), 280.

[55] J. Hoffman Cohn, *I Have Fought a Good Fight* (New York, 1953), 219.

The younger Hoffman Cohn had his share of altercations as a youth. Once during his high school years he was missionizing in Brooklyn's Williamsburgh section, where he would sometimes ascend five or six flights of stairs in order to distribute circulars: "By the time I reached the top floor of a building, the tenants in the lower floors had absorbed the contents of the circulars I had given them. . . . Hot soup was poured down on my head from above; pots and pans were thrown at me from open doors behind which my benefactors were lying in wait for me. Some tried to get hold of me and beat me."[56] What these Jews were doing in late nineteenth-century Brooklyn was not fundamentally different from what their co-religionists were doing in Jerusalem—throwing stones and dead cats at Christians who had come to missionize in the Jewish Quarter, or stoning Turkish soldiers safeguarding the funeral of a co-religionist who had died in a hospital operated by missionaries. These acts of reckless resistance in both Brooklyn and Jerusalem were in many ways a continuation of the combative and defiant stance taken by medieval Jews in Northern Europe toward the symbols and representatives of Christianity. When their religion was on the line, and not only in situations of potential martyrdom, mild Jews could become wild Jews—urinating provocatively on the cross in medieval Europe or attacking Christian missionaries with such weapons of the weak as dead cats and hot soup in the nineteenth century.

JEWISH FIGHTERS

During the early decades of the twentieth century such Jewish boxers as Benny Leonard (né Leiner) and Barney Ross (né Rasofsky), both of whom were born on New York's Lower East Side and raised in observant families, became heroes for many young Jews. Leonard's impact was wonderfully captured by Budd Schulberg in an essay written more than half a century after the great lightweight's retirement as champion in 1925 (when Schulberg was eleven): "To see him climb in the ring sporting the six-pointed Jewish star on his fighting trunks was to anticipate sweet revenge for all the bloody noses, split lips, and mocking laughter at pale little Jewish boys who had run the neighborhood gauntlet."[57]

During the late 1920s and early 1930s Jewish champions dominated world boxing in nearly all categories except "heavyweight," admittedly a

---

[56] Ibid., 42.

[57] Schulberg, "The Great Benny Leonard," *Ring Magazine* (May 1980): 32–37, quoted by Peter Levine, *From Ellis Island to Ebbets Field: Sport and the American Jewish Experience* (New York, 1993), 155.

major exception.[58] Perhaps the most colorful Jewish fighter of the 1930s was "Slapsie Maxie" Rosenbloom (1904–1976), who won the light heavyweight crown in 1930 against a fellow Jew in his native New York City and lost it, also to a co-religionist, in that same city four years later. Rosenbloom, who was known as "Playboy of the Ring" on account of his active social life, admitted that he "always hated to hit hard," preferring the open glove style of attack, which earned him the sobriquet "Slapsie Maxie"—conferred by none other than Damon Runyan.[59]

The lasting impact of these great Jewish pugilists on the hearts and minds of American Jews is also poignantly reflected in Philip Roth's memoir of his father, who would take him as a boy to the Thursday night fights at Newark's Laurel Garden, where the elder Roth had once seen Barney Ross in action. On a visit to his dying father in 1989 Roth brought along a copy of *The Jewish Boxers' Hall of Fame* which he had found while browsing in a Judaica store on upper Broadway. After reminiscing about such great fighters as Abe Attell, Leonard, and Ross, Herman Roth mentioned the name of "Slapsie Maxie" Rosenbloom. "Do you know," asked his son, "that Slapsie Maxie fought another Jew for the light heavyweight title?" Nearly sixty years after the event (which took place on October 22, 1930) Herman had little trouble remembering that this was Abie Bain, whom Rosenbloom knocked out in the eleventh round. "They were all bums," the elder Roth added.

> You know how it was: these kids grew up, they had a tough life, the slums, no money, and they always had an adversary. The Christian religion was an adversary. They fought two battles. They fought because they were fighters, and they fought because they were Jews. They'd put two guys in the ring, an Italian and a Jew, an Irishman and a Jew, and they fought like they meant it, they fought to hurt. There was always a certain amount of hatred in it.[60]

A year earlier in his (slightly) fictionalized autobiography, *The Facts*, Philip Roth had discussed his own adolescent fascination, during the 1940s, with the heritage of Jewish boxing.

---

[58] For five years (1926–1931) the junior welterweight title was held consecutively by two Jews: Mushy Callahan (born Vincent Morris Schneer) and Jackie ("Kid") Berg (born Judah Bergman), and for most of the five years between 1929 and 1934 the welterweight crown was held by either Jackie Fields or Barney Ross. See Allen Bodner, *When Boxing Was a Jewish Sport* (Westport, Conn., 1997), app. B.

[59] Riess, "A Fighting Chance," 243; Robert Slater, *Great Jews in Sports* (rev. ed., New York, 1992), 206–8; Joseph Siegman, *Jewish Sports Legends*, (3rd ed., Washington, D.C., 2000), 62–64.

[60] Philip Roth, *Patrimony: A True Story* (New York, 1991), 201–2.

From my father and his friends I heard about the prowess of Benny Leonard, Barney Ross, Max Baer, and the clownishly nick-named Slapsie Maxie Rosenbloom. And yet Jewish boxers . . . remained, like boxing itself, "sport" in the bizarre sense, a strange deviation from the norm and interesting largely for that reason: in the world whose values first formed me, unrestrained physical aggression was considered contemptible everywhere else. I could no more smash a nose with a fist than fire a pistol into someone's heart. And what imposed this restraint, if not on Slapsie Maxie Rosenbloom, then on me, was my being Jewish.

Being Jewish, for the adolescent Philip Roth in the aftermath of the Holocaust, was still associated (perhaps above all else) with contempt for "unrestrained physical aggression." And yet, perhaps for that very reason, boxing held a certain transgressive fascination. As an adolescent Roth "could recite the names and weights of all the champions and contenders, and even subscribed briefly to *Ring*, Nat Fleischer's colorful boxing magazine." Like the Jewish newspapers eulogizing Benny Leonard upon his retirement from the ring in 1925, Roth too resorted to the metaphor of Einstein in order to describe Jewish pugilistic prowess. "In my scheme of things," he later recalled, "Slapsie Maxie Rosenbloom was a far more miraculous phenomenon by far than Dr. Albert Einstein."[61]

Roth was later to exchange rhetorical blows with another Jewish "heavyweight," the popular novelist Leon Uris, after the publication of the latter's bestselling *Exodus* and its conversion into a blockbuster film. Uris had given an interview to the *New York Post* in which he roundly condemned "a whole school of Jewish American writers, who spend their time damning their fathers, hating their mothers, wringing their hands and wondering why they were born." Their work (which clearly included Roth's *Goodbye Columbus*), said Uris, "is obnoxious and makes me sick to my stomach." He wrote *Exodus*, he candidly explained, because he "was just sick of apologizing—or feeling that it was necessary to apologize." And he no less candidly revealed what he had learned while researching the book: "That we Jews are not in truth what we have been portrayed to be. In truth we have been fighters."[62] Roth riposted by ripping into Uris with a rhetorical uppercut: "So bald, stupid, and uninformed is the statement that it is not even worth disputing," he wrote. By setting out his new image of the fighting Jew, Roth argued, Uris was merely "swapping one simplification for the other."[63]

---

[61] Roth, *The Facts* (New York, 1988), 28.
[62] Quoted by Philip Roth in his 1961 essay "Some New Jewish Stereotypes," reprinted in Roth, *Reading Myself and Others* (London, 1975), 138. I thank Steven Whitfield for bringing this essay to my attention.
[63] Ibid.

FROM FREUD TO ORWELL

And indeed he was. But the oversimplification Uris (and later Kahane) sought to overturn had powerful roots not only in Christian discourse but in modern Jewish writing. Sigmund Freud, in one of the most famous passages in his *Interpretation of Dreams*, recalled hearing from his father Jakob about the latter's humiliation, as a young man in Moravia, while walking one Saturday, sporting a new fur cap on his head. He was accosted by "a Christian" who "with a single blow" knocked his cap off into the mud and shouted, "Jew! Get off the pavement." When young Sigmund asked his father how he had reacted, Jakob responded quietly: "I went into the roadway and picked up my cap." Freud later recalled contrasting his father at that moment with Hamilcar Barca, Hannibal's father, who "made his boy swear before the household altar to take vengeance on the Romans." From that point on, he acknowledged, "Hannibal had had a place in my phantasies"[64]—a place not all that different, I might add, from that occupied several decades later by Benny Leonard in the fantasies of "pale little Jewish boys" like Budd Schulberg, who had endured "bloody noses, split lips, and mocking laughter" while running the gauntlets of America's toughest neighborhoods.

During the 1930s, however, as the threat of Nazi terror began to loom large over the European continent, the "unheroic conduct" represented by Freud's story of his father's timidity increasingly gave way to the sorts of responses later celebrated by Uris and Kahane. In his celebrated *Berlin Diary*, the English writer Christopher Isherwood described a scene that had occurred one evening along the Kleiststrasse, where he saw a crowd gathered around two young women seated in a car and two young Jews standing nearby on the pavement, "engaged in a violent argument with a large blond man who was obviously drunk." What had led to this?

> The Jews, it seemed, had been driving slowly along the street, on the look-out for a pick-up, and had offered these girls a ride. The two girls had accepted and got into the car. At this moment, however, the blond man had intervened. He was a Nazi, he told us, and as such felt it his mission to defend the honor of all German women. . . . The Jews didn't seem in the least intimidated; they told the Nazi energetically to mind his own business. Meanwhile, the girls . . . slipped out of the car and ran off down the street. The Nazi then tried to drag one of the Jews with him to find a policeman,

[64] Sigmund Freud, *The Interpretation of Dreams* trans. A. A. Brill, (New York, 1950), 98–99. On various treatments of this story and its implications, see H. J. Kieval, "Imagining 'Masculinity' in the Jewish Fin de Siècle," in *SCJ* 16 (2000) (*Jews and Gender: The Challenge to Hierarchy*, ed. Jonathan Frankel): 148–50.

and the Jew whose arm he had seized gave him an uppercut which laid him sprawling on his back. Before the Nazi could get to his feet, both young men had jumped into their car and driven away.[65]

The audacious conduct of the two Berlin Jews after being boisterously threatened by a blond Nazi, whom one of them sent sprawling with an uppercut, may also be seen against the background of the pugilistic prowess to which Schulberg later composed his proud paean. In 1935, the year in which the Nuremberg Laws were instituted and "Slapsie Maxie" Rosenbloom ceded his title to a fellow Jew (Bob Olin), the English welterweight H. P. Hollander stressed the wider significance of Jewish pugilistic prowess, asserting that "once he could get into the ring, the Jew could show the world that he could fight—and fight with brain and with strength and with courage. No one could deny him that he was a man amongst men."[66]

The need to make such an assertion in interwar England is evident from such works as *The Jew at Bay*, published there in 1933, whose author (hiding pusillanimously behind the pseudonym H. S. Ashton) had claimed that "it does, in truth, seem that the Jews lack that glorious spirit which will urge the majority of mankind to stand up in defence of their dignity and fight back." The Jew, Ashton asserted, is "long-suffering and resentful . . . but he does not carry the fight into the enemy's territory . . . He inevitably, as history has shown us, gains his end by pacific propaganda, and he eschews physical combat."[67] Ashton, if he was still alive in 1938, was probably greatly surprised at the response of the Labor MP Emanuel (later Lord) Shinwell, who had been born in 1884 in London's East End, when he was interrupted while addressing Parliament on foreign affairs by a fellow MP (Commander Bower) who told him to "go back to Poland." Although Bower was reputed to have been a former heavyweight boxing champion of the Royal Navy, Shinwell, who had boxed in his youth, approached his colleague and "struck him on the side of his jaw."[68] As a young man the future Lord Shinwell had probably followed the distinguished pugilistic career of Ted ("Kid") Lewis (born Gershon Mendeloff), who became England's youngest champion (as a featherweight) in 1913, and had been world welterweight champion in 1915–1916 and 1917–1919.[69]

---

[65] C. Isherwood, *Goodbye to Berlin: A Berlin Diary* (London, 1939), 294.

[66] Quoted from the *Detroit Jewish Chronicle* in Levine, *Ellis Island*, 164.

[67] Ashton, *The Jew at Bay* (London, 1933), 69.

[68] Michael Berkowitz, *The Jewish Self-Image: American and British Perspectives, 1881–1939* (London, 2000), 127–29.

[69] Lewis fought in six different weight divisions (winning 155 fights, 65 by knockout) during his impressive twenty-year career, which ended in 1929; Siegman, *Jewish Sports Legends*, 47, 58–59; Bodner, *When Boxing Was a Jewish Sport*, App. A, B, F.

Eric Blair, who was at Eton when Lewis won his world-championship bouts, may not have followed them with the same enthusiasm as had his "down and out" Jewish contemporaries in London's East End. Yet by the time he was working as a journalist under the name George Orwell he certainly had some knowledge of Jewish pugilistic prowess in early twentieth-century England, and perhaps even of the earlier career of Daniel Mendoza. Nonetheless he insisted that Jews, or rather Jewish males, could not inflict violence with the same abandon as other men. In 1945 Orwell witnessed a Jewish interrogator at an American camp for captured Germans kicking an SS general while shouting "Get up, you swine." Describing the soldier's behavior later for the *Tribune*, he wrote: "I concluded that he wasn't really enjoying it, and that he was merely— like the man in a brothel, or a boy smoking his first cigar, or a tourist traipsing around a picture gallery—telling himself that he was enjoying it."[70] A Jew, thought Orwell, could no more enjoy kicking an SS general than a boy could really enjoy a cigar. Both could only pretend (unconvincingly) to be real men.

FEMINIZED JEWS AND THE MODERN IMAGINATION

While Orwell was witnessing the Jew's interrogation of the German general, Jean-Paul Sartre was writing his *Reflexions sur la question juive* (1946), which included, as noted above, his description of the Jews as "the mildest of men, passionately hostile to violence." Sartre's reflections on the "Jewish question," and in particular his essentialist (and some might say racist) remarks on the Jewish character, have elicited various responses in the half-century since they were published, some implicit and some overt, some mild and some passionate.[71] The American critic Harold Rosenberg, for example, noted upon the book's appearance in English that "Sartre has cut the Jews off from their past," and alleged that "Sartre has consciously permitted himself to accept the anti-Semite's stereotype of the Jew. His disagreement with anti-Semitism reduces itself

---

[70] Orwell, "Revenge is Sour," 3–6, in *The Collected Essays, Journalism, and Letters of George Orwell, 4: In Front of Your Nose*, quoted by John Sack, *An Eye for an Eye: The Untold Story of Jewish Revenge Against the Germans* (2nd ed., New York, 1995), 190.

[71] On various reactions to Sartre's work, including her own, see Suleiman, "The Jew in Sartre's *Reflexions sur la question juive*," 201–18. See also Menachem Brinker, "Sartre on the Jewish Question: Thirty Years Later," *The Jerusalem Quarterly* 10 (Winter 1979): 117–32.

to arguing that these Jewish traits . . . are not so bad."[72] More recently Elaine Marks has argued that "Sartre is transformed in the third part of his essay into the antisemite against whom he rails in the first part."[73]

Sartre's essay, which sought to combat European anti-Semitism, seems, rather ironically, to have perpetuated a number of its stereotypes, including those of the Jew's "obstinate sweetness" and passionate hostility to violence, stereotypes which may arguably be seen as the modern equivalent of the Jew's alleged effeminacy. Late in the eighteenth century, as John Efron has noted, Abbé Gregoire could remark that Jewish men "have almost all red beards, which is the usual mark of an effeminate temperament," and early in the nineteenth, as Sander Gilman has shown, the pioneering anthologist of Jewish humor, L. M. Büschenthal, found a fundamental similarity between Jews and women in the nexus between weakness and wit. "Jews, when oppressed," he asserted, "can attack only verbally. In that they are like women, whose lack of strength is compensated for by their wit."[74] This line of thinking later found expression, as many scholars have recently noted, in Otto Weininger's immensely popular *Geschlecht und Charakter* (1903), which went through six German editions before it was published in English (as *Sex and Character*) in 1906. Weininger, a former Viennese Jew who had converted to Protestantism, saw the Jew basically as a male with a female sensibility. "The homology of Jew and woman becomes closer the further examination goes," he claimed, asserting also that his age was "not only the most Jewish but the most feminine."[75] As John Hoberman has aptly noted, "by the time Weininger absorbed it, this intuitive sense of the Jew's deficient masculinity had been germinating for centuries, dating from the Middle Ages."[76]

---

[72] See Harold Rosenberg, "Sartre's Jewish Morality Play," in Rosenberg, *Discovering the Present: Three Decades in Art, Culture, and Politics* (Chicago, 1973), 270–87. The quoted passages appear on 276, 281–82.

[73] Elaine Marks in *The French Review* 45 (1972): 784, quoted (with approval) by Suleiman, "The Jew in Sartre's *Reflexions sur la question juive*," 201, 208.

[74] J. M. Efron, *Defenders of the Race: Jewish Doctors and Race Science in Fin-de-Siècle Europe* (New Haven and London, 1994), 182n11; Sander Gilman, *Difference and Pathology: Stereotypes of Sexuality, Race, and Madness* (Ithaca, 1985), 180–81, on the basis of L. M. Büschenthal, *Sammlung Witziger Einfalle von Juden . . .* (1812).

[75] On Weininger's feminization of the Jew, see George Mosse, *Nationalism and Sexuality: Respectability and Abnormal Sexuality in Modern Europe* (New York, 1985), 145; Bram Dijkstra, *Evil Sisters: The Threat of Female Sexuality and the Cult of Manhood* (New York, 1996), 401–2, and especially the essays in N. A. Harrowitz and Barabara Hyams, eds., *Jews and Gender: Responses to Otto Weininger* (Philadelphia, 1995).

[76] John Hoberman, "Weininger and the Critique of Jewish Maculinity," in *Jews and Gender*, 143.

The feminized view of the Jewish male was also internalized, as Gilman has shown, by such figures as the Viennese rabbi and scholar Adolf Jellinek, who wrote in 1869: "In the examination of the various races it is clear that some are more masculine, others more feminine. Among the latter the Jews belong." Jellinek added that "a juxtaposition of the Jew and the woman will persuade the reader of the truth of the ethnographic thesis."[77] Jellinek would appear to have been recasting into nineteenth-century terms the traditional dichotomy between Jacob and Esau in Jewish self-perception, a dichotomy in which Esau's association with his diabolical descendant Amalek often lurks beneath the surface.

The dichotomy between the two biblical brothers was cast into explicitly gendered terms by Jules Michelet, nineteenth-century France's foremost historian, and an author who probably had more direct influence on Sartre than any of those we have yet mentioned. In a study on the Bible published in 1864 Michelet asserted that its God always preferred "the weak over the strong," and thus, over "the valiant Ishmael and the strong Esau" preferred Jacob, "delicate and sweet ["fin et doux"] like a woman."[78] Michelet had also expressed radical doubt concerning the massacres alleged by the Bible to have been perpetrated by the Hebrews upon the tribes of Canaan, for "their numerous servitudes rendered them far removed . . . from the warrior's life of the Arabs and their glorification of carnage." Although he made a point of stating for the record "j'aime les juifs,"[79] this was certainly a backhanded compliment, as was the later observation by the great French Orientalist Ernest Renan that the Jews "are full of pity for the poor fools who pass their life cutting each other into pieces, instead of enjoying the pleasures of a peaceful life as they do."[80]

The Sartrian perception of the feminized Jew incapable of violence had important literary antecedents not only on the Continent, but in Britain as well, as the passages we have cited from biblical commentaries and travel accounts clearly indicate.[81] Charles Dickens, as Murray Baumgarten

---

[77] See Gilman, *Freud, Race*, 42–43, quoting from Jellinek's *Der jüdische Stamm* (Vienna, 1869), 89–90. For another instance of Jewish internalization of the feminized image of the Jew, see Gilman, *Difference and Pathology*, 119.

[78] See J. Michelet, *La Bible de l'humanité* (Paris, 1864), 374, cited and discussed (but mistranslated) by Shmuel Almog, "The Racial Motif in Renan's Attitude to Jews and Judaism," in Almog, ed., *Antisemitism Through the Ages*, trans. N. H. Reissner (Oxford, 1988), 272.

[79] Michelet, *La Bible*, 381–82. For the latter quotation, see Gabriel Monod, "Michelet et les juifs," *REJ* 53 (1907), xix.

[80] Renan, *History*, 3:354. The original French edition appeared between 1887 and 1893.

[81] Another biblical commentator, the Aberdeen minister Alexander Davidson, asserted that many of the Jews "who come into contact with Christians are mean and servile earthworms, who will do anything for wordly gain." See his *Lectures, Expository and Practical, on the Book of Esther* (Edinburgh, 1859), 316.

has recently noted, represented the Jew Riah, in *Our Mutual Friend*, as "the unmanned Jew" who wears skirts throughout the novel, "the mark of his Judaism as feminization."[82] A relatively neglected figure, however, in discussions of the nineteenth-century construction of the Jew is William Lecky (1838–1903), the great Victorian historian of European rationalism and morals. In an otherwise generally sympathetic essay (a review of *Israel Among the Nations* by Anatole Leroy-Beaulieu) Lecky wrote of his Jewish contemporaries that "nothing is more conspicuous among them than their unhealthy colouring, their frail, bent, and feeble bodies," adding that "their nervous organization is extremely sensitive, and . . . they are very liable to insanity and to other nervous and brain disorders." Leroy-Beaulieu himself had challenged the view that Jews, like other Semites, were essentially a "feminine race" in possessing "a high degree of receptivity" though little originality, but he acknowledged that the Jew's "feebleness often gives him a somewhat unmanly appearance."[83] Similarly, Lecky acknowledged that "many Jews no doubt serve in the great continental armies with honour," but confidently asserted that "the Jew is naturally a pacific being, hating violence and recoiling with a peculiar horror from blood."[84]

The Dublin-born Lecky had read, we know, Henry Hart Milman's *History of the Jews* (first published in 1829), upon the death of whose author he wrote an eloquent essay, asserting that "very few historians have combined in a larger measure the three great requisites of knowledge, soundness of judgement, and inexorable love of truth."[85] In Milman's oft-reprinted *History of the Jews* Lecky (and thousands of other readers for a century between 1830 and 1930) would have read of the "furious collision" that occurred between Christians and Jews in the fifth century after "great, and probably not groundless, offence" was taken by the former "at the public and tumultuous manner in which the Jews celebrated the feast of Purim"; and of the violent death, upon a cross, of a Christian child in Inmestar, Syria—a subject to which we shall return in the next chapter.[86] They would also have read about Jewish violence against Christians after the Persian conquest of Jerusalem in 614, when the Jews "washed away

[82] Murray Baumgarten, "Seeing Double: Jews in the Fiction of F. Scott Fitzgerald, Charles Dickens, Anthony Trollope, and George Eliot," in *Between "Race" and Culture*, ed. Bryan Cheyette (Stanford, 1996), 52–53.

[83] Leroy-Beaulieu, *Israel Among the Nations*, 163. He also commented that "in many countries" Jews are "manifestly unfit for heavy work" (ibid., 247).

[84] W. E. H. Lecky, "Israel Among the Nations," reprinted in Lecky, *Historical and Political Essays* (London, 1908), 122, 128.

[85] Ibid., 266.

[86] Milman, *History*, 3:192–93, 199–200.

the profanation of the holy city in Christian blood,"[87] a subject to which we shall also soon return. Yet the nineteenth-century stereotype of the feminized Jew was evidently potent enough to allow someone as learned as Lecky, who had read and praised Milman's work, to describe the Jew as "naturally a pacific being, hating violence and recoiling with a peculiar horror from blood."

[87] Ibid., 241. For other instances of Jewish anti-Christian violence in Milman's third volume, see ibid., 195, 240, 350–51.

8

Ancient Jewish Violence and Modern Scholarship

"THE SOMEWHAT RIOTOUS FESTIVITIES OF PURIM"

> The people being solemnly assembled at this feast [of Haman] committed a thousand extravagancies; for as they read the history of this enemy of their religion, the men and women made a frightful noise . . . as often as the name of Haman was pronounced. After the devotion followed the debauch; as is the custom of all feasts celebrated for some deliverance. The Christians took little notice of these follies.

IN THIS manner the Huguenot historian Jacques Basnage (1653–1723) described the celebration of Purim among fifth-century Jews of the Byzantine Empire in his multivolume *History of the Jews from the Time of Jesus Christ to the Present*, aptly described as "one of the boldest publishing endeavors of the Enlightenment."[1] Basnage, who had emigrated to Holland in 1685 after the Protestant church in Rouen where he served as minister was razed to the ground, drew attention, although it is not clear precisely on what basis, to the practice of making "frightful" noises at the mention of Haman's name during the public reading of the book of Esther, and to the heady 3-*d* combination of deliverance, devotion, and debauch (the alliteration appears also in the French original), which characterized, he believed, the Jewish manner of celebrating Purim. Basnage went on to add, however, that if these relatively innocent "follies" of the festival did not much attract the attention of contemporary Christians, there were others, of a somewhat more menacing variety, which clearly did.

> But they [the Jews] were used to set [ting] up a great gallows, and to hang up Haman's effigies, and 'twas imagined they designed to insult the Christians upon the death of Jesus Christ. . . . *And perhaps this was true enough; for indeed they changed the gibbet into a cross, and afterwards burnt the cross,*

---

[1] Adam Sutcliffe, *Judaism and Enlightenment* (Cambridge, 2003), 81.

with the figure fastened to it; which was not done without maledictions, which
reflected upon the Messiah we adore. Theodosius II having notice of it, forbid
the raising and burning of these sorts of gibbets . . . because it was not fit
they should insult the mysteries of Christianity. (emphasis added)

Despite the emperor's legislation, however, the Jews of Inmestar (near
Antioch, in Syria), wrote Basnage, "fell into an excess. Debauchery prevailed over the respect that was due to the Prince's laws; for they fastened
a young Christian to Haman's gibbet, and whipped him so cruelly, that
he died.[2] The fifth-century historian Socrates, on whom Basnage and all
subsequent scholars relied for information about the incident, had made
no mention of Haman, stating only that the child was bound "to a cross."
Nonetheless Basnage, like the Jewish historian Heinrich Graetz after him,
saw it most likely that the Jews' violent "excess" at Inmestar had been
rooted in Purim "debauchery."

Basnage's balanced treatment of the question of Jewish anti-Christian
behavior on Purim, whether as part and parcel of the holiday's jocular festivity or beneath its innocent mask, goes to the heart of the dark issue,
pointing to the tension between truth and imagination in evaluating the
"extravagancies" which characterized Purim's observance over the centuries. Though imagination may sometimes impede perception of the truth,
it is no less often vital to the process of its acquisition, and Purim joys of the
past cannot be perceived until they are imagined. And we must imagine not
only what Jews were doing, but what they imagined themselves to be
doing, and also what they imagined others to be making of their deeds.

Like Basnage, the nineteenth-century Jewish historian Graetz was able
to imagine more than one explanation for the Theodosian law of 408 prohibiting Jewish mockery of Christianity and its symbols on Purim. "On
this day," he wrote, "the merry youths [die lustige Jugend] were accustomed to hang in effigy the arch-enemy of the Jews, Haman, on a gallows,
and this gallows, which it was the custom to burn, had, *by design or by
accident,* the form of a cross" (emphasis added).[3] His contemporary, however, Ferdinand Gregorovius, the Prussian-born historian of Rome, presented the matter in a somewhat more one-sided way. Gregorovius, in
sharp contrast to Graetz, belonged to the school of scholarship that
tended to regard the Jews as being themselves "responsible for the

---

[2] Basnage, *History*, 550 (bk. 6, chap. 15). On this work, see Sutcliffe, *Judaism and Enlightenment*, 81–89, and the literature cited there.
[3] Heinrich Graetz, *Geschichte der Juden. (vom Untergang des jüdischen Staates bis zum
Abschluss des Talmud)* (Berlin, 1853), 4:454; Graetz, *History of the Jews: from the Downfall
of the Jewish State to the Conclusion of the Talmud*, trans. J. K. Gutheim, 2nd rev. ed. (New
York, 1873), 296. On changes in later editions, see further below.

contempt" with which they were often held. It is hardly surprising, there-fore, that he saw the Theodosian law as forbidding the Jews "to celebrate a certain festival [Purim] at which they were *accustomed to give sly expres-sion to their hatred for the crucified Saviour.*" According to Gregorovius, on that day "they represented Haman as crucified and . . . burned him in effigy amidst shouts and revelry *as if he were Christ*" (emphases added).[4] As he saw (and heard) it in his imagination, there were no two ways about it. The Jews of the fifth century hated the crucified Messiah and gave "sly expression" to their hatred by venting it "amidst shouts and revelry" on the day of Purim.

The Theodosian law of 408 alluded to by all three of these scholars had instructed the governors of the provinces, as mentioned earlier, to "pro-hibit the Jews from setting fire to Aman in memory of his past punish-ment, in a certain ceremony of their festival, and from burning with sacrilegious intent a form made to resemble the saint cross in contempt of the Christian faith, lest they mingle the sign of our faith with their jests."[5] Graetz, who stressed the weakness of the Jews caught between the Chris-tianized Eastern and Western Roman empires of the fifth century, saw their attacks upon the Christian religion and its symbols as one of the few forms of resistance open to them. It was in this context that he placed both the Theodosian edict of 408 and the Inmestar incident, which, according to the *Ecclesiastical History* of Socrates, occurred in approxi-mately 415 when the Jews of that small town in Syria "were amusing themselves in their usual way with a variety of sports." Socrates, the only source for the incident, continued:

> In this way they indulged in many absurdities, and at length impelled by drunkenness they were guilty of scoffing at Christians and even Christ him-self; and in derision of the cross and those who put their trust in the Cruci-fied One, they seized a Christian boy, and having bound him to a cross, began to laugh and sneer at him. But in a little while, becoming so trans-ported with fury, they scourged the child until he died under their hands.[6]

In contrast to Graetz, his late nineteenth-century Hebrew translator S. P. Rabinowitz not only omitted any mention of the early fifth-century

---

[4] F. Gregorovius, "Der Ghetto und die Juden in Rom," in Gregorovius, *Wanderjahre in Italien*, 5th ed. (Leipzig, 1878); Gregorovius, *The Ghetto and the Jews of Rome*, trans. Moses Hadas (New York, 1948) 43–45. His essay was written in 1853, the year in which Graetz's fourth volume, discussing the background to the same law, first appeared.

[5] Linder, *Roman Imperial Legislation*, 236–38.

[6] I have quoted the translation of Socrates in *A Select Library of Nicene and Post-Nicene Fathers of the Christian Church*, 2nd ser. ed. P. Schaff and H. Wace (reprint, Grand Rapids, 1983), 2:161.

incident, but also neglected to mention the possibility that the gallows upon which effigies of Haman were customarily burned, according to the edict of 408, "had by design" and not merely by chance "the form of the cross."[7] Rabinowitz was evidently anxious about the possibility of fueling accusations of anti-Christian behavior against the Jews, especially the charge that Jews were in the habit of killing Christian children, whose blood they allegedly required for ritual purposes. The ritual-murder accusation, to which we shall return below, had first surfaced in twelfth-century Europe and had repeatedly raised its ugly head in the nineteenth century, most notably in the "Damascus Affair" of 1840. More recent accusations had occurred in Russia (Saratov, 1860), Hungary (Tisza-Eszlar, 1882–1883) and Germany's Rhineland (Xanten, 1891–1992). As Graetz himself evidently recognized, however, there was little point in withholding potentially embarrassing material from the reading public when—like the last chapters of the book of Esther—it was so widely available in a variety of languages.

Socrates' *Ecclesiastical History* was originally written in Greek, but from the sixteenth century had appeared in numerous Latin editions. It was translated twice into French during the seventeenth century, and an English edition had appeared as recently as 1888.[8] The passage concerning Inmestar, moreover, had been cited as early as 1693 by the Christian Hebraist Johannes Wagenseil.[9] Several years later Sigismund Hosmann, who had consulted Wagenseil's work, mentioned both the Theodosian law of 408 and the Inmestar incident in the extensive chapter devoted to "Jewish hostility against Christians" in his *Das Schwer . . . Juden Hertz* (1699).[10] And early in the eighteenth century the Frankfurt Orientalist Johann Schudt, who had consulted Hosmann's work, included both the Theodosian law and the crucifixion of a Christian child at Inmestar in the chapter on Purim in his *Jüdische Merckwurdigkeiten*.[11] Basanage too, as noted above, discussed the two in tandem, and this trend continued in modern historiography.[12]

---

[7] Graetz, *Divrei*, 2:443; Horowitz, "And It Was Reversed," 138.

[8] For editions and translations between the sixteenth and nineteenth centuries, see Schaff and Wace, *A Select Library*, 2:xvi–xvii.

[9] Wagenseil, *De Infundibuli . . .* (Altdorf, 1693), 132, quoted in *Das Juden-Buch des Magister Hosmann*, ed. Heinrich Conrad (Stuttgart, 1919), 149.

[10] The chapter is excerpted in Conrad, *Juden-Buch*, 139–92. See there 146, 148–49.

[11] Schudt, *JM*, 2:309 (chap. 35).

[12] See, for example, Palmer, *History*, 90; James Parkes, *The Conflict of the Church and the Synagogue: A Study in the Origins of Antisemitism* (London, 1934), 234; J. E. Seaver, *Persecution of the Jews in the Roman Empire (300–438)* (Lawrence, Kans., 1952), 16–17; Linder, *Roman Imperial Legislation*, 236–38; Thornton, "Crucifixion of Haman," 424; Fergus

During the nineteenth century scholars devoted considerable, and sometimes rather animated, discussion to the anti-Christian practices of fifth-century Jews. In his *History of the Jews* (1829) Henry Hart Milman, as noted earlier, described the "furious collision" that occurred between Christians and Jews after "great, and probably not groundless, offence" was taken by the former "at the public and tumultuous manner in which the Jews celebrated the holiday of Purim." Milman, like Basnage before him, also referred to the death of a Christian child at Inmestar, although he did not link the incident to Purim festivity. "Some drunken Jews," he wrote, "began, in the public streets, to mock and blaspheme the name of Christ," and even "went so far as to erect a cross, and fastened a Christian boy to it, whom they scourged so unmercifully that he died."[13]

Some years later the religiously eccentric naturalist Philip Henry Gosse (1810–1888), whom we have also encountered previously, suggested to the (missionary) London Society for Promoting Christian Knowledge that he produce for them a *History of the Jews*, which he managed to complete within about two years. Not surprisingly, the book drew heavily on Milman's popular work. And like Milman before him, Gosse juxtaposed the anti-Christian "indignities" described in the 408 edict with the incident at Inmestar where, he asserted, "the maddened Hebrews proceeded to more dreadful extremities."[14] In 1856 Alfred Edersheim, who was minister of the Scottish Free Church in Old Aberdeen but had been born to a Viennese-Jewish family in 1825 (he was later Grinfield Lecturer on the Septuagint at Oxford), wrote of the custom among fifth-century Jews "during the somewhat riotous festivities of Purim . . . to pour special contempt upon Christianity, and particularly instead of hanging Haman on the gallows, to nail him to a cross, with a too manifest allusion to the Crucifixion." Although Edersheim did not refer to the town of Inmestar by name, he added that in 415 "the Jews in the neighborhood of Antioch carried these provocations so far as . . . to affix a Christian child to a cross, and to scourge him to death."[15] Edersheim, like Basnage and Graetz before him, saw the Inmestar incident as linked to what he called, with characteristic Victorian understatement, "the somewhat riotous festivities of Purim," but there were other nineteenth-century scholars who were less restrained in their comments.

Millar, "The Jews of the Graeco-Roman Diaspora between Paganism and Christianity," in *The Jews among Pagans and Christians in the Roman Empire*, ed. J. Lieu, J. North, and T. Rajak (London, 1992), 117–18.

[13] Milman, *History*, 3:192–93.

[14] *Ibid.*, 229.

[15] Edersheim, *Jewish Nation*, 553; rev. and ed. by H. A. White (London, 1896), 513. On Edersheim (1825–1889), see D. L. Pals in *DBI*, 1:316–17.

DAMASCUS, BLOOD, AND PURIM

During the course of the nineteenth century the holiday of Purim had increasingly been linked not only with "riotous festivities" but also, especially after 1840, with ritual murder. In early February of that year Father Thomas, a Capuchin monk in Damascus, and his servant Ibrahim Amarah disappeared and were later found dead, giving rise to what became known as the "Damascus Affair." Readers of the London *Times* on May 9 of that year could learn that in searching for the monk's remains there had also been found "the remains of more ancient victims . . . who had been immolated like the first by the barbarity of the Jews." Several weeks later they would have been able to read, under the title "A Mystery Hitherto Concealed," excerpts (in translation) from a recently republished work, purportedly by an ex-Moldavian rabbi who had become an Orthodox monk. In that work, which had supposedly first been published in Moldavian-Romanian in 1803 before being translated into Greek in 1834, six specific purposes were given for the Jewish use of Christian blood. In addition to the "obvious" uses of Christian blood for Passover and the circumcision ceremony (both of which were time-honored allegations), the list included such new ones as its use as one of the ingredients in Purim pastries.[16] As Jonathan Frankel has recently stressed, however, the *Times* and other British newspapers were generally more balanced in their accounts of the "Damascus Affair" than those of the Continent. In the years after 1840 many Europeans came to reconsider the question of Jewish blood lust—a question that, as two German jurists (Hitzig and Häring) noted in their 1842 book on the affair, had "so long [been] denied."[17]

In that same year the German philosopher Ludwig Feuerbach received a letter from Georg Friedrich Daumer, a dominant figure in what came to be known as the Nuremberg school of biblical studies, which stressed the importance of human sacrifice in ancient Near Eastern religion. Daumer excitedly claimed to have discovered that Purim was originally a festival in which human blood was ritually imbibed, "as some medieval Jews are supposed to have done."[18] As Jonathan Frankel has noted, both Daumer and his fellow Nuremberg theologian F. W. Ghillany "saw in the Damascus

[16] Frankel, *Damascus Affair*, 145, 264.

[17] Ibid. 137–46, 412.

[18] *Ausgewählte Briefe von und an Ludwig Feurbach*, ed. W. Bolin, (Leipzig, 1904), pt. 2, 13:97 (letter no. 132). Daumer's letter is mentioned by Julius Carlebach, *Karl Marx and the Radical Critique of Judaism* (London, 1978), 389n28. I thank Jonathan Elukin for bringing this citation to my attention.

case prima facie evidence in support of their thesis that the rite of human sacrifice had stubbornly survived in the midst of the Jewish people for some three thousand years."[19]

In 1846 a two-volume work appeared in Paris under the title *Relation Historique des Affaires de Syrie depuis 1840 jusqu'en 1842*, the second volume of which contained, in the words of Frankel, "almost every document, scrap of evidence, and argument put together in Damascus during the affair to prove the guilt of the Jews."[20] Among the diverse materials included was a lengthy excerpt from the alleged Moldavian ex-rabbi's exposé of the Jewish religion which devoted much attention to Jewish hostility toward Christians and the various uses for Christian blood. On the holiday of Purim, it was claimed, the Jews would annually perform a homicide in hateful memory of Haman, and if they managed to kill a Christian, the rabbi would bake the latter's blood in triangular pastries, which he would send as *mesloi-mounès* [*mishloah manot*] (*sic!*) to his Christian friends. The combination of the triangular shape and Christian blood, it was further claimed, was intended as an affront to the Holy Trinity.[21] In addition to the 1839 Romanian edition utilized by the author(s) of the *Relation Historique*, the alleged Moldavian ex-rabbi's work was republished in that language twice during the 1870s, and appeared in Italian translation in 1883.[22]

Even prior to those editions, the work's claims concerning the anti-Christian nature of Purim festivity resurfaced in Henri Roger Gougenot des Mousseaux's *The Jew, Judaism, and the Judaization of the Christian Peoples* (with a preface by Father Voisin, head of the Paris Foreign Mission Seminary) in 1869.[23] Gougenot des Mousseaux's French book, which has been described as "the Bible of modern antisemitism," appeared in both Austria and Romania in 1876, and a decade later it was republished in

---

[19] Frankel, *Damascus Affair*, 412. In 1842 Daumer published his *Der Feuer und Molochdienst der alten Hebräer als . . . Cultus der Nation*, and Ghillany his *Die Menschenopfer der alten Hebräer; Eine geschichtliche Untersuchung*. On Daumer, see more generally Frankel, *Damascus Affair*, 412–15, and the literature cited there.

[20] Frankel, *Damascus Affair*, 415.

[21] Achille Laurent, *Relation Historique des Affaires de Syrie depuis 1840 jusqu'en 1842*, 2 vols. (Paris, 1846), 2:390–91. As Frankel (*Damascus Affair*, 416) notes, since Laurent is otherwise unknown, there has been speculation that its true author was perhaps Count de Ratti-Menton, who had been French consul in Damascus during the affair. There may also have been several authors hiding behind Laurent's name.

[22] Frankel, *Damascus Affair*, 264; *Il Sangue cristiano nei riti ebraici della moderna sinagoga* (Prato, 1883), 30–32 (on Purim).

[23] Gougenot des Mousseaux, *Le Juif*, 227.

France.[24] In 1881–1882, the semiofficial Vatican periodical *Civiltà Cattolica* published a series of articles on Jewish ritual murder, including one asserting that the 1840 murder of Father Thomas at Damascus had been connected with the holiday of Purim, during which Jews were allegedly obligated (according to the work attributed to a Moldavian ex-rabbi) to kill a Christian in memory of Haman.[25]

In 1889 another influential French work appeared which reiterated the claims concerning Jewish violence against Christians in connection with the holiday of Purim, quoting both from Socrates on Inmestar and the alleged Moldavian ex-rabbi's revelations concerning the use of Christian blood in the three-cornered holiday pastries. This was *Le Mystère du sang chez les juifs de tous les temps* by Henri Desportes, with a preface by the noted anti-Semite Edouard Drumont, who in his own bestselling *La France juive* (1886) had already made reference to the revelations of the alleged Moldavian ex-rabbi.[26] Desportes, whose book quickly became "a readily accessible source for everybody and anybody eager to prove the validity of the [ritual-] murder accusation," also repeated the claim, advanced in the *Civiltá Cattolica,* that Father Thomas had been killed in Damascus as part of a Purim rite.[27] During the "Dreyfus Affair" of 1894 and in its aftermath the works of Gougenot des Mousseaux and Desportes enjoyed renewed popularity in France.[28]

In Russia too there emerged in the late nineteenth century a quasi-scholarly literature devoted to the uses of blood in Jewish ritual, most notably Ippolit Liutanskii's 1876 work, *The Question of the Use by Jewish-Sectarians of Christian Blood for Religious Purposes . . .*, which was reissued in augmented form in 1880. Although such scholars as Daniel Chwolson (Khvolson) of St. Petersburg, the Vilna-born Orientalist who had converted to Russian Orthodoxy in 1855 but never lost his sense of Jewish identity, published learned rejoinders to Liutanskii's work, the

---

[24] On *Le Juif* and its influence, see R. F. Byrnes, *Antisemitism in Modern France* (New Brunswick, N.J., 1950), 113–14; Norman Cohn, *Warrant for Genocide* (London, 1967), 41–44; Natalie Isser, *Antisemitism During the French Second Empire* (New York, 1991), 115–18; Frankel, *Damascus Affair*, 418–19.

[25] "Cronaca contemporeana," *Civiltà Cattolica* 33:10 (1882): 214–16; Charlotte Klein, "Damascus to Kiev: *Civiltà Cattolica* on Ritual Murder," in *The Blood Libel Legend: A Casebook in Anti-Semitic Folklore*, ed. A. Dundes (Madison, 1991), 186–87 [the article originally appeared in *WLB* 27 (1974): 18–25]; Frankel, *Damascus Affair*, 420.

[26] E. Drumont, *La France juive*, 2 vols. (Paris, 1886), 2:411.

[27] Henri Desportes, *Le Mystère du sang chez les juifs de tous les temps* (Paris, 1889), 191, 305, 311–14, 366; Frankel, *Damascus Affair*, 422–23.

[28] See especially Stephen Wilson, *Ideology and Experience: Antisemitism in France at the Time of the Dreyfus Affair* (London, 1982), 521, 528, 540, 551–53.

ritual-murder accusation continued to thrive in late nineteenth-century Russia.[29] Although Chwolson did not attempt, even in the third edition of his work on the ritual-murder accusation, which appeared in German in 1901, to bury the evidence regarding the Inmestar incident, he did stress that according to Socrates the Jewish "criminals" (Chwolson's term) who scourged the Christian child were heavily drunk.[30] A year later, however, the noted Hungarian-Jewish scholar Samuel Krauss referred to the conduct of the Jews at Inmestar as merely "an innocent jest" (une innocente facétie).[31]

Knights in Scholarly Armor: Sir Richard Burton and Sir James Frazer

Krauss may have been reacting apologetically to the use made of the Inmestar incident not only in anti-Semitic writing in France, but in scholarly writing in England, especially in the work of two figures who were no less controversial than they were legendarily learned: Sirs Richard Burton and James Frazer. In the final chapter of his essay on "The Jew," which was published posthumously in 1898, the English explorer, scholar, translator, and diplomat Sir Richard Burton (1821–1890) explained why the subject of his essay should be seen as "the deadly enemy of all mankind":

> His fierce passions and fiendish cunning, combined with abnormal powers of intellect, with intense vitality, and with a persistency of purpose which the world has rarely seen, and whetted moreover by *a keen thirst for blood engendered by defeat and subjection*, combined to make him the deadly enemy of all mankind, whilst his unsocial and iniquitous Oral Law contributed to his wild lust of pelf [money], and to justify the crimes suggested by spite and superstition. (emphasis added)[32]

---

[29] In 1884, for example, ten Jews in the small community of Nizhnii Novgorod were murdered with axes by an inflamed mob after reports circulated that a missing Christian child had been kidnapped for her blood. See J. D. Klier, *Imperial Russia's Jewish Question, 1855–1881* (Cambridge, 1995), 423–33.

[30] D. A. Chwolson (Khvolson), *Die Blutanklage und sonstige mittelalterliche Beschuldigungen der Juden* (Frankfurt, 1901), 224. Note also Parkes, *The Conflict*, 234, and Seaver, *Persecution*, 69, both of whom stress, as the former wrote, that "it is a mistake to call this a case of 'ritual murder.'" Nonetheless, according to the latter, it was "certainly a black mark on the Jewish record."

[31] S. Krauss, "Antioche," *REJ* 45 (1902): 46.

[32] R. F. Burton, *The Jew, the Gypsy, and El Islam*, ed. W. H. Wilkins (Chicago, 1898), 117.

Burton's contentious diplomatic career had included a stint as British consul in Damascus during the years 1869–1871, where he ran afoul of some Jewish moneylenders based in Syria who were under British protection. He seems to have begun his essay on the Jews (part of which has never been published) between his removal from that consulship and his transfer to Trieste in 1873. His biographers generally agree that it was after his altercations with Jewish moneylenders that Burton began to make inquiries first into the circumstances of Father Thomas's death at Damascus in 1840 and then, after his return to London, into the general question of Jewish ritual murder.[33]

In the fifth chapter of his essay (which seems to have been completed by 1874) Burton provided his readers with a convenient hand-list of atrocities purportedly committed over the centuries both by the Jews and against them. Those in the latter category, he suggested, must have had some reasonable justification, since they could not have been perpetrated merely "for simply diabolical barbarity," or for such trivial economic crimes as coin-clipping or usury. His list commenced with the fifth-century case of Inmestar (where "some Jews . . . tied a Christian child upon a cross and mocked it, and . . . afterwards scourged it until it died") and concluded with more than ten instances from the nineteenth century, including, of course, that of Damascus in 1840 (where the "the Jews murdered Padre Tomaso and [his servant] Ibrahim Amarah").[34] Among the many medieval cases Burton cited was that of Norwich (England), where in 1135 (*sic*), he reported, "the Jews crucified a boy."[35]

The Norwich case, which was rooted in the disappearance of a Christian boy named William shortly before Easter of 1144 and which gave rise to one of the earliest instances (if not the first) of the ritual-murder accusation in Europe,[36] could conceivably be linked, then, with the Inmestar incident several centuries earlier. This possibility was again raised in 1896 when two distinguished Cambridge scholars, Augustus Jessopp and M. R. James, jointly published an edition and translation of *The Life and Miracles of St. William of Norwich* by the twelfth-century monk Thomas of Monmouth, the single manuscript of which James (who was also director of the Fitzwilliam Museum) had discovered in 1889. In one of the introductory chapters which he authored James sought to provide some background as to how Thomas had come to believe that the Jews of

---

[33] See the preface by Wilkins to Burton, *The Jew* . . . , (previous note), vii–viii; Thomas Wright, *The Life of Sir Richard Burton*, 2 vols., (London, 1906), 1:218–19; Colin Holmes, *Anti-Semitism in British Society, 1879–1939* (London, 1979), 49–62.

[34] Burton, *The Jew* . . . , 117, 120–29.

[35] Ibid., 121.

[36] See McCulloh, "Jewish Ritual Murder"; Yuval, *Two Nations*, 181–83.

Norwich had indeed tortured and crucified the twelve-year-old William in 1144, for no such accusation had previously been made in medieval Europe. James aptly noted in this connection that "the earliest occurrence of child-murder by Jews in literature is in a passage of . . . Socrates," and duly provided both the Greek original and an English translation of the passage from the latter's *Ecclesiastical History* describing the violent incident at Inmestar.[37]

James, who later published several volumes of ghost stories, was convinced, however, that the incident described by Socrates was not one of premeditated ritual murder: "It began in rough horse-play and ended, seemingly owing to the drunkenness of the Jews, in actual violence, which had not been contemplated by the perpetrators." Like Graetz—whom he had read, though he claimed to have come upon the explanation independently—James believed that raucous Purim revelry provided the context to the drunken violence at Inmestar. "As it is known that parallels were drawn by the Jews between Haman the Hung and Jesus Christ, it is conceivable," he wrote, "that the child who came by his end at Inmestar was the representative of Haman and Christ, partly one and partly the other."[38]

It is no great surprise that the 1896 edition by Jessopp and James of *The Life and Miracles of St. William of Norwich* came to the attention of their no less distinguished Cambridge colleague James Frazer (then a fellow of Trinity College), who promptly cited it in the second edition of his *Golden Bough* (1900). There, citing the Theodosian law of 408, he noted the Jewish custom "from an early time . . . to burn or otherwise destroy effigies of Haman" on Purim, mentioning in that connection the testimony of Socrates concerning the violent death of a Christian child at Inmestar in the early fifth century. "The Christian historian does not mention, and perhaps did not know the name of the drunken and jovial festival which ended so tragically," noted Frazer, "but we can hardly doubt that it was Purim, and that the boy who died on the cross represented Haman."[39]

Frazer was aware that both the testimony of Socrates and his interpretation thereof (which adhered closely to that of his Cambridge colleague James) had implications for the more recent history of the ritual-murder accusation, and he did not shy away from them. "We may hesitate to dismiss as idle calumnies all the charges of ritual murder which have been

---

[37] *The Life and Miracles of St. William of Norwich*, ed. Augustus Jessopp and M. R. James (Cambridge, 1896), lxii–lxiii.

[38] Ibid. lxiii–lxiv. On James as author of ghost stories, see Julia Briggs, *Night Visitors: The Rise and Fall of the English Ghost Story* (London, 1977), 124–41.

[39] Frazer, *Golden Bough*, 2nd ed., 3:173–74. Frazer was aware, apparently through Jessopp and James, that Graetz had made a similar argument.

brought against the Jews in modern times," he wrote, adding that "there would be no reason for surprise if among the most degraded part of the Jewish community there should be from time to time a recrudescence of primitive barbarity."[40] No less controversially, Frazer put forward the suggestion, in the second edition of the *Golden Bough*, that there were even "some positive grounds" for thinking that the Jews "may at one time have burned, hanged, or crucified a *man* in the character of Haman" (emphasis added). He went, in fact, so far as to suggest that Jesus himself may have been crucified as part of such a violent Purim ritual.[41]

These views elicited sharp criticisms, as one might imagine, from both Christian and Jewish scholars. One of the more prominent among the latter was Rabbi Moses Gaster, who was both an eminent folklorist and *Haham* of the English Sephardic community. In his impassioned review in the journal *Folklore* (one of several in that issue devoted to Frazer's second edition) Gaster censured the author for his "promiscuous use of late and recent facts in juxtaposition with the oldest on record" in suggesting that Jews in ancient Jerusalem had practiced a custom "thus far known to the imagination of the author alone."[42] The eminent Cambridge anthropologist was apparently chastened, though not quite overwhelmed, by these and other criticisms. In the section of the entry on "Purim" he contributed, shortly afterward, to the *Encyclopaedia Biblica*, Frazer prudently relegated to a footnote his own recent "conjecture" that "the Jews may have borrowed from the Babylonians the custom of putting a malefactor to death at Purim in the character of Haman, and that Jesus may have suffered in that character."[43] Similarly, when he published the famous *Scapegoat* volume of his greatly expanded (and final) third edition in 1913, Frazer moved his controversial crucifixion theory to a supplementary note at the back of the volume.[44]

By then the second edition of the *Golden Bough*, which had appeared in French translation between 1903 and 1911, had been scathingly reviewed not only by Haham Gaster of London, but by his Parisian colleague Israël Levi, in the *Revue des études juives* of which Rabbi Levi was editor. Much of Levi's extensive review, in which he criticized Frazer for his "dalliance in the vulgar discourse of the blood libel," was devoted to the latter's

[40] Ibid., 175.

[41] Ibid., 188–98. For the background to these comments, as well as some responses, see Ackerman, *J. G. Frazer*, 168–69; Robert Fraser, *The Making of the Golden Bough: The Origins and Growth of an Argument* (London, 1990), 151–54.

[42] For Gaster's review, see *Folklore* 12 (1900): 226–30.

[43] *Encyclopaedia Biblica* (1902), s.v. "Purim" (sec. 6) 3:3982n1.

[44] This was noted and discussed by Ackerman, *J. G. Frazer*, 170–71, 248–50.

treatment of Purim.[45] Levi acknowledged that Frazer had relied upon Graetz in linking the Inmestar incident with the holiday of Purim, but he himself was less convinced of this "conjecture," which he saw as characteristic of the Jewish historian's "naïve passion" for extravagant hypotheses. In his view, the incident described by Socrates was a one-time event rather than a rite periodically performed.[46]

Frazer's theories concerning ritual violence on Purim were also bluntly dismissed by the Jewish historian and anthropologist Joseph Jacobs in the famed eleventh edition of the *Encyclopaedia Britannica*. In his entry on "Purim," the Cambridge-educated Jacobs asserted unequivocally that Frazer's suggestion "that the ironical crowning of Jesus with the crown of thorns and the inscription over the Cross . . . had anything to do with the feast of Purim, must be rejected."[47] Jacobs, who was, among other things, a historian of medieval Anglo-Jewry and had reviewed the edition by Jessopp and James of *The Life and Miracles of St. William of Norwich*, was well aware of the proposed connections between the incident at Inmestar the holiday of Purim, and the later history of the ritual-murder accusation. In his entry on Purim for the *Britannica*'s eleventh edition he referred both to Inmestar, where "the Jews . . . ill-treated a Christian child during some Purim pranks and caused his death," and to the suggestion that the incident "gave rise to the myth of the blood accusation in which Jews are alleged to sacrifice a child at Passover." Jacobs, however, dismissed the suggestion as "unlikely, since it has never been suggested that this crime was committed in connection with Purim."[48]

This, as we have seen, was not quite true, for although it had not been claimed that Jews required a Christian *child* for their Purim festivities, it had indeed been asserted quite frequently (as recently, in fact, as 1889) that they required the blood of Christians for preparing their three-cornered Purim pastries. If Jacobs was not aware of the connection between Purim and ritual murder in the writings of Gougenot des Mousseaux and Desportes, Israël Levi presumably was, which explains why his review of *The Golden Bough* was so heavily devoted to Frazer's relatively brief discussion of the holiday. Rabbi Levi's fears concerning the latter's "dalliance in the vulgar discourse of the blood libel" were not unfounded. In 1914, a year after the appearance of his review, the French journalist Albert Monniot—who like Desportes also had close ties with

---

[45] See his review in *REJ* 66 (1913): 141–56, and the brief discussion by Ivan Strenski, *Durkheim and the Jews of France* (Chicago, 1997), 103.

[46] Lévi, *REJ* 66 (1913): 155.

[47] Joseph Jacobs, s.v. "Purim," *EB* 22:661.

[48] Ibid. For his extensive review of *The Life and Miracles of St. William of Norwich*, see *JQR*, o.s. 9 (1897): 748–55.

Edouard Drumont—published *Le Crime rituel chez les juifs*, in which he also quoted many passages from the alleged Moldavian ex-rabbi's work, including those concerning Purim violence against Christians and the use of their blood for preparing holiday pastries.[49]

The assertion that Jews require Christian blood for Purim seems first to have been put forward by Ernst Ferdinand Hess, a late sixteenth-century Jewish convert to Christianity, in his *Juden Geissel* or *Flagellum Judaeorum*.[50] In the early nineteenth century, as we have seen, the allegation surfaced in the work purportedly written by a Moldavian ex-rabbi, and after the "Damascus Affair" of 1840 it circulated widely, especially in France, where it was revived during the "Dreyfus Affair" and repeated as late as 1914 by Albert Monniot. Not surprisingly, it spread to Germany as well, where, in 1921, Albert Rosenberg, the future Nazi ideologist, published a new translation of Gougenot des Mousseaux's anti-Semitic classic.

PURIM AND JEWISH RITUAL MURDER AFTER 1933

In 1933, the year of Hitler's rise to power, two young Anglo-Jewish scholars weighed in on the subject of Inmestar. In his *Purim, or the Feast of Esther* published in that year, N. S. Doniach, who had been a fellow at Oxford's Wadham College, mentioned the incident at Inmestar, where the Jews "it is said . . . went so far as to erect a cross on which they fastened a Christian boy whom they proceeded to whip without mercy." Doniach, however, chose not to mention that it was also "said" by the same source that the Christian boy had died.[51] In that very same year Cecil Roth, who had also studied at Oxford, published a pioneering article on Purim and the origins of the ritual-murder accusation. Following Frazer, Roth acknowledged both that "the Jews were in fact accustomed to commit . . . at the Purim season, some contemptuous formality in which an effigy of Haman figured," and that this was occasionally "transferred to the person of a human being—generally Jewish, exceptionally Christian."[52] Although Roth was willing to acknowledge that Jews had

---

[49] A. Monniot, *Le Crime rituel chez les juifs* (Paris, 1914), 112–13.

[50] Hess's claims concerning uses made by Jews of Christian blood were summarized by Chwolson (Khvolson), *Die Blutanklage*, 181–84. On Purim, see 183. On Hess, see Schreckenberg, *Adversus-Judaeos*, 2:642–43; S. G. Burnett, *From Christian Hebraism to Jewish Studies: Johannes Buxtorf (1564–1629) and Hebrew Learning in the Seventeenth Century* (Leiden, 1996), 66–67; Carlebach, *Divided Souls*, 99, 151–52, 203, 209.

[51] Doniach, *Purim*, 174.

[52] Roth, "Feast of Purim."

sometimes used Christians as human effigies in their rougher Purim festivities, he was not, however, willing to include the case of Inmestar in his
model—asserting that it "was almost universally agreed" that the incident
reported by Socrates, if indeed founded in fact, "was merely an outrage
committed by some drunken ruffians on the occasion of Purim,"[53] and
not a premeditated action. In this respect, his reading of the Inmestar
incident was quite similar to that of Israël Levi, who had since become
chief rabbi of France.

Shortly afterward Simon Dubnow, in the fourth (and final) edition of
his *History of the Jews* (1934–1938), acknowledged that the Jews of
Inmestar had indeed set up a gallows for Haman in the shape of a cross,
but he insisted that it was merely a wooden effigy that they crucified and
scourged, and not a Christian child.[54] It was during that same period that
Dubnow, as mentioned previously, had declared in a letter that "we are at
war with Amalek," and his blatantly apologetic treatment of the Inmestar
incident would appear to reflect that siege mentality. In May of 1934 the
Nazi journal *Der Stürmer*, edited by Joseph Goebbels, devoted a special
issue to the subject of Jewish ritual murder—including an article on the
alleged "slaughter" of Father Thomas at Damascus, under the title,
"Purimmorde."[55] Some three years later *Der Stürmer* published a special
issue on the subject of "Judaism versus Christianity," in which readers
were informed, "Today everyone knows that it is the custom of the Jews
at the festivals of Purim and Passover to murder non-Jews and use their
blood for ritual purposes."[56]

But it was not only in Nazi Germany that such views were then given
public expression. In 1938 Arnold Leese, a British Fascist who had been
indicted two years earlier after publishing an article accusing Jews of ritual murder, published *My Irrelevant Defense*, in which he asserted that
"hatred of Christianity is a tradition among the Jews; just as hate of
England is a sort of perverted religion among an inferior class of Irishmen."
Echoing *Der Stürmer* and some of the nineteenth-century works discussed above, Leese acquainted his readers with some of the Jewish "laws"
of ritual murder:

> The two principal feast-days associated with Ritual Murder have been
> (1) Purim, and (2) Passover, the latter at Easter and the former about a
> month before it. When a Ritual Murder occurred at Purim, it was usually

---

[53] Ibid., 522.

[54] S. Dubnow, *History of the Jews: From the Roman Empire to the Early Medieval Period*,
vol. 2, translated by M. Spiegel from the Russian 4th rev. ed. (South Brunswick, N.J.,
1968), 191.

[55] Trachtenberg, *Devil and the Jews*, 243n6; Frankel, *Damascus Affair*, 430–31.

[56] Quoted in *The Jewish Chronicle*, April 9, 1937, 32.

that of an adult Christian who was murdered for his blood; it is said that the blood was dried and the powder mixed into triangular cakes for eating; it is possible that the dried blood of a Purim murder might be sometimes used for the following Passover.[57]

In his book Leese also provided a chronological list of alleged ritual murders which appeared to him "worthy of record." The first, as we might expect, was Inmestar.[58]

THE PERSIAN CONQUEST OF JERUSALEM
AND THE JEWISH THIRST FOR CHRISTIAN BLOOD

Apparently unknown to Leese (who would certainly have been pleased to cite its learned author as an authority) the Inmestar incident had earlier appeared first on the list of alleged Jewish atrocities included by Richard Burton in the final chapter of his essay on "The Jew," in which he argued that "the cruel and vindictive" teachings of their religion had always rendered the Jews bitterly hostile to adherents of other faiths. "From the earliest ages to these modern days, and not in one place, but the world over," he wrote, "the hatred of the Jew against the non-Jew has been of the fiercest."[59] Burton clearly recognized that some saw the relatively civilized behavior of nineteenth-century European Jews as evidence that their co-religionists of the past were "incapable" of committing the "atrocities" commonly attributed them, but he sharply disagreed: "Because under the present enlightened Governments of the West the Jews have lost much of their ancient rancor, and no longer perpetrate the atrocities of the Dark Ages, Europe is determined to believe that the race is, and ever has been, incapable of such atrocities. The conclusion is by no means logical."[60]

Among the ancient atrocities allegedly perpetrated by the Jews, Burton cited the testimony of Eutychius, the tenth-century Egyptian Christian chronicler mentioned previously, that after the capture of Jerusalem in 614 "the Hebrews of Galilee . . . join[ed] the Persian army under Chosroes" in perpetrating a "great slaughter" of the local Christians. According to Eutychius, the Jews had purchased Christian captives "for the sole purchase of butchering them."[61] This, in fact, was hardly the only testimony

---

[57] Arnold Leese, *My Irrelevant Defense: Being Meditations Inside Gaol and Out on Jewish Ritual Murder* (London, 1938), 50.

[58] Ibid., 50. On Leese, see Holmes, *Anti-Semitism in British Society*, 160–74.

[59] Burton, *The Jew* . . . , 115, 120.

[60] Ibid., 117.

[61] Ibid., 116.

concerning the alleged purchase of and subsequent massacre of Christian captives in 614. Among the seventh-century accounts that have been preserved are those of the Armenian bishop Sebeos and the Palestinian monk Antiochus Strategos of Mar Saba. The former, in his *History of Heraclius*, wrote that "when the Persians approached Palestine, the remnant of the Hebrew people rose against the Christians. They committed great crimes out of national zeal and did many wrongs to the Christian community."[62]

Those "great crimes" and "many wrongs" were described in considerable detail by the eyewitness Strategos in his *Capture of Jerusalem*, the Georgian text of which fills sixty-six large octavo pages of thirty-three lines each.[63] Strategos devoted particular attention to the massacre perpetrated by the Jews in "the reservoir of Mamel [Mamilla Pool]" after thousands of Christians were confined there by the conquering Persians:

> Thereupon the vile Jews ... rejoiced exceedingly, because they detested the Christians, and they conceived an evil plan. ... And in this season then the Jews approached the edge of the reservoir and called out to the children of God, while they were shut therein, and said to them: "If ye would escape from death, become Jews and deny Christ; and then ye shall ... join us. We will ransom you with our money and ye shall be benefitted by us." But their plot and desire were not fulfilled ... because the children of Holy Church chose death for Christ's sake rather than to live in godlessness. ... And when the unclean Jews saw the steadfastness of the Christians and their immovable faith, then they were agitated with lively ire ... and therupon imagined another plot.

The "plot," Strategos explained, was that they would first redeem the Christian captives, and then butcher them:

> How many souls were slain in the reservoir of Mamel! How many perished of hunger and thirst! How many priests and monks were massacred by the sword! ... How many maidens, refusing their abominable outrages, were given over to death by the enemy! How many parents perished on top of their own children! How many of the people were brought up by the Jews and butchered, and became confessors of Christ! ... Who can count the multitude of the corpses of those who were massacred in Jerusalem![64]

---

[62] Quoted (and translated) from F. Macler's 1904 French edition by R. L. Wilken, *The Land Called Holy: Palestine in Christian History and Thought* (New Haven, 1992), 204.

[63] F. C. Conybeare, "Antiochus Strategos' Account of the Sack of Jerusalem in A.D. 614," *EHR* 25 (1910): 502. For a recent bibliography of the various editions and translations of both the Georgian and Arabic versions, see B. M. Wheeler, "Imagining the Sasanian Capture of Jerusalem: The 'Prophecy and Dream of Zerubbabel' and Antiochus Strategos' 'Capture of Jerusalem,'" *OCP* 57 (1991): 72n14.

[64] Conybeare, "Antiochus Strategos' Account," 508–9, partially quoted in F. E. Peters, *Jerusalem* (Princeton, 1985), 172, and Wilken, *The Land Called Holy*, 206.

Strategos, for one, thought he could. He cited a total number of 66,509 Christian corpses, of which 24,518 were allegedly found at Mamilla, many more than were found anywhere else in the city.[65] Later chroniclers, such as the Greek Theophanes (d. ca. 818), cited the number of Christian dead as being as high as 90,000,[66] which became a favorite among modern historians, although it was often cited with polite skepticism. And although the veracity of the claim by Strategos (and later Theophanes) that Jews purchased Christian captives for the purpose of butchering them has been challenged by many scholars, it has been taken quite seriously, even in recent years, by leading Byzantinists.[67]

Early in the eighteenth century the Huguenot historian Jacques Basnage, following Theophanes, asserted that after Jerusalem's conquest, the Jews purchased Christian prisoners from the Persians "to satisfy their hatred," and that "ninety thousand persons perished by their hands upon that occasion."[68] Later in that century Edward Gibbon stated more cautiously (though not more accurately) that "the massacre of ninety thousand Christians is imputed to the Jews and Arabs [sic], who swelled the disorder of the Persian march."[69]

In the nineteenth century the events of 614 were dramatically described by several British scholars, who seem to have been struck by the surprising ferocity of the massacre attributed to the stereotypically unwarlike Jews. In one of the more memorable passages of his *History of the Jews*, Henry Hart Milman wrote:

> It had come at length, the long-expected hour of triumph and vengeance; and they did not neglect the opportunity. They washed away the profanation of the holy city in Christian blood. The Persians are said to have sold the miserable captives for money. The vengeance of the Jews was stronger than their avarice; not only did they not scruple to sacrifice their treasures in the purchase of these devoted bondsmen, they put to death all they had purchased at a lavish price. It was a rumour of the time that 90,000 perished.

[65] Conybeare, "Antiochus Strategos' Account," 515–16.

[66] See *The Chronicle of Theophanes . . . (A.D. 602–813)*, trans. Harry Turtledove (Philadelphia, 1982), 11: "In this year [614] the Persians took . . . Palestine, and its holy city in battle. At the hands of the Jews they killed many people in it; some say, 90,000. The Jews, according to their means, bought the Christians and then killed them."

[67] See A. N. Stratos, *Byzantium in the Seventh Century*, 4 vols. (Amsterdam, 1968–1978), 1:109 ("The Jews raised a fund to which each contributed according to his fortune, ransomed the prisoners, and slew them."); Cyril Mango, *Byzantium: The Empire of New Rome* (London, 1980), 92 (". . . in 614, the Jews bought Christian captives and put them to death.").

[68] Basnage, *History*, 565 (bk. 6, chap. 18).

[69] Edward Gibbon, *The History of the Decline and Fall of the Roman Empire*, 7 vols., ed. J. Bury (3rd. ed., London, 1908), 5:70. The last three volumes of Gibbon's work were originally published in 1788.

"Every Christian church," added Milman, "was demolished; that of the Holy Sepulchre was the great object of furious hatred."[70] In 1841 his fellow Etonian, the Reverend George Williams (1814–1878), accompanied Bishop Michael Solomon Alexander (né Pollack), Jerusalem's first Anglican bishop, to the Holy City, where he then spent two years. Shortly afterwards, Williams published *The Holy City: Historical and Topographical Notices of Jerusalem*, a revised and expanded edition of which appeared in 1849. In his work, for which he received a medal for literary merit from the king of Prussia, Williams wrote that in 614 "the usual horrors attendant on the sacking of a city by a barbarian army were enhanced by the malice of the Jews." These, he continued, "had followed the Persians from Galilee, to gratify their vengeance by the massacre of the believers, and the demolition of their most sacred churches. They were amply gutted with blood. In a few days 90,000 Christians of both sexes, and of all ages and conditions, fell victim to their indiscriminating hatred."[71]

By the time Williams's book had been published, several years after the "Damascus Affair," the alleged blood lust of the Jews had, as we have seen, become a prominent theme in scholarly discourse, and this would appear to be reflected in his reference to the churches of seventh-century Jerusalem as having been "amply gutted with blood." Shortly before the appearance of Williams's work in its revised edition, Philip Henry Gosse published his *History of the Jews*, in which he too provided an account of the bloodshed in 614. Describing the Persian forces that converged upon Syria and Judea in that year, Gosse noted that in these campaigns King Chosroes "disdained not to avail himself of the rancorous bigotry of the Hebrew race." In the conquest of Jerusalem, he reported, a "furious band of twenty-six thousand Jews" took part, who had "gathered to the heathen standard . . . for the sake of imbruing their hands in the blood of those whom they regarded . . . as their deadliest enemies." These, of course, were the Christians, whose places of worship "were destroyed together with the greater portion of the city."[72] Gosse then added:

> The malice of the vindictive Jews was not to be satiated by the demolition of edifices, however sacred, nor the acquisition of spoils, however rich and venerable; they thirsted for Christian blood. And they were gutted with it; for ninety thousand human victims of both sexes, and of all ages and conditions, perished by their hands in the blood-stained streets of Jerusalem.[73]

[70] Milman, *History*, 3:241.

[71] George Williams, *The Holy City: Historical and Topographical Notices of Jerusalem* (London, 1845), 192; Williams *The Holy City: Historical, Topographical, and Antiquarian Notices of Jerusalem*, 2 vols. (rev. ed., London, 1849), 300–301.

[72] Gosse, *History*, 241–24.

[73] Ibid., 243.

In describing the Jewish allies of the Persians as having "thirsted for Christian blood," Gosse would appear, even more than his contemporary Williams, to have been influenced by the renewed and widespread discussion, in the wake of the "Damascus Affair," of the various ritual issues to which the Jews allegedly put the blood of Christians. Side by side with the venerable stereotype of Jewish timidity, the nineteenth century witnessed an increasing tendency to attribute to the Jews a peculiar lust for Christian blood, whether for purposes of ritual or merely revenge. Yet Jewish historians of that century were nonetheless less inclined than those of the twentieth to downplay evidence of anti-Christian violence on the part of their co-religionists—perhaps even taking a certain perverse pleasure in recounting deeds that, as Burton recognized, had become unthinkable after the modern Jews had "lost much of their ancient rancor."

Acknowledging Jewish Atrocities: Munk and Graetz

Milman, Williams, and Gosse all cited only one estimate (90,000) of the number of Christian dead in 614. Both in citing that number, the highest offered by any Byzantine chronicler, and in speaking openly of Jewish vengeance against the Christians of Jerusalem, they were matched by two of the greatest Jewish scholars of the nineteenth century, Salomon Munk and Heinrich Graetz, both of whom had been trained at German universities. The Silesian-born Munk (1803–1867), who was later praised by Graetz as having "possessed all the virtues of the Jews without their faults," was a distinguished Orientalist who translated Maimonides' *Guide of the Perplexed* into French and succeeded Ernest Renan to the professorship of Semitic languages at the Collège de France. In 1845 he published *Palestine: description géographique, historique, et archéologique.* Concerning the conquest of Jerusalem in the early seventh century, Munk wrote that the Persian Army was accompanied by 26,000 Jews, who, upon reaching the Holy City, "took revenge upon the Christians for the cruel persecutions and many humiliations they had suffered over the centuries. It is claimed that 90,000 Christians perished."[74] In a footnote, however, Munk dismissed the claim that these had been first bought by the Jews as slaves, on the grounds that so large a number of prisoners would not have let themselves be butchered without resistance.

Similarly Graetz, then lecturer at Breslau's Jewish Theological Seminary, wrote in 1860: "Ninety thousand Christians are said to have perished in

---

[74] S. Munk, *Palestine: description géographique, historique, et archéologique* (Paris, 1845), 612–13. On Munk, see G. A. Kohut, *Solomon Munk: An Appreciation* (New York, 1902) (for the quotation from Graetz, see ibid., 5) and J. R. Berkowitz, *The Shaping of Jewish Identity in Nineteenth-Century France* (Detroit, 1989), 133–34, 145–46, 241–42.

Jerusalem but the story that the Jews bought the Christian prisoners from the Persians, and killed them in cold blood, is pure fiction."[75] Graetz, who implicitly admitted that Jews had played a major role in the massacre, felt impelled to add that "only in the heat of battle or intoxicated by the rites of conquest would they have been capable of doing to their mortal enemies what the latter would have done had they been victorious. In a period when religion clouded men's minds and desiccated their hearts, humaneness was not to be found in any of the religious camps."[76] He went on to assert unflinchingly that "the Jews relentlessly destroyed the Christian sanctuaries. All the churches and monasteries were burnt down, and the Jews undoubt-edly had a greater share in this deed than did the Persians."[77] This was not all that different from what the British scholar George Williams had written just over a decade earlier, except that Graetz's words elicited an immediate defensive reaction on the part of their author: "Had not Jerusalem, the original possession of the Jews, been torn from them by violence and treachery?" asked Graetz. "Were they not obliged to consider that the holy city was foully desecrated by the adoration of the cross and of the bones of the martyrs as by the idolatries of Antiochus Epiphanes and Hadrian?" The contrapuntal movement of Graetz's discourse on Jewish violence against Christians and their sanctuaries in seventh-century Jerusalem reflects not only the historian's deep personal engagement with his material but also his unwillingness to sweep Jewish religious violence under the rug, or to dismiss, as would many later Jewish historians, all Christian accounts thereof as tainted by bias.

614 IN TWENTIETH-CENTURY SCHOLARSHIP

In his honest and eloquent treatment of the events of 614, Graetz was closely followed by Simon Dubnow. Although the latter explicitly rejected the number of 90,000 Christian dead as an exaggeration, he acknowledged that "in hostile acts toward the Christians, the Jews did not lag

---

[75] Heinrich Graetz, *Geschichte der Juden vom Abschluss der Talmud (500) bis zum Aufblühen der jüdisch-spanischen Cultur* (1027) (Magdeburg, 1860), 34. I have followed the translation in Graetz, ed., with partial trans. by Bella Löwy, *History of the Jews: From the Earliest Times to the Present Day (Specially Revised for this English Edition by the Author)* (London, 1892), 3:21.

[76] Graetz, *Geschichte der Juden vom Abschluss der Talmud*, 35. These words were deleted in the English edition cited in note 75, above, as well as in the French of Moïse Bloch, *Histoire des juifs* (Paris, 1888), 3:259. In a rare, but unfortunately silent, act of homage, the latter sentence was lifted from Graetz by the Italian historian Angelo Pernice. See Pernice, *L'imperatore Eraclio: saggio di storia byzantina* (Florence, 1905), 65. See there also 23.

[77] Graetz, *Geschichte der Juden vom Abschluss der Talmud*, 35. Note that Graetz's brave "allerdings," rendered accurately as "undoubtedly" by his English translator, became somewhat more timidly "il est probable" in Bloch's French translation of 1888.

behind the Persians." Dubnow then added, with a bit more pathos than had Graetz, that "the bitter resentment that had accumulated in the oppressed people for centuries had now found an outlet in atrocities." According to Dubnow, "the Jewish detachments . . . demolished churches and monasteries with the same frenzy the Byzantine mob had shown previously in sacking Jewish synagogues."[78]

Similar in this regard was the philo-Semitic English scholar James Parkes. In his path-breaking *The Conflict of the Church and the Synagogue. A Study in the Origins of Antisemitism* (published in the year following Hitler's rise to power), Parkes did not flinch from discussing the question of Jewish involvement in the massacre of Christians after the Persian conquest of 614. "The popular story, which is repeated in most of the chroniclers," he wrote, "is that the Jews purchased 90,000 Christian prisoners from the Persians for the pleasure of putting them to death." Like Graetz, Parkes rejected the claim that the Jews had purchased Christians for the purpose of slaughtering them, and like the former he was willing to acknowledge that they had engaged in anti-Christian violence on a massive scale: "That Jews took part in the attack upon Jerusalem and in the massacres and destruction of churches which followed, it would be difficult to disbelieve. They had every reason to hate the Christians and to exult in the destruction of the Christian buildings of the city."[79]

These words, it should be stressed, were written by an ordained Anglican priest—albeit one unconventional enough to have recommended P. T. Moon's *Imperialism and World Politics* for Lenten reading.[80] In an important article published in the year following the appearance of Parkes's book, Joshua Starr, one of Salo Baron's first students at Columbia, also acknowledged the "irreconcilable hostility" between Jews and their Christian neighbors during the final decades of Byzantine rule in Palestine, noting also that "there was . . . no dearth of violent forms of hostile expression on *both* sides."[81] Yet he too, as we shall see below, could not fully acknowledge the extent of Jewish violence against Christians in the late sixth and early seventh centuries.

---

[78] Dubnow, *History*, 2:216. Dubnow, in contrast to Munk and Graetz, decided simply to ignore the claim that Jews had purchased Christians as slaves in order to massacre them.

[79] Parkes, *The Conflict*, 260–61; Parkes, *A History of Palestine from A.D. 135 to Modern Times* (New York, 1949), 81–82.

[80] On Parkes's view that "hostility against Jews had been a manifest characteristic of historical Christianity almost from the outset" and the tension between that view and his religious beliefs, see G. I. Langmuir, *History, Religion, and Antisemitism* (Berkeley and Los Angeles, 1990), 25–28. On his mischievous advice for Lenten reading, see Parkes's autobiography, *Voyage of Discoveries* (London, 1969), 78.

[81] Joshua Starr, "Byzantine Jewry on the Eve of the Arab Conquest (565–638)," *JPOS* 15 (1935): 280–82.

The first signs of historiographical stonewalling appear in another work published in 1935: Samuel Klein's history of the Jewish community in Palestine from the close of the Talmud until modern Zionism. The Hungarian-born Klein (1886–1940), who was professor of the historical topography of Palestine at the Hebrew University, made no mention in his book of the conquest of Jerusalem in 614 or of the anti-Christian violence that ensued. Klein did cite the report by the seventh-century apostate Jacob that the Jews of Acre had forced a Christian priest to convert, but he dismissed the testimony as unreliable on the grounds that "the Jews in Palestine were then persecuted, and certainly would not have dared to do such a thing."[82] Klein could just as well have argued that *because* the Jews were persecuted they were motivated to do such a thing, but writing in 1935 he may have had before his eyes the modes of response of Central European Jewry, among whom he had served as a rabbi for many years, to *their* most recent persecutors. Four years later (and a year before his death) Klein announced that he would soon be publishing (in *Zion*) an article on Jewish participation in the Persian conquest of Jerusalem, but it never appeared.[83]

Evenhanded assessments of the reciprocal role of violence in Jewish-Christian relations were to become increasingly rare in post-Holocaust Jewish historiography, both in the land of Israel and in the Diaspora. One important exception, which in certain ways proves the rule, was Joseph Braslavski's Hebrew study, *War and Self-Defense among the Jews of Palestine: From the Aftermath of the Bar-Kochba Revolt until the First Crusade*, published during World War II by the press of the United Kibbutz Movement. Although Braslavski (later Braslavi) was, like the older Klein, who had also been educated in Berlin, primarily a historical geographer, their two books could hardly be more dissimilar in their treatments of Jewish violence against Byzantine Christians in late antiquity.

On a Saturday afternoon in the summer of 1940, the year of Klein's death, Braslavski was on his way from En Harod to deliver a lecture at the neighboring kibbutz Tel Yosef, but found himself in a situation well known to many—he had not yet chosen a topic. The one which suddenly appeared in his head became the title of the book he published three years later, in the same year (1943) in which the Haganah first clashed with British forces at Kibbutz Ramat ha-Kovesh. As his opening reference to

---

[82] Samuel Klein, *Toledot ha-Yishuv ha-Yehudi be-Eretz Yisrael* (Tel-Aviv, 1935), 21. Note also his twenty-page entry on "Jerusalem" in *JL*, 3:190–209, where nothing more is said concerning 614 than that the city was conquered by the Persians. Contrast David Ben-Gurion and Yitzhak Ben-Zvi, *Eretz Israel Past and Present* in (Yiddish) (New York, 1908), 39.

[83] Klein, introduction to *Sefer ha-Yishuv*, 25. Note there his comments about the "imaginary stories" of the Armenians.

the book's conception following the fall of France made clear, Braslavski was not interested in the subject merely for antiquarian reasons, but was searching for a "usable past." "In these trying times for the Jewish settlement [in Palestine]," he wrote there, "it is worthy and desirable to raise up from our obscure past in this land instances of self-defense, bravery, and self-sacrifice," especially during those periods in which the Jews enjoyed no political autonomy.[84]

Braslavski, who had served in the Turkish Army during World War I, was interested in demonstrating that even after the failed Bar-Kochba Revolt, the Jews of Palestine continued to actively resist their enemies, and called upon his readers to learn from their brave example: "If the remains of a people . . . could find the inner strength to struggle for their survival, a people reborn, returning to build their historic homeland, should certainly be capable thereof." This present-minded posture presented the author with a number of challenges, among them the delicate question of what to do about the massacre of 614 and the events surrounding it.

Rather than racing embarrassedly through the bloody narrative of death and destruction in 614, Braslavski devoted more than seven pages to the painful story and to a critical analysis of its sources. Although he somewhat naïvely denied the possibility that anyone (even in the seventh century) would purchase captives in order to kill them, he did assert unequivocally that "the Jews of Palestine undeniably participated most zealously" in the massacre of Jerusalem's Christians. In explaining their motivation Braslavski made a point of citing the Italian historian Angelo Pernice, who wrote that "in a single day the Jews avenged themselves against their eternal enemies, the Christians, for centuries of servitude, hatred, and persecution."[85] Thus, even during the dark days of the Holocaust, a common historiographical view of the events of 614 could still unite Palestinian Jews and European Christians.

In the post-Holocaust years, however, this consensus began to unravel as Jewish (especially Israeli) historiography concerning the degree of Jewish involvement in the violence against Christians in 614 took a decidedly new turn. In 1946 Michael Avi-Yonah, then assistant curator at the Rockefeller Archaeological Museum in Jerusalem, published his Hebrew study of the Jews of Palestine under Roman and Byzantine rule, *Bi-ymei Roma u-Vizantiyon*, which subsequently went through five editions, and was eventually translated into both German and English. Although it undoubtedly still sold fewer copies than Sartre's *Reflexions sur la question juive*, the

---

[84] Braslavski, *Milhama ve-Hitgonenut shel Yehudei Eretz-Yisrael* (En Harod, 1943), introduction.

[85] Braslavski, *Milhama ve-Hitgonenut*, 54–61; Pernice, *L'imperatore Eraclio*, 64.

Lemberg-born and London-educated Avi-Yonah shared one thing with the French existentialist philosopher—a decided reluctance (or inability) to acknowledge the Jewish capacity for vengeful violence. And although he announced in the introduction to his book (written, as he acknowledged, "by a Jew about Jews") that "polemics with enemies of our people are right and proper in the present, but a historian should approach the past *sine ire et studio*," Avi-Yonah sometimes had trouble obeying his own precept. Concerning the many reports of Jewish participation in the massacre of Christians after the Persian conquest of Jerusalem, for example, Avi-Yonah had the following to say: "Christian writers, including modern ones have much to tell about the cruelty with which the Christians in Jerusalem were treated by the Jews. Such complaints," he asserted, "have one basic source—the opinion that Jews have *eo ipso* less [*sic*] rights than Christians, and that the latter are allowed to do what is forbidden to the former."[86]

This alleged double standard seems to have provided Avi-Yonah with the justification for omitting from his narrative—in contrast to such predecessors as Munk, Graetz, and Dubnow—not only the highest figures cited by chroniclers of the total number of Christian victims in 614, but even the lowest. And it seems to have permitted him to cite in his text only the lower estimate of the number of Christian captives brought to the Mamilla pool (as Michael Ish-Shalom noted), while relegating to an endnote the generally accepted (five-fold) higher estimate.[87] The allegation on the part of several chroniclers that the captives were bought by Jews and then massacred was omitted even from the notes.

In discussing the 614 conquest of Jerusalem, Avi-Yonah chose to rely heavily upon the (then) recently re-edited *Sefer Zerubavel*, whose apocalyptic vision purportedly takes place during the Babylonian captivity but which was evidently composed in early medieval times, possibly as late as the seventh century.[88] Privileging this enigmatic Hebrew source over the

---

[86] Avi-Yonah, *Bi-ymei Roma u-Vizantiyon* (Jerusalem, 1946), 195. These words, written with understandable bitterness in the mid-1940s, were still left by Avi-Yonah to stand some four decades later in the book's second English-language edition.

[87] This was still true in the fifth edition of 1980. See there 231, 260, and note Michael Ish-Shalom, *Christian Travels in the Holy Land* (in Hebrew) (Tel-Aviv, 1965; 2nd ed., 1979), 71n103.

[88] See Avi-Yonah, *Bi-ymei Roma u-Vizantiyon*, 231–34; Y. Even-Shmuel, ed. *Midreshei Geulah* (Jerusalem, 1943). Before Even-Shmuel, the argument that *Sefer Zerubavel* was written in Palestine during the third and fourth decades of the seventh century was influentially advanced by Israel Lévi, "L'apocalypse de Zerobabel et le roi de Perse Siroés," *REJ* 71 (1920): 57–65. For more recent discussions of *Sefer Zerubavel* and its historical setting, see Martha Himmelfarb's introduction to her translation of the work in *Rabbinic Fantasies*, ed. David Stern and M. J. Mirsky (Philadelphia, 1990), 67–90, as well as Wheeler, "Imagining the Sasanian Capture of Jerusalem," 72–85, and Wilken, *The Land Called Holy*, 209–13.

more straightforward Byzantine Christian accounts allowed Avi-Yonah to state rather tersely that "there was much killing, plunder, and destruction" in Jerusalem, without specifying by whom. And in sharp contrast to Graetz, who was willing to assert that "the Jews undoubtedly had a greater share" in the burning of Jerusalem's churches and monasteries than did the Persians, Avi-Yonah suggested that only the latter had participated in the destruction of Christian places of worship.[89]

This strategy of denial served Avi-Yonah with regard to related events as well, such as the murder and mutilation, early in the seventh century, of Patriarch Anastasius II of Antioch by the city's Jews, who had been temporarily expelled from the city late in the sixth century, after one of their co-religionists was accused of urinating on an image of the Virgin Mary.[90] Neither the murder of the patriarch nor the expulsion were included in *Bi-ymei Roma u-Vizantiyon* or in any of the subsequent editions or translations of that 1946 work.[91]

Avi-Yonah was perhaps extreme, but hardly unique, in this post-Holocaust apologetic tendency. Another Galician-born historian, Salo Baron, writing on the other side of the Atlantic in the revised edition of his *Social and Religious History of the Jews*, did mention the late sixth-century expulsion of the Jews from Antioch, but he laced his account with subtle doses of lachrymosity—despite his famous (and repeated) critiques of that tendency in earlier Jewish historiography. Baron referred rather one-sidedly to the "humiliating punishment meted out to their entire community for the transgression of a single coreligionist," but buried deep in a Baronian-length footnote the information that the said co-religionist "had at one time insulted the image of the Virgin Mary," and gave no hint

---

[89] Avi-Yonah, *The Jews under Roman and Byzantine Rule* (2nd ed., Jerusalem, 1984), 265: "Having done their work, and set fire to many of the main churches of the city, . . . the Persian army withdrew." Although Avi-Yonah recognized that "at a certain point" the author of *Sefer Zerubavel* "leaves reality behind and launches his imagination on pure fantasy" (261), he nonetheless seems to have clung to it as an alternative to heavy reliance upon the Christian sources.

[90] For the first, see, for example, E. S. Bouchier, *A Short History of Antioch* (Oxford, 1921), 199, and for the second, Parkes, *The Conflict*, 293. For a more graphic description, see recently D. M. Olster, *Roman Defeat . . . and the Literary Construction of the Jew* (Philadelphia, 1994), 4.

[91] In his important review of the first edition, H. Z. Hirschberg noted the brevity and superficiality, but not the apologetic bias, of Avi-Yonah's treatment of the late Byzantine period in general, and of Jewish "cooperation" with the Persians in particular. See his review of Avi-Yonah in *Kiryat Sefer* 24 (1946): 93. See also Ish-Shalom, *Christian Travels*, 71n103, who criticizes Avi-Yonah's misleading manner of citing the estimates of Christian casualties, and Wilken, *The Land Called Holy*, 321n42, who sees Avi-Yonah's handling of the sources as "uncritical."

as to the precise nature of the insult.[92] Baron thus allowed (or constructed) his narrative to suggest that the local Byzantine-Christian authorities simply had it in for Antioch's Jews.

Moreover, by thus presenting the 592–593 expulsion as cruelly arbitrary, he was able to put a rather positive spin on the "sanguinary riot" (not "bloody massacre"!) which the Jews of Antioch "staged" in 610, during which they "killed the patriarch." According to Baron, this was part of the "score" the Jews had "to settle" with the local authorities for their earlier expulsion—a score which could look quite different to anyone who knew that the "humiliating punishment" had been assigned the Jews after one of their co-religionists had allegedly urinated on an image of the venerated Virgin. Rather than challenge the accusation, Baron, like his student Joshua Starr two decades earlier, chose simply to sanitize the transgression.[93]

Although both Graetz and Braslavski had omitted the alleged urination on the image of the Virgin and the subsequent expulsion of the Jews from Antioch, neither minced words about the manner in which its Jews had behaved in 610. According to the former, the Jews "fell upon their Christian neighbors . . . and retaliated for the injuries which they had suffered; they killed all that fell into their hands, and threw their bodies into the fire, as the Christians had done to them a century before. The Patriarch Anastasius, an object of special hate, was shamefully abused by them, and his body dragged through the streets before he was put to death." What I have called Graetz's "contrapuntal" style allowed him to speak openly of Jewish violence against Christians as long as he could present such actions as having been justified or provoked. Thus, before describing the bloody events of 610, during which the Jews "were carried away to a deed of brutal violence," he confidently asserted that "the arbitrariness of the officials and the arrogance of the clergy must have [first] caused intolerable suffering among them."[94]

Graetz was understandably vague about the precise nature of the provocation he posited, but later historians, especially Samuel Krauss, were willing to fill in the lacuna with the assertion that the emperor Phocas (602–610) had issued a decree requiring the Jews to be forcibly baptized. This assertion

---

[92] See Baron, SRH, III: 19, 236. On Baron's critiques of lachrymosity, see Robert Liberles, Salo Wittmayer Baron: Architect of Jewish History (New York, 1995), 344–46.

[93] See Starr, "Byzantine Jewry," 283, who described the act vaguely as "a sacrilege perpetrated by an individual Jew." Twenty years later Andrew Sharf, in his "Byzantine Jewry in the Seventh Century," Byzantinische Zeitschrift 48 (1955): 105 (Sharf, Jews and Other Minorities in Byzantium [Ramat-Gan, 1995], 98), wrote a bit more specifically that "a Jew had been accused of insulting a holy picture."

[94] Graetz, Geschichte der Juden vom Abschluss der Talmud, 32–33; Graetz, History of the Jews, 3:19. See also Braslavski, Milhama ve-Hitgonenut, 47.

was based on the dubious testimony of Pseudo-Dionysius of Tel-Mahre in the late eighth century, the relevant section of whose chronicle was first published in 1894. Early in the twentieth century, Krauss first linked the otherwise (to him) inexplicably violent behavior of Antioch's Jews with the alleged decree of Phocas, a view later accepted by James Parkes. "In reaction against the order for their compulsory baptism in the reign of Phocas," the latter wrote, "the Jews broke into a riot, and seizing the Patriarch Anastasius, murdered him with every brutality and dragged his body through the streets."[95]

In his treatment of the matter, Parkes combined Krauss's view with Graetz's contrapuntal style—referring to the Jews' brutal murder of the patriarch and mutilation of his body (based on Theophanes) *after* first asserting that they had been reacting to a compulsory baptism decree. By contrast, Joshua Starr, writing a year later, rejected the testimony of the widely deprecated Pseudo-Dionysius that Phocas had issued such a decree.[96] This would seem to explain why, in his article on "Byzantine Jewry on the Eve of the Arab Conquest," he made no mention of so central an event as the murder and mutilation by Jews of the patriarch of Antioch. Without being able to point to a justifiable motive it would have been uncomfortable for a Jewish historian, especially after the rise of Nazism, to mention such a crime. Even Graetz had to posit some "intolerable suffering" which had been caused the Jews by the "arbitrariness of the officials and the arrogance of the clergy."

Baron, though he shared Starr's doubts about the alleged forced-conversion decree under Phocas, was willing to report that in their 610 riots the Jews of Antioch had "killed the patriarch," but unlike Graetz, Parkes, or Braslavski before him, he did not mention the mutilation by Jews of the former's body, even in a footnote. This may well have been for reasons of propriety. According to one modern translation of the passage in Theophanes, "the Jews of Antioch . . . disemboweled the great Patriarch Anastasius, and forced him to eat his own intestines"; according to another, "they hurled his genitals into his face."[97]

[95] J.-B. Chabot, "Trois épisodes concernant les juifs," *REJ* 28 (1894): 290–92; Samuel Krauss, s.v. "Antioch," *JE*, 1:632; Krauss, *Studien zur byzantinisch-jüdischen Geschichte* (Leipzig, 1914), 22; Parkes, *The Conflict*, 245. On the problematic character of Pseudo-Dionysius's testimony, see the note 96, below.

[96] Starr, "Byzantine Jewry," 284–85. See also the reservations of Baron, *SRH*, 3:237n21, and Andrew Sharf, *Byzantine Jewry from Justinian to the Fourth Crusade* (London, 1971), 48. On the widespread disrepute of Pseudo-Dionysius among scholars since the 1890s, see the references in Witold Witakowski, *The Syriac Chronicle of Pseudo-Dionysius of Tel-Mahre: A Study in the History of Historiography* (Uppsala, 1987), 27.

[97] For the first quote, see D. M. Olster, *The Politics of Usurpation in the Seventh Century: Rhetoric and Revolution in Byzantium* (Amsterdam, 1993), 102; for the second, see *The Chronicle of Theophanes*, trans. H. Turtledove, 7.

Nevertheless, it is difficult to avoid the sense that Baron, like Jewish historiography in the United States in general during the mid-1950s, was caught in a rather apologetic mood while composing the sixteenth chapter of his *Social and Religious History*.[98] His brief treatment of the 614 Persian conquest of Jerusalem provides perhaps the best illustration. Although by the mid-1950s Avi-Yonah had conceded that, "according to the lowest estimate," 30,000 Christians had been slain in Jerusalem,[99] Baron avoided citing any numerical estimate of the number of Christian dead, stating only that the Persians deported "some 37,000 Christian inhabitants," and that "many more thousand Christian captives were sold to the Jews, who allegedly slew all those who refused to adopt Judaism."[100]

The placing of the word "allegedly" is quite significant. Did Baron really have grounds for believing that the testimony regarding the sale of Christian captives to the Jews was more trustworthy than that concerning the massacre of the former by the latter? In contrast to Munk and Graetz who accepted the historicity of the massacre but explicitly rejected that of the prior purchase of captives, Baron was more confident that Jews had purchased Christian captives than that they had slain them. Moreover, after citing the latter allegation, he added: "More circumspectly, Eutychius spoke of Jews together with the Persians killing innumerable Christians." Baron neglected, however, to inform his readers that the more "circumspect" testimony of Eutychius (d. 940) was three centuries later than that of the Palestinian monk Strategos, who claimed that Jews had purchased Christians and then killed them. Baron, who followed Avi-Yonah in utilizing the Hebrew *Sefer Zerubavel* (which made no mention of the massacre of Christians) as a source for the events of 614 and their aftermath, argued even more forcefully than had the latter that "Persians rather than Jews were responsible for the carnage," on the grounds that the failure to bury the corpses "ran counter to Jewish practice" and accorded with that of the Zoroastrians.[101] Readers of both historians (as opposed to their nineteenth-century precursors) could come away with the impression that during the massacre of 614 not a single Jew had shed a drop of Christian blood.

---

[98] On the still strong "apologetic note" in American Jewish historiography of that time, see the frank assessment by Joshua Trachtenberg (Baron's own student) in Trachtenberg, "American Jewish Scholarship," in *The Jewish People Past and Present*, 4 vols. (New York, 1946–55), 4:439, quoted by Langmuir, "Tradition, History, and Prejudice," 164n15 (*Toward a Definition of Antisemitism*, 360n13).

[99] See note 89, above.

[100] Baron, *SRH*, 3:22.

[101] Ibid., 22–23. See also 238, nn. 24–25.

ANCIENT HISTORY IN THE SERVICE OF THE MODERN STATE

In 1965 two books appeared in Israel on the subject of Christians in the Holy Land which dealt with the events of 614 in diametrically different ways. In his *Short History of Christianity in the Holy Land*, Saul (Paul) Colbi noted laconically that during the Persian conquest of Jerusalem in 614 "most of its Christian inhabitants were done to death [*sic*] [and] churches were burnt down." Dr. Colbi, who had put his Roman training in Canon Law to use as head of the "Christian desk" in Israel's Ministry of Religious Affairs since 1948, omitted any mention of the Jewish alliance with the conquering Persians of which Braslavski, among others, had been so proud. He did note, however, the "deep hatred" which the Mono-physite Christians allegedly harbored for their Orthodox co-religionists who had long discriminated against them, and the "vindictiveness" which had prompted the former "to side openly with the Persians." Readers of Colbi's book (whose bibliographical list was headed by Avi-Yonah's *Bi-ymei Roma u-Vizantiyon*) could reasonably have concluded that the Persians' primary accomplices in the massacre of Jerusalem's Christians were the vindictive members of the Monophysite minority.[102] Whereas Jewish vengeance played no role in Colbi's brief narrative of the events of 614, Michael Ish-Shalom's 1965 anthology (in Hebrew) of Christian travel writing from the Holy Land included a frank discussion of Jewish involvement in the atrocities of the Persian conquest, and even mentioned the alleged 90,000 Christian dead.[103] Ish-Shalom reiterated his version of Jewish violence against Christians during the Persian conquest in a subse-quent volume published a decade later, which proved, like Braslavski's before him, to be little more than a voice in the Judaean wilderness. His was not the version of 614 which was to achieve recognition in the semi-official publications of the Jewish state.

In the *The Jews in Their Land*, the volume conceived and edited by David Ben-Gurion after his retreat to Kibbutz Sdeh Boker, Ben-Zion Dinur, the well-known Hebrew University historian who had also served as Ben-Gurion's minister of Education (1951–1955), took it upon him-self to describe the Jewish role in the Persian conquest of Palestine in 614 and in the subsequent rule of Jerusalem: "It appears," he wrote, "that they greatly assisted the conquest, fighting in the Persian ranks . . . in spe-cial battalions," which "took part in the storming of Jerusalem." As a con-sequence, Dinur asserted, "for three years the Jews were apparently in full

---

[102] Saul (Paul) Colbi, *A Short History of Christianity in the Holy Land* (Tel-Aviv, 1965), 16. On the author, s.v. "Colbi, Paul Saul" in *Who's Who in World Jewry* (Baltimore and New York, 1987), 96–97.

[103] Ish-Shalom, *Christian Travels*, 67–71.

control of Jerusalem; recalcitrant Christians were firmly held in check, many apostates were sentenced to death as idolators, and materials were gathered for the rebuilding of the new Temple."[104] Dinur, like Avi-Yonah before him, rather uncritically relied upon *Sefer Zerubavel* for information about Jewish control of Jerusalem and plans to rebuild the Temple. Although he conceded that Jews were only "apparently in full control" of the city, he neglected to mention the thousands of Christians who were no less "apparently" slaughtered and their houses of worship that were no less "apparently" razed according to the Byzantine sources cited above. Instead Dinur told his readers euphemistically, in language that might have (justly) offended him if used with regard to Jews, that "recalcitrant Christians were firmly held in check." Death appears in Dinur's 1966 account of 614 only as the punishment to which "many apostates were sentenced . . . as idolators."

The tendency in Israeli historiography, both academic and popular, to ignore the slaughter of Jerusalem's Christians in 614 and/or the Jewish role therein only strengthened after the city came under exclusive Jewish rule as a consequence of the Six Day War. In 1969 Colbi (of the Ministry of Religious Affairs) published an expanded version of his *Short History* under the title *Christianity in the Holy Land: Past and Present*, but saw no reason, even after the appearance of Ish-Shalom's book, to expand the section dealing with 614. A similarly titled book which appeared in the same year—*Jerusalem: Past and Present*, edited by Naftali Arbel—was also quite reticent regarding the events 614. Although Arbel's book was also clearly reaching out to a Christian audience (it included a picture of Pope Paul VI kissing the Stone of Appointment), it had only the following to say about the Persian conquest of the city in 614: "Chosroes took Jerusalem, and many of its fine *buildings* were razed" (*my emphasis*).[105] No mention was made of the ecclesiastical character of those buildings, nor of the thousands of Christian casualties.

In 1969 another important publication appeared: the three-volume *History of the Jewish People*, edited by H. H. Ben-Sasson. Shmuel Safrai, Ben-Sasson's colleague in the Hebrew University's Department of Jewish History, and author of the section on the "era of the Mishna and Talmud," included therein a rather selective discussion of the events of 614 which, like those of Avi-Yonah and Dinur, privileged the Hebrew *Sefer Zerubavel* over the more numerous Christian sources. Safrai quoted from the chronicle of the Armenian bishop Sebeos that "the remnants of the Jewish

---

[104] David Ben-Gurion, ed., *The Jews in Their Land*, trans. M. Nurock and M. Louvish (London, 1966), 198.

[105] Naftali Arbel, ed., *Jerusalem: Past and Present*, trans. I. Tastlit (Tel-Aviv, 1969), 12, 127. Arbel had previously edited *The Six Day War* (Tel-Aviv, 1967) and *The Sword and the Plowshare: Israel 1948–1968* (Tel-Aviv, 1968).

people rose against the Christians," and made common cause with the Persians against them, but deleted the bishop's aforementioned assertion that the Jews "committed great crimes out of national zeal and did many wrongs to the Christian community."[106] Instead, he wrote that after receiving control over the city (a matter mentioned only by the visionary if not hallucinatory *Sefer Zerubavel*) the Jews "proceeded with the expulsion of the Christians and the removal of the churches." Not a word was said concerning Christian casualties in the volume from which thousands of Israeli high school and university students have learned about their nation's past.

The treatment of the events of 614 was somewhat more candid in perhaps the most influential of the post-1967 spate of illustrated books on Jerusalem—Teddy Kollek and Moshe Pearlman's *Jerusalem: Sacred City of Mankind* (1968), which was subsequently translated into French, German, Italian, and Spanish. Pearlman had been director of the Israel Broadcasting Service and then of the Government Information Service during the period in which Kollek, the reunited city's first mayor, had been director of the Office of the Prime Minister. Their terse account of the violence in 614 reads, not surprisingly, like a government press release: "With the capture of Jerusalem, many Christians were killed and churches destroyed and damaged."[107] The authors mentioned the sad fate of the city's Christians, but they did not indicate how many were killed, nor by whom, nor who destroyed their churches.

Readers during the late 1960s hungry for more information could have turned, for example, to Jacques Boudet's recently published (and extensively illustrated) *Jerusalem: A History*, which bore the *Nihil obstat* authorization of the Roman Catholic Church. There they would have read that, in 614, "assisted by the Israelites who were bent on revenge for the humiliation of Byzantine domination, the [Persian] soldiers massacred, looted, and set fire to churches and convents."[108] Boudet used the

---

[106] S. Safrai in H. H. Ben-Sasson, ed., *History of the Jewish People* (Cambridge, Mass., 1976), 362. For the Hebrew original, see vol. 1 of the 1969 ed., 348.

[107] Teddy Kollek and Moshe Pearlman, *Jerusalem: Sacred City of Mankind* (Jerusalem, 1968), 152.

[108] J. Boudet, *Jerusalem: A History* (New York, 1967), 212 (the work orginally appeared two years earlier in French). Two years later readers could have turned to Fosco Maraini's text accompanying Alfred Bernheim's photographs in *Jerusalem: Rock of Ages*, where they would have learned that in 614 "a double religious fanaticism—of Persians and Jews—encouraged not only the massacre of the inhabitants but also the destruction of the buildings. . . . The accumulated splendors of three hundred years disappeared in one blow" (Maraini, *Jerusalem: Rock of Ages*, trans. J. Landry [New York, 1969], 93–94. The last sentence is taken from Michel Join-Lambert, *Jerusalem*, trans. C. Haldane (London, 1958), who also wrote that the Persian soldiers "helped by the Jews, launched into massacre, rape, and pillage in every direction" (*Jerusalem*, 141–42).

term "revenge" with regard to Jewish conduct in 614, as had both Jewish and Christian historians quite routinely in the nineteenth century, but in the latter half of the twentieth such words began to disappear from the discourse of Jewish historians when describing the conduct of their co-religionists.

The twentieth volume of the Hebrew general encylopaedia, *Enzyclopedia ha-'Ivrit*, containing a mammoth entry of more than 120 pages on "Jerusalem," appeared in 1971, shortly after the city's reunification during the Six Day War. The subentries on Roman and Byzantine Jerusalem were written by Michael Avi-Yonah, who also contributed the sections on Roman and Byzantine Jerusalem to the parallel entry in the (English) *Encyclopaedia Judaica*, which came out around the same time. In both his post-1967 entries we read that the Persian army besieged Jerusalem in 614 "with the help of its Jewish allies," and in both the Jews vanish mysteriously from the narrative just after the conquest: "The city wall was breached, many *inhabitants* were slain, and the patriarch Zacharias and the 'True Cross' were taken into exile," wrote Avi-Yonah in the *Encyclopaedia Judaica*, revealing the precise identity of neither the slayers nor the slain. The Jews reappear in his narrative only after the bloodshed, to receive (as *Sefer Zerubavel* suggests) rule, albeit brief, over of the city. Mamilla appears in the *Encyclopaedia Judaica*'s entry on Jerusalem only in the section on "water supply," where it is tersely noted that the Mamilla pool is "first mentioned in the Byzantine period," but no mention is made of the context.[109]

In 1975, a decade after the appearance of his tome on Christian travel writing, Michael Ish-Shalom published *In the Shadow of Alien Rule*, a history of the Jewish community in Palestine from the aftermath of the Bar-Kokhba revolt until the Ottoman conquest. In contrast to (his teacher) Samuel Klein's similar volume, published four decades earlier, the problematic Persian conquest was not skipped over. Rather, like Munk and Graetz in the nineteenth century and Braslavski in his own, Ish-Shalom acknowledged "considerable Jewish involvement" in the destruction of churches and the massacre of Christians in Jerusalem, but rejected the claim that the Christian victims had first been bought by the Jews or encouraged by them to convert.[110]

---

[109] Michael Avi-Yonah, s.v. "Jerusalem: Roman and Byzantine," (in Hebrew) *Encyclopedia Hebraica* (Jerusalem, 1971), 20:291; Avi-Yonah, s.v. "Byzantine Jerusalem," *EJ*, 9:1407, 1539; In the former it is more hesitantly claimed that "Jewish rule was *apparently* established" (my emphasis).

[110] Michael Ish-Shalom, *In the Shadow of Alien Rule: History of the Jews in the Land of Israel* (in Hebrew) (Tel-Aviv, 1975), 56–59. For his earlier relationship with Klein, see the introductions to Ish-Shalom, *Kivrei Avot* (Jerusalem, 1948).

Ish-Shalom's somewhat "old-fashioned" book was published by a small Tel-Aviv press and barely noticed.[111] By contrast, several major institutional publications which appeared in Israel shortly before the war in Lebanon continued the conspiracy of silence, implicitly denying Jewish complicity in the 614 massacre. In 1980 the Ministry of Defense published a two-volume *History of Eretz-Israel*, in which the chapter on Roman and Byzantine times was a posthumous publication of the same Hebrew University professor to whom the *Enzyklopedia ha-'Ivrit* and the *Encyclopaedia Judaica* had turned a decade earlier for the equivalent sections in their entries on Jerusalem—Michael Avi-Yonah. "The *Persians*," he wrote in that immensely popular work, "conducted a wholesale slaughter of Jerusalem's Christian population, and burned many churches, including that of the Holy Sepulcher" (my emphasis). After completing the conquest they left Jerusalem and handed it to over to "their allies the Jews, who maintained strict rule over the city and imposed order on the anarchy that was left after the conquest."[112] Jews as imposers of order and maintainers of rule (but not as participants in massacres) certainly fit in with the self-image still maintained by Israel and its defense forces on the eve of the Lebanon War—a view as appropriate to its times as was Braslavski's archaeology of Jewish virile militancy published by the United Kibbutz Movement in the dark days of 1943.

BETWEEN LATE ANTIQUITY AND THE MIDDLE AGES

In the same year in which Braslavski's Hebrew volume on *War and Self-Defense among the Jews of Palestine* appeared, the American rabbi Joshua Trachtenberg, who had been a student of Baron, published his classic (and then timely) study *The Devil and the Jews: The Medieval Conception of the Jew and Its Relation to Modern Anti-Semitism*. In his chapter on the ritual-murder accusation, Trachtenberg included the incident at Inmestar, which "while not an instance of the ritual-murder charge, nonetheless closely paralleled it and may have influenced its later resurrection." Like the Anglo-Jewish scholars Doniach and Roth ten years earlier, Trachtenberg saw the early fifth-century incident as having taken place "during the Purim celebration," but unlike the former, he did not neglect to mention that the Christian child had died. Like Doniach, however, he was less than certain that the 408 edict of Theodosius against mocking the cross on Purim reflected Jewish intentions rather than Christian perceptions.

[111] The only review I have located is an unsigned brief notice in *Kiryat Sefer* 51 (1976): 400.
[112] Avi-Yonah, in Y. Rafel, ed., *Toledot Eretz Yisrael*, 2 vols. (Tel-Aviv, 1980), 2:362. In 1986 the work went through its eleventh printing.

"The execrations traditionally heaped upon the head of Haman in jest," he wrote, "and the carnival aspect of the Purim celebration could have easily led to imprudent and offensive remarks and gestures, and might just as easily have been misinterpreted by hypersensitive Christians."[113]

During the dark decade between 1933 and 1943 it was particularly tempting for Jewish historians to present Christian accusations of anti-Christian behavior on the part of their co-religionists in the past as stemming from misunderstanding and hypersensitivity. Rabbi Trachtenberg's unequivocal acceptance of the testimony of Socrates that at Inmestar a Christian boy was killed by drunken Jews is therefore worthy of admiration, and stands in stark contrast to the dismissive treatment by most post-Holocaust Jewish historians (including his own teacher, Salo Baron) of the Byzantine testimonies concerning the Jewish massacre of Christians in 614. Like Cecil Roth, Trachtenberg linked the Inmestar incident with the Purim execution of a Christian in late twelfth-century France. That event, as presented both by medieval chroniclers (Christian as well as Jewish) and historians of the nineteenth and twentieth centuries, shall concern us in the next chapter, within the context of what Trachtenberg correctly called "the carnival aspect of the Purim celebration."

[113] Trachtenberg, *Devil and the Jews*, 127; Doniach, *Purim*, 172–73.

9

Purim, Carnival, and Violence

Bacchanalia Judaeorum

IN 1888, the same year in which Claude Montefiore's controversial essay on "Purim Difficulties" appeared in London's *Jewish Chronicle*, the Viennese rabbi and historian Moritz Güdemann published the third and final volume of his cultural history of medieval European Jewry. In that pioneering, if somewhat eccentric, work, Güdemann described Purim as "the Jewish *Fastnacht*," which, like its Catholic counterpart, was characteristically celebrated with copious amounts of food and drink, as well as masquerade.[1] This was, as we shall see, a largely accurate description, though Güdemann, as he must have known, was hardly the first to equate the late-winter Jewish holiday with the pre-Lenten Fastnacht of German-speaking Europe—the northern equivalent of the raucous festival known as *carnevale* in Italy and *carnaval* in France. The entry on "Jewish festivals" for the best-known German encyclopedia of the nineteenth century had also described Purim in this manner, and in the eighteenth century such noted German Hebraists as Schudt, Kirchner, and Bodenshatz had either referred to it as the Jewish *Fastnachtsfeste* or compared its earthy observances with those of the latter.[2] In the seventeenth century the Italian former Jew Giulio Morosini noted that Purim was called "the Jewish Carnival," adding that "indeed there is not much difference."[3]

[1] M. Güdemann, *Geschichte des Erziehungswesens und der Kultur der abendländischen Juden* (Vienna, 1888), 3:134–35: "erlustigte man sich durch Mummenschanz und Speise und Trank."

[2] G. W. Fink, "Feste der Juden," 315 in *Allgemeiner Enzyklopädie der Wissenschaften und Künste*, ed. J. S. Ersch and J. G. Gruber 1:43 (1846). Among eighteenth-century authors, see Schudt, *JM* 2:377 ("Es gehet daher wie bei unartigen Christen auf die Fastnacht"); Johann Bodenschatz, *Kirchliche Verfassung der heutigen Juden* (Frankfurt, 1748–1749), 2:252 ("Von Purims—oder Fastnachtsfeste").

[3] Morosini is quoted by Riccardo Calimani, *The Ghetto of Venice: A History*, trans. K. S. Wolfthal (New York, 1987), 196. For a similar expression in the seventeenth century, see René Moulinas, *Les Juifs du pape en France* (Paris, 1981), 195.

Although Güdemann would certainly have agreed, the similarities between the late-winter festivals of Jews and Catholics in premodern Europe clearly caused him considerable discomfort. After briefly mentioning the robust pleasures which characterized Purim's observance he abruptly altered his course, and sought rather to demonstrate that Jews, unlike their Christian neighbors, had not exceeded the boundaries of good taste in their pursuit of these amusements—especially that of drink.[4] Rather than quoting from Hebrew sources which referred to drunkenness and cross-dressing, he preferred to cite one (*Sefer Maharil*) which advocated relative sobriety, contrasting it with the numerous German sources—from which he *did* quote liberally—describing the drunken carousing of Christians during *Fastnacht*. Purim, for Güdemann, may have been "die jüdische Fastnacht," but it was a decidedly more dignified version thereof.

This apologetic tendency became more pronounced in the appendix on "Purim und Fastnacht" which Güdemann included at the end of his 1888 volume, in which he polemicized with the overtly anti-Semitic Semiticist, Paul de Lagarde (1827–1891) of Göttingen, against whom he had done so already in Vienna's *Freie Presse*.[5] Lagarde, who has been aptly described by Jacob Katz as a scholar who "combined devastating criticism of traditional Christianity . . . with deep-seated animosity not only toward Judaism as a religion, but also toward Jews as a group,"[6] had in 1887 published a study entitled *Purim. Ein Beitrag zur Geschichte der Religion*. This learned monograph was ostensibly devoted to the common origins in ancient Persia of the Jewish Purim and the Christian All Saints Day. Yet Lagarde saw fit to carry forward his study, in which Purim was characterized equally by carnal excess and hostility to adherents of other

---

[4] Güdemann's tendency to treat the Jews more leniently than their Christian contemporaries, stressing those sources which highlighted the ignorance and immorality of the latter while underplaying those sources which pointed to similar characteristics among the Jews, was already noted by Ludwig Geiger, "Zur Kritik der neusten jüdischen Geschichtschreibung," *ZGJD* 3(1889): 379–86. See also Alexander Marx, "Moritz Güdemann, (Necrology)," *PAJHS* 28 (1922):276–81.

[5] M. Güdemann, *Geschichte des Erziehungswesens*, 3: 270–74; Güdemann, "Der 'deutsche Nationalheilge' Paul de Lagarde," *Freie Presse* Feb. 12, 1887, cited by Elisabeth Hollender, "Verachtung kann Unwissenheit nicht entschuldigen. Die Verteidigung der Wissenschaft des Judentums gegen die Angriffe Paul de Lagarde's 1884–1887," *FJB* 30 (2003), 196.

[6] Jacob Katz, *From Prejudice to Destruction: Anti-Semitism, 1700–1933* (Cambridge, Mass., 1980), 305–6. On Lagarde, see also Leo Strauss, "Paul de Lagarde," *Der Jude* 8 (1924): 8–15; Fritz Stern, *The Politics of Cultural Despair: A Study in the Rise of the German Ideology* (New York, 1965), 25–128; Schreckenberg, *Adversus-Judaeos*, 3:744–45; and most recently Gesine Palmer, "The Case of Paul de Lagarde," in *Antisemitismus, Paganismus, Völkische Religion*, ed. H. Cancik and U. Puschner (Munich, 2004), 37–53.

religions (a feature prudently omitted by Güdemann), as far as modern times—drawing even upon an 1862 "Purimspiel" which had appeared in Breslau under the title "Haman der grosser Judenfresser." Lagarde's conclusion was that among the Jews the festival had become one of gluttonous amusement amid obligatory drunkenness, in an atmosphere made hateful by arrogant preaching ("den Hass und Hochmuth predigenden Schlemmerei").[7]

A historian of Güdemann's stripe could hardly ignore such words, especially since they had a more than indirect bearing upon the perception of European Jewry during his own day.[8] He therefore challenged Lagarde to visit such Jewish communities as that of his native Göttingen to see whether *Schlemmerei* was practiced there on Purim, asserting further— although not very honestly—that the Talmudic injunction to become heavily intoxicated on that day had always been regarded as hyperbolic. In response to Lagarde's negative comments concerning the custom of cross-dressing on Purim, Güdemann cited a fifteenth-century work which suggested that this had been practiced only by young men. And in response to the claim that Purim celebrations had been characterized by animosity and arrogance, Güdemann was willing to concede that perhaps some of the former had been lurking beneath the surface, but could not imagine, he claimed, whence medieval Jews would have drawn any sense of arrogance.[9] His reply to Lagarde, despite its polemical tone, was essentially a concession to the latter's anti-Semitic agenda. Rather than accepting that Jews of the past could get boisterously drunk and even arrogantly angry one day in the year, he sought to demonstrate that his co-religionists had always adhered to bourgeois standards of polite conduct during their Purim celebrations.[10]

---

[7] Paul de Lagarde, *Purim. Ein Beitrag zur Geschichte der Religion* (Göttingen, 1887), 56–57. On nineteenth-century reactions to Purim observances, see also Wilhelm Marr's 1862 letter published (in translation) by Moshe Zimmerman, in *Wilhelm Marr: The Patriarch of Anti-Semitism* (New York, 1986), 117.

[8] See most extensively, Ismar Schorsch, "Moritz Güdemann: Rabbi, Historian, and Apologist," *LBIYB* 9 (1966): 53–66. On Güdemann's relationship to Lagarde, see ibid., 55.

[9] Güdemann, *Geschichte des Erziehungswesens*, 3:271 ("Woher den Juden im Mittelalter der Hochmuth hätte konnen, ist mir unbegreiflich"). Güdemann's translator, A. S. Friedberg, chose not to include the polemical appendix in the Hebrew edition of the work. It was his opinion that polemics with enemies of the Jews "have already filled our sinews and souls with their bitterness" And there was no point in pursuing them further. See *Ha-Torah veha-Hayyim be-Arzot ha-Ma'arav bi-Mei ha-Beinayim*, 3 vols. (Warsaw, 1897–1899), 3:204–5.

[10] Compare James Picciotto, *Sketches of Anglo-Jewish History*, rev. and ed. and with a prologue by Israel Finestein (London, 1956[1875]), 171, 197, who made a point of stating that "Jews have rarely been guilty of deeds of violence" and that indulging in "fiery liquors" was "contrary to Jewish habits."

PURIM JOYS LOST, FOUND, AND REBURIED

Although Claude Montefiore had been careful, in his 1888 essay, to stop short of explicitly calling for the abolition of Purim, some of his co-religionists, including such prominent Anglo-Jewish figures as Samuel Montagu and Oswald Simon, reacted, as we have seen, rather angrily.[11] Evidently unknown both to Montefiore and his critics, a similar suggestion had been made nearly a century earlier in an anonymous article that appeared in the *Berlinische Monatsschrift* under the title "A Proposal for the Jews to Abolish the Holiday of Purim." The author had suggested that just as members of his (obviously Protestant) faith had freed themselves from spiritual fetters through the abolition of unnecessary festivals, so too could the Jews, through the abolition of one very offensive festival ("eines sehr anstössigen Festes"), lay the ground for their own moral improvement. The Jewish protagonists of the book of Esther, it was asserted, were hardly heroes worthy of emulation. Mordecai, was merely a headstrong person (*Starrkopf*), who for some unknown reason, refused to show honor to the prime minister. The slaughter by the Jews of their enemies was rendered particularly cruel by the latter's failure to resist, and when their modern co-religionists read the story, the author claimed, they think of Christians rather than Persians. Replying anonymously to the 1790 article, David Friedländer, one of the more radical Jewish proponents of Enlightenment in Germany, distinguished between the customs of Purim, many of which he acknowledged to be offensive (*anstössig*) later accretions, and the holiday itself. Similarly, he distinguished between Jews in general and his Prussian co-religionists, who did not consider their Christian neighbors to be their enemies.[12]

In addition to the immediate responses to Montefiore's controversial essay, a less direct response appeared in an editorial published in the *Jewish Chronicle* some two years later—(15 Adar) March 7, 1890—whose author ruefully observed that "Purim has unhappily lost most of its good rollicking humours." The modern world, he asserted, "is quite as pleasure-seeking as ever, but our amusements are sadder than in the past." Looking

---

[11] *Jewish Chronicle*, March 9, 1888, 6.

[12] "Vorschlag an die Juden, das Purimfest abzuschaffen," *Berlinische Monatsschrift* 15 (1790): 377–81, 563–77. I thank Margaret Kimball of the Stanford University library and Steven Zipperstein for arranging for me to get a photocopy of these pages. See also Michael Meyer, *The Origins of the Modern Jew* (Detroit, 1967), 61. On Friedländer (1750–1834), see also David Sorkin, *The Transformation of German Jewry, 1780–1840* (New York, 1987), 73–78, and now Shmuel Feiner, *The Jewish Enlightenment*, trans. Chaya Naor (Philadelphia, 2004), 108–10, 315–20.

backward somewhat nostalgically the anonymous author called the attention of his readers to the "flavour of delightful abandon and child-like
enjoyment in the medieval carnival of which Purim was the Jewish copy.
Its pleasures were perhaps rough, but they were real, and they were
picturesque."

The picturesque pleasures of past Purims were soon to be paraded before
the English reader in inimitable fashion by Israel Abrahams, then of London's Jews' College, who would appear to have played a major role in draft-
ing the 1890 editorial—if he was not its sole author. Abrahams, who had
founded the *Jewish Quarterly Review* with Montefiore in 1889, had
undoubtedly seen his colleague's provocative Purim piece published the
previous year. In fact, one can discern a dialogue between the two friends
emerging first in the pages of the *Jewish Chronicle* and then finding its way
into other publications. To the claim made by Montefiore that Purim celebrations were of "doubtful propriety," the 1890 editorial implicitly
responded with the reminder that Christians too had their "rough pleasures" during the carnival of which Purim, it asserted, was a Jewish version.
And rather than its "crude vengeance," the editorial stressed the holiday's
"delightful abandon." The matter of vengeance was taken up more explicitly a year later in an editorial which, in a similar tone, discussed the once
vigorous but nearly forgotten customs of noise-making in the synagogue at
the mention of Haman's name: "No doubt there was much that was rep-
rehensible in these customs; they looked ugly to an outsider, they were
indecorous in the extreme, and their gradual abolition is a fact on which we
must rejoice. But they were really not altogether so ugly as they seemed."[13]

This nostalgically revisionist posture toward past Purim pleasures was to
find expression some five years later in Abrahams's path-breaking *Jewish
Life in the Middle Ages* (1896), where in the holiday was described as the
"carnival of the European Jews." As Abrahams saw it, "on Purim everything, or almost everything, was lawful; so the common people argued.
They laughed at their Rabbis, they wore grotesque masks, the men attired
themselves in women's clothes and the women went clad as men."[14] The
latter practice was, of course, technically an infringement of Jewish law,
but, according to Abrahams, "on Purim the frolicsomeness of the Jew
would not be denied," and the rabbis learned not to be stern in their
expectations on that day, more or less turning a blind eye "towards such
innocent and mirth-provoking gambols."[15]

[13] *Jewish Chronicle*, March 20, 1891, 5–6.

[14] Abrahams, *Jewish Life*, 260–62. On that work and on Abrahams as scholar and Jew, see
Horowitz, "Israel Abrahams."

[15] On the beginnings of Purim cross-dressing and its halakhic problems, see Horowitz, "And
It Was Reversed," 155–56, and the literature cited there.

As described by Abrahams, the frolicsome Jew enjoying "uproarious fun" on his day of Carnival is, of course, a far cry from the repressed Jew, incapable even of momentary arrogance, described by Güdemann. Abrahams's joyful celebrant was also relatively—and deliberately—distanced from the crudely vengeful Jew of Purim evoked, in their different ways, both by Lagarde and by Montefiore, and by the tradition of biblical scholarship to which they were both heirs. If Güdemann's account of medieval Purim festivities is unmistakably informed by an apologetic sensibility, that of Abrahams, while more adroitly parrying the objections to various improprieties, nevertheless betrays also a powerful sense of nostalgia for a former age when Jews, he believed, still knew how to have fun.

During the 1820s two of London's leading synagogues had prohibited even children from interrupting the reading of the scroll of Esther with "Hamman Clappers"—a subject to which we shall return.[16] In 1888, when both Abrahams and Montefiore were thirty years old, the *Jewish Chronicle* reported that four hundred pupils in the Birmingham Hebrew Schools were entertained, in good Victorian fashion, at "the third annual Purim Tea."[17] Abrahams's passionate portrayal of Purim in the Middle Ages as a day of uproarious fun on which "much joyous license was permitted even within the walls of the synagogue" must undoubtedly be seen against this background. In contrast to Güdemann's overly guarded presentation of Purim in the past and Montefiore's expressed hope that a holiday of such "doubtful propriety" disappear in the future, we can sometimes hear in the background of Abrahams's measured cadences the faint echo of Shylock's ringing words: "hath not a Jew hands, organs, dimensions, senses, affections, passions?"[18]

In 1896, the same year in which Abrahams nostalgically evoked past Purims in his *Jewish Life in the Middle Ages*, New York's *Jewish Messenger* was reminding its readers of "the good times fashionable Israel in the large cities used to enjoy" at the brilliant masquerade balls held on Purim. It also felt that it knew quite precisely where to lay the blame for the holiday's unfortunate decline. For in many of those cities the forces of Reform had been gaining ground and calling, as in the case of the famous Charleston "Memorial" of 1824, for the removal not only of "see-sawing" during the prayers and the use of "profane tunes," but also for "most strictly" prohibiting "the ceremony of striking the impious Haman at the

[16] Todd Endelman, *The Jews of Georgian England, 1714–1830* (Philadelphia, 1979), 162.

[17] *Jewish Chronicle*, March 2, 1888, 15.

[18] W. Shakespeare, *The Merchant of Venice*, 3:1. For more explicit examples of his use of Shakespeare as a subtext see Abrahams, *Jewish Life*, 307; and Abrahams, *Festival Studies* (Philadelphia, 1906), 39.

festival of Purim."[19] "No wonder," commented the *Jewish Messenger* in 1896,

> it has fallen into disuse when modern rabbis try to drive it out of the calendar, make no provision for its celebration in the revised prayer book, and ridicule the good old story of Mordecai as an exploded myth. The new Judaism gives us little compensation for the ceremonies and feasts that have been discarded. . . . Better one night of Purim than a dozen revised and dreary services.[20]

The desiccation and decline of Purim observance in nineteenth-century America is clear from the surprise and enthusiasm shown by American-Jewish visitors upon encountering the more spirited celebration of the holiday in less-Westernized countries. Cyrus Adler, who was born in Arkansas (in 1863), grew up in Philadelphia, and earned his doctorate in Semitics at Johns Hopkins University in Baltimore, visited Cairo during Purim of 1891. He was then traveling as the congessionally appointed commissioner of the World's Columbian Exposition (which was to take place in Chicago) to Turkey, Persia, Egypt, Tunis, and Morocco. "The celebration . . . was more exciting than I had ever seen or heard in any synagogue. . . . Besides the usual noise that attends Purim eve celebration, some young people were setting off fire-crackers." Adler, who, before his 1890–1891 trip to the East, had "never been further away from home than Chicago," observed that "Purim is so well recognized as a time of Jewish carnival that the streets were practically given over to the Jews"[21]—something he clearly could not imagine occurring anywhere in America.

Similarly Herbert Friedenwald, who belonged to a prominent Baltimore Jewish family (into which Adler later married) and who was in charge of the Department of Manuscripts at the Library of Congress, reported a year later that "Purim in Cairo is very different from Purim in Philadelphia

---

[19] The 1824 document is considered to be the earliest expression of the impulse toward Reform in American Judaism. See *A Documentary History of the Jews in the United States: 1654–1875*, ed. Morris Schappes (3rd ed., New York, 1971), 176–77. The earliest effort in Reform circles to do away with the noise-making on Purim was in the 1810 regulations for the synagogues of Westphalia. See Michael Meyer, *Response to Modernity: A History of the Reform Movement in Judaism* (New York and Oxford, 1988), 36, 158.

[20] Quoted by Philip Goodman, "The Purim Association of the City of New York (1862–1902)," *PAJHS* 40 (1950): 160. In 1861 an editorial in the same publication called for the organization of a full-scale Purim Ball at which there would be "a few hours of real pleasure" (ibid., 138).

[21] C. Adler, *I Have Considered the Days* (Philadelphia, 1941), 75, 118, 364–65.

or New York." For one, there had been spirited noise-making in the synagogue: "The mention of the name of Haman was met with shouts and stamping of feet, and one small boy . . . had the temerity to set off a firecracker," a proceeding which, he was surprised to discover, aroused little interest or concern. Moreover, "during the day, masqueraders took full possession of the town, and went about from street to street thoroughly enjoying their lark."[22] He too was clearly struck both by the spirited joy of the holiday and the confident freedom with which it could spill over into the city's streets.

The overall sense among Anglo-American Jewry that the true joys of Purim had been lost to the distant past is acutely captured in Alice Braham's poem "Purim, 1900," which concludes on a distinctly mournful note: "Israel forgets thee, Purim, thou art dead."[23] Five years later, on March 17, 1905, London's *Jewish Chronicle* editorialized: "Time was when Purim was welcomed in the Jewish home as the brightest of the minor feasts; today it is relegated to the cold shade of neglect . . . ""[24] This editorial too appears to bear the imprint of Israel Abrahams, who contributed an unabashedly nostalgic essay under the title "Lost Purim Joys" to that issue's special holiday supplement. "It is unquestionable," observed Abrahams, "that Purim used to be a merrier anniversary than it is now." The explanation for this shift was, according to his mind, "simple," but his own feelings about it were considerably more complex. "In part," he wrote

> the change has arisen through a laudable disinclination from pranks that may be misconstrued as tokens of vindictiveness against an ancient foe or his modern reincarnations. As a second cause may be assigned the growing and regrettable propensity of Jews to draw a rigid line of separation between life and religion, and wherever this occurs, religious feasts tend toward a solemnity that cannot, and dare not, relax into amusement.[25]

---

[22] Herbert Friedenwald "Purim in Cairo," in the *American Hebrew* 50, no. 6 (March 11, 1892), 105, reprinted in Goodman, *Purim Anthology*, 46–47. On Adler's marriage to the former Racie Friedenwald (daughter of Moses), see *I Have Considered the Days*, 55, 262–63.

[23] Friedlander, *Standard Book of Jewish Verse*, 348.

[24] *Jewish Chronicle* March 17, 1905, 8. In a fictional vignette, "Purim in a Ghetto Chevra," contributed to that week's supplement by a certain "G.S.C.," the author writes of an old Esther scroll brought into the synagogue: "could it but speak, what stories it would tell of the Purim of past-days, of Bacchanalian revels, of masked revellers, and of whole-hearted merrymaking."

[25] I. Abrahams, "Lost Purim Joys," reprinted in Abrahams, *The Book of Delight and Other Papers* (Philadelphia, 1912), 271. This tendency, continued Abrahams, was "eating at the very heart of Jewish life, and ought to be resisted by all who truly understand the genius of Judaism."

On the positive side Abrahams welcomed the decline of Purim pranks "that may be misconstrued," presumably by Christians, "as tokens of vindictiveness" against the enemies of the Jews. By this he seemed to suggest both that the Purim mischief of the past (centering on the figure of Haman) was not truly vindictive, and that vindictiveness, or even its appearance, had no place in the good clean fun that he favored.[26] Here Abrahams had more in common with Güdemann's apologetic stance than he might have cared to admit. On the negative side, however, which was the one he stressed in his essay, Abrahams mourned the fact that in the observance of Jewish feasts a wedge had been driven between life and religion, so that relaxed amusement had given way to stiff solemnity. For the medieval Jew, he believed, things had been quite otherwise, for he "drew no severe line between sacred and profane."[27]

Even before publishing his *Jewish Life in the Middle Ages* (1896), Abrahams had given expression to his profound nostalgia for a time when Purim was still "a day of mirth and sociability, of wine-bibbing and of cracking of jokes, of buffooneries and mummings, of choruses and rollicking wine songs." In a brief article, which had originally been presented as a lecture to the Jewish Historical Society of England, he discussed a highly stylized Hebrew letter by the Spanish Jew Solomon ha-Levi of Burgos that had allegedly been written in London on Purim in 1389. What made the letter of particular interest, other than its vivid description of Castilian Purim festivities, was that its author was, as Abrahams noted, "no ordinary Jew," but rather one who soon after its composition converted to Christianity and eventually served as bishop of Burgos under the name Pablo de Santa Maria. Upon his arrival (on a diplomatic assignment) in England, which had expelled its Jews in 1290, Solomon was still, as described by Abrahams, "a very observant and orthodox Jew," who therefore "found himself a stranger in a strange land." Yet "isolation seems not to have preyed his spirits until a day came whereon isolation was intolerable to a medieval Jew." That day, for Abrahams, "was Purim," and, in his (sympathetic) view, "to be alone and sober on such a day was more than Solomon Levi could tolerate."[28]

In that letter, Solomon bemoaned his sad fate of having to spend the festive holiday in such inhospitable surroundings, a fate with which Abrahams himself, in staid London some five hundred years later, would

---

[26] On Abrahams and Jewish religious reform, see most recently H. W. Meirovich, "Israel Abrahams: Master Teacher of Liberal Judaism," *European Judaism* 34, no. 1 (2001): 4–16.
[27] Abrahams, "Lost Purim Joys," 269.
[28] I. Abrahams, "Paul of Burgos in London," *TJHSE* 2 (1894–1895): 148–52 [hereafter I] Saul/Paul's letter had first been published by M. Roest, "Brief von Salmo ha Lewi . . . aan Meir Algudez," *Israelitische Letterbode* 10 (1883–1884): 78–85.

seem to have had considerable sympathy. In fact Abrahams came back to the 1389 letter some five years later, republishing its Hebrew text in the *Jewish Quarterly Review*, together with a partial English translation. "Today I am unable to drink deep, as one ought to do on Purim," wrote Solomon, "I can bless Mordecai and curse Haman. My senses retain their nicety . . . Alas for such a Purim!"[29] In contrast to Heinrich Graetz, who regarded the poetic composition to which this letter was appended as merely satirical, Abrahams saw it as "a genuine expression of medieval Judaism." In his view, "its exaggeration of the virtue of wine-drinking on Purim . . . its warm love of the ceremonies, its quaint association of piety with the joys of the table . . . its total lack of overstrained asceticism, its playful seriousness, its sane humour—all these qualities stamp the letter as the work of a man still imbued with the sentiments of the medieval Rabbis."[30]

In those sentiments Abrahams found room for "warm love of the ceremonies," but not bitter hatred of Christianity. Consequently, in his nostalgic 1905 essay on "Lost Purim Joys" he observed that "probably the oldest of Purim pranks was the bonfire and burning of an effigy [of Haman]," mentioned, as he noted, in a recently published medieval Geonic responsum. He also discussed the efforts of James Frazer, whose colleague at Cambridge he had recently become, to link the Purim bonfire with primitive spring tide conflagrations and with sympathetic magic, connections that Abrahams did not find entirely convincing.[31] Yet he conspicuously omitted the earliest, and perhaps most famous, evidence for the practice of burning an effigy of Haman, namely the 408 edict of Theodosius II discussed in the same (second) edition of Frazer's *Golden Bough*, to which he made explicit reference in his essay.[32]

Frazer had not only cited the Theodosian edict and the custom of Jews "to burn or otherwise destroy effigies of Haman" as part of their Purim rites but had suggested, quite controversially, that there were even "some

---

[29] I. Abrahams, "Paul of Burgos in London," *JQR*, o.s. 12 (1900): 257, 259 [hereafter II]. I follow his characteristically elegant translation.

[30] Ibid., 258. On Solomon/Pablo, see also Baer, *Christian Spain*, 2:139–50. Baer argued (ibid., 140) that the 1389 letter was sent by Solomon from Aquitane in France (then under English rule) rather than from London. What is more important for our present purposes, however, is that Abrahams, who was writing in London, *thought* that his historical subject had been writing from there as well. For more recent discussions of the letter, see also J. G. Krieger, "Pablo de Santa Maria, the Purim Letter, and *Siete edades del mundo*," *Mester* 7, no. 2 (1988): 95–103.

[31] Abrahams, "Lost Purim Joys," 266–68. For the Geonic responsum, see Louis Ginzberg, "Genizah Studies," *JQR*, o.s. 16 (1904): 650–52; Ginzberg, *Geonica*, 2 vols. (reprint, New York, 1968), 3:1–3.

[32] Frazer, *GB*, 3:172.

positive grounds for thinking" that the Jews "may at one time have burned, hanged, or crucified a real man in the character of Haman."[33] As noted earlier, one of the prominent Jews who took public offense at Frazer's theory linking Haman, Jesus, and Purim was Moses Gaster, who censured Frazer for suggesting that Jews in ancient Jerusalem had practiced a custom "thus far known to the imagination of the author alone." Furthermore, he asserted (not very honestly) in response to Frazer's suggestions concerning Jewish ritual violence on Purim that "to drink, to feast, and to offer gifts is all that has been enjoined and carried out throughout the ages."[34]

Gaster's heated denials in response to Frazer's imaginative excesses (reminiscent of Güdemann's response to the excesses of Lagarde) were matched by Abrahams's clearly deliberate omission of the Theodosian edict from his essay on "Lost Purim Joys," despite its direct relevance to the custom of effigy-burning discussed there. The edict had been explicitly mentioned, as we have seen, by many prominent scholars, Jewish as well as non-Jewish, with whose work Abrahams would have been familiar.[35] The omission then, could hardly have been other than apologetically motivated, for the Theodosian edict accused the Jews of "contempt of the Christian faith"—a subject with which Abrahams (like most Jewish scholars of his generation) was never particularly comfortable, and whose associations with Purim, especially after the publication of Frazer's controversial second edition, had become a bit too hot to handle.

Festive Fury in France

In his 1905 essay, Abrahams also omitted any reference to the execution on Purim, in late twelfth-century northern France, of a Christian who had murdered a Jew—an incident concerning which he could have learned a great deal (and probably did) from Heinrich Graetz, whose work he admired greatly.[36] It had also been discussed by Gougenot des Mousseaux in his controversial work on *The Jew, Judaism, and the Judaization of the Christian Peoples*. The French aristocrat, drawing upon d'Arbois de Jubainville's multivolume history of Champagne (1865), had described the Christian's execution as an act of ritual murder, in which "these miserable

---

[33] Ibid., 173–75.

[34] M. Gaster, review of Frazer, in *Folklore* 12 (1900): 226–30.

[35] Abrahams had even reviewed one such book! See Cassel, *Esther*, 224, and the brief review in *JQR*, o.s. 1 (1889): 184.

[36] I. Abrahams, "H. Graetz, the Jewish Historian," *JQR*, o.s. 4 (1892): 165–93.

ones gave themselves the joy of yielding to the demand of their cult and re-enacting the scenes of [Christ's] Passion upon a Christian."[37]

Had Gougenot des Mousseaux, also consulted Graetz's *History of the Jews* on the late twelfth-century incident in what most modern historians have called "Bray" (but may have been "Brie"),[38] he would have learned something that would have interested him greatly, namely that whether by "malignant design or accident, the execution took place on Purim."[39] The aristocratic anti-Semite had included the holiday of Purim among those ritual occasions for which Jews allegedly required Christian blood, and the execution by medieval Jews of a Christian on that holiday would only have added grist to his mill. But did the execution at Bray-sur-Seine (or possibly Brie-Comte Robert) really take place on Purim, and, if so, why was this known to the German-Jewish historian Graetz but not to his learned contemporary d'Arbois de Jubainville, the archivist of the Aube *départe-ment* in north-central France?

The latter relied exclusively upon Latin chroniclers, primarily Rigord's *Gesta Philippi Augusti*,[40] whereas Graetz also consulted R. Ephraim of Bonn's *Sefer ha-Zekhira*—first published in 1858.[41] R. Ephraim, in

---

[37] M. H. d'Arbois de Jubainville, *Histoire des ducs et comtes de Champagne*, 6 vols. (Paris, 1859–1866), 4:71–72; Gougenot des Mousseaux, *Le Juif*, 188–89. See also the early discussion by G.-B. Depping, *Les Juifs dans le moyen age: essai historique* (Paris, 1834), 133–34.

[38] On the precise location of the incident, see Bernhard Blumenkranz, "Bray-sur-Seine," *EJ*, 4:1321–22, and the sources cited there, and more recently Jordan, *French Monarchy*, 36, 271 who argues convincingly for Brie (in Comte-Robert) rather than Bray. The most thorough, if flawed, discussion of the incident remains Robert Chazan, "The Bray Incident of 1192: Realpolitik and Folk Slander," *PAAJR* 37 (1969): 1–18.

[39] See Graetz, *Geschichte . . . (von Aufblühen der jüdisch-spanischen Cultur (1027) bis Maimuni's Tod)* (1st ed., Leipzig, 1861), 6:249. For the English translation utilized here, see the London edition of 1892 "edited and in part translated by B. Löwy" and "specially revised . . . by the author," 3:416. In the American edition, however (Graetz, *History*, 3:404), the important word "malignant" was dropped, apparently for apologetic reasons. Its German original ("boshafter"), however, was retained by Graetz in the second and third German editions of 1871 and 1894, respectively. On Graetz's treatment of the execution, see further below.

[40] For the Latin text of Rigord's account see H. F. Delaborde, ed., *Gesta Philippi Augusti* (Paris, 1882–1885), 118–19, and (from there) Patricia Hidiroglou, "Les Juifs d'apres la littérature historique latine, de Philippe Auguste à Philippe le Bel," *REJ* 133 (1974): 434. Another medieval source used by many historians is the popular thirteenth-century *Speculum Historia* by Vincent of Beauvais, (bk. 30, chap. 8), which drew upon Rigord's account. It was translated into French in the early fourteenth century and printed in Paris in the late fifteenth century.

[41] For more modern publications, see Neubauer-Stern, *Hebräische Berichte*, 70 [German trans., 205–6]; *Sefer ha-Dem'aot*, 1:246–47; Haberman, *Gezerot*, 128. For an (abbreviated) English translation of the passage, see *Church, State, and the Jew in the Middle Ages*, ed. Robert Chazan (New York, 1980), 304–5. On the chronicle, see also Chazan, "R. Ephraim of Bonn's *Sefer Zechirah*," REJ 132 (1973): 119–26.

addition to stating that the execution took place (after the Jews had bribed the countess) on the holiday of Purim, gave its date as 4951/1191—rather than 1192, as had Rigord and the other Latin sources. There were also discrepancies with regard to both the number of local Jewish casualties as a consequence of the swift reprisal by Philip Augustus, with whom the murderer had some sort of feudal tie,[42] and the precise manner of their deaths. Rigord reported that eighty Jews had been burned in Bray/Brie, and a later Latin source (Guillaume le Breton's poetic rendition of Rigord's *Gesta*) expanded the number to ninety-nine. R. Ephraim, however, described their deaths within the narrative conventions of medieval Jewish martyrdom—asserting that sixty were slaughtered preemptively by one of their co-religionists (in order to preclude their possible apostasy) and all others over the age of thirteen were burned to death.

Leopold Zunz included the "martyrs" at Bray/Brie in his lachrymose essay on Jewish suffering in the middle ages (which originally appeared as a chapter in his 1855 survey of medieval Hebrew liturgical poetry) choosing, not surprisingly, the higher figure (ninety-nine) of the two reported by medieval Latin sources. According to Zunz, one of the founding fathers of the "Science of Judaism," not only was the number of martyrs great, but their Purim behavior had been thoroughly innocent. In his version of the tragic events that had occurred there, no Christian murderer had been executed in Bray/Brie; rather, the local Jews had "simply gibbeted a figure of Haman."[43] Zunz, who wrote his essay shortly before the publication of R. Ephraim's Hebrew chronicle, might have been less adamant about denying that the Jews did indeed execute a real Christian had he seen this confirmed in a contemporary Hebrew chronicle. The only Hebrew source he knew concerning Bray/Brie was Joseph ha-Kohen's sixteenth-century *Emek ha-Bakhah*, according to which the Christian murderer was freed by the king on Purim rather than executed by the Jews.[44] Yet whereas the sixteenth-century chronicler had given the number of Jewish victims as eighty, Zunz cited the higher figure of ninety-nine given by Guillaume le Breton. Evidently, for Zunz, there were some things for which Christian chroniclers could be relied upon!

---

[42] On the nature of the relationship between the murderer and Philip Augustus, see the judicious comments of Jordan, *French Monarchy*, 270n77.

[43] Zunz, *Synagogale Poesie* [1855], 26; Zunz, *The Sufferings of the Jews during the Middle Ages*, trans. A. Löwy, rev. and ed. by G. A. Kohut (New York: 1907), 43 (*Miscellany of Hebrew Literature* [1872], 1:184). For a critique of Zunz's tendency to see the mere existence of the Jews as their sole proven crime, see S. W. Baron, "The Jewish Factor in Medieval Civilization," in Baron, *Ancient and Medieval Jewish History* (New Brunswick, N.J., 1972), 261 (originally published in *PAAJR* 12 [1942]).

[44] *Emek Habaca: Historia Persecutionum Judaeorum*, ed. M. Letteris (Vienna, 1852), 45–46.

Rather different was the treatment of the incident some six years later by the younger Graetz, who was generally less apologetic about the Jewish past than was Zunz, and whose historical writing was certainly more engaged with it—for better or for worse.[45] In 1861, when he first addressed the events in Bray/Brie, Graetz wrote: "*By malignant design or accident* the execution [of the Christian] took place on the Purim festival, and this circumstance reminded the people of Haman's gallows, *and perhaps of something else*" (emphases added).[46] This rich and rather engaged historical rhetoric invites further examination. Graetz's artful, though provocative, hedging on the question of "malignant design or accident" in the choice of Purim as the day of the Christian's execution clearly echoes his earlier hedging on the related question as to whether, in the fifth century, the gallows onto which Haman was raised by the Jews had "by design or by accident, the form of a cross." One wonders whether Graetz's consistent ambiguity was itself a matter of design or accident. I suspect that as a Jew who identified with his people's history, Graetz leaned toward the "intentionalist" thesis, but as a responsible scholar he exercised (not only for scholarly reasons) greater caution. Nevertheless, his attempt to reconstruct the mentality of the twelfth-century Jews of Bray/Brie and to imagine what they might have been thinking to themselves when they saw the despised Christian murderer hanging on Purim is quite tantalizing. Graetz was quite certain that they were reminded of Haman on his gallows, but he also suggested that their memories had room for a view, in this instance, of Christ crucified.

It should be stressed that it was not merely his own imagination, but the Latin accounts of the execution (which he read side by side with R. Ephraim's Hebrew chronicle) that led Graetz in this direction. These accounts, as his French contemporary d'Arbois de Jubainville also recognized, describe the Jews of Bray/Brie as having executed the Christian after first leading him through town while being scourged, with his hands bound behind his back and his head crowned with thorns, in a clear re-enactment of Christ's passion.[47] Graetz evidently recognized that it was possible to give credence to these accounts, especially if they described Purim behavior, without necessarily acknowledging the validity of ritual-murder accusations.

His Hebrew translator, S. P. Rabinowitz, who had already omitted, as we have seen, mention of the scourged Christian child at Inmestar, also exercised considerable editorial freedom with regard to the Bray/Brie

---

[45] See Ismar Schorsch, ed., *Heinrich Graetz: The Structure of Jewish History*, 49.

[46] In the German original the emphasized words are: "Aus boshafter Absicht oder zufällig geschah . . . , und vielleicht an etwas Anderes." See Graetz, *Geschichte* (1st ed.), 6:249.

[47] See Hidiroglou, "Les Juifs d'apres la littérature historique latine," 434–38.

incident. Whereas Graetz had asserted that the execution of the Christian on Purim "reminded the people of Haman's gallows, and perhaps of something else," his Hebrew translator rendered him as suggesting, far less provocatively, that the Jews of Bray/Brie "might also have been reminded of King Philip Augustus, a king as tough as Haman."[48] Rabinowitz, however, was not the only one to introduce a significant change into Graetz's problematic passage—so, eventually, did the author himself, in what appears to have been a loss of nerve on his part. Although the second edition (1871) of the relevant volume (six) carried the sentence unaltered, by the third edition (1894), Graetz's dark hint about "something else" in the minds of the Jews witnessing the hanging of a Christian on Purim evidently seemed to him inappropriate. The once brazenly suggestive sentence was toned down to read merely that the Jews of Bray/Brie "were reminded then perhaps of Haman's gallows," with no further possibility dangled before the historical imagination.[49]

One must suspect that the discreet deletion, and the corresponding failure of nerve that it suggests, were at least partly due to Heinrich von Treitschke's vehement and much-publicized criticism of Graetz and his *History of the Jews* in 1879, in which Graetz was accused of a savage or even deathly hatred (*Todhass*) of Christianity.[50] Although Graetz valiantly defended himself, he subsequently became a bit gun-shy about the question of Jewish antagonism toward Christianity and its symbols. He may have been especially cautious with regard to the specific question of anti-Christian hostility on Purim after the appearance of Lagarde's rather hostile 1887 study, which, as we saw above, had so exercised Graetz's younger Viennese colleague Moritz Güdemann.

Although Graetz had expressed some doubt as to whether it was by design or accident that the Christian's execution took place on Purim, he was certain that the Jews themselves had done the deed. This was also the view, decades later, of Cecil Roth, who, even in the dark days of 1933, inferred from R. Ephraim's account that the Jews of Bray/Brie had obtained permission "to execute the murderer *with their own hands*" (emphasis added), although he denied that they intentionally chose the

---

[48] Graetz, *Divrei*, 4:271.

[49] Graetz, *Geschichte* (2nd ed.), 6:231; Graetz, *Geschichte* (3rd ed., Leipzig, 1894), 6:10–11. Although the third edition of volume six appeared after Graetz's death, no indication is given that it was revised by a hand other than the author's.

[50] See the polemical exchanges between Graetz and Treitschke from the years 1879–1880 collected in W. Boehlich, ed., *Der Berliner Antisemitismusstreit* (Berlin, 1965), especially 9, 28, 39, 47. On these exchanges, see also Abrahams, "H. Graetz," 188–90; Schorsch, ed., *Heinrich Graetz: The Structure of Jewish History*, 58–59; M. A. Meyer, "Heinrich Graetz and Heinrich von Treitschke," *Modern Judaism* 6 (1986): 1–11.

day of Purim for his death.[51] By contrast, Robert Chazan has argued that the relevant passage in the Hebrew chronicle (*va-yitluhu be-yom Purim*: "and he was hanged on the day of Purim") is "vexingly ambiguous," since it is not clear whether the hanging was done by the Jews or by those normally charged with such responsibilities. As noted above, all of the major Latin chronicles of the event, including that of Rigord, describe the Jews as having executed the Christian, whether by hanging or crucifixion, after leading him through town with his hands bound behind his back and his head crowned with thorns. Chazan, however, rejects their historicity— finding their accounts "strikingly similar to those of the supposed crucifixion of William of Norwich and Harold of Gloucester." All of these medieval descriptions, he has claimed, may be traced to "a common source, the Gospel versions of the Passion."[52]

Yet it must be stressed that Rigord, for one, did not assert that the Jews of Bray/Brie had crucified the scourged Christian, but rather that he was hanged from a gallows (*et postea patibulo suspenderunt*).[53] His account cannot therefore be easily dismissed as merely paraphrasing "the Gospel versions of the Passion." Moreover, R. Ephraim's testimony that the Christian "was hanged [*va-yitluhu*] on the day of Purim" does not exclude crucifixion, since the same verb was used in Hebrew for both hanging and crucifixion. Jesus himself, as is well known, was commonly referred to by medieval Jewish authors (including R. Ephraim himself) as *ha-taluy*.[54]

In Rigord's Latin chronicle, the date on which the Jews were punished for their rash act is given as March 18, which would place it, as Chazan has noted, some two weeks after Purim—at the end of the normally merry month of Adar. In his estimate, therefore, "Ephraim's suggestion that the hanging took place on Purim day seems questionable," for that "would mean a fifteen-day delay between the execution and Philip Augustus's peremptory punishment."[55] Against such cautious skepticism, however,

---

[51] Roth, "Feast of Purim," 522. See also Depping, *Les Juifs*, 133; Simon Schwarzfuchs, *Les Juifs de France* (Paris, 1975), 56.

[52] Chazan, "Bray Incident," 6, 10–13.

[53] See also Hidiroglou, "Les Juifs d'apres la littérature historique latine," 423–24, who notes (without reference to Chazan) that whereas Guillaume le Breton refers to crucifixion, Rigord speaks only of hanging.

[54] Haberman, *Gezerot*, 27, 189; Ben-Yehuda, *Dictionary*, s.v. *teliah*. On *ha-taluy* as a common term for Jesus, see, for example, Zunz, *Synagogale Poesie*, 466, 470; Rosenthal, *Joseph Hamekane*, 48, 52–53, 56, 86. For its use by R. Ephraim himself, see *Sefer 'Arugat ha-Bosem*, ed. E. E. Urbach, 4 vols. (Jerusalem, 1939–1963), 4:47.

[55] Chazan, "Bray Incident," 4–7. Salo Baron was even more skeptical, asserting that all that can be known after comparing R. Ephraim with Rigord is that "sometime during the

one might argue that on no day other than Purim would the Jews of medieval Europe be likely to commit such a recklessly joyous act, especially one of crucifixion, and on no other day would their recklessness be presumably fueled by alcohol as much as animosity.[56]

Purim, like the various forms of Carnival, was often characterized by an attitude of "creative disrespect," and presented an occasion when "the collective expression of envy, anger, and enmity" could be considered (at least by the Jews themselves) legitimate.[57] Scholars such as Emannuel Le Roy Ladurie and Edward Muir have linked Carnival festivity with religious and political violence, the former describing the 1580 Carnival in the French town of Romans as "a time of masks and massacres for the divided citizenry."[58] And June Nash, who has engaged in field work among Bolivia's tin-mining communities, has described Carnival there as "not a wild excess of sex and drink, but a precise channeling of some very deep passions and sentiments."[59]

If the Jews of medieval Bray/Brie had little hope that local Christians would recognize their right to such collective expression, they could perhaps hope that the former would forgive their follies as simply the "legitimate" consequences of festive inebriation. Sometimes the gamble, as in the case of Bray/Brie, would result in dozens of Jewish deaths, but this, I submit, was part of the Purim rite to be reckless. "I sometimes think," the anthropologist Melvin Konner has written, that "the more reckless

---

Third Crusade there occurred a persecution of the Jews in the small community of Bray." See Baron, *SRH* 4, 129. According to Baron, it was not even clear (despite R. Ephraim's testimony) that the Jews did anything to provoke this "persecution." His version of the events is thus surprisingly close to that of Zunz, whose lachrymose approach he famously criticized.

[56] The exhortation to become so drunk on Purim that one could not distinguish between cursing Haman and blessing Mordecai already appeared in the Babylonian Talmud (*Megillah* 7b). Note also the twelfth-century testimony of R. Abraham b. Isaac of Narbonne in Assaf, *Sifran shel Rishonim*, no. 41, excerpted in Dinur, *Israel in the Diaspora*, 2:5, 218.

[57] On the "creative disrespect" of Carnival, see Peter Stallybras and Allon White, *The Politics and Poetics of Transgression* (Ithaca, 1986), 19, and on its presenting an occasion for "the collective expression of envy, anger, and enmity," see John Bossy, *Christianity in the West 1400–1700* (Oxford, 1985), 43.

[58] See E. Le Roy Ladurie, *Carnival in Romans*, trans. Mary Feeney (New York, 1979); Edward Muir, *Mad Blood Stirring: Vendetta and Factions in Friuli during the Renaissance* (Baltimore, 1993), esp. 191–214.

[59] Whenever its people discussed political repression and revolution, she has noted, "they concluded by asking me, 'But have you ever been here during Carnival?'" June Nash, "Religion, Rebellion, and Working Class Consciousness in Bolivian Tin Mining Communities," 460–62, in *Religion and Rural Revolt*, ed. J. M. Bak and Gerhard Benecke (Manchester, 1984).

among us may have something to teach the careful about the sort of immortality that comes from living fully every day"—or, it might be added, even one day.[60]

PURIM AND PASSION IN PROVENCE

The case of Bray/Brie was not the only medieval instance in which European Jews are reported, apparently reliably, to have reenacted elements of Christ's Passion as part of their violent Purim festivities. Another instance was that of Manosque, a town in Provence, where in 1306 the Jews were accused of insulting the Christian faith on Purim while executing "rough justice" on some of their own co-religionists. The case of Manosque would have been a welcome addition to the anti-Semitic arsenal of such French authors as Gougenot des Mousseaux and Desportes, but it came to light only in 1879, a decade after the former published his influential tract on *The Jew, Judaism, and the Judaization of the Christian Peoples.* Camille Arnaud, who in that year published a brief study of medieval Provençal Jewry, cited two related instances from the archives of Manosque, both of which had occurred in 1306. In one, a Jew was said to have been flogged while being dragged naked through the Jewish quarter after having been found with "a certain woman," in another, a man had reportedly been led through the streets dressed in women's clothing (*ad modum mulieris*) during that same "holiday called Purim." Arnaud, with unconcealed disdain, found it appropriate to add: "Thus proceeded Jewish justice. But the perpetrators of this rude exhibition were required to account for their conduct before Christian justice as well."[61]

The first scholar to link the case of Bray/Brie with that of Manosque was Cecil Roth, in his 1933 article on "The Feast of Purim and the Origins of the Blood Accusation." Roth, who rightly saw the Purim season as "the sole occasion for a certain degree of licensed libertinism in the Jewish calendar," suggested that the twelfth-century incident may represent a stage in the development of a Purim rite of symbolic mockery in which Haman's effigy was replaced by "the person of a human being—generally Jewish, exceptionally Christian."[62] In advancing this argument Roth, as he acknowledged, was following in the footsteps of the person he respectfully,

---

[60] Melvin Konner, *Why the Reckless Survive . . . and Other Secrets of Human Nature* (New York, 1990), 139.

[61] "C'est ainsi que procéda la justice Juive. Mais les auteurs de cette exhibition malhonnête durent rendre compte de leur conduite devant la justice chrétienne." C. Arnaud, *Essai sur la condition des juifs en Provence au Moyen-Age* (Forcecalquier, 1879), 48–49.

[62] Roth, "The Feast of Purim," 522–25.

but not without a tinge of irony, called "the omniscient Frazer," whose *Scapegoat* volume in the mammoth (and enormously popular) third edition of the *Golden Bough* had by then been in print for two decades.[63]

Roth was not in position either to ignore or to summarily dismiss the assertions, coming as they did from the pen of one of the most formidable figures in the intellectual world of the time. Frazer had by then become a cultural hero who, as Mary Douglas has put it, came to dominate "the whole horizon of thoughts about man and his nature . . . within which the widest literary efforts were engaged."[64] Roth chose, therefore, to meet the great Sir James halfway rather than head-on, acknowledging that Jews had "on occasion" done violence to a real man rather than an effigy on Purim, but asserting that the effigy-burning was the more ancient custom, and the other a later, unfortunate development thereof. This was, after all, 1933, which also helps to explain why Roth made the apologetic gesture of referring to the entire custom as a "contemptuous formality."[65] Roth argued that the "justice" executed by the Jews of Manosque must be seen within the carnivalesque context of Purim, and hence as a continuation of the tradition of inflicting punishment upon an effigy of Haman—who, in this instance, was represented by a fellow Jew. He suggested further that the flogging of a naked Jew may have been perceived by Christians as a "blasphemous parody of the Passion."[66]

Four decades later Joseph Shatzmiller, in his meticulous study of the Jews of Manosque during the late Middle Ages, returned to the Purim incident of 1306, publishing further documentary material concerning the trial, and concluding that the punishments carried out by the Jews were not actual ones, but rather humoristic parodies performed in the spirit of Purim.[67] Citing the Theodosian edict of 408 in this regard, he saw the hostile reaction in Manosque as testifying to the "remarkable

---

[63] There, Frazer repeated one of the controversial suggestions regarding Purim that he had made in the second edition, namely that "there are some positive grounds for thinking" that Jews in former times "may at one time have burned, hanged, or crucified a real man in the character of Haman." See Frazer, *Golden Bough* (3rd ed.), 9:394. On the impact of the *Golden Bough*, see Ackerman, *J. G. Frazer*, esp. chap. 14–15; and Mary Beard, "Frazer, Leach, and Virgil: The Popularity (and Unpopularity) of the Golden Bough," *CSSH* 34 (1992): 203–24, especially 212ff.

[64] Mary Douglas, "Judgements on James Frazer," *Daedalus* (Fall, 1978): 151 (*PAAAS* 107, no. 4). See also Beard, "Frazer, Leach, and Virgil," 214.

[65] Roth, "The Feast of Purim," 525.

[66] Ibid., 521.

[67] "Une parodie humoristique de procès, faite dans le cadre de la fête du Purim." See Joseph Shatzmiller, *Recherches sur la communauté juive de Manosque au Moyen Age* (Paris, 1973), 127–28. Shatzmiller also supported Roth's suggestion that the flogging may have been perceived by Christians as a "blasphemous parody of the Passion" (ibid., 129n3).

continuity" between the perception of Purim practices on the part of Christians in late antiquity and in late medieval Europe. With regard to the accuracy of the various accusations of anti-Christian conduct made against the Jews during that long period, Shatzmiller took the prudent position that the problem could not yet be treated on account of the paucity of extant documentation.[68]

I am reckless enough to argue, however—as I have argued throughout this book—that the "remarkable continuity" to be noted here applies no less, and probably more, to Jewish patterns of behavior and expression than to Christian perceptions (or misperceptions) thereof. And the medieval documentation, it must be said, is less sparse than one might imagine. R. Meir Abulafia of Toledo (d. 1244), a leading rabbinical figure in thirteenth-century Spain, composed a blatantly anti-Christian poem for Purim with clear allusions to Jesus, the New Testament, and the bread and wine of the Mass. Later in that century, as Jean Régné noted long ago, charges were brought against the Jews of Villafranca, near Barcelona, concerning their behavior on Purim of 1291.[69] At around the same time—as Shatzmiller himself has noted—the great Spanish rabbi Solomon ibn Adret (d. 1306) discussed the case of two Jews who, when visiting friends in Marseille whose house was near that of the bishop, engaged in Purim "amusements" that were seen by the local Christians as an offense to their religion.[70] Futhermore accusations leveled against the Jews of Lunel (in 1319) and of Hyères (in 1343) for insulting the Christian faith seem also to have been related to their Purim antics.[71]

It must be stressed that Purim antics, like festive license in general, could be multivalent, so that a verifiable "internal" Jewish meaning would not exclude an additional (hostile) message directed toward the Christian environment. This would appear to have been the case in Manosque, where the Jews chose the day of Purim, 1306, for publicly flogging a man found with "a certain woman" and for grotesquely representing a couple found *in flagrante delicto*. We may, perhaps, compare Purim license with that of "misrule" in the late medieval French

---

[68] Ibid., 130–31.

[69] Bernard Septimus, *Hispano-Jewish Culture in Transition: The Career and Controversies of* Ramah (Cambridge, Mass., 1982), 14; Horowitz, "And It Was Reversed," 142–43; J. Régné, *History of the Jews in Aragon: Regesta and Documents*, 1213–1327, ed. Yom Tov Assis (reprint, Jerusalem, 1978), 446.

[70] Shatzmiller, *Recherches*, 130n3. See Solomon ibn Adret, *Responsa*, vol. 3 (reprint, Tel-Aviv, 1973), no. 389.

[71] Shatzmiller, *Recherches*, 129–30; Maurice Kriegel, *Les Juifs à la fin du Moyen Age dans l'Europe méditerranée* (Paris, 1979), 35–36.

countryside, which, as Natalie Davis has noted, was not merely rebellious, but rather, "very much in the service of the . . . community."[72] Similarly the anthropologist David Gilmore has described the modern European Carnival as a customary time "to purge the wrongheaded of their evil ways, to punish deviants and wrongdoers." Gilmore, on the basis of his field work in Andalusia, has stressed the role of internally generated aggression in Carnival festivity.[73]

The execution of justice by medieval Jews on their day of Carnival, whether applied to a Christian murderer in Bray/Brie or a Jewish adulterer in Manosque, could certainly be a festive occasion, especially when normal circumstances prevented such justice from being done. But not only then, for "in punishment," as Nietzsche perceptively wrote, "there is much that is festive."[74] In 1569 a Mantuan jurist suggested that the most appropriate punishment for a Jew who had carnal relations with a Christian woman was for him to be castrated publicly during Carnival, which, he believed, would provide *un belissimo spettacolo*. Such a punishment, in fact, had indeed been meted out to a Jew in late fourteenth-century Avignon.[75]

Earlier in that century the Jews of nearby Manosque incorporated festive punishment in their carnivalesque celebration of Purim when representing, in drag, the female member of the adulterous couple, whose male partner was not merely dramatically paraded in the Jewish quarter,[76] but also flogged while being dragged naked through its streets. The cross-dressing and the nude floggings were not at cross-purposes, but rather represented two sides of the festive inversion characteristic of Purim: partying and punishment. In addition to the settling of accounts within the community there was, in Manosque, the larger account traditionally settled with Christianity and its symbols on the holiday of Purim. The Jews, by openly and unabashedly flogging one of their own, may well have found ways of suggesting that they had someone else in mind as well—Someone whose Passion, as Graetz boldly suggested, may have been in the Purim thoughts of the Jews in late twelfth-century Bray/Brie. The Manosque authorities, who accused the local Jews of having, "in their audacity, put aside their fear of God," could perhaps more accurately have accused them of having, in their (traditional Purim) audacity, put aside (for a day) their fear of Christianity.

[72] N. Z. Davis, *Society and Culture in Early Modern France* (Stanford, 1975), 107.

[73] D. D. Gilmore, *Aggression and Community: Paradoxes of Andalusian Culture* (New Haven, 1987), 8, 12, 99, 120–21.

[74] Friedrich Nietzsche, *On the Genealogy of Morals*, trans. W. Kaufmann and R. J. Hollingdale (New York, 1967 [1887]), 67.

[75] Shlomo Simonsohn, *History of the Jews in the Duchy of Mantua* (Jerusalem, 1977), 115n49; Moulinas, *Les Juifs du pape*, 116. See also Trachtenberg *Devil and the Jews*, 251.

[76] On "comic pairs" in carnivalesque festivity, see Mikhail Bakhtin, *Rabelais and His World*, trans. H. Iswolsky (Bloomington, Ind., 1984), 201.

The violent undertone of medieval Purim festivity, which surfaces vividly in Bray/Brie and in Manosque, but which has been only weakly acknowledged in Jewish scholarship, runs parallel to a similar strain in the European tradition of Carnival celebration. Carnival, as we have seen, was historically a time of license to engage not only in acts of sensual gratification but also in acts of ritualized aggression.[77] These dimensions of Purim are evident also in the 1389 Purim letter by the Spanish Jew Solomon ha-Levi of Burgos, written while he was abroad—and shortly before he converted and became Pablo de Santa Maria. There the author is reminded of "those merry throngs who are today joyously celebrating the feast in Burgos" at which wine flows freely, "all tongues are loosed, incoherence prevails, and a wild scene of mingled love and rage ensues."[78]

One is reminded of Gilmore's recent description of Carnival in Andalusia:

> During the four days of freedom, the celebrants enthusiastically flail each other with bamboo poles. When they tire of that they screech obscenities at rivals, bombard one another with choice bits of embarrassing gossip, pass on stories, revile comrades, divulge secrets, betray confidences. . . . The streets echo not only with good cheer, but also with spiteful epithets, luscious insults, treachery. Scores are settled as men and women pound each other with ribald tirades composed lovingly weeks beforehand.[79]

Solomon Levi's description of Purim as a time when "incoherence prevails, and a wild scene of mingled love and rage ensues" is rendered according to the elegant but restrained translation provided by Israel Abrahams in 1900. Yet for "incoherence" one could just as well have rendered "obscenity" (cf. Isa. 9:16), and Abrahams's "love and rage" might today be translated as "sex and violence." Solomon's letter refers, in a section not translated by Abrahams, to those who give free expression on Purim to "their loves, their hates, their jealousies" (cf. Eccles. 9:6), and to those "who make their way about the city reeling and staggering [cf. Ps. 107:27] as they go, gashing themselves with knives and spears, according to their practice, until blood streams over them."[80]

The last passage is lifted directly from the verse in 1 Kings (18:28) describing the attempts of the prophets of Baal to bring down fire from on high in response to Elijah's repeated taunts, and artfully catches the tone of ritualized violence which became characteristic of Purim. For the biblical author such cultic violence was something to be mocked, but for

[77] Peter Burke, *The Historical Anthropology of Early Modern Italy: Essays on Perception and Communication* (Cambridge, 1987), 186; Scott, *Domination*, 173–74. See also M. Boiteux, "Carnaval annexé: Essai de lecture d'une fête romaine," *Annales E.S.C.* 32 (1977): 365.

[78] Abrahams, "Paul of Burgos in London" (II) 257, 260.

[79] Gilmore, *Aggression and Community*, 8.

[80] Abrahams, "Paul of Burgos in London," (II), 260.

lonely Solomon of Burgos, whose "warm love of the ceremonies" and
"total lack of overstrained asceticism" were adduced by Abrahams as proof
of his continuing loyalty to "the sentiments of the medieval Rabbis,"[81] the
rites of violence on Purim (which may have included punishments of the
sort administered in Manosque) were as longingly recalled as the freely
flowing Spanish wine. They were not, of course, as longingly recalled by
Jewish historians, even those who, like Abrahams, allowed themselves to
wax nostalgic about "lost Purim joys."

WHEN IN ROME . . .

In his *Jewish Life in the Middle Ages* (1896), Abrahams made no mention
of the carnivalesque Jewish violence at Bray/Brie, but he did discuss the
many "indignities" and occasional deaths suffered by the Jews of Rome,
from the fifteenth century onward, during their forced participation in the
footraces that were part of the city's famous Carnival season. Quoting
from Abraham Berliner's then recently published study of Roman Jewish
history, Abrahams reported that on the first day of Carnival several Jews
were forced to open the footraces: "Half clad, often amid heavy showers
of rain, whipped and jeered at, they were compelled amid the wild shouts
of the mob to cover the whole length of the race-course, which was about
1100 yards long. Occasionally the poor victims succumbed to their exer-
tions and fell dead on the course."[82] Berliner had noted that it was during the 1460s, under Pope Paul II, that the Jews of Rome were first
forced to participate in these humiliating exercises, and that only in 1668,
under Clement IX, were they allowed to exempt themselves from running
the gauntlet of the Corso—in return for a hefty payment of 300 gold
scudi. They were still obliged, however, to present the prizes at Carnival's
end. Moreover, from the early seventeenth-century masked processions
called *giudate*, based on mock imitation of Jewish rites, became a common feature of the Roman Carnival.[83]

Earlier in the nineteenth century Ferdinand Gregorovius had described
the traditional Jewish race on the first day of Carnival with great pathos:
"They ran," he wrote "from the Arch of Domitian to the Church of

---

[81] Ibid., 258. On cultic violence in Spain between Jews and Muslims in 1389, see Nirenberg,
Communities of Violence, 181.

[82] Abrahams, *Jewish Life*, 256; A. Berliner, *Geschichte der Juden in Rom*, 2 vols. (Frankfurt,
1893), 2:47.

[83] Berliner, *Rom*, 2:48. See also the discussions of A. Ademollo, *Il Carnevale di Roma*
(Rome, 1883), 1–11, 64; Ettore Natali, *Il ghetto di Roma* (Rome, 1887), 96–106; and especially Boiteux, "Juifs dans le Carnaval," 745–87.

St. Mark at the end of the Corso at full tilt, amid Rome's taunting shrieks of encouragement and peals of laughter, while the Holy Father stood upon a richly ornamented balcony and laughed heartily." Gregorovius was hardly a philo-Semite, but he was impressed by the Jews's age-old "power to endure," which he found "so remarkable that I confess I cannot explain it." He also described the Jews as being "bold and aggressive despite all submissiveness."[84]

One instance of the latter tendency occurred in late February of 1609, when the first of that year's Carnival *giudate* took place, featuring a mock Jewish funeral. The Jews of Rome, despite having experienced personal humiliations during Carnival for nearly a century and a half, reacted quite violently to this mockery of their religion, hurling down upon the procession a variety of household items (including, one suspects, chamber pots). The police had to be called and no less than 140 Jews were arrested.[85]

The *giudata* was a mirror image, in some respects, of the Jews using their Carnival to mock Christianity. Italian Catholics would have been aware of such practices, especially when Purim (as was often the case) overlapped with Lent. In 1575 members of an apostolic delegation to Cremona (in the Duchy of Milan) were told by local Christians that "during Lent the Jews celebrate their own Carnival and roast their meat in the ovens of Christians." This, of course, may have been nothing more than a nasty rumor, however the testimony does possess a fair degree of verisimilitude. Roasting Jewish meat in Christian ovens during Lent, a practice more in keeping with the laws of Kashrut than might first appear,[86] would reflect the traditional double-edged Purim recklessness— daring, on the one hand, to bend (but not to flout) divine laws in the name of festivity, and, on the other, to scoff at Christian pieties while being "swept away" by the same surge of festive joy. Jewish meat in Christian ovens would have been, for some eyes, a ritual reversal no less striking than the more common Purimtide confounding of two types of flesh: men in women's clothing, and women in men's.[87] And it would have possessed, for at least some Jews, the no less attractive feature of literally rubbing Christian noses in the pungent odors of Jewish transgressive activity.

[84] Gregorovius, *Ghetto*, 23–24, 46, 49–50.

[85] Boiteux, "Juifs dans le Carnaval," 757–58.

[86] On the plausibility of the claim that Jews were roasting their meat in Christian ovens during Lent, see Horowitz, "And It Was Reversed," 161–62, and now I. M. Ta-Shma, "Reicha Milta: A Chapter in the Development of Medieval Halakha" (in Hebrew), *Sidra* 19 (2004):177–88.

[87] S. Simonsohn, ed., *The Jews in the Duchy of Milan*, 4 vols. (Jerusalem, 1982–1986), 3:1616. On Purim cross-dressing, see Horowitz, "And It Was Reversed," 155–56, 161–62.

Italian Jews also had other means of using the festival of Purim to express their hostility toward the alien religion based in Rome. The custom, first mentioned in thirteenth-century Latin sources, of smashing a jar on Purim while expressing the hope that, like Haman, Christendom too would soon be smashed, may be reliably confirmed by at least one Hebrew manuscript of fifteenth-century Italian provenance.[88] Late in that century the Franciscan priest Bernardino di Busti included this Purim practice in his *Consilium contra Judaeos* (1488), composed at the request of the Duke of Milan, for the purpose of a trial being conducted against thirty-eight Jews accused of having vilified the Christian religion. Although it is possible, as has been suggested, that Busti learned of this practice from Latin sources, it seems more likely that he drew his knowledge from Jewish apostates, with whom he is known to have been in contact.[89]

In 1547 a Roman Jew met his death running (involuntarily) in one of the annual Carnival races. Four years later some Roman Jews were arrested after drunkenly harassing and then robbing a Christian passerby. They sought to explain their behavior by pointing to the fact that it had occurred during "the week of our Carnival."[90] Whether or not their aggressive behavior had been fueled by memories of what had recently befallen their co-religionist during the Christian Carnival, they evidently expected the local authorities to understand that the Jewish Carnival could include not only boisterousness but also brutality. As noted above, when in the seventeenth century Giulio Morosini reported that Purim was called "the Jewish Carnival," he added that "indeed there is not much difference."[91]

---

[88] See Alexander Patschovsky, ed., *Der Passauer Anonymus: eine Sammelwerk . . . aus der Mitte des 13. Jahrhunderts* (*Schriften der Monumenta Germaniae historica*, vol. 22) (Stuttgart, 1968) 180. This work was kindly brought to my attention by Y. Deutsch. See also Chen Merchavia, "La polemica di Bernardinus di Busti contro gli ebrei ed il Talmud," (in Hebrew) *Michael* 1 (1973): 236n30; Alonso de Espina, *Fortalitium fidei* (Nuremberg, 1494), 841b. The Hebrew manuscript is Frankfurt 8° 130 (formerly Merzbacher, no. 84), 103a, where the verse to be recited while smashing the jar is from Isaiah 30:14 ("And its breaking is like that of a potter's vessel, which is smashed so ruthlessly that among its fragments not a sherd is to be found . . .").

[89] According to Busti it was Jewish custom while smashing the jars to recite the words: *"Sicut contritus fuit Aman, sic regnum christianorum subito conteratur."* See A. Antoniazzi Villa, "Per la storia degli ebrei nel dominio sforzesco; un episodio di antisemitismo nel 1488," *RMI* 46 (1980): 323–38; Villa, *Un processo contro gli ebrei nella Milano del 1488* (Bologna, 1985); Shulvass, *Milan*, 1094–95 (no. 2160), Horowitz, "And It Was Reversed," 159–61.

[90] Thomas Cohen, "The Case of the Mysterious Coil of Rope: Street Life and Jewish Persona in Rome in the Middle of the Sixteenth Century," *Sixteenth Century Journal* 19 (1988): 210, 218–21; Natali, *Il Ghetto*, 100.

[91] Calimani, *Ghetto of Venice*, 196.

EIGHTEENTH-CENTURY ESCAPADES

Early in the eighteenth century the recklessness that Jews often allowed themselves with regard to Purim reared its head in yet another way. In 1715, while awaiting formal permission to inaugurate their new synagogue, the Jews in the small Piedmontese town of Alba (southwest of Turin) decided, somewhat impetuously, to hold Purim services there anyway. They did so, in fact, quite noisily rather than surreptitiously, causing their Christian neighbors to report them to the ecclesiastical authorities.[92] Some two and a half decades later Giovanni Mercurino Arborio Gattinara, the bishop of Alessandria (also in the Piedmont), sought to have the Jews residing in the vicinity of his cathedral either expelled or relegated to the local Ghetto (which would have required expansion). One of several arguments advanced by the bishop in his memorandum to the king of Savoy was that the local Jews were in the habit of reciting curses against Christians as part of their Purim celebrations. Although Ludovico Dani, the king's legal advisor, rejected some of the bishop's accusations, he acknowledged that on Purim the Jews of Alessandria merely did what their co-religionists elsewhere did—they smashed jars into pieces and expressed the wish that Christendom too would quickly be smashed.[93]

Dani's relative indifference toward this practice may have been rooted in his recognition that Purim was "the Jewish Carnival." This was indeed explicitly acknowledged in 1751 by a later bishop of Alessandria, Alfonso Miroglio, who complained on March 21 of that year that the Jews had staged, in a local theater, a satirical comedy (*La Contessina*) during the holy days of Lent, despite having been denied permission to do so. The Jewish actors of Alessandria had been arrested during their second performance and detained for two days in the local citadel. The first performance had taken place on March 12—which in that year coincided with Shushan Purim (the day after the holiday), when some vestigial recklessness was presumably still in force.[94]

A year earlier Frederick the Great of Prussia, in his charter of 1750, had conditioned the privileges of the Jews under his rule upon their refraining

---

[92] J. Sessa, *Tractatus de Judaeis* (Torino, 1717), 131; Vittorio Colorni, *Gli ebrei nel sistema del diritto commune* (Milan, 1956), 47; Segre, *Piedmont*, 2:1345 (no. 2589).

[93] Segre, *Piedmont*, 3:1605–606 (no. 2907). Dani, who quoted the imprecation in Latin, may well have taken it from Busti's *Consilium*, which had been published several times— once (in 1548) on its own and five times (between 1498 and 1588) as part of his *Rosarium Sermonum Predicabilium*. Busti's comments on Jews and Judaism had also been copied by other authors. See Horowitz, "And It Was Reversed," 163–64.

[94] Segre, *Piedmont*, 3:1728–29 (no. 3062); Horowitz, "And It Was Reversed," 164.

from prayers (e.g., 'Aleinu) that could give offense to Christians and "from all improper excesses in their festivals, particularly during the so called Feast of Haman, or Purim."[95] Although this reference to improper excesses ("ungebührlichen Ausschweifungen") was seen by Jacob Marcus as an allusion to the custom of hanging Haman in effigy, it is likely that King Frederick also had other amusements in mind.[96]

In 1756 the Jews of Sugenheim, in Franconia, included in their communal statutes (approved by the local barons) the warning that "no one shall dare mask himself or run around in clown's garb or with candles or torches on Purim under penalty of a florin to be paid the civil authorities." Such behavior, which evidently would otherwise occur, was deemed improper, although again not necessarily for the reason given by Marcus, namely that "such hilarity often ended in a row."[97] Rather, the underlying motive would appear to be the same as that behind the prohibition, in the very same statutes, of throwing fruits and candies to the parading children on the holiday of Simhat Torah—the repression of popular forms of festivity in which sacred and profane elements intermingled in ways that, by the eighteenth century, had become increasingly problematic.[98] This had important implications for the way that Purim came to be observed, or rather, for the ways in which those in positions of power (rabbinic or communal) sought to refashion the festival.

The tendency to delegitimize forms of festivity that had previously been acceptable may be seen, for example, among the leaders of the Portuguese community of Amsterdam who decided, two weeks before Purim of 1640, to prohibit hammering in the synagogue during the reading of the Megillah, a custom they considered more appropriate to barbarians than to civilized individuals. The prohibition seems to have had no more than

[95] On Frederick's 1750 privilege, see Ismar Freund, Die Emanzipation der Juden in Preussen, 2 vols. (Berlin, 1912) 2:51, and the translation (with commentary) provided by J. R. Marcus, The Jew in the Medieval World: a Source Book: 315–1791 (reprint, New York, 1969 [1938]), 94–95. On the anti-Christian character of the 'Aleinu prayer in its various versions and on efforts to censor it, see Yuval, Two Nations, 206–9, 212–16.

[96] Marcus, Jew in the Medieval World, 95. Regarding the Jews of eighteenth-century Germany, note the important testimony from 1705 preserved in the Berlin State Archive and published by Selma Stern, Die Preussische Staat und die Juden (Berlin, 1925), no. 277.

[97] See Max Freudenthal, "Die Verfassungskunde einer reichsritterlichen Judenschaft," ZGJD 1 (1929): 49, 67, and Marcus, Jew in the Medieval World, 220. On efforts among Jews in eighteenth-century Italy to prohibit masquerade, see Simonsohn, Mantua, 542–43; A. Milano, "La 'pragmatica' degli ebrei romani del secolo XVII," RMI 7 (1932–1933): 179; Simha Assaf, ed., Mekorot le-Toledot ha-Hinnukh be-Yisrael, 4 vols. (Tel-Aviv and Jerusalem, 1925–1942), 2:200.

[98] Freudenthal, "Die Verfassungskunde einer reichsritterlichen Judenschaft," 67; Marcus, The Jew in the Medieval World, 220.

a limited effect, however, for three decades later it was deemed necessary not only to repeat it, but to increase the fine twentyfold.[99] As Shakespeare well understood: "The brain may devise laws for the blood, but a hot temper leaps o'er a cold decree."[100]

On Shakespeare's own island a Purim riot broke out in London's (Spanish-Portuguese) Bevis Marks synagogue in 1783 when fourteen members refused to honor the "cold decree" recently issued by the *Mahamad* against noisemaking during the *Megillah* reading. Constables appeared in the synagogue after a complaint was made to the city marshal, and the offenders were removed. One of these was Isaac Mendes Furtado, who not long afterward broke with the congregation. Another was the twenty-one-year-old Joshua Montefiore who, however, recanted.[101] Just over a century later his great grand-nephew, Claude Montefiore, published his controversial essay in which he wrote that he would "not be sorry" if Purim "were gradually to lose its place in our religious calendar."

Although his reservations were rooted more in the vengeful nature of the holiday than in its unruly manner of observance, the learned and aristocratic Balliol graduate would probably have known of the Bevis Marks incident from James Picciotto's *Sketches of Anglo-Jewish History* (1875). The latter, in introducing the 1783 riot, informed his Victorian readers: "It was once the custom among the Jews, during the feast of Purim, for unruly boys and silly men to show their reprobation of Haman's conduct by loudly knocking against the Synagogue benches during the celebration of the service. This absurd and irreverent usage had ever been opposed by the congregational authorities"[102]

The incident was embarrassing enough for Moses Gaster, the *Haham* of England's Sephardi community, to omit it entirely from the "authorized version" of the synagogue's history he published in the year of Victoria's

[99] Joseph Kaplan, "The Portuguese Community in Amsterdam in the Seventeenth Century" (in Hebrew), *PIASH*, 7, no. 6 (1986): 181. The noise-making prohibition was later adopted by the Spanish-Portuguese congregation of London. See Moses Gaster, *History of the Ancient Synagogue of the Spanish and Portuguese Jews* (London, 1901), 58. That the prohibition was no mere formality is evident from the account by John Greenhalgh of his visit to the first London synagogue in 1662. "My Rabbi invited me afterwards to come and see the feast of Purim . . . in which they use great knocking and stamping when Haman is named." See A. M. Hyamson, *The Sephardim of England: A History of the Spanish and Portuguese Jewish Community, 1492–1951* (London, 1951), 19.

[100] W. Shakespeare, *Merchant of Venice*, 1:2.

[101] On this incident, see Doniach, *Purim*, 59; Hyamson, *The Sephardim of England*, 196–97; E. R. Samuel, "Anglo-Jewish Notaries and Scriveners," *TJHSE* 17 (1951–1952): 133, 144.

[102] Picciotto, *Sketches of Anglo-Jewish History*, ed. Finestein, 195.

death.[103] A half-century later, however, Albert Hyamson was able to describe the background to the Bevis Marks riot in the following manner: "To express their execration of Haman . . . it was the custom on the part of the more religiously exuberant section of the Congregation to create such a din at every mention of Haman's name as to shock and annoy the more moderate members. The Mahamad decided in 1783 to keep these manifestations of exuberant Judaism within some limits."[104]

What were for one historian "puerile manifestations" of "absurd and irreverent" conduct could be regarded by another, with the passage of time, as legitimate "manifestations of exuberant Judaism." As we have seen, evidence concerning the pleasures and practices of Purim in the past has often clashed with the impression Jewish historians have wished to convey of Jewish life in the present. Some have attempted, out of genteel embarrassment, to suppress its more exuberant elements and to present a decidedly tame picture of past Purim joys, whereas others have been more willing to acknowledge the sometimes raucous pleasures of the past while lamenting the holiday's devolution from relaxed amusement to stiff solemnity. If the attitudes toward the extravagant follies of Purim have varied considerably among scholars, attitudes toward the violent undertones of its celebration, including expressions of anti-Christian sentiment, have been, as we have seen, even more problematic. By recognizing, however, that on Purim Jews did sometimes give raw expression to their hostility toward symbols of both internal and external authority, we can see Purim more fully in the light of Bakhtin's view of Carnival, namely as "a temporary liberation from the prevailing truth and the established order."[105]

PURIM RECONSIDERED

When Claude Montefiore expressed the hope that Purim would one day lose its place in the Jewish religious calendar, he took a strong position not only against the unnamed Maimonides, who had asserted that "the days of Purim shall never be revoked,"[106] but also against the formal resolution earlier recorded in the book of Esther (9:28) that "these days of Purim should never fall into disuse among the Jews, nor should the commemoration of these days cease among their descendants." Precisely fifty years later, in 1938, Schalom Ben-Chorin (a.k.a. Fritz Rosenthal), a

---

[103] See no. 97, above.

[104] Hyamson, *The Sephardim of England*, 161.

[105] Bakhtin, *Rabelais and His World*, 10.

[106] See the concluding paragraph in Moses Maimonides, Laws of Megillah, *Mishneh Torah*, (2:18).

twenty-five-year-old German Jew who had recently emigrated to Palestine, published a polemical pamphlet in which he proposed that both Esther and Purim be eliminated from Jewish life since "both festival and book are unworthy of a people which is disposed to bring about its national and moral regeneration under prodigious sacrifice."[107] His pamphlet, which aroused considerable criticism, nevertheless was able to boast an approbation by Samuel Hugo Bergman (1883–1975), then rector of (as well as Professor of Philosophy at) the Hebrew University of Jerusalem, who had several years earlier been one of the founders of Brith Shalom. Bergman, an observant Jew if not necessarily an Orthodox one, commended Ben-Chorin for having provided a great service to Jewish religiosity. "The holiday of Purim may proceed," allowed Bergman, "as a folk festival." As a religious festival, however, it had in his opinion "only negative value." Its continued observance was to be understood as a consequence of "the deep decay of our people."[108]

Some three decades later, on the eve of the Six Day War, the octogenarian Bergman was still looking for ways to "uproot the Amalek complex from among us," by whom he meant his fellow citizens of the state of Israel. In an essay originally published in 1967, he noted with dismay that in a recently published letter in the Labor daily *Davar* the journalist Mikhael Asaf, who was a member of its editorial board, reported that he had attended Friday night services at a highly respected religious school on the Sabbath before Purim, and had been shocked to hear "Amalek, Nazis, and the Arabs" linked as an unholy trinity.[109] Asaf, who had emigrated to Palestine from Lodz in 1920—the same year that Bergman arrived from Prague—and later edited the Histadtrut's Arabic daily *Al-Yom* (1948–1960), would probably have been no less shocked to witness, as I did in 1994, the continued celebration of Purim in the streets of central Jerusalem after the news broke of the bloody massacre in Hebron. This is one particular instance in which I would agree with Bergman's prophetic assertion that the holiday's continued observance is best understood as a consequence of "the deep decay of our people."

---

[107] S. Ben-Chorin, *Kritik des Esther-Buches: Eine theologische Streitschrift* (Jerusalem, 1938), 5.
[108] Ibid. 3. Among the responses to Ben-Chorin's pamphlet, see Ya'akov Ashkenazi, *Davar be-'Ito* (Jerusalem, 1938); A. Kaminka, "Ha-Kitrug 'al *Megillat Esther*," in Lewinski, *Sefer ha-Mo'adim*, vol. 6, 56–60.
[109] S. H. Bergman, *Ba-Mish'ol* (Tel-Aviv, 1976), 72.

16. This particular copy of *Megillat Saragossa* is modeled on the
original Scroll of Esther, both in its having been written on parchment
and in its wooden handle. Courtesy of the Library of the Jewish
Theological Seminary of America, New York.

10

Local Purims and the Invention
of Tradition

In Saragossa long ago,
The 17th of Shevat,
Our fathers foiled without a blow,
A wicked foeman's plot

Purim of Saragossa,
O happiest of days!
We love to sing its melodies
And dance our roundelays.

PURIM OF SARAGOSSA

THESE charming stanzas were written in 1936, more than half a millennium after the alleged events which led to the establishment of the local Purim known as "The Purim of Saragossa." They were not composed, however, by a member of one of the Mediterranean communities which, even in the early twentieth century, still celebrated this festival on the seventeenth of Shevat (just less than a month before the "real" Purim), but rather by the rabbi of a Reform synagogue in upper Manhattan—Louis Newman of Temple Rodeph Sholom. The two stanzas (which, as one of my students discovered, may be sung to the tune of Simon and Garfunkel's "Scarborough Fair") appear at both the beginning and end of Newman's play *The Miracle of the Scrolls*, which was published in 1947. It had appeared in mimeograph form, however, as early as 1936, apparently for the purpose of being performed in Temple Rodeph Sholom.

Rabbi Newman, who had set his play in early fifteenth-century Aragon, under the rule of the King Alfonso V, had clearly not consulted the

Danish scholar David Simonsen's article cogently arguing that the "Purim of Saragossa" was actually the Purim of Syracuse—in southern Sicily. Rabbi Simonsen had noted that in medieval documents Syracuse was referred to as "Saragusa," and added that in his day descendants of those Jews who had been expelled from Sicily (in 1492–1493) residing in such eastern Mediterranean communities as Salonika and Smyrna (Izmir) would still celebrate a special Purim on the seventeenth of Shevat.[1]

Other scholars had reported that early in the twentieth century there were still some Jewish families in Janina (Ioannina, northwest of Athens) and a larger number in Istanbul who continued, on that date, to celebrate a special Purim.[2] Not only in the Balkans but also in Jerusalem the Purim of Saragossa/Syracuse continued to be observed in modern times. In fact, it seems to have survived longer in Jerusalem than almost anywhere else. In 1882 Moshe Slatki published in Jerusalem a version of *Megillat Saragossa*, recounting the alleged events upon which the eponymous Purim was based. In his introduction, he noted that "here in the Holy City there are about twenty Jews from Saragossa, in whose native city the sixteenth of Shevat is observed each year as a fast, and on the seventeenth they read a scroll written on parchment, partake of a festive meal, and send gifts of food. And here too [in Jerusalem] the same is done each year."[3]

Slatki had no independent way of knowing, of course, that the sixteenth and seventeenth of Shevat were still observed as days of fast and feast, respectively, in the "native city" of Jerusalem's "Saragossans"—whether that city was located in northern Spain or in southern Sicily. But he clearly did not suspect that former residents of that "Saragossa" might have invented a local Purim that had allegedly been observed there before their expulsion, perhaps as a means of enhancing their sense of cultural patrimony, which would include the possession of venerable traditions that it was their sacred duty to perpetuate.

The Jewish communities of the eastern Mediterranean in the early modern period were often composed of émigré subcommunities, each of

---

[1] Newman's *The Miracle of the Scrolls* was republished in his *Pangs of the Messiah and Other Plays, Pageants, and Contatas* (New York, 1957), 117–52. D. Simonsen "Le Pourim de Saragosse est un Pourim de Syracuse," *REJ* 59 (1910): 90–91. Simonsen's claim was later supported by a number of scholars, including Cecil Roth, in his *The History of the Jews in Italy* (Philadelphia, 1946), 261; Roth, "Le-Toledot Golei Sizilia," *Eretz Yisrael* 3 (1954): 233; Yerushalmi, *Zakhor*, 47, Simon Schwarzfuchs, "The Sicilian Jewish Communities in the Ottoman Empire," *Italia Judaica* 5 (1995): 406–10. Contrast, however, Haim Beinart, "Saragossa," *EJ*, 14:863; Joseph Sermoneta, "Syracuse," *EJ*, 15:635.

[2] A. Danon, "Quelques Pourim locaux," *REJ* 54 (1907): 122. See also Roth, "Le-Toledot Golei Sizilia," 233.

[3] M. Slatki, *Ner Moshe* (Jerusalem, 1882), 82b. On this work, see Shoshana Halevy, *The Printed Hebrew Books in Jerusalem during the First Half Century (1841–1891)* (in Hebrew) (Jerusalem, 1963), 122–23.

which was distinguished by the customs and liturgy of its place of origin. The Jews of Istanbul, or example, were divided into separate congregations of Romaniots (of Byzantine origin); Ashkenazim; Italians; and Sephardim—each of whom were themselves divided into many subcongregations.[4] A similar situation prevailed in Jerusalem, where there was no Romaniot community, but the Jews of Levantine origin were divided into separate *Musta'arab* (Morisco) and *Maghrebi* congregations.[5] From the sixteenth century on, as we shall see, Jews originating in Cairo, Crete, and Algiers (to name only three Mediterranean examples) had their own local Purims that could be observed in either their home communities or in those to which they emigrated.[6] The "Purim of Saragossa," the earliest manuscript evidence for which dates only from the mid-eighteenth century,[7] may well have been "invented" by former "Saragossans" eager to maintain their distinct identity in the multicultural Sephardi Diaspora of the eastern Mediterranean.

The somewhat oxymoronic subject of "invented traditions" has, as is well known, occupied historians and anthropologists in recent decades.[8] The term, as Eric Hobsbawm has explained, "includes both 'traditions' actually invented, constructed and formally instituted, and those emerging in a less easily traceable manner within a brief and datable period . . . and establishing themselves with great rapidity."[9] Among the former may be included, for example, the elaborate royal jubilees instituted in Britain during the reign of Queen Victoria: her Golden Jubilee (after fifty years on the throne)

[4] On the Sephardic congregations in the Jewish communities of the Ottoman Empire, see Joseph Hacker, "The Jews of the Ottoman Empire in the Sixteenth Century," 2:109–33, in *Moreshet Sepharad: The Sephardi Legacy*, ed. H. Beinart, 2 vols. (Jerusalem, 1992).

[5] On the Jewish communities of Jerusalem at the beginning of the early modern period, see Abraham David, *The Immigration and Settlement in the Land of Israel in the Sixteenth Century* (in Hebrew), (Jerusalem, 1993), 68–81.

[6] When in 1541 Elijah Capsali established a local Purim in Crete, he explicitly stated that members of the community who moved elsewhere, whether temporarily or permanently, should regard themselves as bound to continue its observance. See E. S. Artom and U. M. D. Cassuto, eds., *Takkanot Kandyah ve-Zikhronoteha* (Jerusalem, 1943), 128.

[7] The oldest dated manuscript of *Megillat Saragossa* (JTSA 5388/2) was copied in mid-eighteenth-century Istanbul. See the comments of H. Rosenberg "Unpublished Works of Hayyim Joseph David Azulai" (in Hebrew), in *Kiryat Sefer* 5 (1928): 160–61.

[8] See especially Eric Hobsbawm and Terence Ranger, eds., *The Invention of Tradition*, (Cambridge, 1983). For some interesting efforts to apply this concept to modern Jewish history, see M. K. Silber, "The Emergence of Ultra-Orthodoxy: The Invention of a Tradition," 23–84, in *The Uses of Tradition: Jewish Continuity in the Modern Era*, ed. Jack Wertheimer (New York, 1992); H. J. Kieval, "Pursuing the Golem of Prague: Jewish Culture and the Invention of a Tradition," *Modern Judaism* 17 (1997): 1–23.

[9] Hobsbawm, "Introduction: Inventing Traditions," in Hobsbawm and Ranger, eds., *Invention of Tradition*.

in 1887, and her Diamond Jubilee a decade later. Although the queen (and empress) agreed to participate in the former "only with the greatest reluctance," as David Cannadine has noted, after the Diamond Jubilee—for which Elgar composed his "Imperial March"—she gloated: "No one, ever, I believe, has met with such an ovation as was given to me passing through these six miles of streets. . . . The crowds were quite indescribable, and their enthusiasm . . . deeply touching." Those crowds, however, were hardly aware that they were participating in an "invented tradition" which possessed, moreover, a decided political dimension. As the archbishop of Canterbury remarked after Victoria's Golden Jubilee: "Days afterward, everyone feels that the socialist movement has had a check."[10]

Europe's socialists, however, were also able to invent traditions. A notable example is the celebration of May Day, which, unlike Britain's royal jubilees, was not formally instituted, but rather "spontaneously evolved within a surprisingly short period"—the last decade of the nineteenth century. The first May Day (1890) was designed, as Hobsbawm has noted, "as a single simultaneous one-day strike and demonstration for the eight-hour day," but as it spread through Western Europe it took on various ritual and even quasireligious dimensions. "The Catholics have Easter," declared the Italian socialist Andrea Costa in 1893, "henceforth the workers will have their own Easter."[11]

During the same decades in which these two "invented traditions" emerged in England and on the Continent, the tradition of a Saragossan Purim, whose precise origins are extremely unclear, reasserted itself with particular vigor in various Jewish communities of the eastern Mediterranean, including that of Jerusalem. In 1882 Moshe Slatki had reported that twenty Jews in the Holy City who regarded themselves as "Saragossans" annually observed the fast and feast during the month of Shevat. Nearly three decades later, when another resident of Jerusalem, Joseph Meyuhas, again published a printed version of the *Megillah,* he reported that it was still customary for some of the city's Jews to observe the Saragossan Purim, gathering annually on the seventeenth of Shevat at the Rabbi Yohanan ben Zakkai Synagogue to hear the *Megillah* read from a parchment scroll.[12]

Meyuhas, however, did not mention the day of fast, which seems by then to have largely fallen by the wayside. In 1930 still another Jerusalemite,

---

[10] David Cannadine, "The Context, Performance, and Meaning of Ritual: The British Monarchy and the 'Invention of Tradition' c. 1820–1977," 131–36, in Hobsbawm and Ranger, eds., *Invention of Tradition.*

[11] Hobsbawm, "Mass-Producing Traditions: Europe, 1870—1914," 283–86, in Hobsbawm and Ranger, *Invention and Tradition.* Hobsbawm's discussion is based primarily on Maurice Dommanget, *Histoire du premier mai* (Paris, 1953).

[12] J. Meyuhas, "Megillot Mishpaha be-Eretz Yisrael" *Yerushalayim* ed. A. M. Luncz 9 (1911): 285–86.

R. Isaac Badhav, again published the text of *Megillat Saragossa* in his *Ma'aseh Nissim*, an anthology of stories recounting the deliverance of Jewish communities from various dangers. In an afterword, Badhav, who had been born in Jerusalem in 1859, reported that in his youth he would accompany his father each year on the seventeenth of Shevat to hear the *Megillah* read from a parchment scroll in the home of a certain Abraham bin Nun. Although in those days, he noted, the "Saragossans" of Jerusalem would observe a fast on the sixteenth of Shevat prior to the festive celebration on the seventeenth, he himself continued to observe only the latter, since the fast was nowhere mentioned in the *Megillah*.[13] After his father's death, Badhav added, he would read the scroll annually in his neighborhood, Yemin Moshe, from the parchment copy he had inherited from him.[14]

Perhaps it was through Badhav's *Ma'aseh Nissim* that the miraculous story behind the "Purim of Saragossa" came to the attention of Rabbi Newman in New York, who brought it, in turn, to the attention of a new English-speaking audience through *The Miracle of the Scrolls*. Newman was certainly aware that there had been other local Purims in Jewish history. The narrator of his play explains to one of the children participating in the modern festivities: "As you know, there are many special Purims. The Purim[s] of Narbonne, Padua, Shiraz, Chios and Lepanto. . . . But for us, the heirs of ancient Saragossa, the 17th day of Shevat is memorable."[15]

It is understandable that Newman did not choose to write a play based on the so-called Purim of Narbonne, the first on his narrator's list, since the 1236 events upon which it was based began, as we shall see, with the unexplained killing of a Christian fisherman by a Jew—not the sort of thing one wanted to stress as the specter of Nazism began to cast its shadow over Europe. The "Saragossa" story, by contrast, fit into a more convenient narrative with which Jewish memory was more comfortable: The betrayal of a Jewish community by an apostate (Marcus) who sought to sour relations between his former co-religionists and their ruler, who in the end discovered the plot (through the timely intervention of Elijah) and had the apostate hanged. This last detail, nonetheless, proved

---

[13] Badhav, *Ma'aseh Nissim* (Jerusalem, 1930), 34–35. Badhav reported that there were still some in Jerusalem who observed the fast.

[14] Ibid., 35. After selling that copy, however, he continued to read the scroll for his neighbors from the printed text published (with, as he noted, many errors) in *Divrei Yemei Yisrael be-Togarmah* (Husiatyn, 1907–1914) by the Bulgarian-born historian Solomon Abraham Rosanes. The few residents of Yemin Moshe who still possessed their own parchment copies preferred, Badhav explained, to hear the *Megillah* read before a proper minyan in Jerusalem's Old City. On the observance of "Purim of Saragossa" in early twentieth-century Jerusalem, see also J. L. Fishman, in Goodman, *Purim Anthology*, 20–21.

[15] L. Newman, *The Miracle of the Scrolls, or the Purim of Saragossa* (New York, 1947), 6.

somewhat troublesome for Rabbi Newman, who preferred to have the Jews petition the king (successfully) for their former co-religionist to be pardoned.

According to the *Megillah*, of which at least ten manuscript copies survive (none, however, predating the eighteenth century),[16] five thousand Jews, divided into twelve communities (each with its own synagogue) lived in "Saragossanos" under the rule of King "Saragossanos." Whenever the king would pass through their marketplace the Jews would take out thirty-six Torah scrolls in their decorative cases, three from each synagogue, in his honor. At a meeting of the community's leaders (at which there were exactly thirty-six dignitaries present), it was decided, however, that rather than perpetrating the sacrilege of honoring an idolatrous king with scrolls of the holy Torah, it would be better to bring out thirty-six empty cases when he passed through. This deception was practiced successfully for twelve years (corresponding, perhaps coincidentally, to the number of local synagogues), before Marcus the apostate decided to reveal it to the king. On the recommendation of the latter's advisors it was decided that during his next procession through the Jewish market the Torah cases would be opened, and if the Jews were indeed perpetrating a ruse they were to be massacred, their wives and children enslaved, their homes looted, and their synagogues burnt to the ground.

Before proceeding to the miraculous ending of the story told in *Megillat Saragossa*, it is worth noting how even its ostensibly more realistic setting contains suspicious signs of the manipulation (or invention) of numbers for the sake of achieving what Gerson Cohen famously called "the symmetry of history." In twelfth-century Andalusia Abraham ibn Daud, as Cohen has skillfully shown, concocted a version of ancient and medieval Jewish history in which certain numbers (such as 7 and 21) kept coming up with a regularity reminiscent of the roulette wheel at Rick's bar in *Casablanca*. Ibn Daud divided history into 7 stages, and important developments in the history of Judaism were often separated, in his imaginative reconstruction, by 7 generations. As Cohen observed:

> The significance of this sequence . . . lies not only in its heptadic character, but primarily in the fact that the culminating point of each stage, i.e., the seventh generation, bears a symmetry with the earlier counterpart in the chain. Thus, in the seventh generation of the Hillelite chain, the Mishna was redacted. In the seventh generation of the subsequent chain, the redaction of the Talmud was begun.[17]

---

[16] Five are in New York (three at the Jewish Theological Seminary of America, and two at Columbia University), three are in Jerusalem (Ben-Zvi Institute, Schocken Library, and a private collection), two are in England (Leeds and London), and one in Paris.

[17] Abraham ibn Daud, *Sefer Ha-Qabbalah: (The Book of Tradition)*, ed. with trans. and notes by G. D. Cohen (Philadelphia, 1967), 206–7.

The point of such numerical manipulations was to stress, as Cohen remarked, "that the hand of Providence moves unceasingly," thereby bringing "consolation to the despised and persecuted nation" of which Ibn Daud was a member.[18] The numbers 12 and 36 would seem to play, for the anonymous author of *Megillat Saragossa*, a role similar to the numbers 7 and 21 for Ibn Daud—reminders, in both cases, that God kept a close watch on the fate of His chosen nation, whose setbacks, therefore, could be no more than temporary.

How, then, did God arrange for the Jews of Saragossa/Syracuse to be saved from the plot of their former co-religionist? On the night before the next royal procession the beadles of each of the 12 synagogues were awakened by the prophet Elijah, who exhorted them to fill the empty cases with real Torah scrolls. When the king asked that one of the cases be opened so that he could see the words of Moses, the Jews of *Saragossanos* reluctantly complied with his request. To their amazement, however, they discovered not only that there was a Torah scroll inside, but that it was opened to Leviticus 26:44: "Yet, even then, when they are in the land of their enemies, I will not reject them or spurn them so as to destroy them . . . for I am the Lord their God." The apostate and informer Marcus was then hanged, as mentioned above, by royal command. This miracle allegedly occurred on the seventeenth of Shevat, although some versions give the year as 1380, and others as 1420.[19]

Newman's somewhat bowdlerized version of the story introduced a number of noteworthy changes. The reluctance of Saragossa's leaders to continue honoring their king with Torah scrolls is rooted, in his retelling, not in the latter's being an idolater, but rather in his being merely "a mortal monarch." More significantly and as previously noted, whereas in all versions of the *Megillah* Marcus the apostate is not only hanged, but his body thrown to the dogs until the flesh was eaten and his bones then burned, Rabbi Newman of Rodeph Sholom felt that it would be more suitable to have the Jews petition the king for their former co-religionist to be pardoned.[20] *The Miracle of the Scrolls* was composed in 1936, a year in which it was not necessarily advantageous to acknowledge the Jewish appetite for rapacious revenge.[21]

---

[18] Ibid., 196, 212–13. See also Yerushalmi, *Zakhor*, 39.

[19] See Simonsen, "Le Pourim de Saragosse," 93. N. Brüll, "Alphons V. von Aragonien und die Juden in Saragossa," *JJGL* 7 (1885): 39–40, suggested emending 1420 to 1428. This date was accepted by Fishman (in Goodman, *Purim Anthology*, 20–21). The date of 1425 given in the entry "Purims, Special" in the *EJ* (13:1399) is only one of the many inaccuracies there.

[20] Newman, *Miracle of the Scrolls*, 10, 19–20.

[21] Cf. R. Wischnitzer, "The Esther Story in Art," in Goodman, *Purim Anthology*, 243.

Newman's dramatic retelling of the "Saragossa" story is also laced with allusions to modern racial anti-Semitism. When Marcus is introduced to the King of Aragon, the court jester exclaims: "My Lord, here is the greatest jest I can cite you. How can the oil of the Orient mix with the water of the baptismal font?" Later in the play the king refers to the Jews as "a proud and stubborn race."[22] These allusions to the plight of European Jewry in the 1930s help to explain why Newman chose *Megillat Saragossa* for dramatic retelling rather another relatively accessible *Megillah* narrating the events leading to the establishment of a local Purim in early sixteenth-century Cairo, the *Megillat Mizrayim*. The "Purim of Cairo," like that of Saragossa, was still observed in the twentieth century, and its *Megillah* had also been published, in various forms, in the late nineteenth and early twentieth centuries.[23] But that scroll dealt with the suffering and salvation of the Jews under late medieval Islam, whereas its Saragossan counterpart could be directed, albeit obliquely, to the darkening clouds over the Jews of Europe.

PURIM OF CAIRO

From the historical perspective, however, there were other major differences between the Purim of Saragossa/Syracuse and that of Cairo. Whereas the events leading up to the former are known only from *Megillat Saragossa* (whose connection with historical reality is clearly tenuous), those leading to the establishment of a local Purim in Cairo, beginning with the revolt of Ahmed Pasha shortly after his installation as viceroy of Egypt by Sultan Suleiman the Magnificent in August of 1523, are well known from a variety of sources, Jewish as well as non-Jewish. Although those sources are not always in harmony, the basic facts are beyond dispute: Ahmed Pasha, known also as Ahmed Shaitan, declared himself sultan of Egypt and built up a private army, comprised largely of Mamluks. In order to fund his revolt, much property was confiscated and extortions were practiced upon local Jews and Christians. In late February of 1524 Ahmed was surprised, while in the bath, by loyalist forces. Although he managed to escape, he was caught and beheaded in early March.[24]

---

[22] Newman, *Miracle of the Scrolls* 7, 11.

[23] It was first published (in three installments) by Herbert Loewe in *Ha-Magid*, 10, nos. 7–9 (February 14–28, 1866); then by G. Margoliouth, "Megillath Missraim, or the Scroll of the Egyptian Purim," *JQR*, o.s. 8 (1896): 274–88 (Hebrew text with English translation); Abraham Kahana, *Sifrut ha-Historia ha-Yisraelit*, 2 vols. (Warsaw, 1922–1923), 2:78–82; I. E. Yahuda, "Megillat Mizrayim," in *Reshumot* 5 (1927): 385–402 (Hebrew and Judeo-Arabic).

[24] For general treatments of the revolt, see especially G.W.F. Stripling, *The Ottoman Turks and the Arabs, 1511–1574* (Urbana, Ill., 1942), 69–70; P. M. Holt, *Egypt and the Fertile Crescent, 1516–1922: A Political History* (London, 1966), 48–51.

Not only can the historical context of Cairo's Purim be independently verified, it is also one of the few local Purims that can be shown to have been observed continuously over several centuries. Whereas the Saragossa/Syracuse Purim cannot be documented before the middle of the eighteenth century—no less than three centuries after the alleged events upon which it was based—the Purim of Cairo is mentioned as early as 1553,[25] less than three decades after Ahmed Pasha's revolt. As several sources testify, it was still being observed in the nineteenth and early twentieth centuries as a two-day affair—a fast on the 27th of Adar followed by a feast on the 28th.[26]

It is not clear, however, when these two consecutive days of fast and feast were first observed. The earliest extant Hebrew account of Ahmed's rebellion and its impact upon the Jews of Egypt, Elijah Capsali's *Hasdei ha-Shem*, which was written shortly after the events themselves, mentions neither the establishment of a local Purim nor the composition of a *Megillah*.[27] Capsali does report, however, that after the renegade viceroy sought unsuccessfully to extort an enormous amount of money from Abraham Castro, the leader of Egyptian Jewry and director of the Sultan's local mint, the local Jews began to suffer hardship and persecution. In response they observed several days of fasting and prayer, so that the normally merry month of Adar "turned to thorns and thistles, and Purim became a day of mourning and pain."[28]

Here we encounter a phenomenon common to several local Purims— the chronological overlap or contiguity between a community's experience of (and deliverance from) mortal danger and its celebration of the triumph of the Jews over their adversaries during the distant days of Mordecai and Esther. When the Jews of Egypt observed the Fast of Esther in 1524, they undoubtedly felt a close connection between their increasingly fragile fate under Ahmed Pasha and the circumstances that led Esther to declare a three-day fast in ancient Shushan. Although in that same year the joy of Purim was also undermined, Ahmed's defeat and decapitation some two weeks after the holiday undoubtedly took on a

---

[25] Ibn Verga, *Shevet Yehudah*, 145. Ibn Verga's work was first published (in Adrianople) in 1553.

[26] See, for example, Herbert Loewe in *Ha-Magid*, 10, no. 7 (February 14, 1866), 53; J. M. Landau, *The Jews in Nineteenth-Century Egypt* (in Hebrew) (Jerusalem, 1967), 123; Raphael Aaron ibn Shimon, *Nehar Mizrayim* (Alexandria, 1908), 6b–7a; Yahuda, "Megillat Mizrayim," 385; B. H. Hary, *Multiglossia in Judeo-Arabic: With an Edition, Translation, and Grammatical Study of the Cairene Purim Scroll* (Leiden, 1992), 124n37.

[27] Elijah Capsali, *Hasdei ha-Shem*, in Capsali, *Seder Eliyahu Zuta*, 2:147–201. This work was evidently completed in 1524. See Charles Berlin, "A Sixteenth-Century Hebrew Chronicle of the Ottoman Empire" *Studies . . . in Honor of I. Edward Kiev*, ed. C. Berlin (New York, 1971), 39.

[28] Capsali, *Hasdei ha-Shem*, 168–69.

Purim-like character, leading to the establishment of a local Purim in Cairo. This, like the original, was a two-day affair: a fast followed by a feast. And like the original, moreover, its observance included the reading of a *Megillah* narrating the events which led to the holiday's emergence.

Although neither Cairo's local Purim nor the scroll written to recount the events of 1524 were mentioned in Capsali's account, both were mentioned later by Joseph ibn Verga in one of the appendices to his father's historical work *Shevet Yehudah*, first published in 1553. Joseph's brief narrative of the tribulations and salvation experienced by the Jews of Egypt during the reign of Suleiman the Magnificent was based, he explained, on a *Megillah* which had been written there, whose contents he could only present in abridged form. His version of the events, however (like that of all versions of the *Megillah* which have survived), made no mention of any attempt to extort funds from Abraham Castro. Rather, early in the month of Adar twelve leaders of the Jewish community were summoned by Ahmed Pasha and informed that they must, under penalty of death, collect from their co-religionists two hundred pieces of silver bullion. As a consequence, "the day of Purim became a day of mourning."

According to ibn Verga's account, the Jews managed to collect a small portion of the demanded sum, but when they brought it to the viceroy's castle they were told that Ahmed was in the bath. While waiting for him to emerge they were informed that he had fled after being attacked in the bath by one of his viziers, Muhammad Beg, who had turned loyalist. Muhammad and his troops chased Ahmed for three days, finally catching up to him on the 27th of Adar, on which day he was decapitated, and his head brought back triumphantly to Cairo. This was also the date given by ibn Verga, on the basis of the *Megillah* he had seen sometime before 1553, for the local Purim celebrated by the Jews of Cairo.[29]

Strangely, however, most extant versions of *Megillat Mizrayim* give the following day, the 28th of Adar, as the date both of Ahmed's beheading in 1524 and the local Purim subsequently observed in Cairo.[30] This was

---

[29] Ibn Verga, *Shevet Yehudah*, 145–46. On ibn Verga's version of the events, see also David Kaufmann, "Joseph ibn Verga's Extract from the Cairo-Megilla," *JQR*, o.s. 11 (1899): 656–57. According to at least one Ottoman source, Ahmed was forced to flee the bathhouse with his beard half-shaven. See Holt, *Egypt and the Fertile Crescent*, 50. It is also reported that his severed head was eventually sent back to Constantinople. See R. G. Merriman, *Suleiman the Magnificent, 1520–1566* (Cambridge, Mass., 1944), 77.

[30] See, for example, Margoliouth, "Megillath Missraim," 280–81 (Hebrew text), 287–88 (English translation); Yahuda, "Megillat Mizrayim," 401; Zvi Malachi, *Studies in Medieval Hebrew Literature* (in Hebrew) (Tel-Aviv, 1971), 59–60. Margoliouth and Malachi each published Hebrew texts of the *Megillah* based on different manuscripts. Yahuda's 1927 bilingual (Hebrew and Arabic) version was based, he claimed, on the *Megillah* as it was then read in Cairo.

also the date given for both Ahmed's execution and the subsequent annual celebration by Joseph Sambari, a native of Egypt, in his historical work *Divrei Yosef*, completed ca. 1672.[31] Sambari's contemporary, David Conforte, who served as a rabbi in Cairo from 1671 until his death some two decades later, also gave 28 Adar as the date upon which the *Megillah* was read annually and a local Purim celebrated in the synagogue of Cairo's *musta'rib* (native Arabic-speaking) Jews.[32]

By the time Louis Loewe (1809–1888), who later became Moses Montefiore's secretary, interpreter, and traveling companion, arrived in Egypt during the late 1830s, Cairo's local Purim had become a two-day affair, a fast on the 27th of Adar and feast on the following day. Several decades later, when he was back in England, Loewe came across a discussion of Cairo's Purim by a fellow scholar (Ludwig Philippson) who had noted the discrepancy in dates between ibn Verga's *Shevet Yehudah* and Conforte's *Kore ha-Dorot*, and sought to determine which was correct. By way of reply, Loewe decided to publish, in the Hebrew journal *Ha-Magid*, the text of the *Megillat Mizrayim* as he had heard it read during his sojourn in Egypt. This was the first appearance in print of the *Megillah*,[33] which had first been composed over three centuries earlier and may well have undergone changes over time. The dates given in Loewe's text represent a hybridization of the two aforementioned versions: Ahmed's capture and decapitation is described as having occurred, as in *Shevet Yehudah*, on the 27th of Adar—which was subsequently observed as a fast. The day of annual festivity, however, is given as 28 Adar—as in the seventeenth-century chronicles of Sambari and Conforte, both natives of Egypt.[34]

The date given by the latter two is clearly correct for their own time. But it is likely that the original date established for Cairo's local Purim was 27 Adar, as reported by Joseph ibn Verga in 1553.[35] By the late seventeenth century, however, the date of its observance was evidently moved to the 28th, perhaps in order to better emulate the "original" Purim, which was celebrated by the Jews on the day following the defeat of their enemies (Esther 9:17). Sometime after that a further change was introduced, evidently in order to make Cairo's Purim even more like its older namesake—a day of joyful festivity preceded by a fast.

---

[31] Joseph Sambari, *Sefer Divrei Yosef*, ed. Shimon Shtuber (Jerusalem, 1994), 291.

[32] David Conforte, *Kore ha-Dorot*, ed. David Cassel (Berlin, 1846), 32b–33a.

[33] See Hary, *Multiglossia*, 128.

[34] Loewe, *Ha-Magid* 10, no. 7 (February 1866), 53; 10, no. 9 (February 1866), 69.

[35] This was the opinion of Kaufmann, "Joseph ibn Verga's Extract," 657n5. See also Danon, "Quelques Pourim locaux," 113.

ELIJAH CAPSALI AND THE PURIM OF CRETE

In truth, however, it is not clear when the Purim of Cairo was first observed. As noted above, Elijah Capsali, in his *Hasdei ha-Shem*, the earliest Hebrew account of the experiences of Egyptian Jewry during the 1524 revolt, mentioned neither the composition of a *Megillah* nor the observance in Cairo of a local Purim. Moreover, in his 1541 chronicle of the events leading to the establishment of a local Purim in his native Crete, Capsali did not cite the proximate precedent of Cairo's Purim—or any other local Purim for that matter.[36]

In the summer of 1538 the island of Crete, which had been under Venetian rule for over three centuries, was under threat of attack by the Turkish fleet of Suleiman the Magnificent. The Jews of Candia (today Heraklion), the largest community on the island, were called upon by the *provveditori* to participate in civil defense work, including the digging of trenches—an assignment which happened to fall on the fast day of 17 Tammuz, commemorating the breaching of the walls of Jerusalem prior to the destruction of both the First and Second Temples. Capsali, who had recently been elected head of the community, sought initially to have the physically taxing assignment (especially during the Mediterranean summer) postponed for a day. When his efforts proved fruitless, however, he ruled that all of the men who were digging trenches would be permitted to postpone their fast until the following day. In that year the 17 Tammuz fell on a Saturday, so the actual fast was postponed, as was standardly the case, to Sunday, and the men of Crete would be fasting on Monday. As a result, only women, children, and the aged members of the community were to be found in Candia's Jewish quarter on Sunday, 18 Tammuz, 1538.[37]

On that day a rumor, originating perhaps in one of the church sermons, that the Jews were harboring Turkish spies surfaced in the central market, prompting a large crowd of islanders, many of them armed, to storm the Jewish quarter. Capsali's first response as head of the community was to announce, as a means of pacifying the hostile intruders, that anyone who had seen Turkish spies and failed to report them would have all of his property confiscated. More slyly, as he himself later acknowledged, Capsali surreptitiously encouraged the Jewish women to react as hysterically as they could, thereby making the situation unpleasant, if not unbearable,

---

[36] The best version of the text appears in Artom and Cassuto, *Takkanot Kandyah*, 118–28.

[37] Ibid., 119–22. Actually, as the editors note, the 17th of Tammuz fell that year on a Sabbath, and the fast was postponed, as is standardly the case, to Sunday the 18th. On the Jews of Crete during this period, see Joshua Starr "Jewish Life in Crete under the Rule of Venice," *PAAJR* 12 (1942): 59–114. On the four synagogues—the Great, the Priests', the Germans', and the Tall—see there, 99.

for the horde of unwelcome visitors. Lastly, Capsali was able to summon the island's governor, Zuan Moro, who arrived with armed members of his constabulary and succeeded in finally quelling the disturbance.

The secret hand of God in this story, as Capsali later saw it, lay in His having kept the community's combustible young men, who were out digging trenches, away from the Jewish quarter when it was stormed by the hostile crowd.

> Otherwise, there is no doubt that the young men, especially the braver and more belligerent among them, would have provoked the gentiles, and would have drawn their swords, which all had in their homes. In their foolish and vainglorious desire to flaunt their valor they would certainly have harmed one of the gentiles . . . which would cause the entire community to be massacred, without exception.[38]

Unlike some modern historians, Capsali had no doubt that his fellow Jews, especially those of the young male variety, were capable, when sufficiently provoked, of reckless violence against members of the Christian majority. If not for God's subtle intervention, he asserted, they would have drawn their swords against the angry horde. And as in the days of Mordecai and Esther, there was also, in Capsali's opinion, a decisive feminine contribution to the salvation of Crete's Jewish community in 1538—the weeping and wailing women who succeeded in softening the hearts of the hostile intruders. Moreover, the narrative of salvation, as he saw it, also included a benevolent ruler—the island's governor, Zuan Moro—who intervened on behalf of the beleaguered Jews at the right moment. Capsali did not refer explicitly to either Esther or Ahasuerus, but the implicit message was clear: God had come through again for the Jews in their time of need, and their salvation should be acknowledged and celebrated for generations.[39]

Rather than moving to establish such a local festival immediately, however, Capsali waited until the conflict between Venice and the Turks had subsided and a peace treaty was signed (in early October, 1540). Early the next summer, on the New Moon of Tammuz, 1541, he gathered the leaders and members of Crete's Jewish community in its main synagogue and formally proposed that henceforward 18 Tammuz would be declared "a day of feasting and merrymaking," and recognized as a minor festival—on which both fasting and the recitation of *tahanun* would be prohibited. Capsali's fellow rabbis not only accepted his proposal, but also undertook to compose liturgical poems to be recited each year on that day in the island's various synagogues. And the general community was so responsive

---

[38] Artom and Cassuto, *Takkanot Kandyah*, 122–24.
[39] Ibid., 124.

to Capsali's proposal that it went a step further, declaring that not only fasting but also work would be prohibited on 18 Tammuz. The relatively restrained form which this "day of feasting and merrymaking" took in Crete was evidently related to its having fallen during the "three weeks" of mourning for the destruction of both the First and Second Temples, between 17 Tammuz and 9 Ab.[40]

It is noteworthy, moreover, that although scholars since Leopold Zunz in the nineteenth century have referred to the holiday established by Capsali as the "Purim of Crete,"[41] Capsali himself (deliberately, one suspects) avoided using the word "Purim" in either his account of the events of 1538 or his formal proposal to the community three years later. He did, however, suggestively use such expressions from the book of Esther as "a day of feasting and merrymaking,"[42] and even quoted an entire verse from that book: "The Jews enjoyed light and gladness, happiness and honor" (8:16). Capsali, it seems, was either still unaware, in 1541, of the precedent set in Cairo earlier in the century for the celebration of a local Purim, or uneasy about using the term "Purim" for a holiday that fell during the normally mournful "three weeks" rather than, as in Cairo, during the merry month of Adar.

Zunz, however, knew of Crete's local festival not from Capsali's account, which was first published only after his own *Die Ritus des synagogalen Gottesdienstes* (1859) had appeared, but from the eighteenth-century halakhic encyclopedia *Pahad Yitzhak* compiled by R. Isaac Lampronti of Ferrara. In one of his entries, Lampronti had referred to an unpublished responsum of Capsali's discussing "the custom of women in the town of Candia not to do work on the 18th of Tammuz, which they have accepted as [a] Purim."[43] Moritz Steinschneider, in his 1903 list of local Purims, the first to be organized chronologically, also included Crete's local festival within that category, but like Zunz before him, knew of it only from Lampronti's entry, and therefore could not cite a date for the beginning of its observance.[44] We now know, however, not only that

---

[40] Ibid., 125–26. On the "three weeks," see *Shulkhan Arukh*, OH 551, and the eponymous (and anonymous) entry in *EJ*, 15:1124.

[41] L. Zunz, *Die Ritus des synagogalen Gottesdienstes* (Berlin, 1859), 128. See also M. Steinschneider, "Candia: Cenni di storia letteraria," *Mosé* 2 (1879): 412; Steinschneider, "Purim und Parodie," *MGWJ* 47 (1903): 286; Danon, "Quelques Pourim locaux," 115.

[42] Artom and Cassuto, *Takkanot Kandyah*, 124, 127, and cf. Esther 9:17–19, 22.

[43] Lampronti, *Pahad Yitzhak*, vol. 2 (Venice, 1743), s.v. "*devarim mutarim ve-aherim nahagu bahem issur*" (81a). On Lampronti, see D. B. Ruderman, *Jewish Thought and Scientific Discovery in Early Modern Europe* (rev. ed., Detroit, 2001), chap. 9, and the literature cited there, 256–57.

[44] Steinschneider, "Purim und Parodie," 286. Steinschneider placed Crete's Purim at the end of his list, together with three others whose dates were not known to him.

the Purim of Crete was established in 1541, but that it was still being observed early in the twentieth century.[45]

KAUFMANN'S PURIM OF NARBONNE

The late nineteenth and early twentieth centuries marked a liminal point in the history of local Purims; a point at which their observance was still a live, though waning, tradition in many communities, and at which they were also made objects of inquiry by the pioneer practitioners of *Wissenschaft des Judenthums*—many of whom had, like vultures, a keen nose for the pungent smell of death. Although all three of the Mediterranean local Purims discussed so far in this chapter (Saragossa/Syracuse, Cairo, and Crete) were still observed, in some form or other, in the early twentieth century, scholars also began then to "discover" local Purims of which no trace existed except for a single poem or a few scribbled lines on a forgotten manuscript. An example of the former, to which we shall soon return, is the so-called "Purim of the Nagid" (or "Purim of Granada"), which, in the opinion of some scholars, was established by Samuel ibn Nagrela in 1038, after allegedly leading the forces of Granada to victory over the army of Almeria. A prime example of the latter is the Purim of Narbonne, in southwest France (Languedoc), which Steinschneider placed at the head of his list in 1903.[46] Its existence had first been posited by the Hungarian scholar David Kaufmann in 1896, shortly after his Danish colleague Simonsen had published an article adding some local feasts and fasts to the initial list published by Zunz in 1859.[47] Kaufmann felt that he had one more local Purim to add.

His "finding" was based on a brief passage, written and signed by a certain Meir b. Isaac on the rear flyleaf of a Hebrew manuscript (R. Isaac Alfasi's commentary on tractate *Megillah*) which had recently surfaced in Jerusalem and had been published by Adolf Neubauer shortly after its acquisition by the Bodleian library at Oxford. The passage reported that on the 20th of Adar, 1236, the Jews of Narbonne had been savagely attacked in their quarter by the Christian populace, but had been saved by the local viscount [Aimeri IV] and his aristocratic allies, who returned to the Jews all that had been taken from them. The cause of the attack was given as follows: "A Jew from northern France [*zarfati*] dealt a Christian

---

[45] Danon, "Quelques Pourim locaux," 115–16, 125ff; Rosanes, *Divrei Yemei Yisrael*, 2:51n15.

[46] Steinschneider, "Purim und Parodie," 283.

[47] David Simonsen, "Freud und Leid: Locale Fest- und Fasttage im Anschluss an Zunzen Fastentabelle," *MGWJ* 38 (1894): 524–27.

[*sheketz*] fisherman a blow on the head with a wooden implement, causing a wound. The victim was brought for treatment to a Christian physician, who, pressed by a Jew-hating fisherman . . . intentionally caused his
death." The passage closes with the following words: "So that this will be
remembered throughout [the city, Neubauer suggests] and so that these
days of Purim shall not cease according to what was written and according to their time [in each, Neubauer suggests] year, amen amen."[48]

This brief passage raises a number of interesting questions, among them:
What caused the Jew to strike the Christian fisherman on the head? Why
did the author make a point of noting that the former was from northern
France, and why did he refer to the latter by the pejorative term *sheketz*
(abomination) while referring to the Christian physician by the more neu-
tral term *goy*? It was, after all, the physician who, by the author's own
account, caused the first fisherman's death at the urging of the second, and
was thus perhaps most responsible for the subsequent rioting against the
local Jews. The account's conclusion, expressing the hope that "these days
of Purim shall not cease," a clear allusion to Esther 9:27–28, is no less cryptic. Was this merely a literary conceit, or were local "days of Purim" actually decreed, or observed, by the Jews of thirteenth-century Narbonne?

As is often the case, some of the gaps in the text were imaginatively
filled in by scholars, frequently adding new layers of information to those
of their predecessors. David Kaufmann, the first to "discover" Narbonne's
local Purim, asserted matter-of-factly that the Jew and the fisherman had
quarreled before the latter was struck on the head.[49] His lead was followed
shortly after by the authors of two separate entries in the *Jewish Encyclopedia*: In the entry devoted to "Purims, Special," Henry Malter wrote
concerning that of Narbonne: "The facts . . . are as follows. In a quarrel
between a Jew of Narbonne and a Christian fisherman the former dealt
the latter a heavy blow."[50] My own quarrel with these "facts" is that in
addition to no quarrel being mentioned in the text, the Jewish assailant is
clearly described as northern French (*zarfati*) rather than Narbonnese—
a matter, as we shall see, of no small importance.[51]

---

[48] Adolf Neubauer, ed., *Mediaeval Jewish Chronicles and Chronological Notes*, 2 vols.
(1887–1895), 2:251; S. A. Wertheimer, *Ginzei Yerushalayim* (Jerusalem, 1896), 44; D.
Kaufmann, "Le Pourim de Narbonne," *REJ* 32 (1896): 129–30.

[49] Kaufmann, "Le Pourim de Narbonne," 129: "Un juif, se querellant avec un pêcheur
chrétien."

[50] Henry Malter, s.v. "Purims, Special," *JE* 10: 281–82.

[51] See Henri Gross, *Gallia Judaica*, ed. S. Schwarzfuchs (rev. ed., Amsterdam, 1969), s.v.
"*Zarfat*," 537–38. Gross noted that in some late medieval sources *Zarfat* might include the
Midi, but never Provence. See also the early thirteenth-century letter from Narbonne pub-
lished by Joseph Shatzmiller, "Toward a Picture of the First Maimonidean Controversy" (in
Hebrew), *Zion* 34 (1969): 143–44.

In the entry on "Narbonne" in the same encyclopedia, Joseph Jacobs asserted that "in 1236 the lives and property of the Jews were put in jeopardy. In consequence of a quarrel between a Jew and a Christian the populace fell upon the Jews and pillaged their houses." Jacobs, who mentioned a "quarrel" but no blow to the Christian's head, also included the information that "Meir b. Isaac, one of the victims of the riot, instituted the Purim of Narbonne in commemoration of the event."[52] Yet, as we have already noted, Meir did not state that he or anyone else instituted a local Purim. He merely expressed the fervent hope, at the conclusion of his brief account, that "these days of Purim shall not pass." If Meir had been referring to a local Purim in Narbonne, he certainly would have given its date, but the only date he mentioned was that on which the Jewish quarter of Narbonne was attacked—20 Adar. Nonetheless, Kaufmann felt confident enough about the existence of a local Purim in Narbonne that he was even willing to assign it a date—21 Adar, and in this he was followed by Malter and many others.[53]

In 1912, Jean Régné, in his study of medieval Narbonne Jewry, also referred, on the basis of Kaufmann's article, to a Purim of Narbonne allegedly celebrated since 1236 on 21 Adar.[54] Some two decades later, Cecil Roth published a *A Jewish Book of Days* in which, beginning with January 1 (rather than with the Jewish New Year), he described an event of importance to Jewish history that had occurred on each day of the year. No less than eighteen of these were cases of local Purims—most real, but at least one imagined. For the date of February 29, Roth provided the following:

> Riot and deliverance at Narbonne, 1236. A Jew, characteristically quarreling with a fisherman about prices, uncharacteristically gave him so heavy a blow that he died from the consequences. This aroused the populace, which attacked the Jewish quarter and sacked it. Fortunately, Don Aymeric . . . appeared on the scene . . . and re-established order. During the riot, the mob had pillaged the house of Rabbi Meir ben Isaac and carried away . . . his library. Overjoyed at its safe return to him, he recorded the event in one of his books; and the anniversary was long observed by his descendants, on Adar 21st, as a special Purim.[55]

Roth's, characteristically, is the most imaginative reconstruction of the events of 1236, though its imagination draws heavily on stereotype. Although Meir b. Isaac had mentioned no quarrel preceding the blow

[52] Joseph Jacobs, s.v. "Narbonne," *JE*, 9:169.

[53] Kaufmann, "Le Pourim de Narbonne," 129; Malter, "Purims, Special," 281.

[54] J. Régné, *Etude sur la condition des juifs de Narbonne du Ve au XIVe siècle* (Narbonne, 1912), 70.

[55] Roth, *Jewish Book of Days*, 50–51.

delivered by the northern Jew to the Narbonnese fisherman, Kaufmann had confidently posited one, and Roth went a step further, boldly filling in the precise content of the quarrel. Whereas arguing about prices was seen by Roth as a characteristic Jewish activity, delivering a fatal blow to a Christian was seen, for reasons discussed earlier, as highly uncharacteristic. Similarly, Roth, who was himself an avid collector of books and manuscripts,[56] was certain that Meir b. Isaac's major joy upon the suppression of the local riot was in the safe return of his own personal library. And he was no less certain that the local Purim allegedly established by Meir in 1236 "was long observed by his descendants."

The continued observance, by later generations, of a local Purim in Narbonne (which had evidently never existed) was also assumed even by Salo Baron. In discussing the decline of Narbonne in the fourteenth century, Baron wrote: "Nevertheless the Jewish community carried on as best as it could, celebrating a special annual 'Purim Narbonne' to commemorate the preservation of its autonomy after a disturbance in 1236."[57] Here too the account's most dramatic event—the violent attack of a Jew upon a Christian fisherman—is omitted, alluded to under the vague rubric of a "disturbance," whereas the much softer "fact" of an annual celebration commemorating the preservation of local autonomy is given prominence. Shortly afterward, Bernhard Blumenkranz, in the entry on Narbonne in the *Encyclopaedia Judaica* asserted that the anti-Jewish riot of 1236 was set off by "a petty brawl between a Jew and a fisherman that ended in an accidental homicide."[58] The quarrel first mentioned by Kaufmann has here escalated into a brawl, accompanied by the misleading information that the homicide was accidental—misleading since Meir b. Isaac's account says nothing of the Jew's intentions, only that the Christian physician *intentionally* precipitated the fisherman's death.

In his *Zakhor*, published just over a decade later, Yosef Yerushalmi included the "Purim of Narbonne" between those of Granada and Saragossa/Syracuse in his brief discussion of Second Purims as "vessels and vehicles of Jewish memory." Following Kaufmann and others, he too asserted that the anti-Jewish riot of 1236 had been "sparked after a Christian was killed by a Jew in a private quarrel."[59] Somewhat earlier, Aryeh

---

[56] See, for example, C. Roth, "Catalogue of Manuscripts in the Roth Collection," *Alexander Marx Jubilee Volume*, 2 vols. (New York, 1950), English section, 503–35 (850 items); Eva Frojmovic and Frank Felsenstein, eds. *Hebraica and Judaica from the Cecil Roth Collection* (Leeds, 1997).

[57] Baron, *SRH*, 10:85.

[58] Blumenkranz, s.v. "Narbonne," *EJ*, 12:829.

[59] Yerushalmi, *Zakhor*, 27, 46–48. Unlike Blumenkranz, however, he did not claim that the homicide was accidental.

Grabois had presented the novel thesis that the anti-Jewish rioting of 1236 should be seen as a response to the influx of Jewish refugees from outlying towns in the south of France, such as Nîmes and Carcassonne, where their conditions were declining. "Certainly," he wrote, "these riots represent no more than an isolated incident [*sic*] in the long history of peaceful and neighborly relations between Christians and Jews in Narbonne," and were provoked, he suggested, by Christian resentment of the considerable privileges then accorded to the Jews.[60]

There may be some truth to this claim, but it is nonetheless striking that Grabois sought to explain both the 1236 riot and the so-called Purim of Narbonne without reference to the basic fact that a northern Jew had violently assaulted a local Christian and caused his death—an incident whose causal role was certainly evident to the medieval scribe Meir b. Isaac. In distancing and sometimes even disengaging its discourse about the 1236 riot, or "disturbance" as Baron called it, from the central and undeniable act of violence perpetrated by a Jew against a Christian, Jewish historiography from the late nineteenth century through most of the twentieth revealed its continuing reluctance to face the problematic subject of Jewish violence—a subject with which medieval Jewish historiography, as we have seen, was considerably more comfortable.

None of the scholars cited above seems to have entertained the possibility that the Jew's blow to the head of the Christian had not been preceded by a quarrel. None has suggested, furthermore, perhaps on account of another pervasive stereotype about Jews, that the assailant may have been inebriated. Yet if we look at the date of the Christian reprisal—less than a week after the holiday of Purim—and consider what we know about the conduct of Jews in Narbonne and its environs on that raucous holiday, we discover that drunken violence was hardly unheard of.

R. Abraham b. Isaac of Montpellier, the head of Narbonne's Jewish court in the twelfth century, devoted one of his responsa to the following question: "When the heart of 'Moses' was merry with wine on Purim he rose against his fellow man and killed him. What shall be done to him?"[61] From the continuation of the responsum it is clear that the drunken assault on Purim was not completely unprovoked, for the (Jewish) victim had called his (Jewish) assailant "son of a prostitute" and had pulled his hair, although it is not clear precisely when.

Both this act of homicide and the later one of 1236 described by Meir b. Isaac involved a wooden implement, but in this case it seems to have

---

[60] A. Grabois, "Les écoles de Narbonne au XIIIᵉ siècle," in M-H Humbert Vicaire and B. Blumenkranz, eds., *Juifs et judaisme de Languedoc* (Toulouse, 1977) (*Cahiers de Fanjeaux* 12 [1977]): 151–52.

[61] Assaf, *Sifran shel Rishonim*, no. 41; Dinur, *Yisrael ba-Gola*, 2:5, 218.

been thrown from a considerable distance ("some 30 cubits"). The distance was seen by R. Abraham as a mitigating factor, suggesting the possibility of a "fluke," but it may also suggest that the assailant was not so heavily inebriated, or that his accuracy in throwing when inebriated stemmed from the frequency of such acts on his part. The incident reminds us, in any case, of the violent possibilities connected with Purim inebriation—a state enjoined by the rabbis and hardly uncommon on that day, as reported by R. Abraham himself: "It may be assumed," he wrote, "that most of the common people get drunk on Purim."

Returning then to Meir b. Isaac's terse account, we may note that the riot against the Jews of Narbonne occurred on the 20th of Adar, six days after Purim, and after the Christian fisherman had already died of his wounds. This raises the serious possibility that the "northern French Jew," as Meir called him, had attacked the Christian on or around the holiday of Purim, perhaps while in a state of inebriation. R. Abraham's responsum, although written nearly a century earlier, testifies to the combustible link between alcohol and physical violence among southern French Jews on that holiday. And although the fatal violence mentioned there transpired between Jews, we have already noted that in northern France, from which the fisherman's assailant hailed, only decades earlier (in Bray or Brie) a Christian murderer had been hanged on Purim. If he had a score to settle with a Christian in Narbonne, the spirit of Purim together with a little help from the local wine could well have pushed him over the threshold. But I would not discount the possibility that another score to be settled here was the ancient one between the Jews and Amalek, whose descendants, as we have seen, were widely believed to reside in Christian Europe.

As is often the case, local Jewish memory of the Narbonne incident clashed with local Christian memory. We do not know in what year Meir b. Isaac composed his Hebrew account, although it is likely that he did so immediately after the events of 1236. Yet in 1253, seventeen years after its occurrence, the riot was remembered by Narbonne's Christians, or at least two members of its municipal council, as having stemmed from the ritual murder of a Christian child ("*puerum christianum*").[62] Both the Hebrew account and the local archival records concur, on the other hand, in attributing to the viscount and his consuls a central role in the suppression of the anti-Jewish rioting which ensued. Jean Régné, the one scholar who compared the Jewish and Christian versions of the incident, suggested that the Christian fisherman mentioned in the Hebrew source may have been a young man or a fisherman's apprentice, thus increasing

---

[62] Régné, *Etude sur la condition*, 68–69.

the likelihood that his death at the hands of a Jew, less than a century after the first blood libels in Norwich and Würzberg, would be inscribed in local Christian memory as an instance of Jewish ritual murder.[63]

In 1253, moreover, the Christians of Narbonne could also "remember" the local events of 1236 through the prism of more recent developments closer to home. In 1247 several Jews in the town of Valréas, northeast of Avignon, confessed under torture to having ritually murdered a two-year-old Christian girl, and some also gave the names of their alleged accomplices. As a result many members of the community were cruelly and publicly executed.[64] And in Saragossa, which had close ties with Narbonne, miracle tales were circulating in 1250 concerning a Christian boy allegedly murdered by Jews—the first appearance of the blood libel on Spanish soil.[65]

Régné's suggestion that the Christian fisherman's death may have been remembered as a case of ritual murder may be buttressed by the use of an otherwise surprising word in the Hebrew account—*sheketz* (abomination)—surprising not in that a Christian was referred to in such negative terms, but in that it was used selectively by Meir to refer to only one of the three Christians in his narrative. However, we know that later in the thirteenth century the author of *Sefer Nizzahon Vetus*, most probably a German Jew, used the term *shekatzim* with clear reference to Christian children.[66] As is well known, this usage continued well into modern times.[67]

Whereas some of Narbonne's Christians were able to fit the 1236 incident, for purposes of memory, into the preexisting narrative of ritual murder, its Jews, or at least the chronicler Meir b. Isaac, resorted to a different narrative, perhaps even a counternarrative, for remembering the events of that year—that of Purim. But what remains to be determined is precisely

---

[63] Moreover, in 1235 there had been no less than four ritual-murder accusations in Germany, the most famous of which occurred on Christmas Eve of that year. See most recently McCulloh, "Jewish Ritual Murder," 717–32; Yuval, *Two Nations*, 181–87, 287–88.

[64] See Grayzel, *Church and the Jews*, 262–67; Jordan, *French Monarchy*, 146–47, and the sources cited there.

[65] Baer, *Christian Spain*, 1:149.

[66] Berger, *Jewish-Christian Debate*, 219 (English section, 155). Berger's English translation does not carry the full force of the original Hebrew. On the *Nizzahon's* time and place, see ibid., 32–35. The use of the term *shekatzim* for Christian children was characteristically noted by Eisenmenger, *Entdecktes*, 1:718–19.

[67] The entry for "shegetz" in *Webster's Third New International Dictionary* (Chicago, 1986) reads: "A non-Jewish boy or youth—often used disparagingly"; the *New Shorter Oxford English Dictionary* (Oxford, 1993), s.v. "shegetz," also gives its usage as "usually derogatory" and defines it as "among Jewish people, a Gentile boy."

how the narrative was used. Were the phrases from the book of Esther inserted into the chronicle's conclusion merely as a means of highlighting the similarly miraculous salvations of the Jews of ancient Shushan and those of medieval Narbonne? The similarity would have been especially evident to the chronicler and his contemporaries through the close proximity in ritual time of the two otherwise distant events—both of which fell in the middle third of the month of Adar. One wonders further whether the reference to "these days of Purim" was not perhaps a hint on Meir's part that the assault on the *sheketz* which started it all actually took on place on the day of Purim.

For over a century, however, the scholarly consensus has been that Meir's reference to "these days of Purim" reflected the establishment of a local Purim in Narbonne to commemorate the events of 1236. David Kaufmann was the first, as mentioned above, to add the Purim of Narbonne to the list of local Purims initiated by Zunz, and it has been incorporated in virtually every list since.[68] But a careful reading of Meir b. Isaac's account raises, as we have noted, serious questions as to whether any evidence exists that the Jews of Narbonne ever observed, or decided to observe, a local Purim.

Perhaps the most obvious problem is the date of its alleged observance. The only date mentioned in Meir b. Isaac's account is 20 Adar, the day upon which Narbonne's Jews were attacked and then saved through the viscount's intervention. Yet Kaufmann, in his 1896 article, gave *21* Adar as that upon which Narbonne's local Purim was celebrated, both in 1236 and in subsequent years—lending the festival not only a date, but also a history. The usually scrupulous Steinschneider followed Kaufmann in this matter rather uncritically, as did Malter and Roth,[69] all of whom could have consulted the Hebrew text of Meir's account in Neubauer's *Medieval Hebrew Chronicles* (Roth could have consulted the original, as I did, in the Bodleian).

The second volume of Neubauer's work, in which Meir b. Isaac's account appeared, was published in 1895. My suspicion is that Kaufmann, upon encountering Meir's account, hastened to the conclusion that its concluding reference to "these days of Purim" merited Narbonne's inclusion in any future list of local Purims. Taking that step, he needed a date for the festival he had "discovered" (or invented). The original Purim, as Kaufmann well knew, marked the day not of victory but rather its morrow,

---

[68] Beyond those of Steinschneider, Malter, Roth, and Yerushalmi cited above, see also Max Joseph, s.v. "Purim," in *JL* 4:1184; Lewinski, *Sefer ha-Mo'adim* 6:297–322; s.v. "Purim," *EJ* 13:1396–1400.

[69] Note, however, that over "Purims, Special" *EJ* 13:1397–98, where the "correct" date of 20 Adar is given.

upon which the Jews "rested from their enemies" (Esther 9:22). He seems to have assumed, therefore, that in medieval Narbonne too the local Purim he had discovered/invented was observed annually on the day upon which its Jews rested from their enemies—the day after which they were saved by the local viscount from rioting and pillage. Neither Kaufmann nor those who came after him bothered to ask, however, whence the Jews of Narbonne might have drawn the inspiration or authority to declare a local Purim, one that was (quite erroneously) recognized by scholars for several decades as the first of its kind.

SCHIRMANN'S PURIM OF GRANADA

In 1936, the same year in which Rabbi Newman of Temple Rodeph Sholom in Manhattan composed his charming play about the "Purim of Saragossa," Jefim (Haim) Schirmann, then a young scholar of Hebrew poetry at Jerusalem's Schocken Institute for Research, discovered a new Purim, that of Granada, in southern Spain. Unlike David Kaufmann's discovery of Narbonne's Purim four decades earlier, however, Schirmann was less interested in adding to the list of local Purims than in reconstructing the biography of Samuel ibn Nagrela (a.k.a. Shmuel Ha-Nagid, 993–1056). The latter had been described in the *Jewish Encyclopedia*, for example, as a "statesman, grammarian, poet, and Talmudist," but Schirmann clearly felt that an additional epithet should have been added—which did, due largely to his own efforts, appear later in the *Encyclopedia Judaica*— "military commander."[70]

Samuel, it had long been known, had served as vizier to the king of Cordoba during the early eleventh century, and his considerable literary output included a sizable corpus of Hebrew poetry,[71] some of which dealt with military themes and described battlefield experiences. Yet until Schirmann's article on Samuel's "wars" (written while Jewish military commanders in the *Haganah* were themselves preparing for battle against hostile Arab forces), the latter's poetry had not been utilized to reconstruct the latter's military career—concerning which the Arabic sources are curiously silent.[72] Schirmann noted that Samuel's war poems were the

---

[70] See the entry by I. Broydé in *JE* 11:24–25, and compare *EJ* 14:816. On the different depictions of Ha-Nagid in nineteenth- and twentieth-century scholarship, see Elliott Horowitz, "The Court Jews and the Jewish Question," *Jewish History* 12 (1998): 118–21.

[71] Note especially *Diwan of Shemuel Hannaghid*, ed. D. S. Sassoon (Oxford, 1934).

[72] See Ross Brann, "Signs of Ambivalence in Islamic Spain: Arabic Representations of Samuel the Nagid," in *Ki Baruch Hu: Ancient Near Eastern, Biblical, and Judaic Studies in Honor of Baruch H. Levine*, ed. Robert Chazan et al. (Winona Lake, Ind., 1999), 446.

first of their genre in medieval Hebrew literature, and that they were heavily influenced by the conventions of Arabic poetry, with which their
author was intimately familiar. Nonetheless, he was confident that they
could be used "as materials for [reconstructing] the history of Samuel
Ha-Nagid's wars."[73]

The first of Samuel's battles discussed by Schirmann, largely on the
basis of the former's poem *Eloha 'oz*, took place on 1 Ellul (August 4)
1038, near the Andalusian village of El Fuente. In that battle, the forces
of Badis, the Berber king of Cordoba, and his Jewish vizier Samuel
defeated those of Zuhair, the "Slavic" ruler of Almeria,[74] and his vizier
Ibn 'Abbas—a personal enemy of his Cordoban counterpart. Samuel
referred repeatedly in his poem to Zuhair as "Agag," and to his forces as
"Amalek, Edom, and the sons of Keturah," boasting that, upon their
defeat, "Amalek's memory had vanished from Spain."[75] What did he
mean by all of this?

In 1910 Haim (Heinrich) Brody, who was later Schirmann's senior colleague at Jerusalem's Schocken Institute, published an edition of Samuel
Ha-Nagid's poems, including *Eloha 'oz*. From Brody's notes it is clear that
he saw these epithets as largely allegorical: Zuhair had been called "Agag"
because of his evil nature, and his soldiers therefore became "Amalekites."
They were divided, according to Brody, into two ethnic groups, Christians ("Edom") and Muslims ("sons of Keturah").[76] In his 1936 article,
Schirmann did not address the specific meaning of these epithets, but
when he later published *Eloha 'oz* in his anthology of Hebrew poetry in
Spain and Provence, he proposed a more literal reading of the poem:
Zuhair was called "Agag" because of his "Slavic" background, since the
"Slavs," in his view, were referred to by Samuel as "Amalekites." Zuhair's
soldiers were therefore divided by the poet into three ethnic groups: Slavs

---

[73] H. Schirmann, "The Wars of Samuel Ha-Nagid" (in Hebrew), reprinted in Schirmann,
Studies in the History of Hebrew Poetry and Drama (in Hebrew), 2 vols. (Jerusalem, 1979)
1:157–58 (the article originally appeared in *Zion* 1 [1936]: 261–83; 359–76).

[74] The Slavs (in Arabic: *Sakaliba*) of Muslim Spain were not all necessarily descendants of
slaves from the Slavic countries of Central and Eastern Europe. As Pierre Guichard has
noted, from the ninth century on "the same name was given to slaves from Christian
Europe, many of these being people captured in the wars against the Northern Spanish
states, or . . . by Andalusi pirates . . . off the coasts of southern Gaul and Italy, and in the
islands of the Mediterranean." See Guichard, "The Social History of Muslim Spain," *in The
Legacy of Muslim Spain*, ed. S. Khadra Jayussi (Leiden, 1992), 992.

[75] For modern editions of the poem (with commentary), see *Ha-Shira ha-'Ivrit bi-Sefarad
u-vi-Provence*, ed. H. Schirmann, 2 vols. (2nd ed., Jerusalem and Tel-Aviv, 1961) 1:85–92
(no. 25); *Shemuel Ha-Nagid: Shirei Milhama*, ed. A. M. Haberman (Jerusalem, 1963),
3–14, 165–69; *Diwan Shemuel Ha-Nagid*, ed. Dov Jarden (Jerusalem, 1966), 4–14.

[76] *Kol Shirei R. Shemuel Ha-Nagid*, ed. H. Brody (Warsaw, 1910), 125, 129.

("Amalek"), Spanish Christians ("Edom") and Muslim Arabs ("sons of Keturah").[77]

In Schirmann's view, then, Samuel was able to see the defeat of Zuhair/Agag and his forces, which included other "Amalekites," in religious terms as a victory, albeit only a local one, over the archenemy of both his people and his God—reminiscent of earlier such victories in the days of Moses, Samuel, and Mordecai. This dovetailed with Schirmann's earlier claim, first advanced in 1936, that Ha-Nagid "had informed the Jews of [North] Africa, Egypt, Palestine, and Babylonia [Iraq] of his salvation from the hands of his enemies, and established the day of his victory as a special Purim." Fifteen years later, Schirmann again asserted that "the ignominious death of the new Haman, Ibn Abbas, led Samuel to bid his coreligionists to celebrate the day of victory as a new festival of Purim."[78]

This claim, however, which other leading scholars were later to accept uncritically, was made exclusively on the basis of the highly rhetorical lines with which Samuel concluded his 1038 poem. Those lines, loosely translated, read:

> And a second Purim celebrate in honor of He who has again
> the evil Amalek mightily slain
> . . . And make it a sister
> to the festival of Mordecai and Esther
> And write it in your books, so that
> it shall be remembered forever.

It is not clear, though, why these lines should be taken any more literally than the concluding lines of another triumphant poem composed two years later by Samuel upon the death of yet another of his enemies (Ibn Abu Musa): "Now be quiet, and write down these verses! Read them aloud as the weekly portion on the Sabbath."[79] Yet neither Schirmann nor

---

[77] *Ha-Shira ha-'Ivrit bi-Sefarad u-vi-Provence*, 1:85–87. This interpretation was later accepted by two other Jerusalem scholars: Jarden (see n. 76, above), and Dan Pagis, *Change and Tradition in the Secular Poetry: Spain and Italy* (in Hebrew) (Jerusalem, 1976), 76. On the problems with this interpretation, see Horowitz, "From the Generation of Moses," 438–39.

[78] Schirmann, "The Wars," 159; Schirmann, "Samuel Hannagid, the Man, the Soldier, the Politician," *JSS* 13 (1951): 109, 121. Contrast, among earlier scholars, A. A. Harkavy, "Le-Toledot Rav Shemuel Ha-Nagid," *Me-Assef* 1 (1902): 22.

[79] "Leha osher," in Schirmann, *Ha-Shira ha-'Ivrit bi-Sefarad u-vi-Provence*, 1:103–5 (no. 29), partially translated in *The Penguin Book of Hebrew Verse*, ed. and trans. T. Carmi (New York, 1981), 289–90. On this poem and its background, see also Schirmann's posthumous *The History of Hebrew Poetry in Muslim Spain*, (in Hebrew) edited, supplemented, and annotated by Ezra Fleischer (Jerusalem, 1995), 196, 211–12.

any other scholar has claimed, so far as I know, that Samuel Ha-Nagid sought to replace, or even supplement, the traditional Torah reading with verses from his own poetry.

Schirmann's readiness to regard Samuel's clearly rhetorical call for the celebration of a special Purim as sincere was evidently based, in part, on the understandable assumption (rooted in the usually reliable scholarship of Kaufmann and Steinschneider) that a local Purim had been established by the Jews of thirteenth-century Narbonne. Had that indeed been the case, it would not be entirely surprising if the custom of establishing a Second Purim could be rolled backward two centuries, as well as southward, to eleventh-century Andalusia. Both the so-called Purim of Granada and that of Narbonne, however, are each based on a single piece of highly literary evidence, and in neither case is there the slightest sign of their having been observed after their alleged dates of establishment. Yet just as Kaufmann's 1896 "discovery" of a local Purim in Narbonne remained unchallenged for over a century, so too has Schirmann's "discovery" four decades later of Ha-Nagid's Purim left its indelible mark on twentieth-century scholarship.

In 1956, the "Purim of Granada" appeared among the local Purims listed by the folklorist Yom-Tov Lewinski in the volume on Purim in his *Sefer ha-Mo'adim*.[80] By then Schirmann had more than a hundred publications to his name and was editor of *Tarbiz*, the leading Hebrew journal of Jewish Studies.[81] In 1966 the historian Eliyahu Ashtor, Schirmann's colleague at the Hebrew University, accepted both the latter's reconstruction of Samuel's military career and his claim that after the victory at Al Fuente in 1038 Ha-Nagid had exhorted his co-religionists in several countries to "remember the day each year, establishing it as the Purim of Granada." A decade later, Schirmann's colleague (and former student) Dan Pagis also drew similar conclusions from the poem *Eloha 'oz*.[82] By that time the "Purim of Granada" had already been recognized in the *Encyclopedia Judaica*.[83]

---

[80] Lewinski, *Sefer ha-Mo'adim* 6:305.

[81] A year later he was awarded the prestigious Israel Prize. See Ezra Fleischer and Dan Pagis, s.v. "Schirmann, Jefim," *EJ*, 14:968–69; *A Bibliography of the Writings of Prof. Jefim (Haim) Schirmann*, ed. D. Pagis, E. Fleischer, and Y. David (in Hebrew) (Jerusalem, 1983).

[82] Pagis, *Change and Tradition*, 76. Pagis seems to have assumed that Second Purims were already being observed before Ha-Nagid's time. Note also Schirmann's posthumous *History of Hebrew Poetry*, 195, which was "edited, supplemented, and annotated" by another former student, Ezra Fleischer.

[83] See the two entries, "Samuel Ha-Nagid," *EJ*, 14:816, and "Purims, Special," *EJ*, 13:1399–1400. In the latter, however, Ha-Nagid's Purim is listed under the category of "Family Purims" and given the date of 1039.

It was not only in Israeli scholarship, moreover, that Schirmann's Purim of 1038 came to be recognized as the first of its type. In his highly influential *Zakhor*, published in 1982, Yosef Yerushalmi briefly discussed the phenomenon of "Second Purims," and gave several notable examples in chronological order, the first two of which were Granada (1038) and Narbonne (1236). After the victory at El Fuente, asserted Yerushalmi, Samuel Ha-Nagid "declared a Second Purim, and sent forth copies of a magnificent Hebrew poem he had composed for the occasion [*Eloha 'oz*] to Tunis, Palestine, and Babylonia, asking that the Purim be celebrated there as well."[84] As we have stressed, however, both Ha-Nagid's declaration of such a Purim and his request that it be observed by Jewish communities throughout the Islamic world were highly rhetorical flourishes and, as in the case of the "Purim of Narbonne," there is not a shred of evidence that it was ever observed.

MADE IN THE MEDITERRANEAN

When, then, was the tradition of local Purims actually invented? The first hard evidence of such festivals being both declared and observed comes from Cairo and Crete, though not necessarily in that order. That of Cairo was based on events that had occurred in 1524, but its observance cannot be verified, as we have seen, until nearly three decades later. By that point the "Purim of Crete," based on an incident that had occurred in 1538, had been observed for over a decade.

These were not the only local Purims established among Mediterranean Jewish communities during the sixteenth century. In late 1541, only a few months after the "Purim of Crete" was established, the Jews of Algiers instituted a "Purim Edom" (in Arabic: *Purim al-Nasara*) on the fourth of Heshvan—commemorating the failed efforts of Charles V's Spanish fleet, commanded by Admiral Andrea Doria, to seize their city from its Ottoman ruler, Khair al-Din Barbarossa.[85] Less than four decades later the Jews of neighboring Morocco established a local Purim of their own commemorating a similar defeat. In 1578 Dom Sebastian, the young king of Portugal, had landed with a crusading army, and the local Jews feared that they would be forcibly baptized, as had been the case with Portuguese Jewry in 1497. After Sebastian was defeated and killed in the "Battle of

---

[84] Yerushalmi, *Zakhor*, 46–47. Contrast, however, the more careful formulation of Cohen, *Sefer Ha-Qabbalah*, 277.

[85] Its existence was already noted by Zunz, *Die Ritus*, 129, in 1859. See also Steinschneider, "Purim und Parodie" 284; H. Z, Hirschberg, *A History of the Jews in North Africa*, 2 vols. (in Hebrew) (Jerusalem, 1965), 1:327; David Corcos, s.v. "Algiers," *EJ*, 2:622.

the Three Kings" at Alcazaequebir, a local Purim, known alternately as "Purim Sebastiano" and "Purim de los Cristianos," was observed on the first of Ellul. On this occasion a specially written scroll was also read, as was customary in Cairo.[86]

Between the two North African Purims of 1541 and 1578, a local Purim was established in Rome, although it is not clear with what degree of success. In early 1555 a young Christian child was found dead, and the local Jews were accused of having killed it for ritual purposes. Fortunately, the true murderer, a Christian of Spanish origin was found and executed on the orders of Pope Paul IV. The Jews of Rome declared a local Purim on the third of Iyyar to be observed by their co-religionists throughout the Papal States, but as Abraham David has recently noted, there is no evidence that it actually gained acceptance, either in Rome or elsewhere.[87]

Although it is not clear which was the first actually observed local Purim in Italy, we do know that even in the twentieth century the tradition of establishing such local festivals was still alive in that country. In the fall of 1927, after an unsuccessful attempt by local Fascists to torch the Ashkenazi synagogue of Padua, its rabbi, Mazal-Tov Castelbolognesi, instituted a local Purim to be observed annually on the Sabbath of *Parashat Toledot*, when the failed arson attempt took place.[88] The Jews of Padua had, in fact, been observing a local Purim in late summer (on the tenth of Ellul) since the late seventeenth century. In 1684 the imperial armies were besieging Buda, the capital of Hungary, in a effort to drive out the Turks. Rumors began to spread throughout Italy that the Jews of Buda were collaborating with the Turks and perpetrating atrocities against Christians. In Padua, one of the Italian cities closest to Hungary, such rumors were particularly rife, and on August 20th of that year the local ghetto was

---

[86] Among the many discussions of this Purim and its background, see J. M. Toledano, *Ner ha-Ma'arav* (Jerusalem, 1911), 92–94; J. R. Marcus, "Notes on Sephardic Jewish History," *Hebrew Union College Jubilee Volume* (Cincinnati, 1925), 384–91; A. I. Laredo, "Les Purim de Tanger," *Hesperis* 35 (1948): 193–99; Hirschberg, *History of the Jews in North Africa*, 2:211–14; Yerushalmi, *Zakhor*, 47, 119n36. For the Hebrew text of the scroll, see M. Ginsburger, "Deux Pourims locaux," *HUCA* 10 (1935): 447–48. This Purim, however, is not to be confused with Tangier's "Purim de los Bombas," which commemorates events that occurred in 1844. This confusion appears in Simonsen, "Freud und Leid," 526; Steinschneider, "Purim und Parodie," 284, and Roth, *Jewish Book of Days*, 184–85. The distinction between the two Moroccan Purims was made clear by J. M. Toledano in *HUCA* 8–9 (1931–1932): 481–92, and Laredo, "Les Purim de Tanger."

[87] See Steinschneider, "Purim und Parodie," 284; D. Kaufmann, "Délivrance des juifs de Rome, en l'année 1555," *REJ* 4 (1882): 95–96, and most recently Abraham David "Iggeret Nissim," in *Italia* 13–15 (2001): 109–17 (Hebrew section).

[88] Umberto Nahon, "Batte Keneseth d'Italia in Israele," in Nahon, ed., *Scritti in memoria di Sally Mayer (1875–1953): Saggi sull'ebraismo italiano* (Jerusalem, 1956), 270.

attacked and systematically sacked. Only after the intervention of the doge in Venice was order restored. In memory of those events the Jews of Padua established a local festival, which they called "Purim of Buda," and in honor of which a local rabbi, Isaac Vita Cantarini (1644–1723), composed a Hebrew poem.[89]

Two Purims of Verona

Padua's local Purim was still being observed in 1924 when Cecil Roth published a brief article (in French) announcing his discovery that the Jews of Verona, also in the Veneto, had an even older local festival allegedly instituted after they moved into their ghetto, near the city's Piazza Erbe, in 1600. Roth's primary piece of evidence dated, however, not from the early seventeenth century, but from the late eighteenth—a 1765 sermon delivered by R. Menahem Navarra on the New Moon of Shevat, the day upon which the Jews of Verona *then* observed a synagogal ritual marking their move to the ghetto. Roth also cited a festive liturgical poem for the occasion, which he believed to have been composed by R. Mordecai Bassan, who served as Verona's rabbi during the late sixteenth and early seventeenth centuries.[90] On the basis of this rather flimsy evidence Roth, who was then only twenty-five, was willing to assert that the Veronese festival, which he referred to as "the strangest and the most paradoxical of the local Purims," seems "to have been observed regularly during approximately two centuries."[91]

In his aforementioned *Jewish Book of Days*, published in 1930, Roth listed under January 16th the festival allegedly established by the Jews of Verona in 1605, five years after their removal to the ghetto, which he

---

[89] Roth, *Book of Days*, 196–97; Roth, *Venice*, 283–85; *Anthologie der Hebräischen Dichtung in Italien*, ed. Jefim Schirmann (Berlin, 1934), 348–49.

[90] Roth, "La fête de l'institution du ghetto: une célébration particulière à Vérone," *REJ* 79 (1924): 163–69 (also in Italian in *RMI* 3 [1927]). Roth neglected to note the possibility that the poem could also have been composed by a later R. Mordecai Bassan (or Bassani) of Verona, who died in 1703, and whose entry in the *Encyclopedia Judaica* was later composed by Cecil Roth himself. See Roth, "Bassani, Mordecai," *EJ* 4:315. On the earlier Mordecai Bassan, see the many references in *Minutes Book of the Jewish Community of Verona* (in Hebrew), ed. Y. Boksenboim, 3 vols. (Tel-Aviv, 1989–1990), vols. 2–3 infra. For a different opinion as to the poem's authorship, see note 93, below.

[91] Roth, "La fête," 167. Roth's evidence for stretching the observance forward to the late eighteenth century was a fragment from an anonymous journal evidently composed during the years that R. Joseph Marini was rabbi of Verona from 1799 and 1802 (Roth, "La Fête," 166).

again referred to as a local Purim. He also commented again on the strange and paradoxical character of such an observance.

> It would be natural to believe that this indignity would have appeared to them an unmixed calamity. But, as a matter of fact, they thoroughly appreciated the security and the solidarity engendered by living at last in a quarter of their own. . . . This strangest and most paradoxical of local Purims continued to be observed until the French Revolution.[92]

Roth's "discovery" of Verona's paradoxical Purim did not go unnoticed. In 1938 Isaiah Sonne, who was then head of the Italian rabbinical seminary which had (after the rise of Fascism) moved to Rhodes, published the first of two pioneering articles on the history of the Jews in early modern Verona.[93] His 1938 article, which appeared in the Hebrew journal *Zion* (in which Schirmann had recently heralded the "long-lost" Purim of Samuel Ha-Nagid), opened with a frontal attack on Roth's cavalier claims about, and "romantic" attitude concerning, Verona's festival of the ghetto. In contrast to the latter, who based his claims almost exclusively on a single late sermon, Sonne proposed to show what the community's archives had to say about the subject.

One thing they indicated clearly was that although the Jews of Verona modestly celebrated the completion of the synagogue they built in their new ghetto, there was no evidence for any kind of annual celebration until many years later. Sonne showed, moreover, that the *Hallel Gadol* for the annual celebration, which Roth had attributed to R. Mordecai Bassan, had, when published in 1759, been to attributed to another Veronese rabbi—the physician Samuel Meldola, who was still alive in 1660 and was probably no more than a child when the Jews entered their ghetto sixty years earlier. Although Sonne did not posit an alternate date for the beginning of the annual celebration in Verona, he noted that Meldola was first mentioned in records of the community in 1614.[94] He also published an

---

[92] Roth, *Book of Days*, 14–15. See also Roth, *Venice*, 273–74, for a similar formulation without, however, using the word "Purim."

[93] Sonne, "Material on the History of the Jews in Verona," (in Hebrew), part 1, *Zion* 3 (1938): 123–69; part 2: *Kobez 'al yad* 3, no. 13 (1940): 143–84.

[94] Sonne, "Material" (part 1), 135–39. It now appears that Meldola may have been in Verona as early as 1610, at which point he was still clearly a young man, serving as a private tutor. See Boksenboim, *Minutes Book*, 3:150. On his later activities in, and on behalf of, the community, see Moses Shulvass, "A Chronicle of the Misfortunes that Occurred in Italy," *HUCA* 22 (1949): 18–19 (Hebrew section); E. Horowitz, "Jewish Confraternities in Seventeenth-Century Verona: A Study in the Social History of Piety," (Ph.D. diss., Yale University, 1982), 214–21.

entry from the community's minute-book, dated 20 Tammuz 1607, reporting that several days earlier "a great miracle" had occurred when, in the aftermath of hostile efforts to have the Jews locked into their ghetto from the outside, the Jews of Verona were given the keys to the gates, so that they could lock themselves in.[95]

Sonne's 1938 article, which criticized Roth's thesis concerning a local Purim allegedly observed annually, on the New Moon of Shevat, by the Jews of Verona for nearly two centuries, had the clearly unintended effect of replacing Roth's Purim with another—that allegedly observed since 1607 in commemoration of their having received the right to lock themselves into their ghetto. Sonne, who was still alive in 1956 and living in Cincinnati (where he had been on the faculty of the Hebrew Union College since 1940) could not have been particularly pleased to discover that Yom-Tov Lewinski had included a "Purim of Verona" in his list of local Purims published that year—one, moreover, that had allegedly been celebrated on the twentieth of Tammuz since 1607.[96]

There were now two Purims of Verona—Roth's and Lewinski's. When the *Encyclopedia Judaica*, of which Cecil Roth was editor-in-chief, was published in the 1970s, it was ironically Lewinski's "Purim of Verona" (discovered with the help of Sonne) rather than his own (discovered in 1924) that appeared in its list of "Special Purims."[97] And when an Italian rabbi published a survey of "Second Purims in the Communities of Italy" a dozen years later, he too listed for the community of Verona only that allegedly celebrated on the twentieth of Tammuz and unintentionally "discovered" by Sonne—whom he dutifully cited.[98]

But what of the festival marking their entrance into the ghetto that the Jews of Verona were celebrating during the eighteenth century on the New Moon of Shevat? The physician and rabbi Samuel Meldola, who had evidently composed the *Hallel Gadol* recited on those occasions, had lived in Verona until about 1650, before moving on to Mantua.[99] The festival in honor of which he composed the poem must therefore have been established sometime during the first half of the seventeenth century. Although it was purportedly established to commemorate the entrance of

---

[95] Sonne, "Material" (part 1), 131.

[96] Lewinski, *Sefer ha-Moadim*, 6:304.

[97] *EJ*, 13:1399–1400. See also the entry by Shlomo Simonsohn on "Verona" (*EJ*, 16:114) where it is stated that after a ghetto was established there "the community succeeded in securing charge of the keys, an event commemorated by the Verona Jews in the seventeenth and eighteenth centuries by an annual festivity."

[98] Yehudah Nello Pavoncello, "Purim Sheni be-Kehillot Italya," *Yed'a 'Am* 21 (1982): 74.

[99] See Horowitz, "Jewish Confraternities in Seventeenth-Century Verona," 214–21, and the sources cited there.

Verona's heavily Ashkenazic Jewish community into its ghetto during the first decade of the seventeenth century, it may have been stimulated by the local Purim established, further to the north, by Frankfurt's Jews after they returned triumphantly to their own ghetto in early 1616.

GERMAN JEWS AND ENGLISH PROTESTANTS

The local Purim of Frankfurt, the first of its type established north of the Alps, was known as "Purim Vincenz" or "Purim Fettmilch," and named after Vincenz Fettmilch, the self-described Haman and leader of a popular rebellion against Frankfurt's patrician regime. In August of 1614 he had stood at the head of an angry mob of artisans who plundered Frankfurt's Ghetto and drove out its Jews. In early 1616 the old city council returned to power, publicly executed Fettmilch and six of his followers, and permitted Frankfurt's Jews to return to their quarter—an event which they commemorated with a local Purim observed on the nineteenth and twentieth of Adar.[100]

Unlike previous attempts in continental Europe to establish local Purims, the Purim of Frankfurt, which combined days of fast and feast, clearly took root and lasted over time. R. Joseph Yuspa Hahn (Nordlingen), who was present in Frankfurt during the dramatic events of 1614–1616, included a discussion of "Purim Vincenz" and the fast day preceding it in his authoritative halakhic work *Yosif Ometz*.[101] And as in the case of Cairo's Purim, a bilingual scroll was soon written (in this case in Hebrew and Yiddish), which came to be known as *Megillat Vinz* describing (in rhyme) the events leading up to the establishment of Frankfurt's festival. Although the oldest surviving copy dates from 1648, *Megillat Vinz* was apparently first printed as early as 1616.[102] When it was reprinted (under a somewhat different title) in 1880, the *Megillah* included a letter of approbation from R. Simeon Sofer, the chief rabbi of Cracow, who reported that his father, the great Hungarian rabbi R. Moses Sofer (1762–1839), who was a native of Frankfurt, had continued to observe the twentieth of Adar as a minor holiday throughout his life.[103]

---

[100] Among the many discussions see, A. Freimann and F. Kracauer, *Frankfort*, trans. B. S. Levin (Philadelphia, 1929), 73–107; Baron, *SRH*, 14:190–97; Friedrichs, "Politics or Pogrom?" and most recently Ulmer, *Turmoil, Trauma, and Triumph*, 15–88.

[101] Hahn Nordlingen, *Yosif Ometz* (Frankfurt, 1928), 242–43.

[102] See Chone Shmeruk, "Yiddish 'Historical Songs' in Amsterdam" (in Hebrew), in *Studies on the History of Dutch Jewry* 4 (1985): 152.

[103] *Megillah Efah* (Cracow, 1888). For its observance in Frankfurt into the 1870's, see Ulmer, *Turmoil, Trauma, and Triumph*, 79.

During the years that Rabbi Sofer, the leader of Hungarian ultra-Orthodoxy, staunchly preserved the local Purim of his native Frankfurt, Anglican preachers in England were also keeping alive the memory of a local observance rooted in an early seventeenth-century event. This was Guy Fawkes day, celebrated on November 5 and established in the aftermath of the 1605 "Gunpowder Plot"—the abortive conspiracy on the part of several English Catholics to blow up both Parliament and King James I.[104] In *The Churches Deliverance*, published in 1609, Thomas Cooper, a graduate of Christ Church (Oxford) conspicuously used the book of Esther as a frame for reflecting on England's "deliverance from the bloody Papists" some four years earlier. "Surely if my sight fayle me not," wrote Cooper in his introduction, "I see in that deliverance, Ameleck's utter overthrow."[105]

The link between Catholicism and Israel's archenemy was further developed in the 1620s by Thomas Taylor and George Hakewill. In his sermon "An Everlasting Record of the Utter Ruine of Romish Amalek," delivered in London and published in 1624, Taylor asserted that "*Amalek* signifieth a smiting people, and of all Religions, never was any so fierce and smiting as Romish *Amalek*." Like the aggressive Amalekites of old, continued Taylor, the Papists sought to prevent God's people from entering "heavenly Canaan," by "sending into our kingdomes besides forcible instruments of violence . . . innumerable armies of seducing Priests and Jesuits."[106] Two years later, George Hakewill published a pamphlet explicitly comparing England's deliverance from the Gunpowder Plot and the deliverance of the ancient Jews from their enemies, celebrated during the days of Purim. "These daies (the like being scarcely found again in holy scripture)," wrote Hakewill, "I propose to compare with our day of the Powder plott . . . that from thence it may appear that the mercy of God was more cleerely manifested in our Deliverance than in theirs, and that consequently we have greater cause religiously . . . to observe our day then they theires."[107]

The proposal to treat Guy Fawkes day as a Second Purim was clearly taken quite seriously. On November 5, 1704, which in that year fell on a

---

[104] See, for example, Mark Kishlansky, *A Monarchy Transformed: Britain 1603–1714* (London, 1996), 65–67, 76–77; J. E. Carney, s.v. "Gunpowder Plot (1605)," in *Historical Dictionary of Stuart England*, ed. R. H. Fritze and W. B. Robison (Westport and London, 1996), 217–18, and the literature cited there.

[105] Thomas Cooper, *The Churches Deliverance, Contayning Meditations and short notes upon the booke of Hester. In remembrance of the wonderfull deliverance from the Gunpoulder-Treason* (London, 1609). See especially the "Epistle Dedicatory" and "to the Christian and discerning Reader."

[106] Thomas Taylor, *Two Sermons* . . . (London, 1624), 18–20.

[107] Hakewill, *A Comparisone Betweene the Dayes of Purim and that of the Powder Treason* . . . (Oxford, 1626).

Sunday, Bishop William Fleetwood delivered a sermon to the members of the House of Peers which opened with Esther 9:27–28: "The Jews ordained, and took upon . . . their seed, and upon all such as joined themselves unto them . . . that they would keep these two days . . . according to their appointed time every year. And that these days should be remembered and kept throughout every generation." In his sermon, which was delivered in the Abbey Church of Westminster, Fleetwood asserted that the miraculous deliverance of 1605 had been such "the like is scarce to be met with in any History, sacred or prophane, except in this Book of Esther, where we also have a clear Precedent for making a Law for the Publick and Solemn Commemoration of such a Deliverance every year."[108]

A similar sermon, under the title *Haman and Mordecai*, was preached by Thomas Knaggs at St. Paul's Cathedral on November 5, 1716. Even as late as 1843, when again the fifth of November fell on a a Sunday, Thomas Barton Hill preached a sermon at St. Stephen's Church in Islington which opened with the same verses from Esther that Bishop Fleetwood had earlier used, and which Hill cited as "scriptural authority for the observance amongst ourselves of this present day, in which we commemorate so great a deliverance of our Church and nation from Popish cruelty and arbitrary Power."[109] The official *Book of Common Prayer according to the use of the United Church of England and Ireland* published in 1844 included a "PRAYER with THANKSGIVING, to be used yearly upon the Fifth Day of NOVEMBER for the happy Deliverance of King JAMES I and the Three Estates of England, from the most traiterous and bloody-intended Massacre by GUNPOWDER."

During the 1840s the Jews of England, whose liturgy never included a prayer of thanksgiving for their king and country's escape from the Gunpowder Plot—primarily because in 1605 there were no Jews living (openly) in England—began observing their own Second Purim, which was established in response not to local events, but to the "Damascus Affair" of 1840. The "affair," as noted earlier, had begun with the disappearance of a Capuchin monk and his servant just before Purim, and had ended late in the summer of 1840 with the release of all of the Jewish prisoners who were still alive (two had died after torture and a third had converted to Islam) and the Sultan's promulgation of a *firman* declaring the blood libel to be baseless. Among the Jewish dignitaries who had traveled to the Middle East in order to bring the "Damascus Affair" to a successful conclusion was Moses Montefiore, together with his secretary, interpreter, and traveling companion Louis Loewe.

[108] W. Fleetwood, *A Sermon Preach'd Before the House of Peers* . . . (London, 1704), 16.
[109] T. Knaggs, *Haman and Mordecai* . . . (London, 1716); T. B. Hill, *England's Deliverance and England's Duty* (London, 1843), 6–7.

On March 9 (15 Adar), 1841, the second day of Purim (*Shushan Purim*), a special service was held in Montefiore's honor at London's Bevis Marks Synagogue. "Attendance," as Jonathan Frankel has noted, "was by special invitation only, and the eight hundred ticket holders, men and women alike, came dressed in their most splendid attire."[110] According to Frankel, it was "Montefiore's decision to celebrate the end of his mission on Purim."[111] I would surmise, however, that in this matter, as in many others, he had been advised by Loewe, who knew from personal experience of the local Purim celebrated by the Jews of Cairo since the sixteenth century. As in the case of Cairo, moreover, a Hebrew *Megillah* recounting the dramatic events of 1840 in the style of the book of Esther was composed in the aftermath of the "Damascus Affair." Its author was a German Jew residing in the town of Oberdorf, near Württemberg.[112] Curiously, however, the Jews of Damascus themselves did not observe a Second Purim in commemoration of the 1840 affair. And, somewhat ironically, less than half a century after Moses Montefiore introduced a new Purim in London, his great-nephew Claude Goldsmid Montefiore published an article in the London *Jewish Chronicle* calling, in effect, for the abolition of the old one.

Although the latter continued, nevertheless, to be celebrated in late-Victorian and Edwardian England, albeit with tepid tea-parties that provoked in the likes of Israel Abrahams a shameless nostalgia for the rough pleasures of medieval Purims, no evidence exists that Moses Montefiore's "Damascus Purim" survived the death, in 1885, of its centenarian founder. Yet in Yemin Moshe, one of the Jerusalem neighborhoods named after Montefiore, the mysterious "Purim of Saragossa" was still being observed as late as 1930.[113]

In 1953, on the fifth anniversary of the establishment of the State of Israel, its minister of Education and Culture, the Hebrew University historian Ben-Zion Dinur, proposed in a radio broadcast to the nation that Independence Day should be observed in every household with lit candles, flowers, wine, and a festive meal. At the beginning of the meal, Dinur proposed, the 1948 Declaration of Independence, which he referred to in Hebrew as *Megillat ha-ʿAtzmaut* and called "the foundation scroll of the Jewish people," would be read.[114] Although his proposal

---

[110] Frankel, *Damascus Affair*, 382–83.

[111] Ibid., 407.

[112] Ibid., 407–8; J. I. Helfand, "A *Megillah* for the Damascus Affair," 175–84, in *Rabbi J. H. Lookstein Memorial Volume*, ed. Leo Landman (New York, 1980).

[113] Badhav, *Ma'aseh Nissim*, 35.

[114] Dinur's 1953 radio speech is quoted in Lewinski, *Sefer ha-Mo'adim* (Tel-Aviv, 1957) 8:503–4. See also Maoz Azaryahu, *State Cults: Celebrating Independence and Commemorating the Fallen in Israel, 1948–1956* (in Hebrew) (Beer Sheva, 1995), 102–7.

17. In 1996 a terrorist bombing in the center of Tel-Aviv just before Purim put
a damper on most celebrations of the holiday in the Tel-Aviv area, but in
ultra-Orthodox Benei Berak the festivities were as exuberant as ever.
Toy guns and real cigarettes were favorite accoutrements among the
boys, to whom the streets clearly belonged on that day of reversal.
Collection of the author. Photo: Meir Zarovsky.

was clearly influenced by the model of the Seder meal on Passover, it
would appear to have drawn also on the tradition of local Purims with
which Dinur, as a historian, was certainly familiar. In the aftermath of the
1967 war at least one Israeli rabbi argued that the lightning victory over
several Arab armies and the unification of Jerusalem should be marked
with a religious holiday in the tradition of local Purims such as that of
Frankfurt.[115]

On Purim 1991, a century and a half after Moses Montefiore established a special Purim commemorating the "Damascus Affair," the (first)

---

[115] Seraiah Deblitzky, "Keviat Yom Hodaya le-Ahar Milhemet Sheshet ha-Yamim," 61–65,
in *Hilkhot Yom Ha-ʿAtzmaut ve-Yom Yerushalayim*, ed. Nahum Rakover (Jerusalem, 1973).

Gulf War ended with the surrender of Saddam Hussein to the American-led forces that had conquered Iraq. Although the Jews of Israel suffered considerably during the 1991 war—some from the Scud missiles and others from the fear of chemical attack—the chief rabbinate made no attempt to establish a local Purim in its aftermath. The memory of such possibilities had not died out entirely, however. After the massacre at the Tomb of the Patriarchs three years later, at least one local rabbi raised the possibility of establishing a local Purim for the Jews of Hebron and Kiryat Arbah, who had been saved, many insisted, from a savage attack by their Arab neighbors on Purim of 1994, through the "martyrdom of the sainted Doctor Baruch Goldstein."[116]

[116] R. Arnon Sha'arabi, "Purim de-Hevron 5794: Yom Mishteh ve-Simhah," in *Barukh ha-Gever* ed. Michael Ben-Horin (Jerusalem, 1995), 442–44.

Abbreviations

AHR	American Historical Review
AHSS	Annales: Histoire, Sciences Sociales
AJH	American Jewish History
AJHQ	American Jewish Historical Quarterly
BJRL	Bulletin of the John Rylands Library
CSSH	Comparative Studies in Society and History
EHR	English Historical Review
FJB	Frankfurter Judaistische Beiträge
HTR	Harvard Theological Review
HUCA	Hebrew Union College Annual
JAOS	Journal of the American Oriental Society
JES	Journal of Ecumenical Studies
JJA	Journal of Jewish Art
JJGL	Jahrbücher für jüdische Geschichte und Literatur
JJS	Journal of Jewish Studies
JJTP	Journal of Jewish Thought and Philosophy
JMH	Journal of Medieval History
JPOS	Journal of the Palestine Oriental Society
JQR	Jewish Quarterly Review
JRJ	Journal of Reform Judaism
JSQ	Jewish Studies Quarterly
JSOT	Journal for the Study of the Old Testament
JSS	Jewish Social Studies
JTS	Journal of Theological Studies
LBIYB	Leo Baeck Institute Year Book
MEFRM	Mélanges de l'école française de Rome
MERIA	Middle East Review of International Affairs
MGWJ	Monatsschrift für Geschichte und Wissenschaft des Judentums
MLN	Modern Language Notes
OCP	Orientalia Christiana Periodica
PAAAS	Proceedings of the American Academy of Arts and Science
PAAJR	Proceedings of the American Academy for Jewish Research

PAJHS   Publications of the American Jewish Historical Society
PIASH   Proceedings of the Israel Academy of Sciences and
         Humanities
REJ   Revue des études juives
RES   Review of English Studies
RHE   Revue d'histoire ecclesiastique
RHR   Revue d'histoire des religions
RMI   Rassegna Mensile di Israel
RQCAK   Romische Quartalschrift für christliche Altertumskunde und
         Kirchengeschichte
SCH   Studies in Church History
SCJ   Studies in Contemporary Jewry
SIDIC   Service international de documentation judéo-chrétienne
TJHSE   Transactions of the Jewish Historical Society of England
WLB   Wiener Library Bulletin
ZGJD   Zeitschrift für die Geschichte der Juden in Deutschland
ZK   Zeitschrift für Kirchengeschichte

Bibliography

Note: I have included mostly, but not exclusively, works that appear more than once in the notes.

REFERENCE WORKS

American National Biography (ANB). Edited by J. A. Garraty and M. C. Carnes. 24 vols. New York, 1999.

Ben Yehuda, Eliezer. *A Complete Dictionary of Ancient and Modern Hebrew* (in Hebrew). 8 vols. New York, 1960 (reprint).

Dictionary of American Biography (DAB). Edited by A. Johnson. 20 vols. New York, 1928–1936.

Dictionary of Biblical Interpretation (DBI). Edited by J. H. Hayes. 2 vols. Nashville, 1999.

Driver, S. R. *Introduction to the Literature of the Old Testament*, 2nd ed. New York, 1892.

Eisenmenger, J. A. *Entdecktes Judenthum*. 2 vols., n. p., 1700.

Encyclopaedia Britannica (EB). 11th ed. 29 vols. Cambridge, 1910–1911.

Encyclopaedia Judaica (EJ). 16 vols. Jerusalem, 1971–1972.

Frazer, J. G. *The Golden Bough* (GB). 2nd ed. 3 vols. London, 1900.

Ginzberg, Louis. *Legends of the Jews*. 7 vols. Philadelphia, 1909–1938.

Jewish Encyclopedia (JE). 12 vols. New York, 1901–1905.

Jüdisches Lexikon (JL). 5 vols. Berlin, 1927–1930.

McFadyen, J. E. *Introduction to the Old Testament*. London, 1905.

Roth, Cecil. *A Jewish Book of Days*. London, 1931.

Schreckenberg, Heinz. *Die christlichen Adversus-Judaeos-Texte und ihr literarisches und historisches Umfeld (1.–11. Jh.)*. Frankfurt, 1990 (rev. ed.).

———. *Die christlichen Adversus-Judaeos-Texte und ihr literarisches und historisches Umfeld (11–13. Jh.)*. Frankfurt, 1991 (rev. ed.).

———. *Die christlichen Adversus-Judaeos-Texte und ihr literarisches und historisches Umfeld (13.–20. Jh.)*. Frankfurt, 1994 (rev. ed.).

Schudt, J. J. *Jüdische Merckwurdigkeiten* (JM). 4 vols. in 2. Frankfurt, 1714–1718.

Zunz, Leopold. *Die synagogale Poesie des Mittelalters* [1855]. Frankfurt, 1920 (rev. ed.).

HISTORIES OF THE JEWS

Baron, S. W. *A Social and Religious History of the Jews* (SRH). 18 vols. New York and Philadelphia, 1952–1983.

Basnage, J. C. *The History of the Jews, from Jesus Christ to the Present Time*. Translated by T. Taylor. London, 1708.

Dubnow, Simon. *History of the Jews*. II: *From the Roman Empire to the Early Medieval Period*. Translated by Moshe Spiegel. New York and London, 1968.

Edersheim, Alfred. *History of the Jewish Nation: After the Destruction of Jerusalem under Titus*. Edinburgh, 1856.

Gosse, P. H. *The History of the Jews from the Christian Era to the Dawn of the Reformation*. London, 1851.

Graetz, Heinrich. *Geschichte der Juden, von den ältesten Zeiten bis auf die Gegenwart*. 11 vols. Leipzig, 1853–1876 (1st ed.).

————. *History of the Jews*. 6 vols. Philadelphia, 1892–1898.

Graetz, Zvi. *Divrei Yemei Yisrael*. Translated by S. P. Rabinowitz. 9 vols. Warsaw, 1891–1899.

Milman, H. H. *The History of the Jews*. 3 vols. London, 1830 (2nd ed.).

Palmer, E. H. *A History of the Jewish Nation: From the Earliest Times to the Present Day*. Edited by S. F. Smith. Boston, 1875 (rev. ed.).

Renan, Ernest. *History of the People of Israel*. 5 vols. Boston, 1905.

Stanley, A. P. *Lectures on the History of the Jewish Church*. 3 vols. London, 1877 (2nd ed.).

MODERN COMMENTARIES ON ESTHER

Adeney, W. F. *Ezra, Nehemia, and Esther*. New York, 1893.

Baldwin, J. G. *Esther: An Introduction and Commentary*. Leicester, 1984.

Browne, L. E. "Esther." In *Peake's Commentary on the Bible*. Edited by Matthew Black and H. H. Rowley. London, 1962.

Cassel, Paul. *An Explanatory Commentary on Esther*. Translated by A. Bernstein. Edinburgh, 1888.

Clines, D. J. *Ezra, Nehemiah, Esther*. Grand Rapids, Mich., 1984.

Davies, T. W. *Ezra, Nehemiah, and Esther*. London, 1909.

Duff, Archibald. "Esther." In *A Commentary on the Bible*. Edited by. A. S. Peake. London, 1920, 336–40.

Fox, M. V. *Character and Ideology in the Book of Esther*. Grand Rapids, Mich., 2001 (2nd ed.).

Fuerst, W. J. *The Books of Ruth, Esther, Ecclesiastes, the Song of Songs, Lamentations*. Cambridge, 1975.

Holyoake, Austin. *The Book of Esther: A Specimen of What Passes as "the Inspired Word of God."* London, n.d.

Keil, C. F. *The Books of Ezra, Nehemiah, and Esther* [1870]. Translated by Sophia Taylor. Grand Rapids, Mich., 1950.

Levenson, Jon. *Esther: A Commentary*. London, 1997.

Moore, C. A. *The Anchor Bible: Esther*. Garden City, N.Y., 1971.

Paton, L. W. *A Critical and Exegetical Commentary on the Book of Esther*. Edinburgh, 1908.

PRIMARY SOURCES

Assaf, Simha, ed. *Sifran shel Rishonim*. Jerusalem, 1935.

Baer, Fritz (later Yitzhak) ed., *Die Juden im christlichen Spanien*. 2 vols. Berlin, 1928–1936.

Berger, David. *The Jewish-Christian Debate in the High Middle Ages: A Critical Edition of the* Nizzahon Vetus. Philadelphia, 1979.

Bernfeld, S., ed. *Sefer ha-Dema'ot*. 3 vols. Berlin, 1924–1926.

Bonar, A. A., and R. M. McCheyne. *Narrative of a Mission of Inquiry to the Jews . . . in 1839*. Edinburgh, 1842.

Braude, W. G., trans. *Pesikta Rabbati* (PR). New Haven, 1968.

Braude, W. G., and I. J. Kapstein, trans. *Pesikta de-Rab Kahana* (PRK). Philadelphia, 1975.

Buber, S., ed. *Tanhuma*. 2 vols. Vilna, 1885.

Capsali, Eljah. *Seder Eliyahu Zuta*. Edited by A. Shmuelevitz et al. 3 vols. Jerusalem, 1976–1983.

Dinur, B. Z., ed. *Israel in the Diaspora, Part II* (in Hebrew). 6 vols. Tel-Aviv and Jerusalem, 1965–1972.

Eidelberg, Shlomo, ed. and trans. *The Jews and the Crusaders: The Hebrew Chronicles of the First and Second Crusades*. Madison, 1977.

Friedlander, Joseph. *The Standard Book of Jewish Verse*. New York, 1917.

Goodman, Philip, ed., *The Purim Anthology*. Philadelphia, 1949.

Haberman, A. M., ed., *Sefer Gezerot Ashkenaz ve-Zarfat*. Jerusalem, 1945.

Hertz, J. H. *Sermons, Addresses, and Studies*. 3 vols. London, 1938.

Ibn Verga, Solomon. *Shevet Yehudah*. Edited by A. Shohat. Jerusalem, 1947.

Lewinski, Yom-Tov, ed. *Sefer ha-Mo'adim*. Vol. 6 (*Purim, Lag ba-'Omer, Hamisha 'Asar be-Av*) Tel-Aviv, 1955.

Linder, Amnon, ed. and trans. *The Jews in Roman Imperial Legislation* [1983]. Detroit, 1987.

Margaliot, R., ed. *Sefer Hasidim* (Bologna). Jerusalem, 1957.

Montefiore, C. G. *The Bible for Home Reading* (BHR). 2 vols. London, 1896.

Neubauer, A., and M. Stern, eds. *Hebräische Berichte über die Judenverfolgungen während der Kreuzzüge*. Berlin, 1892.

Rosenthal, Judah, ed. *Sepher Joseph Hamekane*. Jerusalem, 1970.

Segre, Renata, ed. *The Jews in Piedmont*. 3 vols. Jerusalem, 1986–1990.

Ulmer, Rivka. *Turmoil, Trauma, and Triumph: The Fettmilch Uprising in Frankfurt am Main (1612–1616) According to Megillas Vintz. A Critical Edition of the Yiddish and He brew Text Including an English Translation. Bein and Frankfurt, 2001.*

Wistinetzki, J., ed. *Das Buch der Frommen* (Parma). Berlin, 1924 (2nd ed.).

Monographs and Articles

Abbott, Lyman. *The Life and Literature of the Ancient Hebrews*. Boston and New York, 1901.

Abrahams, Israel. *Jewish Life in the Middle Ages*. Philadelphia, 1896.

Ackerman, Robert. *J. G. Frazer: His Life and Work*. Cambridge, 1987.

Adler, Cyrus. "Trial of Gabriel de Granada by the Inquisition in Mexico 1642–1645." Translated by D. Fergusson. *PAJHS* 7 (1899).

Aronson, I. M. *Troubled Waters: The Origins of the 1881 Anti-Jewish Pogroms in Russia*. Pittsburgh, 1990.

Baer, Yitzhak. *A History of the Jews in Christian Spain*. Translated by L. Schoffman et al. 2 vols. Philadelphia, 1961.

Bickerman, Elias. *Four Strange Books of the Bible*. New York, 1967.

Boiteux, Martine. "Les Juifs dans le Carnaval de la Rome moderne: (15e–18e siécles)." *MEFRM: moyen age, temps modernes* 88 (1976).

Carlebach, Elisheva. *Divided Souls: Converts from Judaism in Germany, 1500–1750*. New Haven, 2001.

Chase, M. E. *The Bible and the Common Reader*. New York, 1944.

Cheyne, T. K. *Founders of Old Testament Criticism*. London, 1893.

Doniach, N. S. *Purim, or the Feast of Esther*. Philadelphia, 1933.

Frankel, Jonathan. *The Damascus Affair: "Ritual Murder," Politics, and the Jews in 1840*. Cambridge, 1997.

Friedrichs, C. R. "Politics or Pogrom? The Fettmilch Uprising in German and Jewish History." *Central European History* 19 (1986).

Gitlitz, D. M. *Secrecy and Deceit: The Religion of the Crypto-Jews*. Philadelphia, 1996.

Gougenot des Mousseaux, H. R. *Le Juif, le judaïsme et la judaïsation des peuples chrétiens* [1869]. Paris, 1886 (2nd ed.).

Grayzel, Solomon. *The Church and the Jews in the Thirteenth Century*. New York, 1966 (rev. ed.).

Gregorovius, Ferdinand. *The Ghetto and the Jews of Rome*. Translated by M. Hadas. New York, 1948.

Grossman, Avraham. *The Early Sages of France* (in Hebrew). Jerusalem, 1995.

Horowitz, Elliott. "'And It Was Reversed': Jews and Their Enemies in the Festivities of Purim" (in Hebrew). *Zion* 59 (1994).

———. "The Rite to Be Reckless: On the Perpetration and Interpretation of Purim Violence." *Poetics Today* 15 (1994).

———. "'The Vengeance of the Jews Was Stronger than Their Avarice': Modern Historians and the Persian Conquest of Jerusalem in 614," *JSS*, n.s. 4, no. 2 (1998).

———. "*Jewish Life in the Middle Ages* and the Jewish Life of Israel Abrahams." In *The Jewish Past Revisited: Reflections on Modern Jewish Historians*. Edited by D. N. Myers and D. B. Ruderman. New Haven, 1998.

———. "From the Generation of Moses to the Generation of the Messiah: Constructions of Amalek in Jewish History," (in Hebrew). *Zion* 64 (1999).

———. "The Jews and the Cross in the Middle Ages: History and Historiography." In *The Jews of Europe and the First Crusade* (in Hebrew). Edited by Y. Assis, O. Lior et al. Jerusalem, 2000 (rev. English ed.). "The Jews and the Cross in the Middle Ages: Towards a Reappraisal." In *Philosemitism, Antisemitism, and "the Jews"*. Edited by Tony Kushner and Nadia Valman. Aldershot, 2004.

———. "A 'Dangerous Encounter': Thomas Coryate and the Swaggering Jews of Venice." *JJS* 52, no. 2 (2001).

———. "'They Fought Because They Were Fighters and They Fought Because They Were Jews': Violence and the Construction of Modern Jewish Identity." In Peter Medding, ed., *Jews and Violence. SCJ* 18 (2002).

Jordan, W. C. *The French Monarchy and the Jews: From Philip Augustus to the Last Capetians*. Philadelphia, 1989.

Kamil, Omar. "Rabbi Ovadia Yosef and his 'Culture War' in Israel." *MERIA* 4, no. 4 (December 2000).

Klier, J. D. and Lambroza, Shlomo, eds. *Pogroms: Anti-Jewish Violence in Modern Russian History*. Cambridge, 1992.

Leroy-Beaulieu, Anatole. *Israel Among the Nations: A Study of the Jews and Antisemitism* [1893]. Translated by F. Hellman. London, 1895.

Liebman, S. B. *The Jews in New Spain*. Coral Gables, Fla., 1970.

———. *New World Jewry, 1493–1825: Requiem for the Forgotten*. New York, 1982.

Luckert Steven. *The Art and Politics of Arthur Szyk*. Washington D.C., 2002.

McCulloh, J. "Jewish Ritual Murder: William of Norwich, Thomas of Monmouth, and the Early Dissemination of the Myth." *Speculum* 72 (1997).

Mitchell, H. G. *The Ethics of the Old Testament*. Chicago, 1912.

Nirenberg, David. *Communities of Violence: Persecution of Minorities in the Middle Ages*. Princeton, 1996.

Roskies, D. G. *Against the Apocalypse: Responses to Catastrophe in Modern Jewish Culture*. Cambridge, Mass., 1984.

Roth, Cecil. *Venice*. Philadelphia, 1930.

———. *A History of the Marranos*. Philadelphia, 1932.

———. "The Feast of Purim and the Origins of the Blood Accusation." *Speculum* 8 (1933).

———. *The History of the Jews in Italy*. Philadelphia, 1946.

Scott, J. C. *Domination and the Arts of Resistance: Hidden Transcripts*. New Haven, 1990.

Stowe, Harriet Beecher. *Woman in Sacred History*. New York, 1873.

Thornton, T.C.G. "The Crucifixion of Haman and the Scandal of the Cross." *JTS* 37 (1986).

Trachtenberg, Joshua. *The Devil and the Jews: The Medieval Conception of the Jew and Its Relation to Modern Anti-Semitism*. New Haven, 1943.

Walfish, B. D. *Esther in Medieval Garb: Jewish Interpretation of the Book of Esther in the Middle Ages*. Albany, 1993.

Wiznitzer, Arnold. "Crypto-Jews in Mexico During the Seventeenth Century." *AJHQ* 51 (1961–1962).

Wolf, Lucien. *Jews in the Canary Islands*. London, 1926.

Yerushalmi, Y. H. *From Spanish Court to Italian Ghetto: Isaac Cardoso: A Study in Seventeenth-Century Marranism and Jewish Apologetics*. New York, 1971.

———. *Zakhor: Jewish History and Jewish Memory*. Seattle, 1982.

Yuval, Yisrael. *"Two Nations in Your Womb": Perceptions of Jews and Christians* (in Hebrew). Tel-Aviv, 2000.

Index